Beiträge zum
ausländischen öffentlichen Recht und Völkerrecht

Edited by

the Max Planck Society
for the Advancement of Science
represented by Prof. Dr. Armin von Bogdandy
and Prof. Dr. Anne Peters

Volume 315

Patrick Abel

International Investor Obligations

Towards Individual International Responsibility for the Public Interest in International Investment Law

Nomos

The Deutsche Nationalbibliothek lists this publication in the Deutsche Nationalbibliografie; detailed bibliographic data are available on the Internet at http://dnb.d-nb.de

a.t.: Göttingen, Georg-August-Universität, Diss., 2021

ISBN 978-3-8487-8981-8 (Print)
978-3-7489-3317-5 (ePDF)

British Library Cataloguing-in-Publication Data
A catalogue record for this book is available from the British Library.

ISBN 978-3-8487-8981-8 (Print)
978-3-7489-3317-5 (ePDF)

Library of Congress Cataloging-in-Publication Data
Abel, Patrick
International Investor Obligations
Towards Individual International Responsibility for the Public Interest in International Investment Law
Patrick Abel
373 pp.
Includes bibliographic references.

ISBN 978-3-8487-8981-8 (Print)
978-3-7489-3317-5 (ePDF)

1st Edition 2022

Published by
Nomos Verlagsgesellschaft mbH & Co. KG
Waldseestraße 3–5 | 76530 Baden-Baden
www.nomos.de

Production of the printed version:
Nomos Verlagsgesellschaft mbH & Co. KG
Waldseestraße 3–5 | 76530 Baden-Baden

ISBN 978-3-8487-8981-8 (Print)
ISBN 978-3-7489-3317-5 (ePDF)
DOI https://doi.org/10.5771/9783748933175

Onlineversion
Nomos eLibrary

Preface and Acknowledgments

International investment law represents one of the branches of international law in which individuals – natural persons and companies – play a key role both in substantive law and in dispute settlement. Many observers criticise the field to be overly investor-friendly. Do investors enjoy international rights without corresponding obligations? As I started to research the interplay of investment law and human rights in 2015, I came to realise that there is a pattern in investment law theory and practice which answers this question to the negative. In a diffuse, decentral development, investor rights and obligations increasingly go hand in hand. This book aims at comprehensively analysing how international investor obligations have incrementally begun to develop in investment law and how we may situate this finding in the broader debate about the status of individuals in international law. It is a revised version of my doctoral dissertation which I submitted to the Faculty of Law of the University of Göttingen in 2018 and which I defended in 2021. The book takes into account scholarly writing and arbitral jurisprudence until the end of 2021.

Above all, I would like to express my gratitude to *Professor Dr. Peter-Tobias Stoll* who supervised my dissertation. His support and guidance have made this book possible. I am particularly grateful for three fascinating, challenging and inspiring years of working for him as a PhD research fellow at the Institute of International and European Law between 2015 and 2018. I would also like to thank *Judge Professor Dr. Andreas Paulus* for many valuable discussions in Göttingen and Karlsruhe and for his critical and helpful comments as second examiner of my dissertation.

Professor Dr. Armin von Bogdandy and *Professor Dr. Anne Peters* accepted this book into the series of *Beiträge zum ausländischen öffentlichen Recht und Völkerrecht* of the Max Planck Institute for Comparative Public Law and International Law in Heidelberg for which I am much obliged.

Furthermore, my thanks are due to a large group of people who contributed to my dissertation in various ways and in different places. These include firstly, *Professor Dr. Andreas von Arnauld*, *Professor Dr. Christian Walter* and *Professor Dr. Fabian Wittreck* who sparked my interest in academia and especially in national and international human rights law during my studies at the University of Münster. I would also like to thank *Professor Dr. Dapo Akande*, *Professor Dr. Gregory Messenger*, *Professor Dr. Catherine*

Redgwell, *Professor Dr. Dan Sarooshi* and *Professor Dr. Antonios Tzanakopoulos* for the intriguing lectures and discussions during my studies at the University of Oxford which led me to the topic of my dissertation. Furthermore, I am much obliged to *Professor Dr. Nehal Bhuta*, *Professor Dr. Ernst-Ulrich Petersmann*, *Professor Dr. Martin Scheinin* and *Professor Dr. Joanne Scott* for an inspiring time as a visiting PhD researcher at the European University Institute and for taking the time for making valuable remarks on my PhD project.

Among the many colleagues, *Dr. Henner Gött* and *PD Dr. Till Patrik Holterhus* deserve particular mentioning for many discussions and the fruitful collaboration in Göttingen and plenty of other places, as well as for reading and critically commenting drafts. I would also like to thank *Dr. Carsten Bormann* and *Dr. Laura Jung* for their continuous support and *Agata Daszko* for her great help in revising the manuscript.

Moreover, my sincere gratitude is due to the German National Academic Foundation (Studienstiftung des deutschen Volkes) which awarded me a PhD scholarship for this project and to *Professor Dr. Christoph Herrmann* for generously supporting the publication of this book.

Passau, May 2022 *Patrick Abel*

Table of contents

List of Abbreviations

ACHR	American Convention on Human Rights
AfrCHPR	African Charter on Human and Peoples' Rights
AU	African Union
BIT	Bilateral Investment Treaty
COMESA	Common Market for Eastern and Southern Africa
CPTPP	Comprehensive and Progressive Agreement for Trans-Pacific Partnership
CSR	Corporate Social Responsibility
ECHR	European Convention on Human Rights
ECOWAS	Economic Community of West African States
ECtHR	European Court of Human Rights
EIA	Environmental Impact Assessment
EU	European Union
FET	Fair and Equitable Treatment
FTA	Free Trade Agreement
IACtHR	Inter-American Court of Human Rights
IBRD	International Bank for Reconstruction and Development
ICCPR	International Covenant on Civil and Political Rights
ICESCR	International Covenant on Economic, Social and Cultural Rights
ICJ	International Court of Justice
ICSID	International Centre for the Settlement of Investment Disputes
IFC	International Finance Corporation
IHL	International Humanitarian Law
IIA	International Investment Agreement
IISD	International Institute for Sustainable Development
ILC	International Law Commission
ILO	International Labour Organisation
IMF	International Monetary Fund
IMT	International Military Tribunal
ISDS	Investor-State Dispute Settlement
MFN	Most-Favoured-Nation

MIGA	Multilateral Investment Guarantee Agency
NGO	Non-Governmental Organisation
PCA	Permanent Court of Arbitration
PCIJ	Permanent Court of International Justice
SADC	Southern African Development Community
TPP	Trans-Pacific Partnership
UDHR	Universal Declaration of Human Rights
UN	United Nations
UNCITRAL	United Nations Commission on International Trade Law
UNCommHR	United Nations Commission on Human Rights
UNGA	United Nations General Assembly
UNSC	United Nations Security Council
VCLT	Vienna Convention on the Law of Treaties
WTO	World Trade Organisation

Chapter 1.
Introduction: The Need for International Investor Obligations

> Investors' rights are instrumental rights. In other words, investors' rights are defined in order to meet some wider goal such as sustainable human development, economic growth, stability, indeed the promotion and protection of human rights. The conditional nature of investors' rights suggests that they should be balanced with corresponding checks, balances and obligations – towards individuals, the State or the environment. [...]
>
> [A]s investors' rights are strengthened through investment agreements, so too should their obligations, including towards individuals and communities.[1]

More than fifteen years later, this 2003 call by the UN High Commissioner for Human Rights remains topical. In the last few decades, international investment law has provided foreign investors with potent international rights, enforceable against states before international investment tribunals. It is widely believed that, similarly to other non-state actors, foreign investors do not face any corresponding international obligations. This book shall demonstrate otherwise. Its main hypothesis is that international investment law *is already subject to dynamics* aiming to introduce international investor obligations and giving rise to international responsibility of foreign investors.

I. Interactions between foreign investment and the public interest

Reflecting on the international obligations of foreign investors is even more relevant today than it was in 2003. Save for natural catastrophes such as the Covid-19-pandemic, the continuously globalising world economy

1 UN Commission on Human Rights 'Human Rights, Trade and Investment, Report of the High Commissioner for Human Rights' UN Doc E/CN.4/Sub.2/2003/9 (2 July 2003) ‹http://daccess-ods.un.org/access.nsf/Get?Open&DS=E/CN.4/Sub.2/2003/9&Lang=E› accessed 7 December 2021, paras 37, 59.

has led to an ever-increasing volume of foreign investment – defined as an economic activity of a natural or private legal person committing resources across national borders for a specific purpose to earn a profit.[2] The 2020 UNCTAD World Investment Report stipulated the volume of foreign direct investment to amount to USD 1.54 trillion in 2019.[3] Even though the Covid-19-pandemic strongly reduced global foreign direct investment flows by a third to USD 1 trillion in 2020,[4] the volume remains impressive and may recover after the pandemic ends. Given this high economic relevance, foreign investment often has broad social, economic and environmental implications. These are particularly relevant for the states which welcome the investment, the so-called host states.

In the last few years, discussions on the effects of investment law vis-à-vis the public interest have been particularly heated. Notwithstanding, there is no uniform definition of the term 'public interest'. In democracies, it is for the elected state organs to decide what is in the public interest through constitutionally determined processes. Just as most states do, this book will consider certain non-rival and non-exclusive public goods to constitute essential parts of the public interest. These include, for example, a clean environment, the rule of law and a strong economy. In addition to public goods, safeguarding the interests of individuals forms a part of the public interest as well. Protecting the individual is not only relevant for each and every citizen but it also characterises a society which guarantees liberty, equality and dignity as objective values. These different facets of the public interest are interrelated, an insight that brought about the notion of sustainable development.[5]

Legal norms intended to protect the public interest reflect this understanding. On the international level, states have undertaken plenty of obligations which address non-rival, non-exclusive public goods by, for example, signing and ratifying international treaties on environmental protection. Other obligations protect individuals such as international human rights and labour standards which, as shown, also contribute to the public

2 Jeswald W Salacuse, *The Law of Investment Treaties* (3rd edn, Oxford University Press 2021) 30.

3 UNCTAD, *World Investment Report: International Production Beyond the Pandemic* (United Nations Publications 2020) 11.

4 UNCTAD, *World Investment Report: Investing in Sustainable Recovery* (United Nations Publications 2021) 2.

5 On the concept of sustainable development see UNGA 'Transforming Our World: The 2030 Agenda for Sustainable Development' UN A/RES/70/1 (21 October 2015).

interest as understood here. Investment law can interact with these norms in different ways.

On the one hand, one may say that protecting foreign investors can substantially contribute to the public interest. Indeed, foreign investors provide employment. They transfer technology to countries. They build infrastructure and pay taxes. All this can ultimately improve the life of people and help states foster their development in manifold ways, including the protection of human rights, workers' rights and the environment.[6] International law confirms this finding: for example, the International Covenant on Economic, Social and Cultural Rights obliges state parties to realise the embodied international human rights to the maximum of their available resources.[7] Investors may increase these resources. In the same vein, the UN Sustainable Development Goals for 2030 specifically mention the importance of encouraging foreign direct investment to reduce inequality within and among countries.[8] Indeed, a prospering economy qualifies as a public good in itself and foreign investment may have an active role in this regard. In other words, foreign investment can 'harness'[9] or contribute to public interest standards.

On the other hand, foreign investment may endanger and even harm the public interest. After all, investors are private actors who pursue economic profits. These private interests may collide with legal norms that protect public goods and individual rights.[10] Indeed, the UN High Com-

6 On synergies between environmental protection and the promotion of foreign investment see Jorge E Viñuales, *Foreign Investment and the Environment in International Law* (Cambridge University Press 2012) 24–28, 41–58; more broadly on businesses' potentials for furthering human rights and development see John G Ruggie, *Just Business: Multinational Corporations and Human Rights* (Norton 2013) 201.

7 Art 2 (1) International Covenant on Economic, Social and Cultural Rights (adopted 16 December 1966, entered into force 3 January 1976) 993 UNTS 3 (ICESCR).

8 UNGA 'Development Goals' (n 5) No 10.b.

9 On this key term and concept see Pierre-Marie Dupuy and Jorge E Viñuales (eds), *Harnessing Foreign Investment to Promote Environmental Protection: Incentives and Safeguards* (Cambridge University Press 2013).

10 The ambivalent relationship of foreign investment and environmental protection is pointed out for example by Viñuales (n 6) 24–25; for an economic perspective on the impact of multinational enterprises that foreign investors often form part of see Joseph E Stiglitz, 'Regulating Multinational Corporations: Towards Principles of Cross-Border Legal Frameworks in a Globalized World Balancing Rights with Responsibilities' (2007–2008) 23(3) American University International Law Review 451, 474–475.

missioner for Human Rights' 2003 Report on Human Rights, Trade and Investment aimed at raising awareness of the different ways that foreign investment can interact with human rights. It also presented some problematic cases in which investment negatively affected local populations' rights.[11]

A good example illustrating the effect of investment on human rights is the case of the Three-Gorges-Dam in China. This extensive energy project was financed and realised with the support of international private and public investors.[12] While it contributes to the production of clean water energy in the spirit of sustainable development, it not only required local inhabitants to be relocated[13] but also damaged the ecosystem of the Yangtze River.[14]

Therefore, undoubtedly there exists a need for rules which will assure that foreign investments preponderantly further the public interest.[15]

---

11 UNCommHR 'Human Rights, Trade and Investment Report' (n 1) paras 5–19; for a more recent critical account, see UNGA 'Human Rights-Compatible International Investment Agreements. Report of the Working Group on the Issue of Human Rights and Transnational Corporations and Other Business Enterprises' (27 July 2021) UN Doc A/76/238, para 3 which states that 'attracting investment is not a sufficient condition for inclusive and sustainable development' and that 'international investment agreements – if not designed properly – […] can also exacerbate the existing imbalance between rights and obligations of investors and undermine affected communities' quest to hold investors accountable for human rights abuses and environmental pollution.'

12 See ‹http://projects.worldbank.org/P153473?lang=en› accessed 7 December 2021.

13 See for example Yan Tan, *Resettlement in the Three Gorges Project* (Hong Kong University Press 2008).

14 Shilun L Yang, Jianbo Zhang and Xin-Jian Xu, 'Influence of the Three Gorges Dam on Downstream Delivery of Sediment and Its Environmental Implications, Yangtze River' (2007) 34(10) Geophysical Research Letters 37.

15 cf the discussion on the relationship between international investment law and development, for example by UNCTAD 'Investment Policy Framework for Sustainable Development' UNCTAD/DIAE/PCB/2015/5 (2015) and the observation that there is an '[…] awareness that international investment law is related to, and relevant for, development' by Stephan W Schill, Christian J Tams and Rainer Hofmann, 'International Investment Law and Development: Friends or Foes?' in Christian J Tams, Rainer Hofmann and Stephan W Schill (eds), *International Investment Law and Development: Bridging the Gap* (Edward Elgar Publishing 2015) 27.

II. The regulatory setting: Investment agreements and the right to regulate

Setting and implementing investment rules is a core task of the state (1.). Yet, due to the characteristics of investment law (2.), there have been extensive discussions on how the field overly limits host states' right to regulate (3.).

1. Regulating as a function of the state

The purpose of state regulation is to control and channel activities of private actors. It is the traditional task of the host state to balance foreign investors' private interests with the public interest. As part of its sovereignty, the state has the jurisdiction to prescribe and enforce domestic law on its territory in order to set boundaries and incentives for foreign investors. The domestic constitution of a state determines the rules and processes on how policy decisions to that end can be taken, including democratic mechanisms and the choice of a certain economic order. Many states do so successfully while having very different, sometimes completely opposing, regulatory approaches. Indeed, often international law even obliges states to make use of this sovereign right. Such duties may follow from customary international law as well as a myriad of international treaties for the protection of human rights, the environment, labour standards and the rule of law.

However, over the past few years, the capacity of host states to regulate in this manner has been subject to widespread concern due to the disciplining effect of investment law which sets certain boundaries on host states' actions towards foreign investors.

2. Foundations of international investment law

To better understand how investment law affects host states' right to regulate, a short overview of the foundations of international investment law is necessary.

Created in 1959 with the conclusion of the first international investment agreement (IIA) between Pakistan and Germany, investment law aims to protect foreign investors against adverse action by the host state. In IIAs, the state parties agree to reciprocally protect foreign investors that have the nationality of the other party. Most of these investor rights protect foreign investors against host state interference taking place after the host state already admitted the investment to the country. Although each IIA requires a precise assessment of its specific terms,[16] in practice a canon of typical investor rights evolved. These include: the protection against expropriation, the right to fair and equitable treatment (FET), the right to full protection and security, the right to most-favoured nation (MFN) treatment and the right to national treatment.[17] Some more recent IIAs even contain (qualified) market access rights for investors.[18] These international investor rights build on the previously existing customary international law on the treatment of aliens that was, and continues to be, enforced between states through diplomatic protection. States created IIAs to depoliticise the matter by isolating foreign investment protection rules from other, more controversial, topics.[19]

These substantive rights were soon flanked by a particularly effective international enforcement system: international investment arbitration. Investment tribunals allow investors to sue the host state for violating an investor right without need for the home state to take action on their behalf. In earlier times, these arbitral proceedings stemmed from investment arbitration clauses contained in domestic investment contracts concluded between foreign investors and the host state (the so-called contract arbitration). Today, the dominant form of arbitration process is international treaty arbitration – it also constitutes the main focus of this book. In international treaty arbitration, it is only the states, and not the foreign investors, who agree on an investment arbitration clause in the above-mentioned IIAs. Based on this clause, investors can file investment arbitration claims against a respective host state based on the host state's consent to arbitrate embodied in the IIA. To that end, many IIAs build on

---

16 cf on the right to fair and equitable treatment with its particularly diverging expressions in different IIAs Rudolf Dolzer and Christoph Schreuer, *Principles of International Investment Law* (2nd edn, Oxford University Press 2012) 132.

17 On this canon of investment rights see only ibid, 98–215. MFN obligations cause some uniformity of these rights – an effect that one may even describe as a certain multilateralisation of international investment law as observed by Stephan W Schill, *The Multilateralization of International Investment Law* (Cambridge University Press 2009).

18 See further Dolzer and Schreuer (n 16) 88–90.

19 Ibrahim F Shihata, 'Towards a Greater Depoliticization of Investment Disputes: The Roles of ICSID and MIGA' (1986) 1(1) ICSID Review 1, 1–12, 24–25.

multilateral investment arbitration rules such as the ICSID Convention[20] or the UNCITRAL Model Arbitration Rules.[21]

In contrast to the international enforcement of the customary law of aliens through inter-state diplomatic protection, investors have full control over the investment arbitration proceedings independently from the state of their nationality, the home state. They can claim the violation of rights defined in the applicable IIA. If an award is rendered, investors have far-reaching possibilities to internationally enforce it against assets of the host state. Under the New York Convention on the Recognition and Enforcement of Foreign Arbitral Awards[22] and the ICSID Convention, more than 150 states have undertaken the international obligation to recognise and enforce investment awards with only narrow exceptions. In most cases, the host state may only invoke its sovereign immunity to shield itself against such enforcement in a third country.[23]

The purpose of investment law is to provide independent legal protection to foreign investors. In adhering to this, states aim to attract foreign investment by providing more stable market conditions. After all, when in the host state, foreign investors face an unknown legal system. Investment law aims to reduce the investment risk that this exposure entails by providing an independent safeguard against disproportionate or arbitrary host state behaviour. The idea is that foreign investors can be incited to invest abroad if such international protection is available to them. And indeed, investment law has proven a success story – today we see more than 3000 IIAs and a proliferating number of investment arbitration proceedings. For a long time, there was a clear emphasis on IIAs between a developed and a developing country that focused on a unilateral flow of foreign investment from the former to the latter. This political constellation has changed recently: increasingly, states of a similar degree of development conclude

---

20 Convention on the Settlement of Investment Disputes between States and Nationals of other States (adopted 18 March 1965, entered into force 14 October 1966) 575 UNTS 159 (ICSID Convention).

21 UNCITRAL 'Arbitration Rules (With New Article 1, Paragraph 4, as Adopted in 2013)' (16 December 2013) UN Doc A/RES/68/109.

22 Convention on the Recognition and Enforcement of Foreign Arbitral Awards (adopted 10 June 1958, entered into force 7 June 1959) 330 UNTS 3 (NYC).

23 On immunity against the enforcement of arbitral awards in the broader investment arbitration context see August Reinisch, 'Enforcement of Investment Treaty Awards' in Catherine Yannaca-Small (ed), *Arbitration Under International Investment Agreements: A Guide to the Key Issues* (2nd edn, Oxford University Press 2018) paras 29.44–29.63.

IIAs with one another, sometimes in plurilateral settings or in the context of broader agreements, most notably free trade agreements.[24]

3. The right to regulate debate

Despite this success, in the last years we have witnessed a public and scholarly 'backlash'[25] against international investment law as part of the so-called right to regulate debate. Critics argue that investment law favours investors' interests over the public interest represented by the host state. They contend that investor rights constitute international privileges that go much further than protecting against arbitrary host state measures. Effectively, such investor rights would comprehensively shield investors even against a host state which regulates legitimate questions of the public interest – exceedingly curtailing host states' right to regulate. Many critics further emphasise that investment tribunals interpret international investment law in an overly investor-friendly manner. Epistemological effects had contributed to this bias, with many international investment lawyers having a commercial arbitration-background.[26] In addition, some argue that states even pre-emptively abstain from public interest regulation

---

24 John Anthony VanDuzer, 'Sustainable Development Provisions in International Trade Treaties: What Lessons for International Investment Agreements?' in Steffen Hindelang and Markus Krajewski (eds), Shifting Paradigms in International Investment Law: More Balanced, Less Isolated, Increasingly Diversified (Oxford University Press 2016) 172–173.

25 Michael A Waibel (ed), *The Backlash Against Investment Arbitration: Perceptions and Reality* (Wolters Kluwer Law & Business 2010); a comprehensive critique from a global justice-viewpoint presents Steven R Ratner, 'International Investment Law Through the Lens of Global Justice' (2017) 20(4) Journal of International Economic Law 747.

26 On this epistemological criticism see for example Gus van Harten, *Investment Treaty Arbitration and Public Law* (Oxford University Press 2007) 152–184; Moshe Hirsch, 'Investment Tribunals and Human Rights Treaties: A Sociological Perspective' in Freya Baetens (ed), *Investment Law Within International Law: Integrationist Perspectives* (Cambridge University Press 2013) 87–100; on how arbiters' different professional backgrounds influence the drawing of analogies and choice of legal paradigms as interpretive framework in international investment law see Anthea Roberts, 'Clash of Paradigms: Actors and Analogies Shaping the Investment Treaty System' (2013) 107(1) American Journal of International Law 45, 53–57.

because they fear investment arbitration claims for high amounts of compensation – the so-called chilling effect of investment law.[27]

Different conclusions have been drawn from these insights. Some states have decided to terminate their IIAs and to step away from the system of investment law altogether.[28] Other states, international organisations and NGOs have drafted new model IIAs that reconstruct their design aiming to strengthen and clarify the right of host states to regulate,[29] or change the institutional and procedural aspects of investment arbitration.[30] Yet others have proposed to reform investment law from within through a better, more balanced interpretation of IIAs. They call for the IIAs to be read in light of other international treaties that the state parties have concluded and which relate to the public interest, for example, international human rights treaties.[31]

---

27 On the regulatory chill-effect see for example Bruno Simma, 'Foreign Investment Arbitration: A Place for Human Rights?' (2011) 60(3) International & Comparative Law Quarterly 573, 580; Kyla Tienhaara, 'Regulatory Chill and the Threat of Arbitration: A View from Political Science' in Chester Brown (ed), Evolution in Investment Treaty Law and Arbitration (Cambridge University Press 2011); Jonathan Bonnitcha, *Substantive Protection Under Investment Treaties: A Legal and Economic Analysis* (Cambridge University Press 2014) 113–133.

28 This is a policy that for example Ecuador, Venezuela and Bolivia adopted, see Karsten Nowrot, 'Termination and Renegotiation of International Investment Agreements' in Steffen Hindelang and Markus Krajewski (eds), *Shifting Paradigms in International Investment Law: More Balanced, Less Isolated, Increasingly Diversified* (Oxford University Press 2016) 233–265 with further analysis.

29 There is plenty of literature on the precarious right to regulate in international investment law and how to strengthen it, see for example the comprehensive analysis by Aikaterini Titi, *The Right to Regulate in International Investment Law* (Nomos 2014).

30 For an overview of reform proposals for investment arbitration, structured on the basis of constitutional principles that arbitration should live up to, see Stephan W Schill, 'Reforming Investor–State Dispute Settlement: A (Comparative and International) Constitutional Law Framework' (2017) 20(3) Journal of International Economic Law 649; for an overview of the most recent ISDS reforms discussed by UNCTAD, ICSID and UNCITRAL, see José E Alvarez, 'ISDS Reform: The Long View' (2021) 36(2) ICSID Review 253.

31 Among others, Bruno Simma and Theodore Kill, 'Harmonizing Investment Protection and International Human Rights: First Steps Towards a Methodology' in Christina Binder and others (eds), *International Investment Law for the 21st Century: Essays in Honour of Christoph Schreuer* (Oxford University Press 2009) 678–707; Simma (n 27) 581 propose such an interpretation applying Art 31 (3) (c) of the Vienna Convention on the Law of Treaties (adopted 22 May 1969, entered into force 27 January 1980) 1155 UNTS 331 (VCLT).

III. The need for international investor obligations?

Much of the scholarly and public attention to how investment law relates to the public interest has focused on this right to regulate debate. Yet, notwithstanding its importance, in many cases, reclaiming and strengthening the host state's right to regulate is not enough to assure that foreign investments serve the public interest. The reason is that, within the logic that underpins the right to regulate in investment law, the role of third-party rights and public goods remains passive: States can only bring forward the protection of the public interest as a *justification* against investment claims by investors. The right to regulate does not itself express any expectations towards the investors that they should actively align their activities with the public interest as a matter of international law. To that end, the right to regulate relies completely on the host state and its domestic legal system – the state must make use of it. However, in a globalised economy, the host state's ability to do so and regulate foreign investment effectively is often limited in practice.

On a more general level, this concern is subject of the call for corporations' international responsibility (1.). In this light, investment law seems to exacerbate the current lack of international obligations (2.) as can be demonstrated by a hypothetical (but not far-fetched) example (3.).

1. The discussion on the international responsibility of corporations

Private economic actors have become increasingly powerful and influential, especially when operating beyond national borders. There is plenty of academic writing exemplifying that, in many cases, domestic regulation cannot sufficiently address the regulatory challenges posed by globalised economic activity. In this broader picture, foreign investment is part and parcel of the changing role corporations and non-state actors play in international law.

Building on earlier debates,[32] recent years have witnessed intensive discussions, especially on the UN-level, concerning international responsibilities of corporations. In particular multinational enterprises that operate

32 The thinking about binding international standards for multinational enterprises and foreign investors has a long history that goes back to the 1920s and has its more direct origin in the 1970s, for an overview see Peter Muchlinski, *Multinational Enterprises and the Law* (2nd edn, Oxford University Press 2007) 654–674.

across national borders often escape the territorial confines of domestic regulation. The economic power of major multinational enterprises often exceeds the net income growth of smaller states.[33] This economic weight equals power.[34] It is, therefore, self-evident that such private or non-state actors are increasingly regarded as highly important for states and the furthering of the public interest. In 2008, the UN Special Representative of the Secretary-General on the Issue of Human Rights and Transnational Corporations and Other Business Enterprises, John Ruggie, noted in this regard:

> The root cause of the business and human rights predicament today lies in the governance gaps created by globalization – between the scope and impact of economic forces and actors, and the capacity of societies to manage their adverse consequences. These governance gaps provide the permissive environment for wrongful acts by companies of all kinds without adequate sanctioning or reparation. How to narrow and ultimately bridge the gaps in relation to human rights is our fundamental challenge.[35]

Entrusted in 2011 with discerning what international human rights obligations corporations have, if any, John Ruggie presented the UN Guiding Principles on Business and Human Rights which have been widely accepted, received and referenced.[36] These Principles concur with most

---

33 See for example the economic assessment by Stiglitz (n 10) 476; see also Christian Tomuschat, *Human Rights: Between Idealism and Realism* (3rd edn, Oxford University Press 2014) 133 who observes that 'the economic power of a number of multinational corporations by far exceeds the economic capacities of many developing nations' and that '[a]s a result, the corporations are able to act largely without any governmental control by their host states'; but see the differentiated remarks on the relative bargaining power of states and multinational enterprises in different business sectors by Muchlinski (n 32) 104–107.

34 Steven R Ratner, 'Corporations and Human Rights: A Theory of Legal Responsibility' (2001) 111(3) Yale Law Journal 443, 461–463.

35 UN Human Rights Council 'Protect, Respect and Remedy: A Framework for Business and Human Rights. Report of the Special Representative of the Secretary-General on the Issue of Human Rights and Transnational Corporations and Other Business Enterprises, John Ruggie' UN Doc A/HRC/8/5 (7 April 2008), para 3; see further on the particular regulatory problems that multinational enterprises pose, juxtaposed to domestic companies, Stiglitz (n 10) 476–481.

36 On this wide-spread reception see for example Andreas Heinemann, 'Business Enterprises in Public International Law: The Case for an International Code on Corporate Responsibility' in Ulrich Fastenrath and others (eds), *From Bilateralism to Community Interest: Essays in Honour of Judge Bruno Simma* (Oxford University

scholars in considering only states to be bound by international human rights obligations. In contrast, corporations have a moral, non-binding 'responsibility' towards human rights. The prepondering opinion is similar concerning international obligations of corporations that relate to other facets of the public interest such as workers' rights and environmental protection.[37]

The emphasis on the moral responsibilities of corporations has led to a proliferating number of non-binding international CSR norms in the last years, created by states, international organisations and corporations themselves. They serve as guidelines for ethical business conduct and should be given practical effect through voluntary cooperation by companies and consumer pressure. They often build on the UN Guiding Principles on Business and Human Rights and other relevant documents and initiatives such as the UN Global Compact,[38] the OECD Guidelines for Multinational Enterprises[39] or the ILO Declaration on Fundamental Principles and Rights at Work.[40] They reflect the feeling that the setting of norms for private business conduct continues to be a pressing need. Despite the importance of such CSR norms,[41] critics contend that because of their voluntary character, in many situations, they fall short of providing effec-

---

Press 2011) 726–727; Surya Deva and David Bilchitz (eds), *Building a Treaty on Business and Human Rights: Context and Contours* (Cambridge University Press 2017) 2.

37 On environmental law see for example Sandrine Maljean-Dubois and Vanessa Richard, 'The Applicability of International Environmental Law to Private Enterprises' in Pierre-Marie Dupuy and Jorge E Viñuales (eds), *Harnessing Foreign Investment to Promote Environmental Protection: Incentives and Safeguards* (Cambridge University Press 2013) 69–93; on labour standards see for example Katja Gehne, 'Soft Standards and Hard Consequences: Why Transnational Companies Commit to Respect International Labour and Social Standards, and How This Relates to Business and Regulation' in Henner Gött (ed), *Labour Standards in International Economic Law* (Springer International Publishing 2018) 308–315.

38 UN 'Global Compact' ‹www.unglobalcompact.org/what-is-gc/mission/principles› accessed 7 December 2021; see also UNGA 'Towards Global Partnerships: A Principle-Based Approach to Enhanced Cooperation Between the United Nations and All Relevant Partners' UN Doc A/RES/68/234 (20 December 2013).

39 OECD 'Guidelines for Multinational Enterprises' (2011) ‹http://dx.doi.org/10.1787/9789264115415-en› accessed 7 December 2021.

40 ILO 'Declaration on Fundamental Principles and Rights at Work' adopted by the International Labour Conference at its Eighty-sixth Session, Geneva, 37 ILM 1233 (18 June 1998).

41 Generally on the specific advantages of soft law governance approaches see Kenneth W Abbott and Duncan Snidal, 'Hard and Soft Law in International Governance' (2000) 54(3) International Organization 421, 434–450.

tive and adequate human rights protection.[42] The attempt by a group of developing states at the UN Human Rights Council in the Open-ended Intergovernmental Working Group on Transnational Corporations and Other Business Enterprises with Respect to Human Rights to discuss an international treaty that imposes legally binding international human rights obligations on corporations remains inconclusive so far.[43] The first 2017 proposal on Elements for the Draft of a binding human rights treaty called for such binding international obligations of corporations.[44] However, the four subsequently discussed treaty drafts did not adopt this feature and

---

42 See for example International Commission of Jurists, *Needs and Options for a New International Instrument in the Field of Business and Human Rights* (International Commission of Jurists 2014) 17 which considers that the non-binding Guiding Principles on Business and Human Rights are of limited value as an accountability tool because they 'do not create a material or procedural basis for a cause of action by individuals'; David Bilchitz, 'The Necessity for a Business and Human Rights Treaty' (2016) 1(2) Business and Human Rights Journal 203, 205–219 who presents theoretical and practical arguments for binding international obligations of corporations; Barnali Choudhury and Martin Petrin, *Corporate Duties to the Public* (Cambridge University Press 2019) 1–36, 232–237 on the theoretical reasons to impose duties on corporations and why this should include human rights obligations; Jean Ho, 'The Creation of Elusive Investor Responsibility' (2019) 113 AJIL Unbound 10, 13–14 on voluntary compliance as the 'Achilles heel' of the CSR movement. Indeed, the observation that voluntary standards are not enough was the starting-point for expert discussions on international investor obligations by the IISD in 2018, see IISD, *Integrating Investor Obligations and Corporate Accountability Provisions in Trade and Investment Agreements: Report of the Expert Meeting Held in Versoix, Switzerland, January 11–12, 2018* (2018) 1.

43 The Working Group was established by the UN Human Rights Council 'Elaboration of an Internationally Legally Binding Instrument on Transnational Corporations and Other Business Enterprises with Respect to Human Rights' UN Doc A/HRC/RES/26/9 (14 July 2014). At the time of writing, it had seven sessions so far, the last discussing a third revised treaty draft on 25–29 October 2021, see ‹www.ohchr.org/en/hrbodies/hrc/wgtranscorp/pages/igwgontnc.aspx› accessed 7 December 2021.

44 UN Human Rights Council 'Elements for the Draft Legally Binding Instrument on Transnational Corporations and Other Business Enterprises with Respect to Human Rights' (29 September 2017) ‹www.ohchr.org/Documents/HRBodies/HRCouncil/WGTransCorp/Session3/LegallyBindingInstrumentTNCs_OBEs.pdf› accessed 7 December 2021, 6 proposes 'Obligations of Transnational Corporations and Other Business Enterprises', inter alia to 'respect internationally recognized human rights, wherever they operate, and throughout their supply chains', to 'prevent human rights impacts of their activities' and to 'design, adopt and implement internal policies consistent with internationally recognized human rights standards'.

exclusively suggest new international obligations of states towards corporations.[45]

These discussions on corporate actions and international standards, in turn, form part of another, even more general debate: the changing role of non-state actors[46] in international law. In a globalised and further globalising world, non-state actors increasingly take over important (state) functions or impact people's lives in a way a state normally would. To mention but one example, one may refer to the broadening military role that rebel groups, insurgents and other private groups play in armed conflicts.[47] Or one could point to the significant number of international organisations

---

45 These four drafts refer to the 'responsibility' – or, in the most recent draft, the 'obligation' – of corporations only in their preambles. The draft treaty provisions address only the states. Therefore, the drafts seem to adopt the non-binding nature of the Second Pillar of the UN Guiding Principles on Business and Human Rights. See UN Human Rights Council 'Zero Draft Legally Binding Instrument to Regulate, in International Human Rights Law, the Activities of Transnational Corporations and Other Business Enterprises' (16 July 2018) ‹www.ohchr.org/Documents/HRBodies/HRCouncil/WGTransCorp/Session3/DraftLBI.pdf› accessed 7 December 2021; UN Human Rights Council 'Revised Draft Legally Binding Instrument to Regulate, in International Human Rights Law, the Activities of Transnational Corporations and Other Business Enterprises' (16 July 2019) ‹www.ohchr.org/Documents/HRBodies/HRCouncil/WGTransCorp/OEIGWG_RevisedDraft_LBI.pdf› accessed 7 December 2021; UN Human Rights Council 'Second Revised Draft Legally Binding Instrument to Regulate, in International Human Rights Law, the Activities of Transnational Corporations and Other Business Enterprises' (6 August 2020) ‹www.ohchr.org/Documents/HRBodies/HRCouncil/WGTransCorp/Session6/OEIGWG_Chair-Rapporteur_second_revised_draft_LBI_on_TNCs_and_OBEs_with_respect_to_Human_Rights.pdf› accessed 7 December 2021; UN Human Rights Council 'Third Revised Draft Legally Binding Instrument to Regulate, in International Human Rights Law, the Activities of Transnational Corporations and Other Business Enterprises' (17 August 2021) ‹www.ohchr.org/Documents/HRBodies/HRCouncil/WGTransCorp/Session6/LBI3rdDRAFT.pdf› accessed 7 December 2021. For an analysis of how these drafts developed, see Markus Krajewski, 'A Nightmare or a Noble Dream? Establishing Investor Obligations Through Treaty-Making and Treaty-Application' (2020) 5(1) Business and Human Rights Journal 110–112.

46 The term 'non-state actors' is understood as covering all persons other than the state. Thus, it is broader in scope than the term 'individual' as used in this book because non-state actors for example also include international organisations.

47 On the increasing legal importance of the individual in modern international humanitarian law that mirrors the increasing military relevance of non-state actors and armed groups see Kate Parlett, *The Individual in the International Legal System: Continuity and Change in International Law* (Cambridge University Press 2011) 181–196, 208–228.

that make international rules and exert public authority in many different matters, such as environmental protection, regulation of the seas, public health and so on.[48]

Throughout the 20th century, writers have reflected on how international law can adequately grasp the diversification of international actors and the way they interact with or even relativise state sovereignty.[49] International obligations have always formed a focal point in these discussions and continue to do so today. There is the claim that non-state actors should face international legal restraints similar to states if they take over state-like functions or powers[50] – or that international individual rights and accountability should generally go hand-in-hand.[51] There is also a more specific call for international obligations of non-state actors for those situations in which states fail to live up to their international duties. States may be unwilling to confront non-state actors for a variety of reasons. Or they may be unable to enforce their domestic law against them due to a lack of resources and institutions or due to dependencies on the

---

48 See Matthias Ruffert and Christian Walter, *Institutionalised International Law* (Nomos 2015) paras 61–114 who identify an 'institutionalised' international law in this increasing role of international organisation with functionally constitutional elements.

49 For a discussion of various concepts of international personality that try to grasp this increasing diversification see Roland Portmann, *Legal Personality in International Law* (Cambridge University Press 2010) 42–242.

50 The literature is extensive on this matter. For the present introductory purpose, it may suffice to point to a few prominent voices, for example Hersch Lauterpacht who forcefully advocated the individual subjectivity of natural persons in international law, see Hersch Lauterpacht, *International Law and Human Rights* (Garland Publishing, Inc. 1973) 27–72; for a more cautious position see Tomuschat (n 33) 133; for a stance that international law is purely about the relation between states see Dionisio Anzilotti, *Cours de droit international: 1 Introduction, théories générales* (Sirey 1929) 134.

51 For example Ernst-Ulrich Petersmann, *Multilevel Constitutionalism for Multilevel Governance of Public Goods: Methodology Problems in International Law* (Bloomsbury Publishing 2017) 341–358 who argues in favour of an international cosmopolitan and republican form of international multilevel constitutionalism which includes an international accountability of diverse actors including citizens and multinational enterprises. John Ruggie in his mandate as Special Representative of the UN Secretary-General followed an approach of 'principled pragmatism', focusing on a reachable, politically authoritative set of norms instead of a legally binding instrument, see Ruggie (n 6) 42–46.

non-state actor.[52] Moreover, third states – in our context capital-exporting countries – may encounter legal and political barriers when regulating the extraterritorial conduct of non-state actors.[53]

2. International investor rights without obligations?

These general concerns against private actors and corporations also apply to foreign investors. Often, they form part of multinational enterprises or other forms of joint transnational business activities. Many foreign investors engage in activities that support the state in its public functions or even take over such functions following privatisation. Where foreign investors assume a critical role in a host state's economy, for example in infrastructure projects, the state may find itself, to a certain extent, dependent on the investor. What is more, countries may struggle with poor state organisation, corruption or other inabilities to properly enforce domestic laws against foreign investors.

In this scenario, investment law seems to exacerbate the general lack of international obligations of non-state actors: It provides international rights to investors without imposing international obligations. And, as seen, investor rights call into question the host state's right to regulate foreign investors' behaviour under domestic law. In the worst case, investment law shields investors against host states' domestic regulation in a globalised setting, in which even unhindered domestic regulatory capacity may not be enough.[54] In this broad perspective, to reassert host states' right to regulate may be important and necessary but insufficient to reach the

52 IISD, *A Sustainability Toolkit for Trade Negotiators: Trade and Investment as Vehicles for Achieving the 2030 Sustainable Development Agenda* (2017) 5.3.1 mentioning more cautiously the case that 'domestic laws are not complete'.

53 For an analysis that connects the related business and human rights-debate with international investment law see George K Foster, 'Investors, States, and Stakeholders: Power Asymmetries in International Investment and the Stabilizing Potential of Investment Treaties' (2013) 17(2) Lewis & Clark Law Review 361, 393–398; on the most prominent case of domestic law with extraterritorial reach, the US Alien Torts Act, see for example Anja Seibert-Fohr, 'Transnational Labour Litigation: The Ups and Downs Under the Alien Tort Statute' in Henner Gött (ed), *Labour Standards in International Economic Law* (Springer International Publishing 2018).

54 That international investment law may exacerbate the challenge to regulate multinational corporations is emphasised for example by UNHRC 'Protect, Respect and Remedy' (n 35) paras 12–13.

goal of assuring that foreign investment serves the public interest. This points to the need for the development of international obligations of foreign investors.[55]

3. A practical example

Due to the demand for high-end technological knowledge and the promise of potential high returns, foreign investors often engage in commercial exploitation of natural resources in the mining sectors of developing countries. One can picture a situation in which foreign investors do not import the high production standards from their home state but instead heavily pollute the groundwater at the production site, using cheaper technology to maximise profits. This pollution endangers the local population's health.

In this scenario, it appears that, just like any corporation, foreign investors do not have any binding international obligation to respect the population's health nor to protect the environment. Legally binding standards can only follow from the host state's national law. However, the host state may be unwilling to act against the investors because it prioritises furthering its economic development. It may be unable to do so because it heavily depends on the tax payments of the economically powerful investors. Or it suffers from an insufficient domestic administrative and judicial system. In addition, investment law may even protect the investors against any measures of the host state. The investors could sue the host state before an investment tribunal if the state chooses to protect the environment or the local population. The procedural risk of potentially high amounts of damages may deter the host state from taking any action in the first place. Therefore, in this constellation, it seems that investment law would exacerbate the lack of legally binding international obligations of corporations.

55 Indeed, the debate on obligations of foreign investors has a long history reaching back into the 18th century, see Karsten Nowrot, 'Obligations of Investors' in Marc Bungenberg and others (eds), *International Investment Law* (Nomos 2015) para 3.

IV. Exploring investor obligations in investment law

How does investment law grasp, if at all, the need for international investor obligations? Does it in some way reflect the changing and sometimes precarious position of states vis-à-vis potent foreign investors, and the increasing role of non-state actors in general international law? In general terms: could investment law, as a field, center not only around the protection of foreign investors but also contribute to the creation of some form of binding international responsibility? And what would this mean for the role and purpose of investment law within general international law?

This book aims to answer these questions. It will show that already today, investment law increasingly addresses the investors' misconduct towards the public interest independently of the states' national law and its enforcement on the domestic level. Investment law is generating new forms of international standards that foreign investors must observe regarding international human rights, workers' rights, the environment and the rule of law, to name the most relevant examples. As this book shall elaborate in detail, it is remarkable that these norms are of legally binding effect – while at times drawing and building on legally non-binding CSR standards.

To shed light on these dynamics, this book is divided into three Parts. Parts I and II distinguish between two different categories of investor obligations. The first will study 'direct international investor obligations' which constitute binding international standards directly applicable to foreign investors. Such direct obligations may, for example, require the investor to conduct an environmental impact assessment – and to pay compensation to the host state in case of non-compliance.

Part II introduces 'indirect international investor obligations' as a new term. These are standards of conduct for investors which deprive investors of substantive or procedural investment protection in case of non-compliance. Consequently, states cannot directly demand investors to comply with these indirect obligations and claim compensation in case of a breach. Rather, indirect obligations are implied in investor rights. These obligations are already established, to a substantial extent, in arbitral jurisprudence, even though tribunals do not yet identify them as a structural phenomenon. For example, an indirect obligation may also call upon the foreign investor to conduct an environmental impact assessment, as discussed above for direct obligations. Yet, here the consequence of a breach is different: for example, investors may be deprived of the possibility to invoke an investor right against the host state before an investment tribunal.

Lastly, Part III will outline the common implications of both categories of such investor obligations. There, it shall be submitted that while they contribute to rebalancing investment law as a field, they also offer a potentially new function of IIAs – as an international regulatory instrument capable of steering investors' behaviour. In the broader picture, investor obligations give rise to a new form of individual international responsibility prompting reflection on general international law as a whole.

Part I
Direct Obligations

Part I will first address direct international investor obligations. These are obligations construed similarly to obligations in international criminal law: They directly apply to investors and command them to act or abstain from certain action as a matter of international law. Part I will show that such direct obligations have already been created and are being applied in investment law today.

To that end, Part I will begin by addressing preconditions of these direct international obligations. It will show that there are no obstacles for their creation under general international law – even though the existence of such obligations in other branches of international law remains an exception (Chapter 2). Then, this Part will explain and systematise the direct obligations which have recently developed in investment law practice (Chapter 3). Subsequently, the analysis will proceed to a procedural perspective. It will elaborate on counterclaims in investment arbitration. They represent a means for states to internationally enforce direct obligations against investors. It is submitted that they are at states' disposal under many existing IIAs (Chapter 4). Part I concludes that overall, we may already be witnessing the dawn of direct obligations in international investment law (Chapter 5).

Chapter 2.
Preconditions of Direct Obligations

Chapter 2 will introduce the concept of direct obligations more closely and shed light on its preconditions under international law.

The term 'direct obligations' means that international law provides for a directly applicable obligation to investors as non-state actors (I.). Some critics raise fundamental objections against the possibility of creating such direct obligations.[1] However, it will be shown that there is nothing in international law that prevents imposing such obligations onto the investors. First, international law allows for conferring the necessary international subjectivity to investors as a particular group of non-state actors (II.). Imposing such obligations does not violate the principle of *pacta tertiis nec nocent nec prosunt* (III.). Notwithstanding, only very few such obligations exist in international law as of today (IV.). Most consider international investment law to be no different in this regard. In contrast to this book's hypothesis, it is usually perceived to be an asymmetrical branch of international law that accords rights without obligations to investors (V.). The Chapter concludes: direct obligations have few preconditions but also few role-models (VI.).

I. Direct applicability

Part I searches for international obligations that are *directly applicable* to foreign investors. Similar to directly applicable international rights, these are international obligations that do not require a state to implement or transform them into domestic law to have effect. These 'direct obligations' address not the state but the investors and directly demand them to act or abstain from acting.[2]

---

1 See for example Andrew Clapham, *Human Rights Obligations of Non-State Actors* (Oxford University Press 2006) 35–41.

2 On this notion of directly applicable rights see Markos Karavias, *Corporate Obligations Under International Law* (Oxford University Press 2014) 11–12; Karsten Nowrot, 'How to Include Environmental Protection, Human Rights and Sustainability in International Investment Law?' (2014) 15(3/4) Journal of World Invest-

Herein, direct obligations depart from the so-called mediatisation of obligations. In this concept, only states have international obligations. These include duties to prescribe and enforce domestic law. Consequently, states have to adopt or transform these duties' requirements into their domestic legal systems. It is only these domestic obligations that directly apply to non-state actors.[3]

For example: Art 6 (1) ICCPR[4] enshrines the right to life. Mediatisation of obligations means that only the state parties are bound by this obligation. They have to adopt respective legislation in their domestic legal systems to make it applicable to private actors. For example, they may enact domestic criminal law to protect the life of individuals against criminal behaviour of other individuals. Then, it is only domestic criminal law which binds those individuals – not the ICCPR. In contrast, if Art 6 (1) ICCPR was a direct obligation, individuals would be subject to it as a matter of international law, independent of domestic criminal law.

Clearly, direct obligations represent a much more immediate international norm for addressing private actors' behavior. Foregoing the mediatisation by the state may be important in cases when a state is unwilling or unable to enact and enforce domestic law.[5] And directly applicable obligations may constitute grounds for bringing about an international responsibility of foreign investors. Such an active addressing of private actors may correspond with their increasing role in a globalised economy and be desirable even when states are willing and able to enact and enforce domestic law.

---

ment & Trade 612, 636; Anne Peters, *Beyond Human Rights: The Legal Status of the Individual in International Law* (Cambridge University Press 2016) 496–501; see also Jacob K Cogan, 'The Regulatory Turn in International Law' (2011) 52(2) Harvard International Law Journal 321, 346–348 who coins these legal norms as 'unmediated law'.

3 In the purest form suggested by Lassa F Oppenheim, *International Law: A Treatise* (2nd edn, Longmans, Green and Co. 1912) 362–365; on states' obligation to protect see Peters (n 2) 67–71; on how IIAs incorporate international obligations of states to prescribe and enforce domestic law to protect the public interest, see Nowrot, 'Include' (n 2) 638.

4 International Covenant on Civil and Political Rights (adopted 16 December 1966, entered into force 23 March 1976) 999 UNTS 171 (ICCPR).

5 Peters (n 2) 76–78 flagging out the closing of 'regulatory gaps'.

II. International subjectivity

The most fundamental objection against direct obligations lies in the alleged lack of international legal subjectivity of foreign investors. Indeed, such argumentation featured for example in the *Urbaser v Argentina* ICSID proceedings.[6] However, this line of argument is without merit.

The terms 'international subjectivity' or 'international personality', used interchangeably here, have no authoritative definition in international law[7] and continue to remain controversial.[8] This study understands international subjectivity as the capacity of an entity to have rights and obligations under international law – quite similar to how subjectivity is understood in many domestic jurisdictions.[9] Which rights and obligations the respective entity with an acknowledged international legal subjectivity enjoys, if any, is an altogether different and separate question.[10]

In the most traditional understanding, suggested for example by legal positivism in the early 20th century, only states could enjoy international subjectivity.[11] However, throughout the past hundred years, states have accepted the international subjectivity of non-state actors. This is particularly true for individuals, following the recognition of human rights by the

---

6 *Urbaser S.A. and Consorcio de Aguas Bilbao Bizkaia, Bilbao Biskaia Ur Partzuergoa v The Argentine Republic*, ICSID Case No. ARB/07/26, Award (8 December 2016) paras 1193–1194.

7 Peters (n 2) 35; Roland Portmann, *Legal Personality in International Law* (Cambridge University Press 2010) 9.

8 See for example Rosalyn Higgins, *Problems and Process: International Law and How We Use It* (Clarendon Press 1995) 50; Barnali Choudhury and Martin Petrin, *Corporate Duties to the Public* (Cambridge University Press 2019) 209–210 and the notion of 'subjects as prisoners of doctrine' by Clapham (n 1) 59–63.

9 See the reference and comparison to domestic legal concepts of subjectivity by Portmann (n 7) 7–8.

10 This distinction between subjectivity and the content of rights and obligations is for example affirmed by Steven R Ratner, 'Corporations and Human Rights: A Theory of Legal Responsibility' (2001) 111(3) Yale Law Journal 443, 475–476; Christian Walter, 'Subjects of International Law' in Anne Peters (ed), *Max Planck Encyclopedia of Public International Law* (May 2007) paras 21–22; James Crawford, *Brownlie's Principles of Public International Law* (8th edn, Oxford University Press 2012) 121; see also *Reparation for Injuries Suffered in the Service of the United Nations* (Advisory Opinion) [1949] ICJ Rep 174, 178 in which the ICJ observed that the 'subjects of law in any legal system are not necessarily identical in their nature or in the extent of their rights'.

11 That was for example the position by Oppenheim (n 3) 19; Dionisio Anzilotti, *Cours de droit international: 1 Introduction, théories générales* (Sirey 1929) 134; see also the critical remarks by Portmann (n 7) 42–79.

international community.[12] Indeed, as will be laid out in more detail at a later stage, many consider that states have granted investors individual rights in IIAs, and that they have implicitly accorded them the necessary international personality too.

Not to be confused with this presented understanding of international legal subjectivity are other definitions of the concept that this study does not adopt – but with which it does not conflict either. For example, some understand international legal subjectivity as presupposing a certain minimum corpus of rights such as the capacity to conclude international treaties.[13] Others require the relevant actor to have 'a certain freedom of action on the international level and […] engage in international transactions beyond a framework rigidly fixed once and for all in their constitutive instrument.'[14] Some also require that the entity has the right to create, amend and terminate international law so as to acknowledge that it enjoys subjectivity.[15]

12 Christian Tomuschat, *Human Rights: Between Idealism and Realism* (3rd edn, Oxford University Press 2014) 112–116; on individual rights beyond human rights see for example *LaGrand Case (Germany v USA)* (Judgment) [2001] ICJ Rep 466, para 77; *Case Concerning Avena and Other Mexican Nationals (Mexico v United States of America)* (Judgment) [2004] ICJ Rep 12, para 40; on multinational corporations see Muthucumaraswamy Sornarajah, *The International Law on Foreign Investment* (5th edn, Cambridge University Press 2021) 80–86.

13 Manuel Rama-Montaldo, 'International Legal Personality and Implied Powers of International Organizations' (1970) 44 British Yearbook of International Law 111, 139; cf Peters (n 2) 37.

14 Christian Tomuschat, 'International Law: Ensuring the Survival of Mankind on the Eve of a New Century: General Course on Public International Law' (1999) 281 Recueil des Cours 9, 160. See also the indications of international legal personality that point to state-like entities by Bin Cheng, 'Introduction to Subjects of International Law' in Mohammed Bedjaoui (ed), *International Law: Achievements and Prospects* (UNESCO, Nijhoff 1991) 38.

15 Ian Brownlie, *Principles of Public International Law* (6th edn, Oxford University Press 2003) 57; also at least discussed as a potential consequence of invoking international subjectivity on the example of corporations by José E Alvarez, 'Are Corporations "Subjects" of International Law?' (2011) 9(1) Santa Clara Journal of International Law 1, 23–26, 31–35; see also the overview by Andrea Bianchi, 'The Fight for Inclusion: Non-State Actors and International Law' in Ulrich Fastenrath and others (eds), *From Bilateralism to Community Interest: Essays in Honour of Judge Bruno Simma* (Oxford University Press 2011) 49–52.

Yet, these approaches figure in a different scholarly context.[16] Largely, they address the role private organisations play in the setting of international standards or the deliberating of new international rules. They revolve around the problem that non-state actors may relativise states' sovereign norm-setting authority. The present study has no say in these matters. As will be laid out in more detail, this book engages with states' own initiative to impose obligations on investors. The presented alternative definitions of subjectivity do not challenge states' capacity to do so.[17]

In line with this observation, the Tribunal in *Urbaser v Argentina* explicitly affirmed investors' international subjectivity. It held that

> [a] simple look at the MFN Clause of Article VII of the BIT shows that Contracting States accepted at least one hypothesis where investors are entitled to invoke rights resulting from international law [...]. If the BIT therefore is not based on a corporation's incapacity of holding rights under international law, it cannot be admitted that it would reject by necessity any idea that a foreign investor company could not be subject to international law obligations.[18]

Even more broadly, it found that to perceive international law as governing inter-state relations only had 'its importance in the past'[19] but 'has lost its impact'[20]. Recently, the UNCITRAL Tribunal in *Aven v Costa Rica* has explicitly affirmed this finding, citing the *Urbaser* award.[21]

---

16 The importance of the context when discussing international legal personality becomes clear reading the five different definitory categories of international personality discerned by Portmann (n 7) 13–14.

17 Hence, conceptually, this study claims that investors may enjoy derivative, partial and relative subjectivity similar to how the ICJ accepted international organisations' subjectivity in *Reparation for Injuries* (n 10) 178 and affirmed the individual character of consular rights in *LaGrand* (n 12) para 77; *Avena* (n 12) para 40. On the implicit granting of subjectivity see Walter (n 10) paras 23–26; supported is the partial subjectivity of the investor for example by Tillmann R Braun, *Ausprägungen der Globalisierung: Der Investor als partielles Subjekt im Internationalen Investitionsrecht: Qualität und Grenzen dieser Wirkungseinheit* (Nomos 2012) 162; for a contrary, too narrow position see Andreas Kulick, *Global Public Interest in International Investment Law* (Cambridge University Press 2012) 197. cf the discussion of legal subjectivity of multinational enterprises by Clapham (n 1) 79–80.

18 *Urbaser v Argentina*, Award (n 6) para 1194.

19 ibid.

20 ibid.

21 *David Aven et al. v The Republic of Costa Rica*, Case No. UNCT/15/3, Final Award (UNCITRAL, 18 September 2018) para 738.

III. Non-application of the pacta tertiis principle

However, in contrast to the granting of individual *rights* to foreign investors, the imposing of direct *obligations* may encounter additional concerns. Some argue that states cannot unilaterally impose direct obligations on investors without their consent due to the principle of *pacta tertiis nec nocent nec prosunt*. In this view, because foreign investors are no party to IIAs, they cannot be bound by a direct obligation enshrined in the IIA.[22]

The *pacta tertiis* principle forms one of the elementary rules on the making of international law and is a general principle of law. It stipulates that states cannot be bound by an international treaty without their consent.[23] This follows from the more general principle that all sources of international law go back to the positive sovereign consent of a state to be bound, as reflected in the PCIJ's *Lotus* judgment.[24] The reasons why international law cannot bind a state without its consent are enshrined in the principles of sovereignty and sovereign equality (Art 2 (1) UN-Charter). These give every state freedom on how to arrange its internal and external affairs.

---

22 This position is taken for example by Todd Weiler, 'Balancing Human Rights and Investor Protection: A New Approach for a Different Legal Order' (2004) 27(2) Boston College International and Comparative Law Review 429, 448; Jarrod Hepburn and Vuyelwa Kuuya, 'Corporate Social Responsibility and Investment Treaties' in Marie-Claire Cordonier Segger, Markus W Gehring and Andrew P Newcombe (eds), *Sustainable Development in World Investment Law* (Kluwer Law International 2011) 598; also implicated by James Crawford, 'Treaty and Contract in Investment Arbitration' (2008) 24(3) Arbitration International 351, 364; similarly Martin Jarrett, *Contributory Fault and Investor Misconduct in Investment Arbitration* (Cambridge University Press 2019) 112–113 for what this book understands to be indirect obligations which will be analysed in Part II below.

23 Art 34 VCLT; recognised in *Certain German Interests in Polish Upper Silesia (Germany v Poland)* (Merits) [1926] PCIJ Rep Series A No 7, 29; *Case of the Free Zones of Upper Savoy and the District of Gex (Switzerland v France)* (Judgment) [1932] PCIJ Rep Series A/B No 46, 55–56; *Anglo-Iranian Oil Co. Case (United Kingdom v Iran)* (Preliminary Objection) [1952] ICJ Rep 93, 109; for an in depth-analysis of the principle and its expressions in international law see Christine Chinkin, *Third Parties in International Law* (Clarendon Press 1993); on possible exceptions applicable to states see Christian Tomuschat, 'Obligations Arising for States Without or Against Their Will' (1993) 241 Recueil des Cours 195; Herbert L Hart, *The Concept of Law* (2nd edn, Clarendon Press 1994) 226; Nico Krisch, 'The Decay of Consent: International Law in an Age of Global Public Goods' (2014) 108(1) American Journal of International Law 1.

24 *The Case of the S.S. 'Lotus' (France v Turkey)* (Judgment) [1927] PCIJ Rep Series A No 10, 18.

Similarly, because all states are sovereign, no state can impose a legal norm against the will of another state: *Par in parem non habet imperium*.[25]

But to apply the *pacta tertiis* principle to the relation between states and foreign investors would be misleading. This confusion likely follows from investment arbitration's historical origins in international commercial arbitration. In many domestic legal systems' private law, the *pacta tertiis* rule applies to legal relations between private actors. There, it means that they cannot be bound by a contract with another private actor without their consent. The justification for this domestic *pacta tertiis* rule lies in the private actor's private autonomy and freedom of contract.[26] One cannot simply transfer such domestic legal principles to the international level.

Rather, in international law, foreign investors exist as international subjects only to the extent that states have granted them this status in a certain IIA. In consequence, states have generally wide discretion as to the rights and obligations they wish to attach to this status,[27] safe of course for conflicting rules such as international human rights obligations which will be dealt with at a later point. In granting rights and imposing obligations, they simply exert sovereign powers through international law. There is no difference between a state creating a domestic obligation as a matter of public law and prescribing an international obligation jointly with another state in an international treaty.[28] Precisely this argument was decisive for the International Military Tribunal to justify that states can impose

---

25 Crawford, *Principles* (n 10) 448–449; on the origins and meaning of this notion see Yoram Dinstein, 'Par in Parem Non Habet Imperium' (1966) 1(3) Israel Law Review 407.

26 See for example the brief theoretical contextualisation by Hector L Macqueen and Stephen Bogle, 'Private Autonomy and the Protection of the Weaker Party: Historical' in Stefan Vogenauer (ed), *General Principles of Law: European and Comparative Perspectives* (Bloomsbury Publishing 2017) 274–276.

27 See Chinkin (n 23) 120–122 who rightly observes that '[i]ndividuals as third parties to treaties are not in the same position as third party States or organizations' (121). She argues that states can provide rights and impose obligations on individuals as well as revoke and modify treaties which have accorded individual rights without these individuals having any say under the international law of treaties.

28 cf John H Knox, 'Horizontal Human Rights Law' (2008) 102(1) American Journal of International Law 1, 29 on how international human rights obligations directly applicable to private actors are to be construed.

directly applicable international criminal obligations on private actors.[29] The same holds true for IIAs.[30]

IV. Direct obligations as the exception in international law

While general international law does not hinder states from creating directly applicable obligations, states have only done so to a very limited extent. To determine if this is the case, the traditional methods to identify the content of the sources of international law apply: foremost, treaty interpretation and identification of customary international law.

Direct obligations are most well-established in international criminal law. In 1948, the International Military Tribunal famously confirmed that natural persons are subject to directly applicable obligations.[31] However,

29 'The Signatory Powers created this Tribunal, defined the law it was to administer, and made regulations for the proper conduct of the Trial. In doing so, they have done together what any of them might have done singly […]. With regard to the constitution of the Court, all that the defendants are entitled to ask is to receive a fair trail on the facts and law.', International Military Tribunal, *The United States of America, the French Republic, the United Kingdom of Great Britain and Northern Ireland, and the Union of Soviet Socialist Republics v Hermann Wilhelm Göring and Others* (Proceedings) (1948) XXII Trial of the Major War Criminals Before the International Military Tribunal, 461.

30 Supported for example by Kate Miles, *The Origins of International Investment Law: Empire, Environment and the Safeguarding of Capital* (Cambridge University Press 2013) 359; Karsten Nowrot, 'Obligations of Investors' in Marc Bungenberg and others (eds), *International Investment Law* (Nomos 2015) para 13; Peter Muchlinski, 'Negotiating New Generation International Investment Agreements: New Sustainable Development Oriented Initiatives' 59; Jose D Amado, Jackson S Kern and Martin D Rodriguez, *Arbitrating the Conduct of International Investors* (Cambridge University Press 2018) 90; but see Alvarez (n 15) 23–24 who warns against accepting international subjectivity of corporations as that would possibly require applying the *pacta tertiis* rule in the relation of states to corporations. However, Alvarez uses a more material definition of international subjectivity that presupposes equal rights and obligations of subjects, a concept that is not followed here, see above Chapter 2.I.

31 '[E]nough has been said to show that individuals can be punished for violations of International Law. Crimes against International Law are committed by men not by abstract entities, and only by punishing individuals who commit such crimes can the provisions of International Law be enforced.', *The United States of America and Others v Hermann Wilhelm Göring and Others*, Proceedings (n 29) 466; later confirmed by International Military Tribunal for the Far East, *The United States of America, the Republic of China, the United Kingdom of Great Britain and Northern Ireland, the Union of Soviet Socialist Republics, the Commonwealth*

such obligations prohibit only the gravest forms of atrocities and also do not address corporations.[32] Furthermore, while *ius cogens* is broadly accepted to directly bind non-state actors,[33] it only covers the most elemental norms such as the prohibition of torture. The same is true for international humanitarian law. Because it only applies in situations of armed conflict, it is too narrow in scope to comprehensively cover foreign investment activity – even if some argue that norms on non-international armed conflicts directly apply to non-state actors.[34]

---

of Australia, Canada, the Republic of France, the Kingdom of the Netherlands, New Zealand, India, and the Commonwealth of the Philippines Against Araki, Sadao and Others (Judgment) (4 November 1948) printed in Bert V Röling and Christiaan F Rüter (eds), *The Tokyo Judgment: The International Military Tribunal for the Far East (I.M.T.F.E.), 29 April 1946–12 November 1948* (University Press Amsterdam 1977) 27–28; ILC 'Principles of International Law Recognized in the Charter of the Nürnberg Tribunal and in the Judgment of the Tribunal' [1950] Yearbook of the International Law Commission, vol II 374–378 subsequently acknowledged by UNGA 'Formulation of the Nuremberg Principles' UN Doc A/RES/488 (V) (12 December 1950); see also Art 25 para 1 Rome Statute of the International Criminal Court (adopted 17 July 1998, entered into force 1 July 2002) 2187 UNTS 3 (Rome Statute); *Prosecutor v Duško Tadić* (Decision on the Defence Motion for Interlocutory Appeal on Jurisdiction) IT-94-1-AR72 (ICTY, 2 October 1995) paras 128–137; *Prosecutor v Duško Tadić* (Judgment) IT-94-1-T (ICTY, 7 May 1997) paras 661–669.

32 There have been early indications in favour of international corporate punishment, see *The United States of America and Others v Hermann Wilhelm Göring and Others*, Proceedings (n 29) 501–517 which declared the Leadership Corps of the Nazi Party, the Gestapo, the Sicherheitsdienst des Reichsführers and the Schutzstaffel to be criminal groups and organisations; and see the investigation of businesses' criminal wrongdoings by *United States v Alfried Felix Alwyn Krupp von Bohlen und Halbach and Others ('The Krupp Case')* (1948) IX Trials of War Criminals Before the Nuernberg Military Tribunals Under Control Council Law No 10 (US Military Tribunal III) 1327–1448 and *United States v Karl Krauch and Others ('The Farben Case')* (1948) VIII Trials of War Criminals Before the Nuernberg Military Tribunals Under Control Council Law No 10 (US Military Tribunal VI) 1132. However, different traditions in civil and common law jurisdictions prevented that such obligations came to be established, see Karavias (n 2) 59–67, 89–115.

33 Supported for example by UN Human Rights Council 'Report of the Independent International Commission of Inquiry on the Syrian Arab Republic' UN Doc A/HRC/19/69 (22 February 2012), para 106; Peters (n 2) 101. But see the opposite view for example by *Kiobel and Others v Royal Dutch Petroleum Co. and Others* (2010) 621 F.3d 111 (US Court of Appeals for the Second Circuit) 148.

34 A prominent example is Common Art 3 of the Geneva Conventions, for example as enshrined in the Geneva Convention for the Amelioration of the Condition of the Wounded and Sick in Armed Forces in the Field (adopted 12 August

Although international human rights have a comprehensive scope, the prevailing view is that non-state actors do not have directly applicable binding human rights obligations.[35] This view, with relation to corporations, is confirmed in the 2011 UN Guiding Principles on Business and Human Rights. Their First Pillar elaborates on the legally binding international human rights duties of states. The Second Pillar lists the non-binding responsibilities of companies, stating that corporations only 'should'[36] comply with international human rights. Some attempt to give these rules a stronger normative effect. For example, the UN Office of the High Commissioner for Human Rights in the FAQs on the Guiding Principles observes that while the Principles were not a legal instrument, they were not voluntary but would reflect 'a minimum expectation of all companies'.[37] However, legally speaking, this statement is not very helpful because it blurs the doctrinal analysis. As a matter of international law, the norms enshrined in the Guiding Principles remain non-binding and voluntary in the sense that companies are free to choose if they comply with the moral expectations expressed therein.

1949, entered into force 21 October 1950) 75 UNTS 31 (GC I); see International Committee of the Red Cross, *Commentary on the First Geneva Convention* (1952) 51 with further references.

35 Peters (n 2) 67–68, 71; Tomuschat, *Human* (n 12) 129–135; Maria Monnheimer, *Due Diligence Obligations in International Human Rights Law* (Cambridge University Press 2021) 17–28; Xuan Shao, 'Environmental and Human Rights Counterclaims in International Investment Arbtiration: at the Crossroads of Domestic and International Law' (2021) 24(1) Journal of International Economic Law 157, 161–162; for an opposite view see Jordan J Paust, 'Human Rights Responsibilities of Private Corporations' (2002) 35(3) Vanderbilt Journal of Transnational Law 801, 810; Weiler (n 22) 440–444; Choudhury and Petrin (n 8), 231; for a more careful position which considers it at least possible to interpret human rights to bind non-state actors see Markus Krajewski, 'A Nightmare or a Noble Dream? Establishing Investor Obligations Through Treaty-Making and Treaty-Application' (2020) 5(1) Business and Human Rights Journal 105, 110.

36 See Principle 11 in UN Human Rights Council 'Guiding Principles on Business and Human Rights Implementing the United Nations "Protect, Respect and Remedy" Framework' UN Doc HRC/RES/17/4 (2011); John G Ruggie, *Just Business: Multinational Corporations and Human Rights* (Norton 2013) 90–93.

37 Office of the UN High Commissioner for Human Rights 'Frequently Asked Questions About the Guiding Principles on Business and Human Rights' HR/PUB/14/3 (2014), 9.

Even where human rights treaties such as the AfrCHPR[38] contain language indicative of international duties,[39] most reject that these norms are directly applicable to non-state actors.[40] Other branches, such as international labour law, are subject to similar discussions. Where the wording of a treaty appears to directly address non-state actors, such a direct application is nevertheless generally equally rejected.[41]

In contrast to these international treaties, it is more generally accepted that UN Security Council resolutions issued under Chapter VII of the UN

---

38 African Charter on Human and Peoples' Rights (adopted 27 June 1981, entered into force 21 October 1986) 1520 UNTS 217 (Banjul Charter).

39 It covers an entire chapter on human rights duties; for a comparative analysis of the institutional and procedural features of the three regional human rights treaties see Patrick Abel, 'Menschenrechtsschutz durch Individualbeschwerdeverfahren: Ein regionaler Vergleich aus historischer, normativer und faktischer Perspektive' (2013) 51(3) Archiv des Völkerrechts 369, 369–392.

40 cf Kofi Quashigah, 'Scope of Individual Duties in the African Charter' in Manisuli Ssenyonjo (ed), *The African Regional Human Rights System: 30 Years After the African Charter on Human and Peoples' Rights* (Martinus Nijhoff Publishers 2012) 123–127, 129–133 who on the one hand rather clearly describes the existence of international duties but on the other hand considers that they are enforceable through the state's legislation, which is indicative of a more sceptical understanding of their direct applicability; Karavias (n 2) 24–25 is cautious as to the binding character due to the generic formulation of the provisions. Direct applicability is rejected for example by Tomuschat, *Human* (n 12) 130.

41 A good example for a treaty that contains wording which seems to indicate directly applicable obligations is the ILO Convention (No 98) Concerning the Application of the Principles of the Right to Organise and To Bargain Collectively (adopted 1 July 1949, entered into force 19 July 1951) 96 UNTS 257 (ILO Convention Collective Bargaining). Its Art 1 (1) states: 'Workers shall enjoy adequate protection against acts of anti-union discrimination in respect of their employment.' Other treaties with similar language are Art III (1) International Convention on Civil Liability for Oil Pollution Damage (adopted 29 November 1969, entered into force 19 June 1975) 973 UNTS 3 (IMO Convention on Civil Liability for Oil Pollution Damage); Art 4 Basel Protocol on Liability and Compensation for Damage Resulting from Transboundary Movements of Hazardous Waste and their Disposal (adopted 10 December 1999) (Basel Protocol); Art II (1) Vienna Convention on Civil Liability for Nuclear Damage (adopted 21 May 1963, entered into force 12 November 1977) 1063 UNTS 265 (Vienna Convention on Civil Liability for Nuclear Damage); Art 3 (1) Convention on Third Party Liability in the Field of Nuclear Energy (adopted 29 July 1960, entered into force 1 April 1968) 956 UNTS 251 (OECD Convention on Third Party Liability in the Field of Nuclear Energy); on these treaties and the question of direct applicability see generally Ratner (n 10) 479–481 with a position favouring direct applicability; more cautiously Peters (n 2) 157–161.

Charter[42] provide for obligations directly applicable to non-state actors. For example, UN Security Council Resolution 1474 (2003) 'stresses the obligation of all States and other actors' to comply with an arms embargo that applied to Somalia.[43] What is more, a particular category of UN Security Council resolutions set the so-called targeted sanctions, especially with the aim of combatting terrorism. They target specific individuals and companies and sometimes issue concrete prohibitions for these private actors, for example asset freezes and travel bans.[44]

This overview shows that in international law, obligations directly applicable to non-state actors are the exception.

V. Investment law's asymmetry

1. The traditional focus on investor rights

The traditional perspective on international investment law is no different from that of general international law. States created IIAs to provide international protection to investors, leaving no room for investor obligations. For that reason, scholars have characterised investment law as being asymmetrical:[45] Only host states have obligations towards foreign investors, not vice versa.

In this concept, the asymmetry dissolves in the interplay of international and domestic law. It is the host state's domestic law which establishes the legal framework within which foreign investors carry out their investment.[46] Therein, states impose obligations on foreign investors to protect

---

42 Charter of the United Nations (adopted 26 June 1945, entered into force 24 October 1945) 1 UNTS XVI (UN Charter).

43 UNSC 'The Situation in Somalia' UN Doc S/RES/1474 (2003) (8 April 2003), para 1.

44 On targeted sanctions see only Thomas J Biersteker, Sue E Eckert and Marcos Tourinho (eds), *Targeted Sanctions: The Impacts and Effectiveness of United Nations Action* (Cambridge University Press 2016).

45 Used for example by *Hesham Talaat M. Al-Warraq v The Republic of Indonesia*, Final Award (UNCITRAL, 15 December 2014) para 659; Patrick Dumberry and Gabrielle Dumas-Aubin, 'How to Impose Human Rights Obligations on Corporations Under Investment Treaties?' (2011–2012) 4 Yearbook on International Investment Law and Policy, 2–3.

46 In the 2018 IISD Expert Meeting on Investor Obligations in Trade and Investment Agreements, participants even considered the fact that investors must observe domestic law in the host state 'too obvious to be included in a trade or

the public interest – just as they do for any other private actors. IIAs serve to discipline how the states regulate investors.

2. Recent integration of CSR norms

Shifting the focus away from the actions of the host state, recently concluded IIAs began to incorporate non-binding international CSR norms.[47]

Some of these IIAs legally bind the state parties to encourage foreign investors to voluntarily comply with such CSR norms. Here, a binding obligation of states is coupled with the voluntary policy approach towards foreign investors. States must adopt or endeavour to adopt respective internal policies. Thus, these provisions do not require states to adopt binding regulation towards foreign investors.[48] To give one example, Art 22.3 CETA[49] stipulates:

> Cooperation and promotion of trade supporting sustainable development [enshrines that] […] each Party shall strive to promote trade and economic flows and practices that contribute to enhancing decent work and environmental protection, including by: […] (b) encouraging the development and use of voluntary best practices of corporate social responsibility by enterprises, such as those in the OECD Guide-

---

investment treaty', see IISD, *Integrating Investor Obligations and Corporate Accountability Provisions in Trade and Investment Agreements: Report of the Expert Meeting Held in Versoix, Switzerland, January 11–12, 2018* (2018) 3.

47 On this general trend see for example Mary E Footer, 'Bits and Pieces: Social and Environmental Protection in the Regulation of Foreign Investment' (2009) 18(1) Michigan State Journal of International Law 33, 57–63; Nowrot, 'Include' (n 2) 639; Nowrot, 'Obligations' (n 30) paras 34–48; on the trend in EU IIAs see Stefanie Schacherer, *Sustainable Development in EU Foreign Investment Law* (Brill 2021) 270–276; specifically on the trend to introduce CSR norms on climate protection see Wendy Miles and Merryl Lawry-White, 'Arbitral Institutions and the Enforcement of Climate Change Obligations for the Benefit of All Stakeholders: The Role of ICSID' (2019) 34(1) ICSID Review 1, 13–14.

48 Jarrod Hepburn and Vuyelwa Kuuya, 'Corporate Social Responsibility and Investment Treaties' in Marie-Claire Cordonier Segger, Markus W Gehring and Andrew P Newcombe (eds), *Sustainable Development in World Investment Law* (Kluwer Law International 2011) 599–605.

49 Comprehensive Economic and Trade Agreement (adopted 30 October 2016) ‹https://investmentpolicy.unctad.org/international-investment-agreements/treaty-files/3593/download› accessed 7 December 2021 (CETA).

> lines for Multinational Enterprises, to strengthen coherence between economic, social and environmental objectives [...].

Other IIAs directly address foreign investors with hortatory language, calling upon them to conform with international CSR standards. Again, this method retains the voluntary approach and does not create any legal obligations for foreign investors. However, by not addressing the states as intermediaries, it is a step more direct in interacting with foreign investors than the method mentioned above. A good example is Art 10.30 of the Pacific Alliance Additional Protocol which in paragraph 2 appeals to foreign investors directly by stating:

> [...] Las Partes recuerdan a esas empresas la importancia de incorporar dichos estándares de responsabilidad social corporativa en sus políticas internas, incluyendo entre otros, estándares en materia de derechos humanos, derechos laborales, medio ambiente, lucha contra la corrupción, intereses de los consumidores, ciencia y tecnología, competencia y fiscalidad.[50]

To be sure, notwithstanding the lack of legally binding effect, including provisions related to CSR into IIAs may have an important practical effect. Such IIA norms reflect the fact that moral expectations towards foreign investors have changed. They provide a point of reference that the public may use to exert pressure on misbehaving foreign investors. What is more, the inclusion of CSR-provisions changes the matters dealt with in an IIA: They expand and generalise its scope beyond the focus on the investor's economic activity.[51] It is also notable that, quite often, it has been the developed countries such as the USA, Canada and the EU that

50 Art 10.30 Additional Protocol to the Framework Agreement of the Pacific Alliance (adopted 10 February 2014, entered into force 1 May 2016) ‹https://investmentpolicy.unctad.org/international-investment-agreements/treaty-files/2940/download› accessed 7 December 2021 (Framework Agreement Pacific Alliance): '[...] The Parties remind the corporations of the importance of these corporate social responsibility standards in their internal policies, including inter alia standards on human rights, labour standards, the environment, corruption, consumers' interests, science and technology, anti-trust and taxation.' (courtesy translation only).

51 cf the general observation of international investment law's generalisation by Peter-Tobias Stoll and Till P Holterhus, 'The "Generalization" of International Investment Law in Constitutional Perspective' in Steffen Hindelang and Markus Krajewski (eds), *Shifting Paradigms in International Investment Law: More Balanced, Less Isolated, Increasingly Diversified* (Oxford University Press 2016).

have supported the inclusion of CSR norms – even though, at least in the IIAs concluded with developing countries, they might still have a stronger interest to protect the rights of their investors.[52]

At the same time though, due to their non-binding character, the inclusion of CSR norms into IIAs necessarily fails to meet the regulatory problems discussed in Chapter 1. The legal asymmetry in receiving binding international rights without corresponding obligations is unchanged. They remain non-enforceable as a matter of law.[53] For these reasons, scholars have criticised the integration of CSR-norms as unsuitable for changing the behaviour of investors.[54] In this vein, already in 2003, the UN High Commissioner for Human Rights demanded a greater balance in IIAs that should include CSR 'both on a voluntary basis and through the recognition of investors' direct accountability for their actions with regard to human rights.'[55]

Therefore, including CSR norms into IIAs is only of limited relevance for the present study into direct obligations, simply because they lack legally binding effect. Nevertheless, it can be said that they broaden the scope of IIAs and introduce a new perspective on foreign investments which was alien to IIAs before. This modest change of perception is useful to keep in mind and, indeed, foreshadows the important interplay between 'soft' and 'hard' law that this study will address at a later stage.[56]

VI. Interim conclusion: Few preconditions, few role-models

General international law does not hinder states from imposing direct obligations.[57] To that end, states can grant investors the necessary international subjectivity, and investors cannot invoke the principle of *pacta tertiis* against their creation. However, in other branches of international

---

52 Hepburn and Kuuya, 'Corporate' (n 48) 607.

53 Too broad Eva van der Zee, 'Incorporating the OECD Guidelines in International Investment Agreements: Turning a Soft Law Obligation into Hard Law' (2013) 33(1) Legal Issues of Economic Integration 33, 52.

54 Dumberry and Dumas-Aubin (n 45) 5.

55 UN Commission on Human Rights 'Human Rights, Trade and Investment, Report of the High Commissioner for Human Rights' UN Doc E/CN.4/Sub.2/2003/9 (2 July 2003) ‹http://daccess-ods.un.org/access.nsf/Get?Open&DS=E/CN.4/Sub.2/2003/9&Lang=E› accessed 7 December 2021, 4.

56 See below Chapter 3.III and Chapter 7.II.3.

57 Supported for example by Monnheimer (n 35) 12.

law, such directly applicable obligations exist only exceptionally, most prominently in international criminal law. The same is true for investment law. As asymmetrical instruments IIAs traditionally focused on providing rights to investors against host states without corresponding international obligations. There is a recent trend of integrating non-binding CSR norms into IIAs. Yet, it does not overcome the field's described *legal* asymmetry.

Chapter 3.
Direct Obligations in Investment Law Practice

Appreciating that direct obligations are possible, but scarce in international law, it is astonishing that they have recently emerged in investment law. Chapter 3 will analyse how they have been introduced in the last years. This development rests on two main pillars.

First, direct obligations appear in several recent IIAs and model BITs of mainly developing countries.[1] The most important examples covered in this Chapter are the 2008 Ghana Model BIT,[2] the 2012 SADC Model BIT Template,[3] the 2016 African Union's Draft Pan-African Investment Code,[4] the 2007 COMESA Investment Agreement,[5] the 2008 ECOWAS Investment Rules,[6] the 2016 Morocco-Nigeria BIT,[7] the 2015 India Model

1 See also the short overview on human rights obligations in recent IIAs by Barnali Choudhury, 'Investor Obligations for Human Rights' (2020) 35(1–2) ICSID Review 82, 88–92.

2 Ghana Model BIT (2008) ‹https://investmentpolicy.unctad.org/international-investment-agreements/treaty-files/2866/download› accessed 7 December 2021 (Ghana Model BIT).

3 Southern African Development Community, Model Bilateral Investment Treaty Template with Commentary (July 2012) ‹https://www.iisd.org/itn/wp-content/uploads/2012/10/sadc-model-bit-template-final.pdf› accessed 7 December 2021 (SADC Model BIT).

4 Draft Pan-African Investment Code (26 March 2016) E/ECA/COE/35/18, AU/STC/FMEPI/EXP/18(II) (Draft Pan-African Investment Code).

5 Investment Agreement for the COMESA Common Investment Area (adopted 23 May 2007) ‹https://investmentpolicy.unctad.org/international-investment-agreements/treaty-files/3092/download› accessed 7 December 2021 (COMESA Investment Agreement).

6 ECOWAS Supplementary Act A/SA.3/12/08 Adopting Community Rules on Investment and the Modalities for their Implementation with ECOWAS (adopted 19 December 2008, entered into force 19 January 2009) (ECOWAS Investment Rules).

7 Reciprocal Investment Promotion and Protection Agreement Between the Government of the Kingdom of Morocco and the Government of the Federal Republic of Nigeria (adopted 3 December 2016) ‹https://investmentpolicy.unctad.org/international-investment-agreements/treaty-files/5409/download› accessed 7 December 2021 (Morocco-Nigeria BIT).

BIT,[8] the 2019 Netherlands Model BIT,[9] as well as the 2015 Brazil Model BIT and the resulting Brazilian BITs with other countries.[10] In addition, important institutions have suggested and supported creating direct obligations to reform investment law, for example in the 2015 UNCTAD Investment Policy Framework for Sustainable Development,[11] the 2005 IISD Model International Agreement on Investment for Sustainable Development,[12] the 2017 IISD Sustainability Toolkit for Trade Negotiators[13] and the 2018 Report of the IISD Expert Meeting on Integrating Investor Obli-

---

8 India Model BIT (28 December 2015) ‹https://investmentpolicy.unctad.org/international-investment-agreements/treaty-files/3560/download› accessed 7 December 2021 (India Model BIT).

9 Netherlands Model BIT (22 March 2019) ‹https://investmentpolicy.unctad.org/international-investment-agreements/treaty-files/5832/download› accessed 7 December 2021 (Netherlands Model BIT).

10 Brazil Model BIT (2015) ‹https://investmentpolicy.unctad.org/international-investment-agreements/treaty-files/4786/download› accessed 7 December 2021 (Brazil Model BIT); Brazil-Angola Investment Cooperation and Facilitation Agreement (adopted 1 April 2015, entered into force 28 July 2017) ‹https://investmentpolicy.unctad.org/international-investment-agreements/treaty-files/4720/download› accessed 7 December 2021 (Brazil-Angola BIT); Brazil-Chile Investment Cooperation and Facilitation Agreement (adopted 24 November 2015) ‹https://investmentpolicy.unctad.org/international-investment-agreements/treaty-files/4712/download› accessed 7 December 2021 (Brazil-Chile BIT); Brazil-Malawi Investment Cooperation and Facilitation Agreement (adopted 25 June 2015) ‹https://investmentpolicy.unctad.org/international-investment-agreements/treaty-files/4715/download› accessed 7 December 2021 (Brazil-Malawi BIT); Brazil-Mexico Investment Cooperation and Facilitation Agreement (adopted 26 May 2015, entered into force 7 October 2018) ‹https://investmentpolicy.unctad.org/international-investment-agreements/treaty-files/4718/download› accessed 7 December 2021 (Brazil-Mexico BIT); Brazil-Mozambique Investment Cooperation and Facilitation Agreement (adopted 30 March 2015) ‹https://investmentpolicy.unctad.org/international-investment-agreements/treaty-files/4717/download› accessed 7 December 2021 (Brazil-Mozambique BIT); Brazil-Peru Economic and Trade Expansion Agreement (adopted 29 April 2016) ‹https://investmentpolicy.unctad.org/international-investment-agreements/treaty-files/5402/download› accessed 7 December 2021 (Brazil-Peru FTA).

11 UNCTAD 'Investment Policy Framework for Sustainable Development' UNCTAD/DIAE/PCB/2015/5 (2015).

12 IISD, *Model International Agreement on Investment for Sustainable Development* (2005).

13 IISD, *A Sustainability Toolkit for Trade Negotiators: Trade and Investment as Vehicles for Achieving the 2030 Sustainable Development Agenda* (2017).

gations and Corporate Accountability Provisions in Trade and Investment Agreements.[14]

Second, there are five recent investment arbitration awards that are indicative of the emerging direct obligations. These are the decisions by the UNCITRAL Tribunals in *Al-Warraq v Indonesia*[15] and *Aven v Mexico*[16] and by ICSID Tribunals in *Urbaser v Argentina*,[17] *Burlington v Ecuador*[18] and *Perenco v Ecuador.*[19] In these cases, states counter-sued the investors after the respective investor had filed an investment claim. In these counterclaims, states contended that the investors had violated a direct obligation and claimed compensation from the investors.

Based on these sources, this Chapter will systematise the direct obligations along different techniques for their creation which include:

- the integration of directly applicable international obligations existing outside of international investment law (I.),
- the diversion of international obligations of states to investors (II.),
- the conversion of legally non-binding CSR standards (III.),
- the elevation of domestic investor obligations to substantive international investor obligations (IV.),
- the original creation of direct obligations (V.),
- the application of domestic investor obligations in international investment arbitration (VI.).

Viewed together, these approaches allow to discern a nascent doctrine of direct obligations which this Chapter will appreciate in the last step (VII.).

---

14 IISD, *Integrating Investor Obligations and Corporate Accountability Provisions in Trade and Investment Agreements: Report of the Expert Meeting Held in Versoix, Switzerland, January 11–12, 2018* (2018).

15 *Hesham Talaat M. Al-Warraq v The Republic of Indonesia*, Final Award (UNCITRAL, 15 December 2014).

16 *David Aven et al. v The Republic of Costa Rica*, Case No. UNCT/15/3, Final Award (UNCITRAL, 18 September 2018).

17 *Urbaser S.A. and Consorcio de Aguas Bilbao Bizkaia, Bilbao Biskaia Ur Partzuergoa v The Argentine Republic*, ICSID Case No. ARB/07/26, Award (8 December 2016).

18 *Burlington Resources Inc. v Republic of Ecuador*, ICSID Case No. ARB/08/5, Decision on Counterclaims (7 February 2017).

19 *Perenco Ecuador Ltd. v The Republic of Ecuador*, ICSID Case No. ARB/08/6, Interim Decision on the Environmental Counterclaim (11 August 2015).

I. Integrating external obligations directly applicable to private actors

Investor obligations could come about by introducing directly applicable international obligations of non-state actors outside of investment law into IIAs and investment arbitration. This approach featured in recent arbitral jurisprudence. This Section will show that as of today, in most cases this concept remains infeasible.

1. Concept

To create direct obligations, IIAs could build on the few existing international obligations that apply directly to foreign investors outside of investment law ('external' obligations). As seen, these are mainly obligations stemming from international criminal law and *ius cogens*.[20] There are two possible means of integration – substantive and procedural.

On a substantive level, an IIA clause may restate or reinforce external obligations. Such a clause can declare them applicable as part of the IIA. It may also modify their content in the process. For example, an IIA clause could reinforce the international obligation of foreign investors not to commit genocide. Then, technically, the IIA creates a new direct obligation the source of which is the IIA as an international treaty. In the example, this obligation exists separately from the prohibition to commit genocide under customary international law.

Alternatively, an IIA could define external obligations as the applicable law in investment arbitration. Here, the integration would operate on a procedural level only: The investment tribunal applies an international norm from a source external to the IIA, for example the above-mentioned customary prohibition to commit genocide. Then, it may serve as basis for a counterclaim by the state against the investor.

Generally, the freedom of states and investors to choose which type of international law is to be the applicable substantive law of an arbitration

20 See Chapter 2.IV.

is widely accepted in the literature[21] and in arbitral decisions[22] – despite the fact that sometimes investment arbitrators appear reluctant to resort to such 'alien' sources.[23] Investment tribunals have already accepted the converse constellation: Investors may base their claims against the host state on international human rights law, provided that the respective jurisdictional clause is broad enough.[24] In ICSID arbitrations, Art 42 (1) ICSID Convention even provides as a residual rule that the tribunal shall apply any relevant international law.[25]

---

21 Such freedom to decide on the applicable law clause is for example supported by Clara Reiner and Christoph Schreuer, 'Human Rights and International Investment Arbitration' in Pierre-Marie Dupuy, Ernst-Ulrich Petersmann and Francesco Francioni (eds), *Human Rights in International Investment Law and Arbitration* (Oxford University Press 2009) 84–85; Christoph Schreuer and Ursula Kriebaum, 'From Individual to Community Interest in International Investment Law' in Ulrich Fastenrath and others (eds), *From Bilateralism to Community Interest: Essays in Honour of Judge Bruno Simma* (Oxford University Press 2011) 1093–1094; Pierre-Marie Dupuy and Jorge E Viñuales, 'Human Rights and Investment Disciplines: Integration in Progress' in Marc Bungenberg and others (eds), *International Investment Law* (Nomos 2015) paras 66–74.

22 See for example *Asian Agricultural Products Ltd. v Republic of Sri Lanka*, ICSID Case No. ARB/87/3, Final Award (27 June 1990) para 21; *Phoenix Action, Ltd. v The Czech Republic*, ICSID Case No. ARB/06/5, Award (15 April 2009) para 78.

23 On this reluctance, described as reticence or *Berührungsangst*, see Bruno Simma, 'Foreign Investment Arbitration: A Place for Human Rights?' (2011) 60(3) International & Comparative Law Quarterly 573, 576; cf the empirical analysis suggesting 'significant potential for ICSID tribunals to broaden their perspective by selecting arguments from materials that are related to other areas of international law' by Ole K Fauchald, 'The Legal Reasoning of ICSID Tribunals – an Empirical Analysis' (2008) 19(2) European Journal of International Law 301, 358.

24 *Biloune and Marine Drive Complex Ltd v Ghana Investments Centre and the Government of Ghana*, Award on Jurisdiction and Liability (UNCITRAL, 27 October 1989) 203; *Chevron Corporation (USA) and Texaco Petroleum Corporation (USA) v The Republic of Ecuador*, Interim Award (UNCITRAL, 1 December 2008) paras 209–210; *Toto Costruzioni Generali S.P.A. v Republic of Lebanon*, ICSID Case No. ARB/07/12, Decision on Jurisdiction (11 September 2009) paras 154–168; Dupuy and Viñuales (n 21) paras 60–65.

25 The provision also includes substantive rules of international law, see Emmanuel Gaillard and Yas Banifatemi, 'The Meaning of "And" in Article 42(1), Second Sentence, of the Washington Convention: The Role of International Law in the ICSID Choice of Law Process' (2003) 18(2) ICSID Review 375, 397; Dupuy and Viñuales (n 21) para 70.

2. The Urbaser v Argentina award[26]

This concept of integrating external obligations into investment law was recently applied and supported in investment arbitration. In an unprecedented manner, the ICSID Tribunal in its 2016 award in *Urbaser v Argentina* held that foreign investors had broad international human rights obligations. These external obligations could serve as a basis for an arbitral counterclaim by the host state.

In this case, the claimants operated water and sewage services in the Area of Greater Buenos Aires which had been privatised by Argentina in the 1990s.[27] The investors contended a violation of various rights under the Spain-Argentina-BIT.[28] They based their claim on the government's conduct in the 2001 Argentinian economic crisis. In their view, Argentina was responsible for the investment's eventual insolvency due to the depreciation of the Argentinian Peso and failed concession tariffs renegotiations.[29]

In the course of the proceedings, Argentina filed a counterclaim based on obligations of the claimants under international human rights law, hence on norms external to the Spain-Argentina-BIT. The state claimed compensation of USD 404.34 million from the investors. Argentina argued that they had violated their human rights obligation to provide access to water to the local population as agreed on in the concession contract. It saw such a violation in the lack of appropriate investment into the water and sewage infrastructure and the insufficient provision of water at

26 This Section 3.I.2 draws on Patrick Abel, 'Counterclaims Based on International Human Rights Obligations of Investors in International Investment Arbitration: Fallacies and Potentials of the 2016 ICSID Urbaser v. Argentina Award' [2018] Brill Open Law 1.

27 *Urbaser v Argentina*, Award (n 17) para 42.

28 Argentina-Spain BIT (adopted 3 October 1991, entered into force 28 September 1992) ‹https://investmentpolicy.unctad.org/international-investment-agreements/treaty-files/119/download› accessed 7 December 2021 (Argentina-Spain BIT).

29 *Urbaser v Argentina*, Award (n 17) paras 34–35. The Tribunal eventually dismissed the claim. Although it found for a violation of the FET standard due to the too abrupt termination of renegotiation talks by the Argentinian government, it held that Argentina did not cause any damage to the investors by this violation because the investors had already operated at loss without any remaining economic perspective. They could not have hoped for any profit because the contractually promised expansion works into infrastructure had not been undertaken, see *Urbaser v Argentina*, Award (n 17) paras 846–847, 997–1009, 1090–1109.

affordable prices.[30] The reason that Argentina based its counterclaim on an *international* obligation was that the Tribunal had previously rejected to exercise its jurisdiction over domestic Argentinian law.[31] The question thus arose, whether the investors had any such obligation under international human rights law and if so, whether the Tribunal's jurisdiction covered this obligation. The Tribunal elaborated on these general aspects in quite some detail even though it eventually dismissed the counterclaim.

a) Direct obligations in human rights law

To recall, the analysis answered the first question if foreign investors have any binding international human rights obligations by large to the negative.[32] Yet, the Tribunal came to a very different conclusion. It proclaimed the existence of broad negative human rights obligations of corporations. Affirming that corporations can be subjects of international law,[33] it argued that private actors had to abstain from harming human rights of others, including the right to water.[34] It derived this obligation from different treaties and declarations such as the ILO Tripartite Declaration of Principles concerning Multilateral Enterprises and Social Policy,[35] the UDHR,[36] the ICCPR and ICESCR. The exact scope of this negative obligation remains blurry. But because Argentina contended the violation of a *positive* 'obligation to perform'[37] access to water to the population in Buenos Aires, the Tribunal dismissed the counterclaim. It held that human

---

30 *Urbaser v Argentina*, Award (n 17) paras 1156–1166.

31 *Urbaser S.A. and Consorcio de Aguas Bilbao Bizkaia, Bilbao Biskaia Ur Partzuergoa v The Argentine Republic*, ICSID Case No. ARB/07/26, Decision on Jurisdiction (9 December 2012) paras 251–254.

32 See Chapter 2.IV.

33 *Urbaser v Argentina*, Award (n 17) paras 35, 1193–1195.

34 ibid 1195–1198.

35 ILO 'Tripartite Declaration of Principles Concerning Multinational Enterprises and Social Policy' adopted by the Governing Body of the International Labour Office at its 204th Session (Geneva, November 1977) and amended at its 279th (November 2000), 295th (March 2006) and 329th (March 2017) Sessions, (1978) 17 ILM 422 (16 November 1977) ‹www.ilo.org/wcmsp5/groups/public/---ed_emp/---emp_ent/---multi/documents/publication/wcms_094386.pdf› accessed 7 December 2021.

36 UNGA 'Universal Declaration of Human Rights' UN Doc A/RES/217 (III) A (10 December 1948).

37 *Urbaser v Argentina*, Award (n 17) para 1210.

rights law had not established such positive obligations (in contrast to negative duties) for private actors.[38]

The Tribunal's reasoning is hard to sustain. Most notably, it disregards the non-binding character of cited soft-law. States explicitly intended not to produce *legally binding* effect through instruments such as the UDHR and the ILO Tripartite Declaration. Given the lack of status as sources of international law, reflected in Art 38 (1) ICJ-Statute, they cannot by themselves establish an international obligation of investors. Neither did the Tribunal indicate how these non-binding norms could have been transformed to binding rules of international law – a matter controversially discussed on a general level in scholarly writing.[39]

To the extent the Tribunal refers in its reasoning to binding human rights law, namely Art 11 (1) and 12 ICESCR, it misinterprets these provisions. More precisely, it misreads Art 5 (1) ICESCR to render all ICESCR rights directly applicable to non-state actors. This provision reads:

> Nothing in the present Covenant may be interpreted as implying for any State, group or person any right to engage in any activity or to perform any act aimed at the destruction of any of the rights or freedoms recognized herein, or at their limitation to a greater extent than is provided for in the present Covenant.

The mentioning of non-state actors in the provision misled the Tribunal to the conclusion that ICESCR rights directly bound private actors in their relation to another – and that for this reason the right to water covered by Art 11 (1) ICESCR, read in conjunction with Art 5 (1) ICESCR, could be understood as an international obligation of corporations.[40] However,

---

38 ibid 1206–1209.

39 On the relationship between soft law and international investment law see Andrea K Bjorklund and August Reinisch (eds), *International Investment Law and Soft Law* (Edward Elgar Publishing 2012). For positions that are more open to accept the Tribunal's findings see Ted Gleason, 'Examining Host-State Counterclaims for Environmental Damage in Investor-State Dispute Settlement from Human Rights and Transnational Public Policy Perspectives' (2021) 21(3) International Environmental Agreements 427, 438–439 who points to transnational public policy; James J Nedumpara and Aditya Laddha, 'Human Rights and Environmental Counterclaims in Investment Treaty Arbitration' in Julien Chaisse, Leïla Choukroune and Sufian Jusoh (eds), *Handbook of International Investment Law and Policy* (Springer 2021) 1841 referring to legal scholarship which accepts that private actors are bound by international human rights law.

40 *Urbaser v Argentina*, Award (n 17) paras 1196–1197. And even if the horizontal effect was established, the Tribunal would have had to elaborate on whether

the clause has a different meaning: it is a provision on the abuse of rights.[41] Similar clauses can be found in Art 5 (1) ICCPR as well as in Art 17 ECHR[42] and Art 29 (a) ACHR,[43] sharing a common origin in Art 30 of the UDHR. The declaration's and treaties' preparatory works show that the parties wanted to rule out the possibility that human rights could be invoked with the sole intention of infringing on the human right of another person. They were particularly concerned that human rights could be interpreted based on extremist and totalitarian ideologies. The purpose of the above clauses is thus to prevent such interpretation. Therefore, they provide interpretive guidance on the scope and *telos* of human rights enshrined in the respective treaty, rather than create obligations.[44]

---

the obligation is owed to the home state, host state or other private actors, or perhaps even to all cumulatively. On these different constructions see Anne Peters, *Beyond Human Rights: The Legal Status of the Individual in International Law* (Cambridge University Press 2016) 110–113.

41 See also Edward Guntrip, 'Urbaser v. Argentina: The Origins of a Host State Human Rights Counterclaim in ICSID Arbitration?' [2017] EJIL:Talk! ‹www.ejiltalk.org/urbaser-v-argentina-the-origins-of-a-host-state-human-rights-counterclaim-in-icsid-arbitration/#more-14978› accessed 7 December 2021.

42 Convention for the Protection of Human Rights and Fundamental Freedoms (adopted 4 November 1950, entered into force 3 September 1953) CETS No 5 (ECHR).

43 American Convention on Human Rights (adopted 22 November 1969, entered into force 18 July 1978) 1144 UNTS 123 (ACHR).

44 This interpretation of the UDHR and the ICCPR clauses is supported for example by Thomas Buergenthal, 'To Respect and to Ensure: State Obligations and Permissible Derogations' in Louis Henkin (ed), *The International Bill of Rights* (Columbia University Press 1981) 86–89; Manfred Nowak, *U.N. Covenant on Civil and Political Rights: CCPR Commentary* (2nd edn, N.P. Engel 2005) Art 5 paras 1, 510; for the ICESCR for example by Philip Alston and Gerard Quinn, 'The Nature and Scope of States Parties' Obligations Under the International Covenant on Economic, Social and Cultural Rights' (1987) 9 Human Rights Quarterly 156, 208; Manisuli Ssenyonjo, *Economic, Social and Cultural Rights in International Law* (Hart Publishing 2009) para 3.36; Ben Saul, David Kinley and Jacqueline Mowbray, *The International Covenant on Economic, Social and Cultural Rights: Commentary, Cases, and Materials* (Oxford University Press 2014) 262–267; for a contrary interpretation albeit without detailed argumentation see Upendra Baxi, *The Future of Human Rights* (Oxford University Press 2002) 146. That the *Urbaser v Argentina* Tribunal erred in finding direct human rights obligations is supported for example by Markus Krajewski, 'A Nightmare or a Noble Dream? Establishing Investor Obligations Through Treaty-Making and Treaty-Application' (2020) 5(1) Business and Human Rights Journal 105, 124–125; Maria Monnheimer, *Due Diligence Obligations in International Human Rights Law* (Cambridge University Press 2021) 28.

The Human Rights Committee supported the interpretation presented here for the identical clause in Art 5 (1) ICCPR for example in the communication No 117/1981 of *MA v Italy*. In this case, the petitioners contended that Italy violated their ICCPR rights by convicting them under penal law for reorganising the dissolved fascist party in Italy. The Human Rights Committee dismissed the communication as inadmissible, *inter alia* because the acts leading to the conviction appeared to the Human Rights Committee to be 'of a kind which are removed from the protection of the Covenant by article 5 thereof.'[45] Thus, the petitioners failed to show the possibility of an ICCPR violation which constitutes an admissibility requirement. *Tomuschat* in his individual opinions in *López Burgos v Uruguay* and *Celiberti v Uruguay* understood Art 5 (1) ICCPR in the same manner. The clause prohibited individuals 'from availing themselves of the same rights and freedoms with a view to overthrowing the régime of the rule of law which constitutes the basic philosophy'[46] of the ICCPR. The European Court of Human Rights similarly interpreted and applied Art 17 ECHR as far back as its very first judgment in *Lawless v Ireland*[47] and continues to do so in cases relating to abusive interpretations of ECHR rights. Art 17 ECHR excludes from protection, for example, the promoting of racist ideologies, terrorism and the overthrowing of democracy.[48] Finally, also

45 *M.A. v Italy* Comm No. 117/1981 (Decision on Inadmissibility) UN Doc Supp No 40 (A/39/40) 190 (1981) (UN Human Rights Committee, 21 September 1981) para 13.3.

46 *Sergio Euben Lopez Burgos v Uruguay* Comm No R.12/52 (Individual Opinion of Mr. Christian Tomuschat) UN Doc Supp No 40 (A/36/40) 176 (1981) (UN Human Rights Committee, 29 July 1981); *Lilian Celiberti de Casariego v Uruguay* Comm No. R.13/56 (Individual Opinion of Mr. Christian Tomuschat) UN Doc Supp No 40 (A/36/40) 185 (1981) (UN Human Rights Committee, 29 July 1981).

47 *Case of Lawless v Ireland (No. 3)* App no 332/57, ECHR Series A no 3 (European Court of Human Rights, 1 July 1961) para 7.

48 *Case of United Communist Party of Turkey and Others v Turkey* App no 19392/92, ECHR 1998-I (European Court of Human Rights, 30 January 1998) para 60; *Case of Refah Partisi (the Welfare Party) and Others v Turkey* App no 41340/98, 41342/98, 41343/98, 41344/98, 13.2.2003, ECHR 2003-II 267 (European Court of Human Rights, 13 February 2003) para 99; *Case of Leroy v France* App no 36109/03, ECLI:CE:ECHR:2008:1002JUD003610903 (European Court of Human Rights, 2 October 2008) para 26; *Case of Paksas v Lithuania* App no 34932/04, ECLI:CE:ECHR:2011:0106JUD003493204 (European Court of Human Rights, 6 January 2011) para 87; *Case of Kasymakhunov and Saybatalov v Russia* App no 26261/05, 26377/06, ECLI:CE:ECHR:2013:0314JUD002626105 (European Court of Human Rights, 14 March 2013) paras 103–104; Jochen A Frowein, 'Artikel 17' in Jochen A Frowein and Wolfgang Peukert (eds), *Europäische Menschenrechts-*

the Inter-American Court of Human Rights in an advisory opinion in 1985 briefly affirmed the same understanding for Art 29 (a) ACHR.[49]

b) Mechanics of integrating external obligations

Despite the fact that the Tribunal's award is not compelling on the existence of broad external obligations in human rights law, it is useful to examine how it dealt with the follow-up question: What are the legal mechanisms to integrate external obligations into an IIA? More precisely: How can a state bring it forward as the basis of a counterclaim against investors? The ICSID Tribunal in *Urbaser v Argentina* offered not one but four different explanations:

1. Systemic interpretation of the IIA as enshrined in Art 31 (3) (c) VCLT,[50]
2. IIA clauses on the applicable law in investment arbitration, in the case Art X (5) Spain-Argentina BIT which declared international law applicable,[51]
3. Art 42 (1) ICSID Convention[52] which defines international law to be applicable in investment arbitrations as a residual rule,
4. peremptory norms of general international law (*ius cogens*).[53]

The Tribunal did not put these approaches into any order. To start with the last on the above list, it is inaccurate to consider the concept of *ius cogens* as a means of integrating external direct obligations into an IIA. *Ius cogens* simply refers to the legal character of a norm.[54] It is of supreme hierarchy: States cannot create norms that conflict with *ius cogens*.[55] From

---

konvention: EMRK-Kommentar (2nd edn, N.P. Engel 1996) paras 1–4; William Schabas, *The European Convention on Human Rights: A Commentary* (Oxford University Press 2015) 611–620.

49 *Compulsory Membership in an Association Prescribed by Law for the Practice of Journalism (Arts 13 and 29 American Convention on Human Rights)* OC-5/85 (Advisory Opinion) Inter-American Court of Human Rights Series A No 5 (13 November 1985) para 67.

50 *Urbaser v Argentina*, Award (n 17) para 1200.

51 ibid 1201.

52 ibid 1202.

53 ibid 1203.

54 *Legality of the Use by a State of Nuclear Weapons in Armed Conflict* (Advisory Opinion) [1996] ICJ Rep 66, para 83.

55 Art 53 and 64 Vienna Convention on the Law of Treaties (adopted 22 May 1969, entered into force 27 January 1980) 1155 UNTS 331 (VCLT); *Prosecutor v Anto*

this negative effect alone, one cannot follow a positive integration into an IIA as a directly applicable norm.[56]

Art 31 (3) (c) VCLT, the so-called method of systemic interpretation, stipulates that interpreting an international treaty, one shall consider, together with the context, '[a]ny relevant rules of international law applicable in the relations between the parties.' The provision helps aligning IIAs with the protection of public goods and interests reflected in international obligations of the parties. Especially, international human rights can be read into investor rights and justification clauses of IIAs.[57] However, Art 31 (3) (c) VCLT only forms one method of interpretation which must

---

Furundžija (Judgement) IT-95–17/1-T (ICTY, 10 December 1998) para 153; for an in-depth analysis of this conflict of norms-effect in the context of other problems and solutions of norm conflicts in international law see Joost Pauwelyn, *Conflict of Norms in Public International Law: How WTO Law Relates to Other Rules of International Law* (Cambridge University Press 2003) 98–99.

56 Abel, 'Counterclaims' (n 26) 12–14.

57 The literature is extensive on this matter, see for example Ernst-Ulrich Petersmann, 'Constitutional Theories of International Economic Adjudication and Investor-State Arbitration' in Pierre-Marie Dupuy, Ernst-Ulrich Petersmann and Francesco Francioni (eds), *Human Rights in International Investment Law and Arbitration* (Oxford University Press 2009) 183 who advocates for interpreting investment law in the light of human rights and principles of justice as part of a constitutional theory of international economic adjudication; Bruno Simma and Theodore Kill, 'Harmonizing Investment Protection and International Human Rights: First Steps Towards a Methodology' in Christina Binder and others (eds), *International Investment Law for the 21st Century: Essays in Honour of Christoph Schreuer* (Oxford University Press 2009) 705 and Simma, 'Foreign' (n 23) 584–586 arguing that concepts such as legitimate expectations and the police powers doctrine should be read in the light of human rights; Jorge E Viñuales, *Foreign Investment and the Environment in International Law* (Cambridge University Press 2012) 151–156 who considers general systemic integration as an interpretive technique for example to allow for different treatment of foreign investors; Ursula Kriebaum, 'Foreign Investments & Human Rights: The Actors and Their Different Roles' (2013) 10(1–17) Transnational Dispute Management, 13–14 on how human rights may influence our understanding of investment treaties; Tarcisio Gazzini, *Interpretation of International Investment Treaties* (Hart Publishing 2016) 210–239 analysing in detail the arbitral and treaty practice on Art 31 (3) (c) VCLT. For general analyses on Art 31 (3) (c) VCLT see for example ILC 'Fragmentation of International Law: Difficulties Arising from the Diversification and Expansion of International Law, Report of the Study Group of the International Law Commission, Finalized by Martti Koskenniemi' UN Doc. A/CN.4/L.682 (13 April 2006), paras 410–480; Mark E Villiger, *Commentary on the 1969 Vienna Convention on the Law of Treaties* (Martinus Nijhoff Publishers 2009) 432–434.

be applied holistically and in concert with the other interpretive rules provided in Art 31 VCLT. The point of departure must always be the actual wording of the provision in question.[58] There is rarely a solid textual basis in IIAs in favour of direct obligations. In the case of *Urbaser v Argentina*, the Spain-Argentina BIT offered no such ground. It appears thus, very hard to read the presence of direct obligations into an IIA given that a majority of states is sceptical about these norms; for this very reason, the ICSID Tribunal in *Blusun v Italy* rejected to consider Art. 19 of the Energy Charter Treaty as an investor obligation to environmental impact assessment (EIA) because the provision 'operates not at the level of individual investors but at the interstate level, as is equally the case with the developing general international law of EIAs'.[59] Therefore, in most cases, systemic interpretation will only have a marginal role to play in bringing about direct obligations.

The only viable concept for integrating a direct obligation was the applicable law clause. In contrast to the approach via Art 31 (3) (c) VCLT, this is a means of *procedurally* integrating an external obligation into an IIA. The applicable law clause in Art X (5) Spain-Argentina-BIT in *Urbaser v Argentina* appeared broad enough to establish the Tribunal's jurisdiction because it explicitly covered international law. The resort to Art 42 (1) ICSID Convention was, therefore, superfluous. This means that the ICSID award in *Urbaser v Argentina* serves as a good example of procedurally integrating a (supposedly existing) external obligation.

c) A desire for direct obligations

All in all, the ICSID award in *Urbaser v Argentina* in its part on counterclaims should be treated with care. Its essential argument that private actors have negative obligations under international human rights law cannot be sustained. Notwithstanding, the Tribunal marks a new approach in the way investment tribunals address international human rights and obligations of investors more broadly. Its willingness to adjudicate on a counterclaim based on a direct obligation towards the public interest is

---

58 See for example *Interpretation of Peace Treaties with Bulgaria, Hungary and Romania (Second Phase)* (Advisory Opinion) [1950] ICJ Rep 221, 229.

59 *Blusun S.A, Jean-Pierre Lecorcier and Michael Stein v Italian Republic*, ICSID Case No. ARB/14/3, Award (27 December 2016) para 275 on Art 19 of The Energy Charter Treaty (adopted 17 December 1994, entered into force 16 April 1998) 2080 UNTS 95; generally on this scepticism see above Chapter 1.III.1.

by itself noteworthy. In doing so, it countered perceptions that investment tribunals focus only on the protection of investors. Importantly, even if mistaken in its conclusions, the Tribunal's line of argument draws on general developments in international law – thus displaying that it was more generally influenced by the change of private actors' normative role in international law. Therefore, the award expresses a new attitude by an investment tribunal sympathetic towards the concept of direct obligations.

3. The Aven v Costa Rica award

Furthermore, the 2018 *Aven v Costa Rica* award is another important arbitral award which discussed the integrating of external investor obligations. While this award affirms that such integration is generally possible, it avoids the methodological mistakes of the *Urbaser v Argentina* award.

In *Aven v Costa Rica*, the UNCITRAL Tribunal had to decide on an environmental counterclaim raised by Costa Rica. The claimants developed a tourism project at the Central Pacific Coast. After receiving the required permits and initiating the project, Costa Rica issued several decisions which shut down the investment to protect sensitive wetlands and forest grounds within the project site.[60] The claimants argued that this had completely devalued the investment project in violation of investment protection rules enshrined in the CAFTA-DR.[61]

During the proceedings, Costa Rica raised a counterclaim and demanded compensation from the claimants for damaging the forest in the investment region by constructing roads, excavating ditches, placing culverts and removing the vegetative strata, for increasing soil sedimentation and for filling and draining wetlands.[62] Costa Rica brought forward that the claimants were internationally responsible for violating domestic law, customary international law and CAFTA-DR provisions on environmental protection.[63]

Citing the *Urbaser v Argentina* award, the Tribunal welcomed and affirmed the idea that investors can have international environmental obliga-

---

60 *Aven v Costa Rica* (n 16) para 6.

61 ibid; see Dominican Republic-Central America FTA (adopted 5 August 2004, entered into force 1 March 2006) ‹https://investmentpolicy.unctad.org/international-investment-agreements/treaty-files/2482/download› accessed 7 December 2021 (CAFTA-DR).

62 *Aven v Costa Rica* (n 16) paras 698–699, 720.

63 ibid 699–700.

tions as subjects of international law, potentially enforceable before investment tribunals:

> [...] It is true that the enforcement of environmental law is primarily to the States, but it cannot be admitted that a foreign investor could not be subject to international law obligations in this field, particularly in the light of Articles 10.9.3, 10.11 and 17 of DR-CAFTA.
>
> Under international law of investments, particularly under DR-CAFTA, the investors enjoy by themselves a number of rights both substantive and procedural, including the right to sue directly the host State when it breaches its international obligations on foreign investment (Section A of Article 10 in DR-CAFTA). What about the investor's obligations arising of the investment according to international law? This Tribunal shares the views of *Urbaser* Tribunal that it can no longer be admitted that investors operating internationally are immune from becoming subjects of international law. It is particularly convincing when it comes to rights and obligations that are the concern of all States, as it happens in the protection of the environment. It is pertinent to recall the observation of the International Court of Justice regarding this kind of obligations: 'In view of the importance of the rights involved, all States can be held to have a legal interest in their protection; they are obligations *erga omnes*'.[64]

However, the Tribunal ultimately dismissed the counterclaim, in part because it did not consider that the CAFTA-DR provisions contained environmental obligations *directly applicable* to foreign investors:

> First, the Tribunal believes that the language of articles Article 10.9.3.c and 10.11 seeks to ensure that States retain a significant margin of appreciation in respect of environmental measures in their respective jurisdictions, but they do not -in and of themselves- impose any affirmative obligation upon investors.[65]

It is submitted that the result of the award is correct, but its reasoning remains incomplete.

---

64 ibid 738–739.

65 ibid 743; for a contrary position see Prabhash Ranjan, 'Investor Obligations in Investment Treaties: Missing Text or a Matter of Application?' in Jean Ho and Mavluda Sattorova (eds), *Investors' International Law* (Hart 2021) 146 who contends that the Tribunal accepted that the CAFTA-DR imposed direct investor obligations, however without accounting for para 743 of the decision.

On the one hand, the Tribunal is methodologically sound in rejecting the argument that the CAFTA-DR contains international investor obligations. The mechanics of integrating external obligations presented above do not apply here. There is no clause in the CAFTA-DR which incorporates an external international environmental obligation which is directly applicable to investors: Art 10.9 (3) (c) CAFTA-DR states that the obligations on performance requirements 'shall not be construed to prevent a Party from adopting or maintaining measures, including environmental measures: [...] (ii) necessary to protect human, animal, or plant life or health; or (iii) related to the conservation of living and non-living exhaustible natural resources'. Art 10.11 stipulates that nothing in the investment chapter of the CAFTA-DR 'shall be construed to prevent a Party from adopting, maintaining, or enforcing any measure otherwise consistent with this Chapter that it considers appropriate to ensure that investment activity in its territory is undertaken in a manner sensitive to environmental concerns.'

Already the wording of both provisions indicates that they safeguard the regulatory leeway of states for environmental protection. The CAFTA-DR only speaks to how states may engage in domestic environmental regulation while at the same time living up to their international investment protection obligations under the treaty.

On the other hand, the Tribunal appears to have overlooked Costa Rica's argument that the claimants had also violated customary international environmental law. Art 10.22 (1) CAFTA-DR, the applicable law clause for the arbitration, states that the tribunal 'shall decide the issues in dispute in accordance with this Agreement and applicable rules of international law' which includes customary international law. If customary environmental obligations directly applicable to investors existed – which, as submitted, they do not, at least in the current state of international law[66] – they could have served as a viable basis for a counterclaim. The Tribunal should have at least elaborated on this aspect.

In addition, it deserves mention that the Tribunal's reference to *erga omnes* obligations in acknowledging individual international subjectivity is misleading. The status of subjectivity and the content of rights and obligations are two separate questions as presented above.[67] As to *erga omnes* obligations, this notion refers to the special status of certain obligations of *states*, namely, that each state owes all other states compliance and is inter-

66 See above Chapter 2.IV.

67 See above Chapter 2.II.

nationally responsible to all states in case of a breach – transferring certain fundamental norms such as human rights from a traditional bilateral to a communal setting.[68] However, the status of *erga omnes* does not mean that private actors are bound to these international obligations as well, as the Tribunal seems to imply. In fact, important human rights obligations considered to exert *erga omnes* effect such as the European Convention on Human Rights require individuals to be victims of human rights violations to raise a human rights claim.[69]

Nonetheless, it is fair to say that the award contributes to recognising that integrating external investor obligations into investment law is, in principle, possible. That the Tribunal affirmed the reasoning in the *Urbaser v Argentina* award is noteworthy on its own as it may contribute to legitimising said reasoning as a *de facto*-precedent.[70] It also shows that the line of reasoning in the *Urbaser v Argentina* award is not exclusive to human rights but can potentially be generalised to cover other aspects of the public interest such as environmental protection.

4. Critique

Other than the awards in *Urbaser v Argentina* and *Aven v Costa Rica*, there is not much material that supports the integrating of external obligations into investment law. This reveals that it is a technique that, by large, may only be relevant in the future – pending the development of international obligations directly applicable to private actors in other areas of international law.[71] Having said that, integrating the few already-existing external

---

68 Bruno Simma, 'From Bilateralism to Community Interest in International Law' (1994) 250(VI) Recueil des Cours 217, 293–295.

69 See Patrick Abel, 'Menschenrechtsschutz durch Individualbeschwerdeverfahren: Ein regionaler Vergleich aus historischer, normativer und faktischer Perspektive' (2013) 51(3) Archiv des Völkerrechts 369, 379–380 with a comparison of the European to the American and African human rights systems, the latter allowing for *actiones populares*.

70 Debadatta Bose, 'David R Aven v Costa Rica: The Confluence of Corporations, Public International Law and International Investment Law' (2020) 35(1–2) ICSID Review 20, 21.

71 This is why Peter Muchlinski, 'The Impact of a Business and Human Rights Treaty on Investment Law and Arbitration' in Surya Deva and David Bilchitz (eds), *Building a Treaty on Business and Human Rights: Context and Contours* (Cambridge University Press 2017) 367 is interested in the potentials of a new interna-

obligations especially from international criminal law[72] could have merit. They address the gravest forms of injustice that investment law should not neglect. While the great majority of investment activities are unrelated to such atrocities, they may still be relevant in exceptional cases. This is for example evidenced by the recent scholarly interest in the interplay between investment and humanitarian law.[73]

In fact, in the ICSID proceedings in *Foresti et al. v South Africa*, the Tribunal almost would have had to adjudicate on a possible *ius cogens* violation by an investor. In this case, investors filed a claim against South Africa which enacted mineral ownership laws to eliminate the consequences of apartheid. Apartheid is prohibited by *ius cogens*. The parties eventually settled and discontinued the case.[74] Otherwise, likely, the Tribunal would have had to enquire if the investors had acquired property through the support of the apartheid regime. This constellation could have been a chance to integrate the external *ius cogens* prohibition of apartheid. It shows that this technique of integrating direct obligations can be relevant in investment law practice.

II. Diverting international obligations of states

Appreciating that there are only exceptional instances of external obligations of private actors, the analysis now turns to the many international obligations of states. In the last years, investment law practice has proposed to divert these state obligations to investor obligations through IIAs. This Section will trace these suggestions and criticise that state obligations are often not suitable for a simple transfer to investors.

---

tional treaty that imposes binding, directly applicable international human rights obligations on corporations.

72 See Chapter 2.IV.

73 The ESIL convened a Colloquium on the topic of 'International Investment Law & the Law of Armed Conflict' in October 2017; from scholarship see only Heather L Bray, 'SOI – Save Our Investments! International Investment Law and International Humanitarian Law' (2013) 14(3) Journal of World Investment & Trade 578; Christoph Schreuer, 'The Protection of Investments in Armed Conflicts' in Freya Baetens (ed), *Investment Law Within International Law: Integrationist Perspectives* (Cambridge University Press 2013).

74 *Piero Foresti and Others v The Republic of South Africa*, ICSID Case No. ARB(AF)/07/1, Award (4 August 2010) paras 54–58, 79–82.

1. Concept

The idea of diverting state obligations is to use the fact that state parties to an IIA often have many international obligations on the protection of the public interest, for example enshrined in human rights, labour standards and environmental protection treaties. IIA clauses could create direct obligations and define their content by referring to these obligations of states. Here, the IIA operates as the device that overcomes the lack of direct applicability to non-state actors for the purpose of the IIA. Outside of the investment context, it is a concept which also the 2003 UN Norms on the Responsibilities of Transnational Corporations and Other Business Enterprises with Regard to Human Rights propose in the business and human rights-debate.[75]

2. IIAs and reform suggestions

So far, no investment tribunal has applied this method of diverting states' international obligations to investors. Rather, the Tribunal in *Aven v Costa Rica* was – rightly – careful in distinguishing a directly applicable external international investor obligation from an international obligation of states. As we have already seen, in this case, Costa Rica raised an environmental counterclaim against the claimants, *inter alia* contending that they had violated environmental obligations under the CAFTA-DR. The Tribunal rejected this counterclaim because the investment protection chapter of the CAFTA-DR only contains environmental provisions related to the regulatory leeway of the host state.[76] In the words of the Tribunal, 'Art 10.9.3.c and 10.11 [...] do not -in and of themselves- impose any affirmative obligation upon investors.'[77] Within the terminology of this chapter, these provisions did not divert the international obligations of the host state to the foreign investors.

---

75 UN Commission on Human Rights 'Norms on the Responsibilities of Transnational Corporations and Other Business Enterprises with Regard to Human Rights' UN Doc E/CN.4/Sub.2/2003/12/Rev.2 (2003) (13 August 2003); for a criticism and contextualisation to international investment law see Muchlinski, 'Impact' (n 71) 364.

76 See above Chapter 3.I.3.

77 *Aven v Costa Rica* (n 16) para 743.

One can find such 'diversion clauses' in several recent IIAs of developing countries. The ECOWAS Investment Rules are a good example. Their Art 13 stipulates:

> (1) Investors and their investments shall prior to the establishment of an investment or afterwards, refrain from involving themselves in corrupt practices as defined in Article 30 of this supplementary Act.
>
> (2) Investors and their investments shall not be complicit in any act described in Paragraph (1) [...].

Art 30 – to which Art 13 refers – obliges the state parties to enact and enforce criminal laws in their domestic jurisdiction against corruption as defined therein. Therefore, the reference in Art 13 to Art 30 diverts the international obligations of the state parties created in the latter provision to the investor. It also means that the investor has the international obligation to abstain from such actions irrespective of whether the host state lives up to its obligations in Art 30 and enacted respective domestic law.

Another good example is Art 14 ECOWAS Investment Rules. Its paragraph 2 states:

> Investors shall not manage or operate the investments in a manner that circumvents human rights obligations, labour standards as well as regional environmental and social obligations, to which the host State and/or home State are Parties.

Notable about this provision is not only that it diverts obligations of states to investors but that it goes even further. By pointing to the obligations of both the host state and the home state, it binds investors to the combined highest standard, preventing them from gaining a competitive advantage in a host state with lower standards. In the same vein, Art 18 Morocco-Nigeria BIT imposes post-establishment obligations to 'uphold human rights in the host state' (para 2), to act in accordance with core labour standards enshrined in the 1998 ILO Declaration on Fundamental Principles and Rights of Work (para 3) and not to circumvent international environmental, labour and human rights obligations of the host state or home state (para 4).[78]

---

78 See for example Niccolò Zugliani, 'Human rights in International Investment Law: The 2016 Morocco-Nigeria Bilateral Investment Treaty' (2019) 68(3) International and Comparative Law Quarterly 761, 766 who stresses that investors must not only respect but also actively uphold human rights while also noting that the provision's 'relevance must not be overestimated' (767); Okechukwu

An example of diverting state obligations without depending on their ratification by one of the IIA's state parties offer Art 14 (4) ECOWAS Investment Rules, Art 15 (2) SADC Model BIT Template and Art 14 (C) IISD Model International Agreement on Investment for Sustainable Development.[79] All three stipulate in a similar way that investors and investments shall act in accordance with fundamental or core labour standards enshrined in the 1998 ILO Declaration on Fundamental Principles and Rights of Work. They set a minimum standard for investors irrespective of the home and host states' own obligations.

Further insightful examples relate to anti-corruption norms. Art 10 SADC Model BIT Template covers a comprehensive anti-corruption obligation for foreign investors. The commentary to the provision states that the language of the obligation is taken from the UN and OECD Conventions on Bribery. The SADC Model BIT Template only added certain language that addresses payments to family members of business associates of an official which was considered to constitute a loophole in the mentioned conventions.[80] Art 15 of the 2003 UN Convention against Corruption[81] and Art 1 of the 1997 OECD Convention on Combating Bribery of Foreign Public Officials in International Business Transactions[82] impose international obligations *on states* to prescribe and enforce criminal legislation against bribes with similar language.

Art 11 of the 2015 India Model BIT[83] even takes over the wording of the UN and OECD Conventions without any change by stipulating:

> The parties reaffirm and recognize that: [...] (ii) Investors and their investments shall not, either prior to or after the establishment of

---

Ejims, 'The 2016 Morocco–Nigeria Bilateral Investment Treaty: More Practical Reality in Providing a Balanced Investment Treaty?' (2019) 34(1) ICSID Review 62, 77 who considers the placing of 'direct obligations on foreign investors [...] a novelty and a remarkable trend'; Krajewski (n 44) 114–115 who considers that the provision lacks legal clarity but understands it to at least make the international human rights obligations of Morocco and Nigeria directly applicable to investors.

79 IISD, *Model* (n 12).

80 SADC Model BIT, 32.

81 United Nations Convention against Corruption (adopted 31 October 2003, entered into force 14 December 2005) 2349 UNTS 41 (UN Convention against Corruption).

82 OECD Convention on Combating Bribery of Foreign Public Officials in International Business Transactions (adopted 17 December 1997, entered into force 15 February 1999) 2802 UNTS 225 (OECD Anti-Bribery Convention).

83 India Model BIT.

> an investment, offer, promise or give any undue pecuniary advantage gratification or gift whatsoever, whether directly or indirectly, to a public servant or official of a Party as an inducement or reward for doing or forbearing to do any official act or obtain or maintain other improper advantage nor shall be complicit in inciting, aiding, abetting, or conspiring to commit such acts.

The chapeau which addresses the state parties favours a reading that understands the provision as a mere interpretive guidance for other articles of the Model BIT. Yet, the chapter that covers Art 11 has the title 'Investor obligations', and number (ii) as well as the Article's other numbers directly address foreign investors with obligatory language. Consequently, one can best understand the provision as creating a direct obligation against bribery that builds on the UN and OECD Conventions. In addition to the India Model BIT, Art 17 (2)-(3) of the Morocco-Nigeria BIT contains similar language.

Apart from these new IIAs, scholars have proposed the diverting of state obligations as a reform option. Some call for making use of international conventions such as the ICCPR, the ICESCR, the ILO Declaration on Fundamental Principles and Rights at Work and the UN Convention against Corruption as treaties that most states have ratified.[84] In addition, they suggest drawing on customary law.[85]

---

84 See for example Patrick Dumberry and Gabrielle Dumas-Aubin, 'When and How Allegations of Human Rights Violations Can Be Raised in Investor-State Arbitration' (2012) 13 Journal of World Investment & Trade 349, 352–358 who explain that international treaties such as the OECD Anti-Bribery Convention and the Convention on the Elimination of All Forms of Discrimination against Women (adopted 18 December 1979, entered into force 3 September 1981) 1249 UNTS 1 (CEDAW) speak to corporate behaviour; while they do not yet create international obligations directly applicable to corporations, states were free to sign BITs that would impose specific human rights obligations on them.

85 See for example José A Rivas, 'ICSID Treaty Counterclaims: Case Law and Treaty Evolution' in Jean E Kalicki and Anna Joubin-Bret (eds), *Reshaping the Investor-State Dispute Settlement System: Journeys for the 21st Century* (Brill 2015) 825 who points to environmental obligations and labour standards under international customary law or accepted as general principles of law.

3. Critique

The greatest advantage of diverting state obligations is that they represent a particularly rich source of binding standards. International treaties and customary law have developed far-reaching obligations of states for the protection of the public interest. IIAs could build on these to create direct obligations in a current state of international law with only few obligations directly applicable to non-state actors. Levelling the international obligations of states and investors appears a feasible reaction to the increasing power that many multinational-enterprises and their investment subsidiaries hold today.

On the other hand, one may oppose the concept of diverting state obligations and argue that there are important reasons why standards for private actors and states should differ. After all, it is solely the state that represents its constituency and is competent to take policy decisions that weigh and balance the different interests of citizens and inhabitants.

This is reflected in the way most international obligations leave states considerable leeway on how to comply with them. Generally, international obligations do not explicitly prescribe how states should act. For example, most obligations do not require the state to take a certain policy action. Rather, they express a certain result the state must accomplish. They leave the selection of means to reach that result to the state. Therein, international obligations provide room for states' internal decision-making processes and account for policy preferences.[86] If one diverted state obligations to investors, this leeway would now be at the disposal of the latter. It would be up to investors to decide on the means to reach the prescribed result of the obligation. But in contrast to states, investors do not provide for internal decision-making processes which represent the interest of the constituency or, for example, follow democratic principles – but rather serve the interests of the investors themselves and their shareholders. Inter-

86 See also the general question how international law should address states' prerogative to regulate private behaviour posed by Steven R Ratner, 'Corporations and Human Rights: A Theory of Legal Responsibility' (2001) 111(3) Yale Law Journal 443, 466. A good example of such leeway are international human rights obligations under the ICESCR: Art 2 (1) requires state parties to take steps to the maximum of their available resources with a view to progressively achieving the full realization of ICESCR rights, see Committee on Economic, Social and Cultural Rights 'General Comment No 3: The Nature of States Parties' Obligations (Art 2, Para 1, of the Covenant)' UN Doc E/1991/23 (14 December 1990), paras 1–14.

national obligations of states have not been created to provide non-state actors with such policy-making power in mind. Consequently, in many instances, the simple diversion of state obligations to investors must be considered ill-placed.

For example: the ICESCR explicitly leaves room for the states to take policy decisions in realising cultural, economic and social rights. They are only subject to certain restrains such as the core minimum standard or the duty to progress according to the abilities of the state. Simply diverting the ICESCR obligations to investors does not answer the question which role private actors should play in the shaping of the cultural, economic and social conditions in society[87] – political questions that states surely do not intend to leave for investors to decide. This shows that it is problematic to analogise and divert state obligations as they might not be suitable to apply to non-state actors.[88] Rather than a simple copy of state obligations, direct obligations must provide further criteria and guidance how exactly investors should behave towards the public interest.

A suggestion in this regard was made by the ICSID Tribunal in its 2016 award in *Urbaser v Argentina* that has been criticised above.[89] It held that private actors must only *abstain from harming* the human rights of others. Positive obligations to fulfil human rights could only follow from a contract with the state.[90] On the one hand, this is a clear-cut pragmatic distinction that relieves foreign investors from providing welfare to citizens, something usually considered a task of the state. On the other hand, it only represents a minimum approach that centres on the defending of freedom of others against investors. Yet, many of the non-binding CSR

87 Ratner (n 86) 493 rightly points out that it is necessary to strike a balance between individual liberties and business interests.

88 Supported for example by Karsten Nowrot, 'How to Include Environmental Protection, Human Rights and Sustainability in International Investment Law?' (2014) 15(3/4) Journal of World Investment & Trade 612, 637; Karsten Nowrot, 'Obligations of Investors' in Marc Bungenberg and others (eds), *International Investment Law* (Nomos 2015) para 16; for an opposite view that too quickly suggests to look into the host and home states' international obligations see Todd Weiler, 'Balancing Human Rights and Investor Protection: A New Approach for a Different Legal Order' (2004) 27(2) Boston College International and Comparative Law Review 429, 445.

89 See Chapter 3.I.2.

90 *Urbaser v Argentina*, Award (n 17) paras 1110–1120.

norms appeal for a more active role of companies and hence reflect a societal expectation to go beyond this purely negative dimension.[91]

This is not the place to decide on the best approach – rather, the award serves as an example of which types of questions an IIA must answer if it aims to divert international obligations of states to investors.

III. Converting legally non-binding standards

Apart from international obligations of states, CSR norms represent another potentially rich source of direct obligations. This Section will show that new IIAs have started to convert these legally non-binding norms to binding direct obligations – and why the blurring of these different types of norms may prove to be counterproductive.

1. Concept

By their nature, CSR norms are legally non-binding. An IIA may convert such soft law to a direct obligation by conferring the missing binding legal effect for the purpose of the IIA.[92]

---

91 For example, Principle 11 of the UN Human Rights Council 'Guiding Principles on Business and Human Rights Implementing the United Nations "Protect, Respect and Remedy" Framework' UN Doc HRC/RES/17/4 (2011) not only calls on enterprises to 'avoid infringing on the human rights of others' but also to 'address adverse human rights impacts with which they are involved'. Similarly, the OECD Guidelines for Multinational Enterprises contain many active responsibilities, for example to '[c]ontribute to economic, environmental and social progress with a view to achieving sustainable development' or, to give a more specific example, to employ 'training programmes' to '[p]romote awareness of and compliance by workers employed by multinational enterprises with respect to company policies through appropriate dissemination of these policies', see OECD 'Guidelines for Multinational Enterprises' (2011) ‹http://dx.doi.org/10.1787/9789264115415-en› accessed 7 December 2021, 19.

92 This is for example suggested with regard to non-binding standards for the protection of indigenous peoples by George K Foster, 'Investors, States, and Stakeholders: Power Asymmetries in International Investment and the Stabilizing Potential of Investment Treaties' (2013) 17(2) Lewis & Clark Law Review 361, 407–408; see also Choudhury (n 1) 92 who considers conversion of soft law by proposing that states could provide CSR norms with binding effect for investors by replacing the word 'expected' with the word 'shall' and by explicitly allowing for counterclaims.

Such converting of soft law has to be distinguished from mere references to CSR in some recent IIAs that leave the voluntary character of the norms untouched, as already discussed above. A conversion as understood here requires specific language in an IIA provision that transforms a rule from non-binding into binding.

2. IIAs and reform suggestions

Such language is provided for in several recent IIAs and model BITs of developed and developing countries.

Belgium and Luxembourg introduced the concept of converting CSR standards to direct investor obligations in their recent 2019 Model BIT for the Belgium-Luxembourg Economic Union.[93] Its Art 18 (1) states that '[i]nvestors shall […] act in accordance with internationally accepted standards applicable to foreign investors to which the Contracting Parties are a party.' The term 'shall' indicates that the BIT binds investors to the otherwise non-binding international CSR standards.

Art 15 of the ECOWAS Investment Rules addresses 'corporate governance and practices' and thus refers to non-binding norms of CSR. Art 15 (1) transfers these non-binding norms into legally binding investor obligations by stating that '[i]nvestments shall comply with and maintain national and internationally accepted standards of corporate governance for the sector involved, in particular for transparency and accounting practices.' Although the article's chapeau provides for certain flexibility through stipulating that the paragraphs must be understood to apply '[i]n accordance with the size and nature of an investment', the formulation 'shall' in contrast to 'should' is evidence of a legally binding character.

Art 16 (1) of the SADC Model BIT even goes further by stating that '[i]nvestments shall meet or exceed national and internationally accepted standards of corporate governance […]'. This provision highlights that the respective soft law applies as a binding minimum standard. In the same vein, Art 12 (3) of the 2008 Ghana Model BIT stipulates that foreign investors '[…] shall behave in accordance with relevant guidelines and other internationally accepted standards applicable to foreign investors.'

93 Belgium-Luxembourg Economic Union Model BIT (28 March 2019) ‹https://investmentpolicy.unctad.org/international-investment-agreements/treaty-files/5854/download› accessed 7 December 2021; in the same vein Krajewski (n 44) 116.

A similar approach features in Art 19 of the 2016 African Union's Draft Pan-African Investment Code that forms part of the Agreement's Chapter 4 titled 'investors [sic!] obligations'. The provision states in paragraph 1 that '[i]nvestments shall meet national and internationally accepted standards of corporate governance for the sector involved, in particular for transparency and accounting practices.' Paragraph 3 further spells out obligations that include 'active co-operation between corporations and stakeholders in creating wealth, jobs and the sustainability of financially sound enterprises' in lit. b as well as the obligation to '[e]nsure that timely and accurate disclosure is made on all material matters regarding a corporation, including [...] risks related to environmental liabilities [...]' in lit. c.

Even more concrete is the obligation laid down in Art 18 (1) of the Morocco-Nigeria BIT which stipulates that '[c]ompanies in areas of resource exploitation and high-risk industrial enterprises shall maintain a current certification to ISO 14001 or an equivalent environmental management standard'. Its Art 19 comprehensively states that '1) In accordance with the size and nature of an investment, a) investments shall meet or exceed national and internationally accepted standards of corporate governance for the sector involved [...]'.

The 2015 Brazil Model BIT offers a nuanced alternative for converting CSR norms into binding international standards. It covers a special provision on CSR in its Art 14. The provision states in paragraph 1 that

> [i]nvestors and their investment shall strive to achieve the highest possible level of contribution to the sustainable development of the Host State and the local community, through the adoption of a high degree of socially responsible practices, based on the voluntary principles and standards set out in this Article.

Paragraph 2 stipulates that '[t]he investors and their investment shall endeavour to comply with the following voluntary principles and standards for a responsible business conduct and consistent with the laws adopted by the Host State receiving the investment:', subsequently listing eleven rules that, for example, call on the investor to '[r]espect the internationally recognized human rights of those involved in the companies' activities' in lit. b. Brazil has adopted this model in several BITs.[94] Sometimes these

94 Art 15 (2) Brazil-Chile BIT; Art 10 Brazil-Angola BIT; Art 9 Brazil-Malawi BIT; Art 13 Brazil-Mexico BIT; Art 10 Brazil-Mozambique BIT; Art 2.13 (2) Brazil-Peru FTA.

treaties' substantive standards go even further. For example, Art 10 Brazil-Angola-BIT provides a longer list of standards than the 2015 Brazil Model BIT, *inter alia* also demanding more explicitly, respect for the environment.[95]

The wording used by the Brazilian BITs indicates a certain conversion of CSR norms by using 'shall', 'deberán'[96] or 'deverão'.[97] Herein, they deviate from the strictly voluntary approach of other IIAs that integrate CSR norms and are careful to use the hortatory expression 'should'.[98] It is also telling that the 2015 Brazil-Colombia-BIT generally follows the 2015 Brazil Model BIT but fails to provide any obligatory language in its Art 13 on Corporate Social Responsibility. Instead, it obliges only the state parties to appeal to investors to comply voluntarily with relevant standards[99] – a sign that, here, Colombia rejected to consent to a provision that would otherwise lead to binding standards for investors.

On the other hand, the Brazil Model BIT does not transform CSR standards to legally binding obligations in a similar extensive manner as the ECOWAS Investment Rules. It does not allow to invoke these obligations in any international dispute settlement procedure but only before domestic courts.[100] What is more, pursuant to the Model BIT, investors must only 'strive' and 'endeavour' to comply with voluntary standards. The most adequate interpretation is that investors have an international due diligence obligation of best effort – an obligation of conduct instead of an obligation of result. Notwithstanding, an obligation of conduct is still a legally binding provision that departs from the purely voluntary

95 Art 10 and Annex II (i) Brazil-Angola BIT; for a broader analysis of the new Brazilian IIA policy, including a comparison to IIAs from other regions, see Geraldo Vidigal and Beatriz Stevens, 'Brazil's New Model of Dispute Settlement for Investment: Return to the Past or Alternative for the Future?' (2018) 19(3) Journal of World Investment & Trade 475, 477, 505.

96 Art 15 (2) Brazil-Chile BIT; Art 13 (2) Brazil-Mexico BIT.

97 Art 10 Brazil-Angola BIT; Art 10 Brazil-Mozambique BIT.

98 See Chapter 2.V.2.

99 Brazil-Colombia Investment Cooperation and Facilitation Agreement (adopted 9 October 2015) ‹https://investmentpolicy.unctad.org/international-investment-agreements/treaty-files/5765/download› accessed 7 December 2021 (Brazil-Colombia BIT).

100 See further Michelle R Sanchez Badin and Fabio Morosini, 'Navigating Between Resistance and Conformity with the International Investment Regime: The Brazilian Agreements on Cooperation and Facilitation of Investments (ACFIs)' in Fabio Morosini and Michelle R Sanchez (eds), *Reconceptualizing International Investment Law from the Global South* (Cambridge University Press 2018) 231–232.

model of international CSR norms. Therefore, Art 15 of the 2015 Brazil Model BIT and the cited other Brazilian BITs serve as an example of an intermediate and careful approach to the converting of international soft law.[101]

3. Critique

The advantage of converting non-binding international soft law is that it makes use of existing norms that already have private actors as their addressees. It does not face the problems that diverting states' obligations bring about, discussed above.[102] Foreign investors form a sub-category of corporations and hence are mostly already subject to these non-binding rules of soft law. Advocates of this conversion approach consider soft law a rich source of internationally consented standards, best suited as orientation for binding obligations.[103]

However, converting these norms' character is also problematic. It changes the regulatory approach these norms originally follow. Creating soft law such as CSR norms serves a specific strategy: to encourage and compel businesses to voluntarily cooperate with states by aligning their activities with the public interest. Often, there is the underlying political belief that such cooperation is more effective than the imposing and en-

101 The same conclusion is drawn by Jose D Amado, Jackson S Kern and Martin D Rodriguez, *Arbitrating the Conduct of International Investors* (Cambridge University Press 2018) 130; Krajewski (n 44) 116–117. For a contrary assessment see Muchlinski, 'Impact' (n 71) 351–352 who understands the Brazilian provisions as remaining legally non-binding, however without explaining why a best-efforts-obligation lacks legal force even though international law acknowledges the binding character of best-efforts-obligations where they apply to states; Nitish Monebhurrun, 'Novelty in International Investment Law: The Brazilian Agreement on Cooperation and Facilitation of Investments as a Different International Investment Agreement Model' (2017) 8(1) Journal of International Dispute Settlement 79, 95–100 who qualifies the provisions as voluntary despite identifying and highlighting the treaty provisions presented here as reflecting a binding best effort obligation; Ranjan (n 65) 131 who considers a lack of specificity to rule out a binding character.

102 The concreteness of non-binding standards is for example highlighted by Foster (n 92) 407–408.

103 For example supported by Patrick Dumberry and Gabrielle Dumas-Aubin, 'How to Impose Human Rights Obligations on Corporations Under Investment Treaties?' (2011–2012) 4 Yearbook on International Investment Law and Policy, 8.

forcing of legal duties.[104] This approach is lost where such norms become obligations that call for compliance independent of investors' will.

This also means that CSR norms were developed for a different, cooperative context. It is quite common that moral or ethical standards demand more from a person than the law does. The latter entails a limitation of freedom and hence require a different weighing and balancing of the positions affected by the norm. Consequently, non-binding standards do not always embody an adequate value judgment that is suitable and directly transferable to a legally binding setting. An emerging international consensus on a CSR standard does not necessarily mean that there is also an emerging consensus on a new *binding* norm.[105]

IV. Elevating domestic investor obligations to international investor obligations

In creating direct obligations, recent investment practice has not stopped at the dualist divide between the national and international legal orders. As this Section will lay out, the UNCITRAL investment Tribunal in *Al-Warraq v Indonesia* and new IIAs have elevated domestic investor obligations to international investor obligations. In comparison to the abovementioned examples, this method, when handled correctly, appears more realistic and capable of introducing obligations to investment law.

1. Concept

IIAs can contain clauses which turn domestic obligations into direct international obligations, for example by drawing on the host state's administrative law or existing domestic contracts with the investor. In such cases, one may speak of an elevation of the domestic investor obligation to an international investor obligation.

The concept of elevating a domestic investor obligation presupposes that one distinguishes between national and international law as different legal

104 cf Peter Muchlinski, *Multinational Enterprises and the Law* (2nd edn, Oxford University Press 2007) 113–114.

105 On this process ibid, 111–112. Some scholars do not sufficiently distinguish between binding and non-binding norms, for example Weiler (n 88) 445–446.

orders.[106] In such a dualist setting, international obligations of states must be transformed or declared applicable within the domestic legal order to take effect in the latter. An elevation in the present sense operates in the opposite direction: a domestic legal norm is brought into the international legal order. In both cases mentioned, such transformation results in two substantive legal norms that exist independently on the domestic and international level.

One can picture this legal technique as a form of a 'reversed umbrella clause'.[107] Umbrella clauses in IIAs require the host state to protect investors' rights enshrined in investment contracts or otherwise found in the host state's domestic legal order as a matter of international law. They elevate the host state's domestic obligations towards the investor to an international obligation of the state.[108] Elevation as understood here works similarly, only that it operates in the reverse direction by elevating investors' domestic obligations towards the state. With the words of the UNCITRAL Tribunal in *Aven v Costa Rica* in the context of domestic environmental law, elevation means that 'any violation of state-enacted environmental regulations [by the investor] will amount to a breach of the Treaty'.[109] Such elevation must also be distinguished from IIA clauses

106 On dualism see the overview by Pierre-Marie Dupuy, 'International Law and Domestic (Municipal) Law' in Anne Peters (ed), *Max Planck Encyclopedia of Public International Law* (April 2011) paras 4–10 who also points to a (controversial) passage in *Certain German Interests in Polish Upper Silesia (Germany v Poland)* (Merits) [1926] PCIJ Rep Series A No 7, 19 which does seem to reflect and illustrate a dualist view on the relation of international and domestic law.

107 Gustavo Laborde, 'The Case for Host State Claims in Investment Arbitration' (2010) 1(1) Journal of International Dispute Settlement 97, 112; cf the reference to umbrella clauses in *Al-Warraq v Indonesia*, Final Award (n 15) para 663.

108 For a general analysis of umbrella clauses see Rudolf Dolzer and Christoph Schreuer, *Principles of International Investment Law* (2nd edn, Oxford University Press 2012) 166–178. Sometimes, scholarly writing identifies the imposition of obligations in IIAs but does not comment on its character as an international obligation, see for example Peter Muchlinski, 'Regulating Multinationals: Foreign Investment, Development, and the Balance of Corporate and Home Country Rights and Responsibilities in a Globalizing World' in José E Alvarez and others (eds), *The Evolving International Investment Regime: Expectations, Realities, Options* (Oxford University Press 2011) 49.

109 *Aven v Costa Rica* (n 16) para 743. The Tribunal rejected that CAFTA-DR contained such a reversed umbrella-clause. On this case and the environmental counterclaim, see above Chapter 3.I.3.

which restate that investors face obligations under the host state's domestic law with declaratory effect only.[110]

Conceptually, it is important to highlight that elevating domestic to international obligations must also be separated from the question of whether domestic obligations are part of the applicable law in an investment arbitration. There is a difference between substance and enforcement. Elevation as understood here operates on the level of substantive international law. It is only the content of such an international obligation which is defined by referring to domestic law. As a corollary, the interpretation of such an international investor obligation follows the rules of Art 31 and 32 of the VCLT. In turn, if an investment tribunal applies domestic obligations in an arbitration, said rules retain their substantive domestic legal character.

Furthermore, elevated investor obligations must be distinguished from the so-called legality clauses in IIAs. These clauses require investors to comply with the host state's domestic law if they want to qualify for protection under the respective IIA. For example, some IIAs contain a provision which defines protected 'foreign investment' as only those investments which comply with domestic law. This means that under these provisions compliance with domestic law forms a requirement of investor rights' substantive scope. Similar provisions exist which require compliance with domestic law as a precondition for access to investment arbitration. All these provisions do not set self-standing obligations on investors – importantly, the state cannot demand compliance and claim compensation in case of non-compliance. Rather, these legality clauses entail *indirect* obligations which will be dealt with at a later stage in Part II of this book.[111]

2. The Al-Warraq v Indonesia award

In the UNCITRAL case of *Al-Warraq v Indonesia*, the Tribunal acknowledged the elevating of a domestic investor obligation.

---

110 Yet, especially in policy suggestions, this point is often missed, see for example IISD, *Toolkit* (n 13) para 5.3.1; see Xuan Shao, 'Environmental and Human Rights Counterclaims in International Investment Arbitration: at the Crossroads of Domestic and International Law' (2021) 24(1) Journal of International Economic Law 157, 164, 174 who follows the umbrella clause-analogy but rather inconsistently considers that the rule still remained domestic in character.

111 See Chapter 7.I.2 and Chapter 7.II.5.

In this case, the claimant conducted an investment in Indonesia as a shareholder of the Indonesian 'Bank Century'. In the course of the global financial crisis of 2008/2009, the bank suffered liquidity problems and received state aid, including a bailout by the Indonesian Central Bank. Following the bailout, Indonesia filed criminal proceedings with several persons involved with Bank Century, including the claimant. The state alleged banking mismanagement, fraud and corruption. Eventually, the claimant was convicted *in absentia*, and his assets were confiscated.[112] In 2011, the claimant instituted an investment arbitration claim under the OIC Investment Agreement[113] and the 2010 UNCITRAL Arbitration Rules. He claimed the violation of a series of investor rights, including the right to adequate protection and security, the protection against expropriation and the FET-right via the MFN-clause.[114]

In the course of the proceedings, Indonesia filed a counterclaim against the investor. The state argued that he unjustly enriched himself in violation of his domestic financial commitments. Indonesia demanded compensation in the amount of the bailout (Rp. 6.7 trillion), alternatively of the sum allegedly stolen by the claimant (USD 360.735.638) or any sum found appropriate by the Tribunal.[115]

The Tribunal found in its 2014 award that, in principle, Indonesia had the right to bring a counterclaim based on the investor's fraudulent behaviour and referred *inter alia* to Art 9 OIC Investment Agreement to that end. This provision stipulates:

> The investor shall be bound by the laws and regulations in force in the host state and shall refrain from all acts that may disturb public order or morals or that may be prejudicial to the public interest. He is also to refrain from exercising restrictive practices and from trying to achieve gains through unlawful means.

112 *Al-Warraq v Indonesia*, Final Award (n 15) paras 73–141.

113 Agreement on Promotion, Protection and Guarantee of Investments among Member States of the Organisation of the Islamic Conference (adopted 5 June 1981, entered into force 23 September 1986) ‹https://investmentpolicy.unctad.org/international-investment-agreements/treaty-files/2399/download› accessed 7 December 2021 (OIC Investment Agreement).

114 *Hesham Talaat M. Al-Warraq v The Republic of Indonesia*, Award on Respondent's Preliminary Objections to Jurisdiction and Admissibility of the Claims (UNCITRAL, 21 June 2012) para 46.

115 *Al-Warraq v Indonesia*, Final Award (n 15) para 655.

While there are voices from the time in which the OIC Agreement was created that see in this provision only the declaratory restating of the host state's right to regulate,[116] the Tribunal gave it a much broader meaning in its award. It is useful to quote the exact reasoning of the Tribunal in this regard:

> Article 9 imposes a positive obligation on investors to respect the law of the Host State, as well as public order and morals. An investor of course has a general obligation to obey the law of the host state, but Article 9 raises this obligation from the plane of domestic law (and jurisdiction of domestic Tribunals) to a treaty obligation binding on the investor in an investor state arbitration. An analogy can be drawn with so called 'umbrella clauses' that elevate contractual obligations to the treaty plane. The fact that the Contracting Parties imposed treaty obligations on investors (which the Claimant assented to by accepting the open offer of investment arbitration made by the Respondent in the OIC Agreement) confirms the interpretation […] that permits counterclaims by the respondent state.[117]

Notwithstanding, the Tribunal dismissed Indonesia's counterclaim for more specific reasons: Indonesia had failed to prove the investor's personal liability as it could not distinguish his actions from other parties that were involved in the fraud but were not subject to the counterclaim.[118] What is more, the fraudulent actions had primarily been committed against the private Bank Century. While the Tribunal generally found it possible that Indonesia could subrogate Bank Century's claims, Indonesia had not demonstrated the relevant facts to that end either.[119] The Tribunal further

---

116 Hasan Moinuddin, *The Charter of the Islamic Conference and Legal Framework of Economic Co-Operation Among Its Member States: A Study of the Charter, the General Agreement for Economic, Technical and Commercial Co-Operation and the Agreement for Promotion, Protection and Guarantee of Investments Among Member States of the OIC* (Clarendon Press 1987) 149–150 who draws a comparison to established practice in other IIAs at that time. His argument that Art 9 of the OIC Investment Agreement reflects the power of a state to uphold public order implicit in other IIAs is close to the contemporary 'right to regulate' debate and focuses on the state rather than, as the provision's wording indicates, on the investor.

117 *Al-Warraq v Indonesia*, Final Award (n 15) para 663.

118 ibid 669.

119 ibid 670.

added that some of the respondent's actions were subject to a separate dispute resolution clause.[120]

Therefore, even though the counterclaim eventually failed to succeed, this was only for specific factual, rather than fundamental legal reasons. Importantly, the Tribunal in its reasoning explicitly affirmed that the OIC Agreement created an international obligation of the investor. It also acknowledged the possibility to hold him accountable through a counterclaim in investment arbitration. The obligation in Art 9 OIC Investment Agreement conforms with the above-mentioned conceptual observations in that it elevates Indonesian domestic law. It serves to protect the public interest in the form of the rule of law against fraudulent behaviour. What is more, apparently, Art 9 OIC Investment Agreement is not limited to issues of fraud and corruption but elevates any other domestic obligation, potentially including environmental and human rights obligations, for example.

3. IIAs and reform suggestions

Elevating domestic to international investor obligations has some ground in other IIAs as well.

One may even consider if ordinary umbrella clauses – which can be found in many IIAs – may, in certain cases, have the effect of elevating not only the contractual obligations of the state as conventionally thought, but also the investor's obligations. In this regard, the precise wording of the umbrella clause appears relevant. Some explicitly state that the state promises the investors to comply with its contractual obligations as a matter of international law – these clauses clearly do not elevate investors' domestic obligations as they only elaborate on the state. Other umbrella clauses, however, require compliance with investment contracts in general without any language that focusses on the state's actions only. Arguably, these umbrella clauses not only elevate the state's but also the investor's domestic contractual obligations. The ICSID Tribunal in its 2002 Procedural Order No 2 in *SGS v Pakistan* commented in this direction that

> [i]t would be inequitable if, by reason of the invocation of ICSID jurisdiction, the Claimant could on the one hand elevate its side of the dispute to international adjudication and, on the other, preclude the

120 ibid 671.

> Respondent from pursuing its own claim for damages by obtaining a stay of those proceedings for the pendency of the international proceedings, if such international proceedings could not encompass the Respondent's claim.[121]

This idea remains to be tested for concrete IIAs. However, many umbrella clauses may contain language which implies that they should only benefit the foreign investor.

Meanwhile, the approach to elevate domestic obligations has received express attention in new IIAs. For example, Art 11 (1) and (2) of the ECOWAS Investment Rules stipulates that

> Investors and Investments are subject to the laws and regulations of the host State. Investors and investments must comply with the host State measures prescribing the formalities of establishing an investment, and accept host State jurisdiction with respect to the investment.

As a post-establishment obligation, Art 14 (1) separately establishes that

> [i]nvestors or investments shall, in keeping with best practice requirements relating to their activities the size of their investments, strive to comply with on hygiene, security, health and social welfare rules in force in the host country. [sic!]

In the same vein, Art 13 COMESA Investment Agreement lays out that 'investors and their investments shall comply with all applicable domestic measures of the Member State in which their investment is made.' That this clause has a more extensive meaning than legality clauses becomes clear from Art 28 (9) COMESA Investment Agreement. This provision specifically allows for counterclaims by host states against investors on the ground that the investor 'has not fulfilled its obligations under this Agreement, including the obligations to comply with all applicable domestic measures'.

Similarly, Art 22 of the AU's Draft Pan-African Investment Code stipulates in paragraph 1 that '[i]nvestors shall abide by the laws, regulations, administrative guidelines and policies of the host State.' The 2008 Ghana Model BIT titles its Article 12 'Responsibilities of Nationals and Companies of a Contracting Party in the Territory of the other Contracting

121 *SGS Société Générale de Surveillance S.A. v Islamic Republic of Pakistan*, ICSID Case No. ARB/01/13, Procedural Order No. 2 (16 October 2002) para 302.

Party' and provides in paragraph 1 that foreign investors '[...] shall be bound by the laws and regulations in force in the host State, including its laws and regulations on labour, health and the environment.'[122]

Somewhat more ambiguous is the way the 2015 India Model BIT addresses foreign investors' compliance with host state law. Art 11 stipulates:

> The parties reaffirm and recognize that: (i) Investors and their investments shall comply with all laws, regulations, administrative guidelines and policies of a Party concerning the establishment, acquisition, management, operation and disposition of investments. [...] (iii) Investors and their investments shall comply with the provisions of law of the Parties concerning taxation, including timely payment of their tax liabilities.

The chapeau favours a reading that the provision merely restates that investors face domestic obligations. But the fact that the subparagraphs only relate to specific domestic laws is a strong argument in favour of understanding the provision as elevating them to international obligations.[123]

Even the Netherlands as a capital exporting state has included a provision which may be read to elevate domestic investor obligations into its new 2019 Model BIT. Art 7 (1) Netherlands Model BIT on corporate social responsibility states:

> Investors and their investments shall comply with domestic laws and regulations of the host state, including laws and regulations on human rights, environmental protection and labor laws.

Interestingly, in addition, Art 7 (4) Netherlands Model BIT elevates certain domestic obligations that are enacted in the *home* state if their violation causes damages in the host state:

> Investors shall be liable in accordance with the rules concerning jurisdiction of their home state for the acts or decisions made in relation to

122 See also Amado, Kern and Rodriguez (n 101) 137–138; on this approach in the broader context of Africa's investment policy, see Makane Moise Mbengue and Stefanie Schacherer, 'The Africanization of International Investment Law: The Pan-African Investment Code and the Reform of the International Investment Regime' (2017) 18(3) Journal of World Investment & Trade 414, 434–436.

123 In the same direction, but more cautiously, based on Art 12 India Model BIT see Muchlinski, 'Impact' (n 71) 350; see Krajewski (n 44) 120 who considers an interpretation as presented here to be possible but questions if such an understanding would add any value.

the investment where such acts or decisions lead to significant damage, personal injuries or loss of life in the host state.

Furthermore, the obligation to comply with domestic law features prominently in policy suggestions and reform proposals, for example by the IISD. The Institute promoted it already in its 2005 Model International Agreement on Investment for Sustainable Development[124] and includes it as feasible policy options in its 2017 Sustainability Toolkit for Trade Negotiators[125] as well as in expert consultations held in 2018.[126]

4. Critique

Clearly, elevating domestic obligations has the great advantage that these norms are tailored to private actors and comprehensively protect the public interest. They do not face the structural disadvantages of other methods of transforming norms discussed in the previous Sections.

Such combining of international and domestic law is not alien to investment law. Rather, *Douglas* famously identified 'hybrid foundations'[127] as a characteristic of international investment arbitration. For example, the right to FET requires an inquiry into the host state's legal system to assess if the investor's legitimate expectations were violated by a change of the regulatory environment. In addition, one may highlight the role of the previously mentioned umbrella clauses.[128] From the perspective of the state, elevating domestic obligations is a sovereignty-friendly technique of creating direct obligations. It may find political support even from states that are otherwise reluctant to create any international obligations directly applicable to non-state actors.

However, this sovereignty-friendly aspect can be problematic as well. Sometimes, investors want to challenge a certain domestic obligation be-

124 Art 11 IISD, *Model* (n 12).

125 IISD, *Toolkit* (n 13) para 5.3.1, Option 1.

126 Nathalie Bernasconi-Osterwalder and others, *Harnessing Investment for Sustainable Development: Inclusion of Investor Obligations and Corporate Accountability Provisions in Trade and Investment Agreements* (IISD, 2018) 9–10; IISD, *Obligations* (n 14) 3–4.

127 Zachary Douglas, 'The Hybrid Foundations of Investment Treaty Arbitration' (2004) 74(1) British Yearbook of International Law 151.

128 More generally on the role of domestic law in international investment arbitration Jarrod Hepburn, *Domestic Law in International Investment Arbitration* (Oxford University Press 2017).

cause they consider it to violate their investor rights under an IIA. There is the danger that the state may counter this claim from the outset, by arguing that said obligation is elevated into an international investor obligation – and that, thus, the investor cannot challenge it. However, it is established that the state cannot bring forward its internal law to justify that it violates its international obligations. This principle is established in Art 27 VCLT and Art 32 of the ILC Articles on the Responsibility of States for Internationally Wrongful Acts.[129] This shows that domestic investor obligations cannot be blindly elevated through an IIA so as to immunise the state against respective claims by the investor. The case of *Al-Warraq v Indonesia* is a good example: Indonesia's counterclaim referred to the investor's allegedly fraudulent actions. As such, it was based on the same reason for which the investor claimed that Indonesia had violated the OIC Investment Agreement.

The solution is a contextual interpretation of 'reverse umbrella clauses' based on Art 31 (1) VCLT: Any domestic law that is subject to elevation must itself conform with the investor rights enshrined in the respective IIA. In consequence, elevation never leads to a simple 'copy' of the domestic obligation. It is contingent on compliance with the rest of the IIA. Thus, the Tribunal must question and examine its legality in the process of elevating it.

Already this interpretation detaches the obligation's content from its origins in the host state's domestic legal system. What is more, it is not necessary that the elevated norm stems from the host state's domestic legal order. For example, it is possible to conceive clauses which additionally refer to the home state's domestic law – as proposed in the 2019 Netherlands Model BIT –, the law of a third party of the IIA (in case there are more than two state parties), or even of a third state that is not a party to the IIA. In these cases, the original domestic norm *de facto* exerts an extraterritorial effect. For example, Art 14 (1) Morocco-Nigeria BIT imposes environmental impact assessment obligations that investors must fulfil '[...] as required by the laws of the host state for such an investment or the laws of the home state for such an investment, whichever is more rigorous in relation to the investment in question.'[130] This shows that elevating domestic obligations does not necessarily mean the taking of the least sovereignty-impairing approach.

---

129 UNGA 'Responsibility of States for Internationally Wrongful Acts' UN Doc A/RES/56/83 (12 December 2001).

130 Art 14 (1) Morocco-Nigeria BIT.

V. Creating direct obligations de novo

1. Concept

Apart from the discussed different means of resorting to pre-existing norms,[131] there is of course also the option that an IIA creates an entirely new direct obligation – without referring to any other norm to define its content.

2. The Al-Warraq v Indonesia award

A good example of such an original creation can be encountered in the already-mentioned UNCITRAL award in *Al-Warraq v Indonesia*. As shown, the Tribunal found that Art 9 OIC Investment Agreement elevates domestic obligations enshrined in Indonesian law to an international obligation.[132] But the award also held that Art 9 enshrined an additional, original international obligation as will be presented in this paragraph.

It is useful to restate the wording of Art 9 OIC Investment Agreement:

> The investor shall be bound by the laws and regulations in force in the host state and shall refrain from all acts that may disturb public order or morals or that may be prejudicial to the public interest. He is also to refrain from exercising restrictive practices and from trying to achieve gains through unlawful means.

Whereas the first half of the first sentence relates to the host state's domestic law, the second half imposes an additional standard by referring to public order, morals and interest. The second sentence then goes even further in proscribing restrictive practices, finishing with another reference to domestic law. One must read these passages between the references to domestic law as additional direct obligations that follow from the IIA itself.

In this vein, the award elaborated on original direct obligations. For example, the Tribunal subsumed the different actions of the investor not only under Indonesian law but also under the autonomous test of preju-

131 cf the general comment on the approach of rule-referencing by Mary Footer, *An Institutional and Normative Analysis of the World Trade Organization* (Nijhoff 2006) 320.

132 See Chapter 3.IV.2.

dice against the public interest, public order and morals.[133] It found, for example that '[t]he Claimant's admission that he undertook the duties on the Board of Commissioners in a major bank without understanding their significance is clearly prejudicial to the public interest prohibited by Article 9.'[134] Unfortunately, the Tribunal failed to clarify the abstract standard against which it measured the claimant's behaviour. Nevertheless, the award is an example for how a tribunal interprets and applies an autonomous direct obligation in an IIA.

3. IIAs and reform suggestions

Original direct obligations can also be found in recent IIAs of developing countries.

For example, the ECOWAS Investment Rules in Chapter III on 'Obligations and Duties of Investors and Investments' create comprehensive original obligations towards the public interest. Art 12 prescribes that investors must conduct a pre-establishment environmental and social impact assessment of the investment. This obligation does not only draw on the respective applicable domestic rules of the host states but provides an additional independent international minimum standard.

Art 14 imposes obligations addressing conduct after the establishment of the investment relating to labour standards and human rights in the workplace. In part, this provision relates both to existing domestic laws and other international obligations that bind states.[135] It also provides for original obligations that do not refer to any other existing norms, for example to 'uphold human rights in the workplace and the community in which they are located'. Further obligations can be found in Art 15 that calls for transparency of the investment contract and for a dialogue and exchange by the investor with the local community.

Chapter III flanks these specific duties with general obligations of conduct in Art 11. It requires investors to 'strive through their management policies and practices, [sic!] to contribute to the development objectives of the host States and the local levels of government where the investment is located' and to provide information to the host state which is required for decision-making and statistical purposes.

---

133 See *Al-Warraq v Indonesia*, Final Award (n 15) paras 632, 644–645, 663.

134 ibid 644.

135 See Chapter 3.II and Chapter 3.IV.

A similar comprehensive approach is represented through Art 12–15 SADC Model BIT Template. Art 15 entitled 'Minimum Standards for Human Rights, Environment and Labour', very comprehensively stipulates in its paragraph 1 that '[i]nvestors and their investments have a duty to respect human rights in the workplace and in the community and State in which they are located.' This general clause does not draw on pre-existing domestic or international human rights norms. It represents a particularly far-reaching approach to bind foreign investors to an international human rights standard. In similarly broad terms, the AU's Draft Pan-African Investment Code imposes 'socio-political obligations' on investors in its Art 20, including in paragraph 1 obligations to provide '(b) respect for socio-cultural values' and '(e) respect for labour rights'. Art 23 (1) separately addresses the exploitation of natural resources. It prescribes that '[i]nvestors shall not exploit or use local natural resources to the detriment of the rights and interests of the host State.'

Furthermore, a rather particular original obligation can be found in Art 16 COMESA Investment Agreement. The provision contains the right of investors to hire qualified personnel from any country. Yet, it also states that investors 'shall accord a priority to workers who possess the same qualifications and are available in the Member State or any other Member State', hence, to privilege personnel of the local market. That this provision is more than a mere condition for the investor right to freely hire personnel is not only indicated by its wording which indicates a self-standing obligation. Also, Art 28 (9) COMESA Investment Agreement allows for counterclaims on the basis that investors have not fulfilled their obligations under the Agreement. This covers counterclaims based on Art 16.

Another example of a quite specific obligation can be found in Art 12 of the 2008 Ghana Model BIT. It states that foreign investors '[...] shall to the extent possible, encourage human capital formation, local capacity building through close cooperation with the local community, create employment opportunities and facilitate training opportunities for employees, and the transfer of technology.' Although the provision contains a qualification that gives due regard to the foreign investor's capacities, it is drafted in obligatory language. It requires investors to assure that their activities directly benefit local communities.

Furthermore, institutions like the UNCTAD[136] and the IISD also suggest creating new direct obligations. For example, the IISD in its 2017 Sustainability Toolkit for Trade Negotiators highlights the including of investor obligations that 'where necessary, supplement the state parties' domestic laws, to abide by internationally recognized standards on CSR and responsible business conduct, and to go beyond what is already provided for under international legal instruments'[137]. While this proposal leaves the precise standard rather elusive, it is evidence of a call for supplementing available domestic and international rules with new binding international standards. It also shows that the different techniques to create direct obligations studied in the previous Sections can be combined. More specifically, the IISD emphasises obligations to conduct human rights- and environmental impact assessments in the pre- and even the post-establishment phase.[138] This resonates in some of the examples of new IIAs of developing countries presented above.

4. Critique

Creating original direct obligations allows state parties of an IIA to express common values and economic policies. The bilateral setting of BITs is especially prone to flexible inter-party solutions. Naturally, creating new obligations 'from scratch' offers an opportunity to go beyond international standards that states have already created. States may agree on standards bilaterally where there is no multilateral consensus. It is also a simple solution to the various concerns that one may raise against the other techniques for creating direct obligations which this Chapter has pointed out above.

However, as a corollary such provisions are less suitable to interlace with a wider net of international obligations. This is problematic from the perspective of investors because, in the worst-case scenario, they would have to adhere to different and separate international standards (in addition to

136 See for example UNCTAD 'Development Indications of International Investment Agreements, IIA Monitor No. 2' UNCTAD/WEB/ITE/IIA/2007/2 (2007), 6.

137 IISD, *Toolkit* (n 13) para 5.3.1, Option 2; Other, similar suggestions can be found for example in Art 13–15 IISD, *Model* (n 12); IISD, *Obligations* (n 14) 11–12.

138 See for example the emphasis on impact assessment obligations in IISD, *Obligations* (n 14) 11–12.

the domestic ones) depending on the respective jurisdiction within which they operate. This causes higher transaction costs and, potentially, greater legal uncertainty. Yet, states may also wish to avoid that direct obligations build on other international norms. In international trade law, it was for example a strategy of the USA to include self-construed labour standards in FTAs in order not having to refer to ILO Conventions and Declarations.[139] Original investor obligations could serve a similar agenda.

All in all, creating direct obligations anew offers flexible and context-sensitive solutions at the price that the IIA is not embedded in a broader frame of international standards.

VI. Applying domestic obligations in investment arbitration

The previous five Sections described techniques to create substantive direct obligations. As will be laid out in this Section, in the investment awards of *Perenco v Ecuador* and *Burlington v Ecuador*, a different approach featured that does not operate on the substantive level of international law at all: the applying of domestic investor obligations in investment arbitration. In these cases, states filed counterclaims on the ground that the investors had violated domestic law – without an IIA that elevated them into international obligations. These have led to the first successful awards against investors. This Section will explain this approach and the awards in more detail. It will show that applying domestic obligations in investment arbitration is functionally equivalent to creating a substantive international obligation. And it will lay out why this is currently the most promising approach for imposing direct obligations on investors.

1. Concept

To understand this concept, it is necessary to elaborate on how the applicable law in an investment arbitration is determined. It is a characteristic feature of arbitration that the disputing parties can decide on this question by consent in an arbitration agreement. As investors are no parties to IIAs,

---

139 See on this issue the in-depth analysis by P. Alston, '"Core Labour Standards" and the Transformation of the International Labour Rights Regime' (2004) 15(3) European Journal of International Law 457, 479, 499–506 who distinguishes between the different generations of US FTAs.

their consent cannot follow from the IIA itself. Instead, one interprets the arbitration clause in the IIA to form a standing unilateral offer to arbitrate by the IIA's state parties. This offer is directed to foreign investors of the other state party's nationality. If investors file an arbitral claim with reference to this IIA, it implicitly covers their acceptance of the state's standing offer. This concludes the arbitration agreement. Its content is defined by the IIA's arbitration clause; hence, it incorporates the IIA's relevant provisions.[140] This means that the IIA defines which disputes the parties may bring before an investment tribunal and which law may apply.

The approaches vary between IIAs. Sometimes, an IIA enshrines a separate clause that explicitly defines the applicable law in an investment arbitration. Some arbitration clauses are narrow and exclude the application of any law other than the norms of the IIA. For example, Art. 14.D.3 USCMA[141] as well as Art 26 (1) Energy Charter Treaty[142] give a tribunal jurisdiction only for disputes regarding USMCA or Energy Charter Treaty violations, respectively. But there is a substantial number of IIAs that have a much broader arbitration clause. For example, China's Model BIT[143] contains a jurisdictional clause that covers '[a]ny legal dispute [...] in connection with an investment [...]'.[144] Such clauses also cover domestic investor obligations. What is more, Art 42 (1) ICSID Convention provides that the host state's domestic law is part of the applicable law in an ICSID arbitration as a residual rule.

If an investment tribunal has jurisdiction for disputes on domestic law, in principle, this may cover both domestic investor rights and obligations. In such a case, if the claimant fulfils all other jurisdiction and admissibility

140 This feature of international investment arbitration has been famously coined 'arbitration without privity' by Jan Paulsson, 'Arbitration Without Privity' (1995) 10(2) ICSID Review 232; on consent and its various forms see Dolzer and Schreuer (n 108) 254–260.

141 Agreement between the United States of America, the United Mexican States, and Canada (adopted 30 November 2018, revised 10 December 2019 by the Protocol of Amendment, entered into force 1 July 2020) ‹https://investmentpolicy.unctad.org/international-investment-agreements/treaty-files/6008/download› accessed 7 December 2021 (USMCA).

142 n 59.

143 The text of the current third version of China's Model BIT, adopted in 1998 (a fourth, updated version has been subject to discussions for several years), can be found in a commented version in Wenhua Shan and Norah Gallagher, 'China' in Chester Brown (ed), *Commentaries on Selected Model Investment Treaties* (Oxford University Press 2013) 145–180.

144 ibid, 172.

requirements,[145] investment tribunals may adjudicate on counterclaims based on domestic obligations. This may include matters of the public interest such as domestic human rights, environmental obligations or workers' rights.[146]

Conceptually, it is important to distinguish this constellation from the elevation of domestic to international obligations discussed above.[147] Here, there is no international treaty provision that creates an international obligation of investors by referring to domestic law. It is only on a *procedural level* that the IIA confers on investment tribunals the jurisdiction to apply domestic law without changing these obligations' domestic legal nature. Notwithstanding, the analysis will point out that tribunals will often internationalise these domestic obligations in the course of the proceedings.

2. The Perenco v Ecuador and Burlington v Ecuador awards

Recent investment awards indicate rather well how applying domestic law in investment arbitration can bring about such an internationalising effect. The awards in question are the 2015 ICSID interim decision on the environmental counterclaim in *Perenco Ecuador Ltd. v Ecuador* (*Perenco v Ecuador*) and the 2017 ICSID award on Ecuador's counterclaim in *Burlington Resources Inc. v Ecuador* (*Burlington v Ecuador*). In both cases, the Tribunals applied Ecuadorian environmental law.

These two separate ICSID proceedings against Ecuador essentially derive from the same facts. The investors, Perenco Ecuador Ltd. (Perenco) and Burlington Resources Inc. (Burlington), were engaged as part of a consortium in the Ecuadorian oil industry in the Amazon region. They conducted the investment on the basis of the so-called production-sharing-contracts with the government. These contracts are a form of public-private-partnership undertaken in Ecuador after the country privatised the sector in 1993.[148] When in 2002 the world oil price increased substantially,

---

145 These will be laid out in more detail in Chapter 4.

146 Supported for example by Schreuer and Kriebaum (n 21) 1094–1095; Tarcisio Gazzini and Yannick Radi, 'Foreign Investment with a Human Face – with Special Reference to Rights of Indigenous Peoples' in Rainer Hofmann and Christian J Tams (eds), *International Investment Law and Its Others* (Nomos 2012) 93; Viñuales (n 57) 103.

147 See Chapter 3.IV.

148 *Perenco Ecuador Ltd. v The Republic of Ecuador*, ICSID Case No. ARB/08/6, Decision on Jurisdiction (30 June 2011) paras 1–14; *Burlington Resources Inc.*

Ecuador changed the agreed distributive scheme for the unexpected surpluses. The government considered that the natural resources' additional value should belong to the state. After the investors refused to pay and negotiations to amend the contract failed, Ecuador eventually seized the investments.[149] Both investors filed separate investment claims, Perenco contending violations of rights under the France-Ecuador-BIT[150] and the applicable investment contracts,[151] Burlington only breaches under the US-Ecuador-BIT.[152]

Key for the present purpose is the fact that in both proceedings Ecuador filed counterclaims for soil and groundwater pollution. The investors had allegedly caused it in the course of producing oil. Ecuador contended the violation of Ecuadorian law, claiming damages of USD 2.797.007.091 from Burlington[153] and USD 2.548.526.259 from Perenco.[154]

In *Burlington v Ecuador*, the Tribunal found Ecuadorian law applicable on the basis of an agreement between Ecuador and Burlington in 2011. In it, the parties agreed on the Tribunal's jurisdiction over the Ecuadorian counterclaims and that Ecuadorian law was applicable in the arbitra-

---

v Republic of Ecuador, ICSID Case No. ARB/08/5, Decision on Liability (14 December 2012) paras 9–15; *Perenco Ecuador Ltd. v The Republic of Ecuador*, ICSID Case No. ARB/08/6, Decision on Remaining Issues of Jurisdiction and on Liability (12 September 2014) paras 62–80.

149 *Burlington v Ecuador*, Decision on Liability (n 148) paras 25–66; *Perenco v Ecuador*, Decision on Remaining Issues of Jurisdiction and on Liability (n 148) paras 81–214.

150 Accord entre le Gouvernement de la République française et le Gouvernement de la République de l'Équateur sur l'encouragement et la protection réciproques des investissements (adopted 7 September 1994, entered into force 10 June 1996, date of termination 23 May 2018) ‹https://investmentpolicy.unctad.org/international-investment-agreements/treaty-files/1052/download› accessed 7 December 2021 (Ecuador-France BIT).

151 *Perenco v Ecuador*, Decision on Jurisdiction (n 148) paras 15–22.

152 Treaty between the United States of America and the Republic of Ecuador concerning the Encouragement and Reciprocal Protection of Investment (adopted 27 August 1993, entered into force 11 May 1997, date of termination 18 May 2018) ‹https://investmentpolicy.unctad.org/international-investment-agreements/treaty-files/1065/download› accessed 7 December 2021 (Ecuador-US BIT).

153 *Burlington v Ecuador*, Decision on Counterclaims (n 18) para 52. In addition, Ecuador filed a contract claim on infrastructural damage caused by a lack of proper maintaining, which will be left aside in this analysis, see *Burlington v Ecuador*, Decision on Counterclaims (n 18) paras 890–1074.

154 *Perenco v Ecuador*, Interim Decision on the Environmental Counterclaim (n 19) para 36.

tion.[155] This conformed with the arbitration clause in Art VI (1) Ecuador-US-BIT. It conferred jurisdiction on the Tribunal by defining that

> [...] an investment dispute is a dispute between a Party and a national or company of the other Party arising out of or relating to [...] (c) an alleged breach of any right conferred or created by this Treaty with respect to an investment.

In contrast, in *Perenco v Ecuador*, the Tribunal was less explicit on its reasons for applying Ecuadorian law.[156] Yet, the France-Ecuador-BIT also covers a broad jurisdiction clause that enabled the Tribunal to apply domestic law. To that end, Art 9 confers jurisdiction on an ICSID Tribunal for '[...] tout différend légal survenant entre cette Partie contractante et un national ou une société de l'autre Partie contractante à propos d'un investissement de ce dernier dans la première.'

In both proceedings, the parties disputed whether the investors were subject to strict- or fault-based liability rules for the causing of environmental damages. It was also contested which party had to bear the onus of proving pollution and causation. It was also controversial which domestic rules applied until 2008 under the applicable Ecuadorian Civil Law code. In addition, in 2008, Ecuador enacted a new Constitution which substantially changed the protection of the environment. The 2008 Constitution gave legal personality to nature itself (the *Pacha Mama*) and instituted a high standard of environmental protection covering fairly detailed provisions. This included that natural resources belonged to the state and a strict-liability system for environmental pollution.[157] The parties disagreed on how the 2008 Constitution related to the Ecuadorian statutory tort law regime for environmental harm. As most of the relevant investment activities had taken place before 2008, the retroactive application of the 2008 Constitution raised another concern. In addition, on a factual level,

---

155 *Burlington v Ecuador*, Decision on Counterclaims (n 18) paras 60–61, 71–72.

156 *Perenco v Ecuador*, Interim Decision on the Environmental Counterclaim (n 19) paras 36–55; cf James Harrison, 'Environmental Counterclaims in Investor-State Arbitration: Perenco Ecuador Ltd v Republic of Ecuador, ICSID Case No ARB/08/6, Interim Decision on the Environmental Counterclaim, 11 August 2015 (Peter Tomka, Neil Kaplan, J Christopher Thomas)' (2016) 17(3) Journal of World Investment & Trade 479, 485.

157 On the 2008 Constitution see *Perenco v Ecuador*, Interim Decision on the Environmental Counterclaim (n 19) paras 73–78; *Burlington v Ecuador*, Decision on Counterclaims (n 18) paras 195–216.

the parties were divided if and to which extent environmental and infrastructural damage was actually caused.[158]

The two Tribunals came to different conclusions in their decisions on the respective counterclaim. In its interim decision in *Perenco v Ecuador*, the Tribunal found Ecuadorian statutory law and standards 'as applied "on the ground"'[159] to be the relevant applicable standard.[160] However, the Tribunal did not reach a final decision. Instead, it first criticised the problematic independency and methodology of the parties' experts who were heard in the proceedings. On this basis, it observed that Perenco will likely be liable for environmental harm arising from some of its investment activities. Yet, it held that there was an insufficient factual basis for a final assessment of the issue. Instead, it appointed its own expert to investigate the matter – not without calling on the parties to come to an amicable solution; as the parties could not settle the matter, in 2019, the Tribunal finally ordered Perenco to pay USD 54.539.517 to Ecuador.[161]

The Tribunal in *Burlington v Ecuador* affirmed that the investor had polluted the environment and violated Ecuadorian law.[162] It found Burlington to be liable in the sum of USD 39.199.373.[163]

3. Investment arbitration's internationalising effect

How could such application of *domestic* law represent the setting and enforcing of an *international* direct obligation?

International law may, of course, come to play if the applicable domestic law itself contains norms of international law. That is the case if domestic law transformed or declared international law applicable, or adopts a monistic system.[164] But even more, also the application of purely domestic

158 See the submissions of the parties, summarised in *Perenco v Ecuador*, Interim Decision on the Environmental Counterclaim (n 19) paras 36–55; *Burlington v Ecuador*, Decision on Counterclaims (n 18) paras 52–57.

159 *Perenco v Ecuador*, Interim Decision on the Environmental Counterclaim (n 19) para 352.

160 ibid 321–352.

161 ibid 581–609; *Perenco Ecuador Ltd. v The Republic of Ecuador*, ICSID Case No. ARB/08/6, Award (27 September 2019) para 1023.

162 *Burlington v Ecuador*, Decision on Counterclaims (n 18) paras 234–247.

163 ibid 889.

164 Régis Bismuth, 'Customary Principles Regarding Public Contracts Concluded with Foreigners' in Mathias Audit and Stephan W Schill (eds), *Transnational Law of Public Contracts* (Bruylant 2016) 324; see also *Wena Hotels Limited v Arab*

obligations in an international investment arbitration can bring about, to a certain extent, an *international* standard for investor conduct. One may distinguish three reasons for its internationalising-effect that follow from the peculiarities of investment arbitration as an international adjudicatory proceeding: the joint application of domestic and international law (a), the interpretation of domestic law by an international investment tribunal (b) and the international enforcement of awards (c). As will be shown, the decisions in *Perenco v Ecuador* and *Burlington v Ecuador* represent good examples in this regard.

a) Joint application with international law

Domestic obligations may interact with international law which may change their content. It is not rare that domestic law is applicable in an investment arbitration *together* with international law – this is even the residual rule in ICSID arbitrations pursuant to Art 42 (1) ICSID Convention. If a Tribunal in certain parts of the decision resorts to international law and only in others to domestic law, this may alter the overall result of the legal analysis – juxtaposed to an isolated application of domestic law.

More specifically, domestic obligations may conflict with international law. Scholars and tribunals have extensively discussed this constellation. A prepondering approach accorded international law a corrective function.[165] Others argued that international law always prevails over conflicting domestic law.[166] While this is not the place to engage in this general discussion, it reflects how domestic obligations may change when applied in conjunction with international law in counterclaims.

Republic of Egypt, ICSID Case No. ARB/98/4, Decision (5 February 2002) para 42 in which the Ad-Hoc Committee stressed that Egyptian law contains '[...] a kind of *renvoi* to international law by the very law of the host State' (italics in the original).

165 See the overview in *Antoine Goetz et consorts v République du Burundi (Goetz I)*, ICSID Case No. ARB/95/3, Award (10 February 1999) para 97; Christoph Schreuer, *The ICSID Convention: A Commentary* (2nd edn, Cambridge University Press 2009) Art 42 paras 214–235; for an example of a view that accords international law a corrective function see William M Reisman, 'The Regime for Lacunae in the ICSID Choice of Law Provision and the Question of Its Threshold' (2000) 15(2) ICSID Review 362, 371–381.

166 Prosper Weil, 'The State, the Foreign Investor, and International Law: The No Longer Stormy Relationship of a Menage À Trois' (2000) 15(2) ICSID Review 401, 409.

The award in *Perenco v Ecuador* illustrates this well. The Tribunal indicated that a domestic environmental obligation of the investor could be subject to review if it conforms with the host state's international obligations. It stated that

> [...] a State has wide latitude under international law to prescribe and adjust its environmental laws, standards and policies in response to changing views and a deeper understanding of the risks posed by various activities, including those of extractive industries such as oilfields. All of this is beyond any serious dispute and the Tribunal enters into this phase of the proceeding mindful of the fundamental imperatives of the protection of the environment in Ecuador.[167]

The statement seems to imply that the state's latitude – while being wide – has its limits, and that the Tribunal reserves itself to examine if the domestic obligation complies with international law. Notably, the Tribunal gave no relevance to the way the Ecuadorian legal system itself defines the hierarchy between domestic and international law.[168]

b) Interpretation by an investment tribunal

Second, investment tribunals may internationalise domestic obligations in the way they interpret them. International arbitrators work independently and decoupled from the host state's legal system. In the process of interpreting and applying domestic law, they can accord domestic obligations an 'autonomous' international meaning.

From a legal perspective, investment tribunals must endeavour to interpret domestic obligations in line with interpretive rules of the relevant domestic legal order, including relevant domestic case law.[169] On the other

167 *Perenco v Ecuador*, Interim Decision on the Environmental Counterclaim (n 19) para 35.

168 Schreuer, *ICSID* (n 165) Art 42 para 200.

169 An international tribunal must seek to apply domestic law as understood in the respective domestic legal order, see *Case Concerning the Payment in Gold of Brazilian Federal Loans Contracted in France (France v Brazil)* (Judgment) [1929] PCIJ Rep Series A No 15, 124–125; *Case Concerning the Payment of Various Serbian Loans Issued in France (France v Yugoslavia)* (Judgment) [1929] PCIJ Rep Series A No 20, 46–47; James Crawford, *Brownlie's Principles of Public International Law* (8th edn, Oxford University Press 2012) 53; affirmed in the context of international investment law for example by *Hussein Nuaman Soufraki v The*

hand, however, states created investment tribunals precisely to independently assess the host state's domestic law. This means that investment tribunals have a certain leeway in how they interpret applicable domestic law. They cannot be bound to blindly apply domestic law in line with domestic courts' decisions or the host state government's contentions.

What is more, every norm interpretation and application to concrete facts with at least some discretion entails the creating of a new, more specific norm.[170] From a sociological perspective, investment arbitration takes place in a different institutional and procedural setting than domestic adjudication. Tribunals may interpret the same norms differently than domestic courts. In most cases, international arbiters do not have the same background as national judges. Many tend to private commercial law or public international law approaches because of their professional experience.[171] Likewise, they have not been socialised in the respective host state legal system. Consequently, they do not experience the professional ties or integration into an epistemic community of domestic jurists. And they do not necessarily participate or picture themselves participating in a domestic discourse. This may affect the interpretive process already for epistemological reasons.

To what extent investment arbitration internationalises a domestic investor obligation in this sense depends on the methodology that the arbiters apply in engaging with domestic law. Some adopt a very self-restrained position that aims at reflecting an unchanged understanding of a domestic obligation as it is established in the respective legal system. Other

---

United Arab Emirates, ICSID Case No. ARB/02/7, Decision of the ad hoc Committee on the Application for Annulment of Mr Soufraki (5 June 2007) para 96; *Fraport AG Frankfurt Airport Services Worldwide v Republic of Philippines*, ICSID Case No. ARB/03/25, Decision on the Application for Annulment of Fraport AG Frankfurt Airport Services Worldwide (23 December 2010) para 236; *Emmis International Holding, B.V. Emmis Radio Operating, B.V. MEM Magyar Electronic Media Kereskedelmi és Szolgáltató Kft. v The Republic of Hungary*, ICSID Case No. ARB/12/2, Award (16 April 2014) para 175; Hepburn (n 128) 109–110.

170 Hans Kelsen, *Reine Rechtslehre* (Franz Deuticke 1934) 94–99 coins this the 'constitutive function' of the judicial decision.

171 Stephan W Schill, 'W(h)ither Fragmentation? On the Literature and Sociology of International Investment Law' (2011) 22(3) European Journal of International Law 875, 888. Generally on sociological insights on international investment law see Moshe Hirsch, 'The Sociology of International Investment Law' in Zachary Douglas, Joost Pauwelyn and Jorge E Viñuales (eds), *The Foundations of International Investment Law: Bringing Theory into Practice* (Oxford University Press 2014) 144–148.

arbiters take the position that it is the purpose of investment tribunals to *control* domestic law. Comparisons to the use of domestic law in other questions of investment law come to mind. One may point, for example, to the much-discussed methodology of tribunals in interpreting and applying the FET standard.[172]

The proceedings in *Perenco v Ecuador* and *Burlington v Ecuador* illustrate the different interpretive approaches to domestic law. The Tribunal in *Perenco v Ecuador* interpreted the Ecuadorian constitution very autonomously.[173] It found that the new Ecuadorian Constitution protected the environment more stringently. Nevertheless, it chose not to derive a strict liability standard from it but to apply Ecuadorian statutory law. It held that this statutory law defined the environmental liability of companies more specifically and had been applied consistently without change after the new Ecuadorian Constitution came into effect.[174] It went on that the application of constitutional 'background values' cannot serve as applicable standards 'as a matter of law in an international arbitration', they could not 'be right as a matter of Ecuadorian law or international law' if in domestic practice the state consistently applied statutory regulation with a fault-based liability standard.[175] The Tribunal, thus, appears to have been guided by a diffuse standard of international law in interpreting the 'right' liability standard of Ecuadorian law.

The Tribunal in *Burlington v Ecuador* came to a very different interpretive conclusion. It held that the 2008 Ecuadorian Constitution introduced a strict liability scheme applicable from 2008 onwards.[176] Similarly to the Tribunal in *Perenco v Ecuador*, it rejected to accord retroactive effect to the Constitution.[177] Yet, the Tribunal found that already from at least 2002 until 2008, a strict-based liability regime had anyway been applied.

172 See on the role of domestic law in international investment arbitration in general the extensive analysis and differentiated conclusions in Hepburn (n 128); there specifically on the FET standard on 13–40; on the problem that internationalising the interpretation of domestic law can lead to contradictory decisions which may harm the coherence of a domestic legal system, see Shao (n 110) 175–178.

173 Harrison (n 156) 486–487.

174 *Perenco v Ecuador*, Interim Decision on the Environmental Counterclaim (n 19) paras 321–326.

175 ibid 348.

176 *Burlington v Ecuador*, Decision on Counterclaims (n 18) paras 225–232.

177 ibid 233.

It grounded this interpretation in Ecuadorian domestic jurisprudence[178] and explicitly mentioned that it understood the leading Ecuadorian cases differently than the Tribunal in *Perenco v Ecuador*.[179] In comparison, the Tribunal in *Burlington v Ecuador* shows a slightly more self-restrained approach by sticking more closely to the decisions of Ecuadorian courts.

Read in conjunction, the decisions' explicitly diverging interpretations show that to apply domestic law does not mean that its content is clear and predefined by a domestic legal system. Tribunals can exert substantial interpretive discretion. Practically speaking, this may lead tribunals to construing standards of conduct which are as autonomous as if they had applied an international obligation from the outset.

c) International enforcement

Investment arbitration further internationalises domestic obligations through the award's enforcement. If the counterclaim based on a domestic obligation is successful, the award against the investor is covered by the rules of the 1958 New York Convention on the Recognition and Enforcement of Foreign Arbitral Awards or (in case of an ICSID arbitration) the ICSID Convention. Neither the ICSID Convention nor the New York Convention are limited to awards against host states but also apply to awards against investors.[180]

At the time of writing, the New York Convention has 168 state parties. They are obliged to recognise and enforce foreign arbitral awards in their domestic legal system. Only under the narrow grounds of Art V of the New York Convention they may refuse to do so. ICSID awards enjoy an even more effective international enforcement. The currently 156 state

---

178 ibid 234–247 with reference to *Perenco v Ecuador*, Interim Decision on the Environmental Counterclaim (n 19) fn 881.

179 *Burlington v Ecuador*, Decision on Counterclaims (n 18) para 248.

180 For Art I New York Convention see Bernd Ehle, 'Article I' in Reinmar Wolff (ed), *New York Convention* (C.H. Beck 2012) paras 138–139; for Art 54 ICSID Convention see Schreuer, *ICSID* (n 165) Art 54 para 7; Meg Kinnear and Paul J Le Cannu, 'Concluding Remarks: ICSID and African States Leading International Investment Law Reform' (2019) 34(2) ICSID Review 542, 545; on a general level, in particular on possible obstacles accruing from a commercial reservation by a state under the New York Convention, see Amado, Kern and Rodriguez (n 101) 152–168; more specifically on the consequences of such a cross-border enforcement see Abel, 'Counterclaims' (n 26) 24.

parties of the ICSID Convention are under an international obligation to treat any ICSID award as a decision of a domestic court of the highest instance as stipulated in Art 53 and 54 ICSID Convention – hence must enforce them automatically without further ado. The only possible way of challenging an ICSID award is through the internationalised annulment procedure conducted by an international ad hoc-Committee pursuant to Art 52 ICSID Convention.

Therefore, through the arbitral award, the originally domestic obligation plays part in the international enforcement network. It potentially gives effect to the domestic obligation far beyond the host state's territory – flanked by international obligations of states that are party to the named conventions. Also in this sense, the obligation is thus internationalised.

4. Critique

Applying domestic obligations in investment arbitration shares some of the advantages that elevating domestic to substantive international obligations entails:[181] It is a sovereignty-friendly solution because only standards that the host state enacts in its domestic legal system are applied. This approach may also be more acceptable to many developed states which so far refuse to impose international obligations on enterprises.

Yet, again, it is suggested that an investment tribunal cannot apply domestic investor obligations without reservation but must review their compliance with the state's international investment obligations – a point that follows from the above-mentioned joint application of domestic and international law. Conversely, the degree of internationalisation depends on the doctrinal approach of the respective investment tribunal and may thus differ from case to case. How strong the obligation is internationalised only crystallises in the process of its interpretation and application in the arbitration proceedings and the enforcement stage.

On the other hand, the greatest appeal of applying domestic obligations in investment arbitration is that it currently has a much broader potential scope of application than the other presented approaches. It has already been pointed out that many IIAs provide jurisdiction to apply domestic law. They may, therefore, be particularly prone to apply domestic obliga-

---

181 See Chapter 3.IV.4.

tions in investment arbitration, subject to fulfilling all other jurisdiction and admissibility requirements.[182]

VII. A nascent doctrine of direct obligations

After the previous six Sections have shed light on different methods of creating direct obligations, this Section will bring these insights together.

The various analysed techniques allow to identify an emerging doctrine of direct obligations in investment law (1.). They prompt two questions about the right construction of the obligations encountered in the analysis. First, who is the bearer of the obligation? It is submitted that the analysed IIA provisions constitute directly applicable obligations in line with this Part's initial hypothesis. Alternative constructions must be rejected, such as to understand them as obligations between the host and the home state (2.). Second, one may ask: To whom do investors owe these obligations? Surprisingly, thus far the investment practice has not reflected on this aspect. It is most convincing to consider the host state as the relevant counterpart (3.). Finally, after having crystallised the shape of the new direct obligations, this Section will discuss how they interact with investor rights. It will show that especially MFN rights bear the risk of undermining them – even though it is more appropriate to interpret them as being compatible (4.).

1. Emerging direct obligations from plural sources

From the rich material studied in the last Sections, one may conclude that direct obligations have emerged in the last years in investment law – not only in the form of important reform suggestions, but even in first existing IIAs and arbitral awards. Although, overall, the relevant IIAs are little in numbers compared to the more than 3000 existing IIAs and despite the fact that most states remain reluctant to adopt binding investor obligations in new IIAs, they do reflect a new qualitative approach. They find support

182 For a full analysis of jurisdiction and admissibility requirements of counterclaims see below Chapter 4. For a criticism that points to states 'becoming increasingly defensive of their domestic jurisdiction over domestic legal issues' see Shao (n 110) 165–168.

not only with developing countries and some developed states but also with important institutions such as UNCTAD.

Moreover, the five awards in *Al-Warraq v Indonesia*, *Aven v Costa Rica*, *Urbaser v Argentina*, *Burlington v Ecuador* and *Perenco v Ecuador* outline that there is a development that goes beyond the creation of new IIAs. These decisions are based on 'conventional' BITs, including treaties to which developed countries are parties, too, namely the US-Argentina BIT, the CAFTA-DR, the US-Ecuador-BIT and the France-Ecuador-BIT.[183] In addition, the new 2019 Netherlands Model BIT contains direct obligations based on domestic obligations enacted in the home and the host state (however, without a possibility to enforce them via ISDS against investors). Thus, they show that there is a basis for integrating direct obligations into already-existing IIAs.

Although the first three mentioned awards eventually dismissed the counterclaims, they contain quite far-reaching reasoning that accepts direct obligations in broad terms. The last two cases, *Burlington v Ecuador* and *Perenco v Ecuador*, even see, for the first time in the history of investment arbitration, investment tribunals awarding damages to a state because the respective investors polluted the environment.

This practice has already developed to a degree that it was possible to systematise the obligations along different techniques for their creation. Each identified approach comes with own advantages and disadvantages. Surely, they differ in the degree they may already be applied under existing IIAs. In international law's present state, solutions that base on domestic obligations are easier to achieve. It is likely that more states support them because they are comparatively sovereignty-friendly.[184]

---

183 *Al-Warraq v Indonesia*, Final Award (n 15) forms the exception because it follows from a claim based on the OIC Investment Agreement. cf with the decision of the UNCITRAL Working Group III on the reform of ISDS to 'consider formulating provisions on investor obligations' in IIAs, UNCITRAL 'Possible Reform of Investor-State Dispute Settlement (ISDS), Multiple Proceedings and Counterclaims' (22 January 2020) UN Doc A/CN.9/WG.III/WP.193, para 41.

184 cf the observation of increasingly extensive domestic due diligence obligations of corporations by Eric de Brabandere and Maryse Hazelzet, *Corporate Responsibility and Human Rights – Navigating Between International, Domestic and Self-Regulation* (Grotius Centre Working Paper 2017/056-HRL) 15–19; cf the analysis of plural 'anchors' and 'entry points' in IIAs for investor diligence in investment law by Jorge E. Viñuales, 'Investor Diligence in Investment Arbitration: Sources and Arguments' (2017) 32(2) ICSID Review 346, 351, 355, 367 which follow a similar systematic approach as the findings of this chapter.

2. Construction as directly applicable norms

To identify emerging direct obligations is all the more intriguing if one takes account of the fact that the individual character of investor *rights* remains contested in investment law scholarship. Some argue that these are substantive rights of the home state, only procedurally enforceable by the investor against the host state.[185] One could question the nature of direct obligations in the same manner. Yet, the present findings on obligations strongly indicate that investor obligations must be understood as international norms directly applicable to investors. The two alternative constructions are inadequate, namely: investor obligations as limitations of investor rights (a) and investor obligations as disguised inter-state obligations (b).

a) Limitations of investor rights' scope?

One could argue that the analysed IIA clauses indicative of direct obligations were just a way of simplifying treaty provisions on investor *rights*. Then, one would understand these provisions as only elaborating on investor rights' scope, functionally similar to limitation or justification clauses.

As an example, one may take a provision which prohibits foreign investors to engage in bribery. Following the presented alternative construction, this clause was a way of expressing that the host state did not owe investment protection to foreign investors who have committed bribery. In other words: a corrupt investor could not invoke an investor right like the protection against expropriation against the host state's misconduct.[186]

However, such an interpretation would fall short of reflecting the true extent of the encountered obligations. All of them express a self-standing norm that require foreign investors to act or abstain from acting in a certain manner. Importantly, in most cases the respective IIAs also allowed to bring claims on the basis of these obligations against the investor.

185 For this position see for example *The Loewen Group, Inc. and Raymond L. Loewen v United States of America*, ICSID Case No. ARB(AF)/98/3, Award (26 June 2003) para 233; sympathetic is also Eric de Brabandere, *Investment Treaty Arbitration as Public International Law: Procedural Aspects and Implications* (Cambridge University Press 2015) 63–67.

186 cf the similar arguments against directly applicable duties in human rights law in Chapter 2.IV.

Conversely, these provisions must have been meant as true obligations and not as a way of circumscribing investor rights' scope.

b) Inter-state obligations?

If one agrees on the presence of obligations, in a second step, one could put the obligations' addressee in doubt – and contend that they do not constitute obligations of foreign investors, but rather obligations of the *states*.

(1) Obligations of the host state

In this view, one could understand the IIA clauses analysed throughout Chapter 3 as obligations of the host states to enact and enforce domestic legislation to protect the public interest. Following this construction, the above-mentioned anti-bribery clause would constitute an obligation of the host state to enact and enforce domestic anti-bribery laws against foreign investors on its territory.

However, also this interpretation is at odds with the provisions' envisaged role and functioning. As seen, states create them to hold foreign investors accountable for *their* misconduct towards the public interest. Again, one must consider the possibility for the host state to file a counterclaim before domestic courts or investment tribunals based on the violation of these obligations. How should a host state file such a motion if it is the host state itself that is the real addressee of these obligations? Therefore, construing the international obligations as targeting the host state leads to paradoxical and uncompelling results.

(2) Obligations of the home state

Alternatively, one may argue that what seem to be investor obligations are in reality obligations of the foreign investor's *home* state. This line of argument resonates in the complementary discussion on the nature of international investor rights in IIAs. As seen, discussions continue on the fundamental question if IIAs grant individual rights to foreign investors.[187] Some understand IIAs to only create obligations and rights between the host and the home state. In this view investors represent their home state before investment tribunals only in a procedural capacity.[188] The distinction between these two approaches is not only theoretical but has practical consequences on issues such as the investor's ability to consent to violations or the doctrine of necessity.[189]

Naturally, supporters of the inter-state model will also be hesitant to recognise the concept of direct obligations in IIAs. If one extends their inter-state logic to the encountered obligations, it seems that one would have to understand them as obligations of the home state. Then, it would also be the home state *in the person of the investor of its nationality* which violates an obligation owed to the host state. To take the above-mentioned example: An IIA clause that prohibits investors from engaging in bribery would have to be interpreted as an obligation of the home state to ensure that the foreign investor of its nationality does not engage in such deeds in the territory of the host state. If the investor committed such acts, the home state would be in breach of this obligation.

But this construction is not compelling either. It is not very likely that states would agree to define their own international obligations as dependent on the actions of a private actor outside of their control. Such a construction would be tantamount to a rule that attributes all actions of investors to their home state on the mere basis of nationality. The home

187 Supported for example by *Corn Products International, Inc. v United Mexican States*, ICSID Case No. ARB(AF)/04/01, Decision on Responsibility (15 January 2008) paras 167–169; *Yukos Universal Limited (Isle of Man) v The Russian Federation*, PCA Case No. AA 227, Interim Award on Jurisdiction and Admissibility (UNCITRAL, 30 November 2009) para 551; ILC 'Articles on Responsibility of States for Internationally Wrongful Acts, with Commentaries' (2001) II(2) Yearbook of the International Law Commission, 31 (53rd session of the International Law Commission, 23 April-1 June and 2 July 2001), 95; Douglas (n 127) 183; Kate Parlett, 'The Individual and Structural Change in the International Legal System' (2012) 1(3) Cambridge Journal of International and Comparative Law 60, 69; Peters (n 40) 317.

188 *Loewen v USA* (n 185) para 233; sympathetic is also Brabandere (n 185) 63–67.

189 For a general discussion of these different models see for example Douglas (n 127) 160–184; on the consequences and implications for international responsibility see Martins Paparinskis, 'Investment Treaty Arbitration and the (New) Law of State Responsibility' (2013) 24(2) European Journal of International Law 617, 621–647; Yun-I Kim, 'Investment Law and the Individual' in Marc Bungenberg and others (eds), International Investment Law (Nomos 2015) paras 15–69.

state could be held responsible for extraterritorial actions without even having effective or overall control over the foreign investor – and even the details of these thresholds for attribution of non-state actors' conduct remain controversial in general international law on state responsibility.[190]

In other words, it is significantly harder to construe a state obligation that draws on foreign investors' behaviour than an international right. The former would bring about the home state's international responsibility for conduct outside of its territory. Only the construction of directly applicable investor obligations accurately describes the phenomena encountered in Chapter 3. The Tribunals in *Al-Warraq v Indonesia* and in *Urbaser v Argentina* have explicitly affirmed this.[191]

3. Direct obligations owed to whom?

However, these observations only clarify the bearers of the direct obligations. In turn, it is necessary to appreciate *to whom* investors owe these obligations.[192] Whereas domestic company law traditionally understands corporations as trustees of their shareholders, the matter is different in the present context on obligations towards the public interest. For example, in human rights law, for a long time it has been controversial if human rights obligations should be construed so that the private actor owes them vertically to the state (a concept of fundamental duties[193]) or whether private actors could owe them horizontally to other private actors.[194]

Astonishingly, the material investigated in Chapter 3 does not address this question at all, that is: if the investor owes direct obligations for example to the local population, employees and consumers, or to the host state where it operates. The focus appears to lie on imposing the international obligation on foreign investors as an extraordinary new feature in

190 See only Art 8 ILC 'Articles on State Responsibility with Commentaries' (n 187); James Crawford, *State Responsibility: The General Part* (Cambridge University Press 2013) 141–165.

191 *Al-Warraq v Indonesia*, Final Award (n 15) para 663; *Urbaser v Argentina*, Award (n 17) paras 1193–1195.

192 cf Amado, Kern and Rodriguez (n 101) 125–126.

193 Christian Tomuschat, 'Grundpflichten des Individuums nach Völkerrecht' (1983) 21(3) Archiv des Völkerrechts 289, 302–313; Peters (n 40) 110–113.

194 Distinguished as converse and correlative duties by John H Knox, 'Horizontal Human Rights Law' (2008) 102(1) American Journal of International Law 1, 2; see also Peters (n 40) 99–113.

investment law – without elaborating on the other party that forms part of the legal relationship any obligation brings about.

One could consider that foreign investors owe their obligations to other private actors. In counterclaims, the host state would then make use of a procedural right granted in the IIA to represent these private actors.[195] Direct obligations which draw on other existing norms appear to favour this perspective: those building on international obligations of states, on domestic law and on CSR norms. These norms themselves define between whom they apply. Some construe a relationship between private actors such as, for example, the prohibition to commit international crimes. In the case of domestic law, it depends on the underlying type of obligation, for example if it stems from administrative or civil law.

However, it is more compelling to construe direct obligations as generally owed by the investor to the host state.[196] As IIAs grant investor rights against the host state, it follows investment law's logics to complement this legal relationship with direct obligations. In addition, the role of counterclaims points to a construction in which host states enforce an own right against the investors. Furthermore, in the case of direct obligations that protect public goods such as the environment and the rule of law, it is the only feasible concept – as there is no identifiable individual that may be harmed. But the obligations encountered in Chapter 3 make no difference in their functioning as to which good or interest is protected. Thus, consistency favours applying the same construction for obligations which directly affect third parties and others that protect a public good.

4. Investor rights as challenges for direct obligations

Having established that investment law has given rise to direct obligations of investors owed to the host state, the analysis will now turn to their interaction with investor rights. Of course, direct obligations do not operate in a vacuum. They impair foreign investors' freedom. As a corollary, they may trigger protection enshrined in international human rights (a) as well as MFN- and national treatment rights of investors (b). Especially MFN

---

195 This corresponds in different facets to the direct claims II and the espousel ('reverse diplomatic protection') models proposed by Amado, Kern and Rodriguez (n 101) 23–24, 42–54.

196 This corresponds to direct claims model III proposed by ibid, 24.

obligations may endanger direct obligations' effectiveness even though it will be shown that, rightly interpreted, they do not contradict another.

a) Human rights of the investor

Direct obligations encroach on foreign investors' international human right to property. Provisions found in regional human rights treaties, such as Art 1 of Protocol I to the ECHR, Art 21 ACHR and Art 14 AfrCHPR, protect this right for natural and private legal persons[197] alike. It cannot make a difference if the state limits this freedom by imposing domestic or international obligations.

However, this observation hardly limits direct obligations' effect. It is well established that encroachments on human rights can be justified. Importantly, all cited regional human rights treaties explicitly allow to limit the freedom of property to protect the 'general interest',[198] the 'interest of society'[199] or the 'interest of public need or [...] the general interest of the community',[200] respectively. If the state conforms with the requirements for such a justification such as the principle of proportionality,[201] international human rights do not contradict investment law's new direct obligations but can be interpreted in harmony.[202]

197 For Additional Protocol I to the ECHR, this follows from Art 34 ECHR, for the ACHR from its Art 21. If corporations have human rights under the Banjul Charter is more controversial. Its Art 2 points to individuals as bearers of human rights as a general principle, but the subsequent specific human rights entail also rights of peoples. The question of the personal scope of protection is hard to clarify because persons have locus standi before the African Commission on Human and People's Rights and the African Court of Human and People's Rights even if they do not claim a violation in their own right, see Frans Viljoen, 'Communications Under the African Charter: Procedure and Admissibility' in Manisuli Ssenyonjo (ed), The African Regional Human Rights System: 30 Years After the African Charter on Human and Peoples' Rights (Martinus Nijhoff Publishers 2012) 102–105.

198 Art 1 (2) ECHR.

199 Art 21 (1) ACHR.

200 Art 14 (1) AfrCHPR.

201 On the condition of proportionality see only Olivier D Schutter, *International Human Rights Law: Cases, Materials, Commentary* (2nd edn, Cambridge University Press 2014) 368–380.

202 The relevant interpretive technique is systemic interpretation as enshrined in Art 31 (3) (c) VCLT, discussed above in Chapter 3.I.2.b).

b) MFN- and national treatment rights of the investor

Similar to human rights, national treatment clauses in IIAs most likely do not conflict with direct obligations. One may argue that investors are not treated like national entrepreneurs because only the former face international and domestic obligations. However, one can at least justify such unlike treatment on the basis that foreign investors and national entrepreneurs are not comparable: Foreign investors receive international rights that national entrepreneurs do not have. Considering these international rights and obligations together, the IIA does not leave the investor worse off than national corporations. One may say, therefore, that there is no competitive disadvantage – the central concern that national treatment and MFN rights aim to prevent.[203]

Although they serve a similar purpose, MFN rights are more problematic. Investors may challenge direct obligations by arguing that the host state treats investors of a different nationality more favourably when they are protected by a different IIA not containing any such obligations. In other words: One could say that IIAs without direct obligations necessarily provide more favourable treatment than IIAs with direct obligations. If that were true, the investor could demand the same treatment, effectively negating direct obligations entirely. Consequently, direct obligations could only enter into effect after the host state has included them in all of its IIAs in force. Then, MFN rights would cause an opposite effect on obligations compared to their multilateralisation of investor rights identified by *Schill*.[204]

Indeed, in the case of MFN rights, it is harder to argue against a competitive disadvantage of the investor who is subject to direct obligations. What is more, arbitral tribunals have interpreted MFN obligations broadly in the past, for example as even covering arbitration clauses[205] – an argument that could be extended to direct obligations.

---

203 Dolzer and Schreuer (n 108) 198–199, 206–207.

204 Stephan W Schill, *The Multilateralization of International Investment Law* (Cambridge University Press 2009) 121–196.

205 Affirming the application of MFN-obligations to arbitration clauses *Emilio Agustín Maffezini v The Kingdom of Spain*, ICSID Case No. ARB/97/7, Decisión del Tribunal sobre Excepciones a la Jurisdicción (25 January 2000) para 64; *Siemens A.G. v The Argentine Republic*, ICSID Case No. ARB/02/8, Decision on Jurisdiction (3 August 2004) paras 94–110; *Gas Natural SDG, S.A. v The Argentine Republic*, ICSID Case No. ARB/03/10, Decision of the Tribunal on Preliminary Questions of Jurisdiction (17 June 2005) paras 24–31, 41–49; *Suez,*

However, it is more compelling to deny such a drastic conflict between direct obligations and MFN rights. As both norms form part of the same IIA, Art 31 (1) VCLT requires them to be interpreted in a systematically consistent way. It would run counter to the purpose of direct obligations in a bi- or plurilateral IIA if they would only have effect if contained in all other IIAs of the host state.[206] There is nothing in the wording or purpose of clauses on direct obligations which justifies treating them differently to other IIA provisions – which always reflect a special agreement reached between the parties applicable only *inter se*. What is more, it is too formalistic to understand the inclusion of investor obligations as automatically providing less favourable treatment. Rather, they represent a different *modus* of addressing foreign investors actions. The actual degree of protection granted to the investor by an IIA – the investor's treatment – depends on how one interprets and applies them to the specific facts of a dispute.

Notwithstanding, also because general doctrinal discussions on MFN clauses remain unsettled in many regards,[207] there is a risk that tribunals

---

Sociedad General de Aguas de Barcelona S.A. and Vivendi Universal S.A. v The Argentine Republic, ICSID Case No. ARB/03/19, Decision on Jurisdiction (3 August 2006) paras 52–68; *National Grid PLC v The Argentine Republic*, Decision on Jurisdiction (UNCITRAL, 20 June 2006) paras 79–93; *Impregilo S.p.A. v Argentine Republic*, ICSID Case No. ARB/07/17, Award (21 June 2011) paras 79–109; *Hochtief AG v The Argentine Republic*, ICSID Case No. ARB/07/31, Decision on Jurisdiction (24 October 2011) paras 58–100; rejecting the application of MFN-obligations to arbitration clauses *Salini Costruttori S.p.A. and Italstrade S.p.A. v The Hashemite Kingdom of Jordan*, ICSID Case No. ARB/02/13, Decision on Jurisdiction (15 November 2004) paras 102–119; *Plama Consortium Limited v Republic of Bulgaria*, ICSID Case No. ARB/03/24, Decision on Jurisdiction (8 February 2005) paras 183–227; *Telenor Mobile Communications A.S. v The Republic of Hungary*, ICSID Case No. ARB/04/15, Award (13 September 2006) paras 90–101; *Vladimir Berschader and Moïse Berschader v The Russian Federation*, SCC Case No 080/2004, Award (21 April 2006) paras 159–208; *Señor Tza Yap Shum v La República del Perú*, ICSID Case No. ARB/07/6, Decisión sobre Jurisdicción y Competencia (19 June 2009) paras 193–220; *Austrian Airlines v The Slovak Republic*, Final Award (UNCITRAL, 9 October 2009) paras 124–140; generally on this controversy see for example Martins Paparinskis, 'MFN Clauses and International Dispute Settlement: Moving Beyond Maffezini and Plama?' (2011) 26(2) ICSID Review 14; Dolzer and Schreuer (n 108) 270–275.

206 On the relation of MFN-clauses and specific arrangements between states see Dolzer and Schreuer (n 108) 207. Similar arguments caused investment tribunals to reject the application of MFN-clauses to the scope of arbitration clauses, see for example *Tza Yap Shum v Peru* (n 205) para 220.

207 Dolzer and Schreuer (n 108) 211–212.

may interpret them in a manner undermining the newly created direct obligations. Therefore, states are best-advised to clarify the respective clauses in IIAs and to revise pre-existing IIAs accordingly.

Chapter 4.
International Enforcement Through Counterclaims

Building on the analysis of substantive investor obligations carried out in the previous Chapter, the analysis will now turn more closely to how states may procedurally enforce such obligations through arbitral counterclaims. It is submitted that under many IIAs, counterclaims are already possible today.

It seems that states have only recently realised the potentials of counterclaims even though investment arbitration has always provided for this instrument (I.). While there are some important jurisdiction and admissibility requirements, these are more lenient than is often believed (II.). Of course, host states always have the possibility to take steps against investors within their domestic legal system. Nevertheless, counterclaims have important advantages as an international enforcement mechanism for protecting the public interest (III.). Yet, by their nature, they remain a reactive instrument, requiring the investor to file an arbitral claim against the host state first. As of today, there is no basis for the host state to initiate a self-standing claim without such a prior, so-called primary claim by the investor (IV.).

I. The discovery of counterclaims for a new purpose

Counterclaims are well-established in different international dispute settlement procedures.[1] They form separate and self-standing claims that the

---

1 For a study on counterclaims before the ICJ see Constantine Antonopoulos, *Counterclaims Before the International Court of Justice* (T.M.C. Asser Press 2011); for a short general overview on the widespread possibility to file counterclaims see Zachary Douglas, 'The Enforcement of Environmental Norms in Investment Treaty Arbitration' in Pierre-Marie Dupuy and Jorge E Viñuales (eds), *Harnessing Foreign Investment to Promote Environmental Protection: Incentives and Safeguards* (Cambridge University Press 2013) 427; see further Hege E Veenstra-Kjos, 'Counterclaims by Host States in Investment Treaty Arbitration' (2007) 4(4) Transnational Dispute Management 1, 4–5; for a historical analysis of early cases see Bradley Larschan and Guive Mirfendereski, 'The Status of Counterclaims in International Law, with Particular Reference to International Arbitration Involving a Private

respondent files against the claimant in response to the latter's primary or original claim. Building on similar instruments in domestic legal systems, their main purpose is to merge the procedure on the primary claim with the respondent's counterclaim to achieve higher procedural economy.[2]

Although investment counterclaims have only recently sparked greater attention, *inter alia* in the UNCITRAL Working Group III on ISDS reform,[3] generally, investment arbitration has always allowed for them. When states created investment arbitration, they modelled it on commercial arbitration. There, the possibility of counterclaims between private actors is well-established. The ICSID Convention even explicitly allows counterclaims in Art 46[4] as well as in Rule 40 of the ICSID Rules of Arbitration.[5] One can find similar wording in the UNCITRAL Arbitration

---

Party and a Foreign State' (1986–1987) 15(1) Denver Journal of International Law and Policy 11, 18–24.

2 Dafina Atanasova, Adrián Martínez Benoit and Josef Ostransky, 'The Legal Framework for Counterclaims in Investment Treaty Arbitration' (2014) 31(3) Journal of International Arbitration 357, 359–360.

3 See for example Maxim Scherer, Stuart Bruce and Juliane Reschke, 'Environmental Counterclaims in Investment Treaty Arbitration' (2021) ICSID Review 36(2) 413, 414; see the discussions and policy suggestions for counterclaims in Art 18 (E) IISD, *Model International Agreement on Investment for Sustainable Development* (2005); UNCTAD 'Investment Policy Framework for Sustainable Development' UNCTAD/DIAE/PCB/2015/5 (2015), 109–110; IISD, *A Sustainability Toolkit for Trade Negotiators: Trade and Investment as Vehicles for Achieving the 2030 Sustainable Development Agenda* (2017) para 5.5.2, Option 4; IISD, *Integrating Investor Obligations and Corporate Accountability Provisions in Trade and Investment Agreements: Report of the Expert Meeting Held in Versoix, Switzerland, January 11–12, 2018* (2018) 15; on the UNCITRAL Working Group III see UNCITRAL 'Possible Reform of Investor-State Dispute Settlement (ISDS), Multiple Proceedings and Counterclaims' (22 January 2020) UN Doc A/CN.9/WG.III/WP.193, paras 32–45.

4 Art 46 ICSID Convention stipulates: 'Except as the parties otherwise agree, the Tribunal shall, if requested by a party, determine any incidental or additional claims or counterclaims arising directly out of the subject-matter of the dispute provided that they are within the scope of the consent of the parties and are otherwise within the jurisdiction of the Centre.'

5 Art 40 ICSID Rules of Arbitration states: '(1) Except as the parties otherwise agree, a party may present an incidental or additional claim or counter-claim arising directly out of the subject-matter of the dispute, provided that such ancillary claim is within the scope of the consent of the parties and is otherwise within the jurisdiction of the Centre. (2) An incidental or additional claim shall be presented not later than in the reply and a counter-claim no later than in the counter-memorial, unless the Tribunal, upon justification by the party presenting the ancillary claim and upon considering any objection of the other party, authorizes the presentation of the claim at a later stage in the proceeding. (3) The Tribunal shall fix a time

Rules, both in their 1976 version in Art 19 (3) and in their 2010 version with a changed wording in Art 21 (3).[6] *Schwebel* pointedly commented that assumptions on arbitration as a one-way street 'are as colorful as they are misconceived'.[7]

And indeed, states have, in the past and on various occasions, filed counterclaims in investment arbitration and before the Iran-US Claims Tribunal. Yet, these only accounted for approximately two percent of the total investment arbitration claims.[8] Many of them related to private law-related matters of the contractual relationship between the host state and the investor. They did not address investors' conduct towards the public interest. It is useful in this regard to recall that in the first years, investment arbitration often built on arbitration clauses in investment contracts rather than IIAs. As a consequence, these disputes often led to rather technical

---

limit within which the party against which an ancillary claim is presented may file its observations thereon.' On the history of the ICSID Convention in this regard see IBRD 'Report of the Executive Directors on the Convention of the Settlement of Investment Disputes Between States and Nationals of Other States' ICSID/15/ Rev.1, 35–49 (18 March 1965) para 13; Thomas Kendra, 'State Counterclaims in Investment Arbitration – a New Lease of Life?' (2013) 29(4) Arbitration International 575, 577–578.

6 Art 19 (3) of the 1976 UNCITRAL Arbitration Rules stipulates: 'In his statement of defence, or at a later stage in the arbitral proceedings if the arbitral tribunal decides that the delay was justified under the circumstances, the respondent may make a counter-claim arising out of the same contract or rely on a claim arising out of the same contract for the purposes of a set-off.' Art 21 (3) of the 2010 UNCITRAL Model Arbitration Rules states: 'In his statement of defence, or at a later stage in the arbitral proceedings if the arbitral tribunal decides that the delay was justified under the circumstances, the respondent may make a counter-claim or rely on a claim for the purpose of a set-off provided that the arbitral tribunal has jurisdiction over it.' On other investment arbitration rules and their position to counterclaims see Guido Carducci, 'Dealing with Set-Off and Counterclaims in International Commercial and Investment Arbitration' (2013) 3 Yearbook on International Arbitration 173, 178–180.

7 Stephen M Schwebel, 'A BIT About ICSID' (2008) 23(1) ICSID Review 1, 5; similarly Jackson S Kern, 'Investor Responsibility as Familiar Frontier' (2019) 113 AJIL Unbound 28, 29–30 who points to the history of international investment law as a 'two-way system'.

8 Mark W Friedman and Ina C Popova, 'Can State Counterclaims Salvage Investment Arbitration?' (2014) 8(2) World Arbitration & Mediation Review 139, 149; José A Rivas, 'ICSID Treaty Counterclaims: Case Law and Treaty Evolution' in Jean E Kalicki and Anna Joubin-Bret (eds), *Reshaping the Investor-State Dispute Settlement System: Journeys for the 21st Century* (Brill 2015) 779.

contractual counterclaims by the host state against the investor.[9] By and large, these counterclaims have remained unsuccessful.[10]

Most cases on counterclaims in investment *treaty* arbitration only came up in the last years.[11] Even then, most counterclaims related to matters that one would consider to belong to contract law, such as the payment of maintenance costs for a vessel in winter or the meeting of obligations under a bank operation certificate.[12] The five awards on counterclaims discussed in Chapter 3 form the forefront of counterclaims on genuine matters of public interest. Therefore, the use of counterclaims for holding investors accountable in their conduct towards the public interest is not the invention of a new IIA feature – but rather the discovery of a pre-existing tool for a new purpose.

II. Lenient jurisdiction and admissibility requirements

In light of the emerging practice of counterclaims with this new purpose, it is necessary to reflect on their jurisdiction and admissibility requirements. Some argue that they are restrictive, admitting counterclaims only in exceptional circumstances.[13] This Section will submit the contrary and show that these requirements are relatively lenient,[14] namely: the consent

---

9 On this trend Hege E Kjos, *Applicable Law in Investor-State Arbitration* (Oxford University Press 2013) 131–133; Julien Chaisse and Rahul Donde, 'The State of Investor-State Arbitration' (2018) 51(1) The International Lawyer 47, 60–61; for an overview on investment contract counterclaims see Vohryzek-Griest, 'State Counterclaims in Investor-State Disputes: A History of 30 Years of Failure' (2009) 15 Revista Colombiana de Derecho Internacional 83, 92–111.

10 Vohryzek-Griest (n 9) 86–87; Mark A Clodfelter and Diana Tsutieva, 'Counterclaims in Investment Treaty Arbitration' in Catherine Yannaca-Small (ed), *Arbitration Under International Investment Agreements: A Guide to the Key Issues* (2nd edn, Oxford University Press 2018) para 17.03.

11 Rivas (n 8) 779.

12 *Antoine Goetz & Consorts and S.A. Affinange des Métaux v Republic of Burundi (Goetz II)*, ICSID Case No. ARB/01/2, Sentence (21 June 2012) para 285.

13 See for example Andrea K Bjorklund, 'The Role of Counterclaims in Rebalancing Investment Law' (2013) 17(2) Lewis & Clark Law Review 461, 461.

14 Similarly for example Stephan Schill and Vladislav Djanic, 'International Investment Law and Community Interests' in Eyāl Benveniśtî and Georg Nolte (eds), *Community Interests Across International Law* (Oxford University Press 2018) 244–245; more cautiously, calling for revisions of IIAs, are Clodfelter and Tsutieva (n 10) para 17.96; for a sceptical perspective see Friedman and Popova (n 8) 152–153.

to arbitrate by the disputing parties (1.), the jurisdiction *ratione personae* (2.) and *materiae* as related to matters of the public interest (3.) and to domestic obligations (4.), and the direct relation to the primary claim's subject matter (5.).

1. Consent by the disputing parties

Just as any investment arbitration claim, a counterclaim must firstly be covered by the jurisdiction of the investment tribunal. Because the counterclaim is nothing but a regular investment arbitration claim, the host state and the investor must both agree to submit it to investment arbitration. This can take place explicitly and *ad hoc*, as done for example by the parties in *Burlington v Ecuador*.[15]

If there is no such explicit agreement, one could argue that there is no consent in case the investor objects against the tribunal's jurisdiction for the counterclaim. Instead, investment tribunals have accepted that the consent to a counterclaim is already present in the arbitration agreement that materialised *through investors' primary claim*.[16] In other words: by filing their primary claim, investors have already consented to a possible counterclaim. To understand this argument, it is necessary to recall how the arbitration agreement materialises: Investors accept the host state's standing offer to arbitrate – embodied in the IIA's arbitration clause – by filing their primary claim. The IIA defines the terms of this arbitration agreement. Building on this construction, one can argue that the arbitration agreement also covers the filing of counterclaims at a later point in time because the IIA allows for such a procedural instrument – for example, because it incorporates counterclaim-friendly third instruments such as the above-mentioned ICSID Convention and UNCITRAL Model Arbitration Rules. What is more, Art 46 ICSID Convention even presumes that the disputing parties consent to counterclaims in their agreement on arbitration for the primary claim.[17]

---

15 *Burlington Resources Inc. v Republic of Ecuador*, ICSID Case No. ARB/08/5, Decision on Counterclaims (7 February 2017) paras 60–61, 71–72.

16 *Syridion Roussalis v Romania*, ICSID Case No. ARB/06/1, Award (7 December 2011) para 866; *Goetz v Burundi (Goetz II)* (n 12) para 278.

17 This follows from the negative formulation: '*Except as the parties otherwise agree*, the Tribunal shall, if requested by a party, determine any incidental or additional claims or counterclaims arising directly out of the subject-matter of the dispute provided that they are within the scope of the consent of the parties and are

Yet, some argue that investors may narrow the scope of their consent when accepting the host state's offer – and may also exclude consent on a future counterclaim. Indeed, this is one of the unsuccessful preliminary objections that the investor raised against Argentina's counterclaim in *Urbaser v Argentina*. Here, the investor contended that it had not accepted Argentina's offer to arbitrate to the full extent – but only as it allows to file the primary claim against Argentina. This argument is about cutting out those parts of the offer that appear unfavourable to the investor. In the case of *Urbaser v Argentina*, the investor even argued to have done this implicitly.[18]

The more compelling position is that the investor must accept the host state's offer to arbitrate as it stands without modification.[19] Following gen-

---

otherwise within the jurisdiction of the Centre.' (emphasis added) The role of the first part of the provision is not entirely clear given that at the end the Article positively demands the parties' consent. Yet, the state parties explicitly chose the negative formulation over a positive one which is best understood as an interpretive presumption of consent for counterclaims if there are no particular indications against it in the arbitration agreement, see also Christoph Schreuer, *The ICSID Convention: A Commentary* (2nd edn, Cambridge University Press 2009) Art 46 paras 6–11; even more strongly advocating a general presumption of jurisdiction for counterclaims is Zachary Douglas, *The International Law of Investment Claims* (Cambridge University Press 2009) para 488; Clodfelter and Tsutieva (n 10) para 17.24.

18 *Urbaser S.A. and Consorcio de Aguas Bilbao Bizkaia, Bilbao Biskaia Ur Partzuergoa v The Argentine Republic*, ICSID Case No. ARB/07/26, Award (8 December 2016) paras 1123–1125; cf Jorge E Viñuales, 'Investment Law and Sustainable Development: The Environment Breaks into Investment Disputes' in Marc Bungenberg and others (eds), International Investment Law (Nomos 2015) para 19.

19 Supported by Walid Ben Hamida, 'L'arbitrage Etat-investisseur cherche son équilibre perdu: Dans quelle mesure l'État peut introduire des demandes reconventionnelles contre l'investisseur privé?' (2005) 7(4) International Law FORUM du droit international 261, 269; Douglas, *International* (n 17) para 491; Douglas, 'Enforcement' (n 1) 429; Kjos (n 9) 135; Jose D Amado, Jackson S Kern and Martin D Rodriguez, *Arbitrating the Conduct of International Investors* (Cambridge University Press 2018) 84–85; for the contrary position see Schreuer (n 17) Art 46 para 94 who argues that consent is restricted to the extent necessary for the investor's specific claim; see also Gustavo Laborde, 'The Case for Host State Claims in Investment Arbitration' (2010) 1(1) Journal of International Dispute Settlement 97, 109 who argues that investors can accept the offer 'for as little as a single dispute, in full, or anywhere in between'; Stefan Dudas, 'Treaty Counterclaims Under the ICSID Convention' in Crina Baltag (ed), *ICSID Convention After 50 Years: Unsettled Issues* (Wolters Kluwer 2017) 404 who observes that the arbitration agreement mirrors the BIT dispute resolution clause only 'most of the times'; Hugo Thomé, 'Holding Transnational Corporations Accountable for En-

eral contract law principles, a modified acceptance of an offer represents a new offer with the respective new terms.[20] Otherwise, the investor could bind the host state to terms against the state's will – contradicting the contractual and procedural equality between the disputing parties. After all, cutting out parts of the state's offer could substantially alter the procedural balance between the parties. The state cannot have an interest to allow a cherry-picking of investment arbitration rules, especially if standardised model rules are supposed to apply. Otherwise, the investor would also, for example, have the possibility to exclude certain procedural rights of the host state to present evidence or gain other advantages – an absurd result. This position against cherry-picking has been affirmed by the ICSID award in *Roussalis v Romania*.[21]

Delving deeper into the possible constellations of consent-giving, two come to mind: First, an investor may file an investment claim with reference to an IIA that allows for counterclaims without explicitly modifying the terms of the state's offer. Such a conduct must be interpreted as affirming the state's offer without modification and hence as consent to possible counterclaims. This was also the conclusion by the Tribunal in *Urbaser v Argentina*.[22] Second, a foreign investor may explicitly rule out to consent to counterclaims but otherwise accept the state's offer, embodied again in an IIA that allows for counterclaims. Here, the investor's filing of an investment claim does not constitute an acceptance of the state's offer to arbitrate because offer and acceptance do not coincide. Therefore, an investment tribunal would have to already reject its jurisdiction for the investor's primary claim.

However, there is a complication if in the second scenario the host state appears before an investment tribunal and argues on any matter without having reserved a preliminary objection against the tribunal's jurisdiction. Under the doctrine of *forum prorogatum*, in such a case, a state implicitly consents to a tribunal's jurisdiction. The PCIJ affirmed this doctrine in the case of *Rights of Minorities in Upper Silesia* and the ICJ has continued to recognise it ever since.[23] However, investment arbitration under institu-

---

vironmental Harm Through Counterclaims in Investor-State Dispute Settlement: Myth or Reality?' (2021) 22(5–6) Journal of World Investment & Trade 651, 675–675 arguing that states 'have the final word and determine the scope of consent'.

20 Ben Hamida (n 19) 269.

21 *Roussalis v Romania*, Award (n 16) para 866.

22 *Urbaser v Argentina*, Award (n 18) paras 1146–1148.

23 *Rights of Minorities in Upper Silesia (Minority Schools) (Germany v Poland)* (Judgment) [1928] PCIJ Rep Series A No 15, 24–25; *The Corfu Channel Case (UK v*

tional rules such as Art 25 (1) ICSID Convention require consent in writing. It depends on how formally one understands this criterion and the concrete actions in the pleadings if the doctrine of *forum prorogatum* may apply – a matter that remains controversial.[24] Therefore, host states are well advised to raise preliminary objections before an investment tribunal to prevent an unfavourable arbitration agreement. Of course, *forum prorogatum* may also apply to the converse situation and produce the necessary consent of the investor to a counterclaim in case of remaining doubt.[25]

All in all, it is the state which defines the terms of investment arbitration through its offer to investors. If the host state's offer to arbitrate encompasses a jurisdiction for counterclaims, the investor must either accept the whole 'package' or step away from the filing of an investment claim.

2. Jurisdiction ratione personae

The last Section has shown how the disputing parties may influence the tribunal's jurisdiction for counterclaims in the way they give their consent. It laid out that IIAs which incorporate the ICSID Convention and the UNCITRAL Model Arbitration Rules are open to counterclaims. However, given that the IIA's arbitration clause *specifies* the terms of the arbitration agreement, it is a separate question if the IIA *itself* allows for the filing of counterclaims or rules them out on a general level. A possible obstacle is that the IIA's arbitration clause contains wording which allows only investors to file claims. As a matter of jurisdiction *ratione personae*, this would rule out the filing of counterclaims by states. Tribunals and scholars approach this question differently. Rather restrictively, some focus only on the wording of the respective clause (a). In contrast, others have very broadly affirmed tribunals jurisdiction for counterclaims '*ipso facto*' (b). It is submitted that one should prefer a holistic interpretive approach that takes account of the wording, context and telos of the arbitration clause – with the consequence that tribunals indeed have jurisdiction over counterclaims under many IIAs (c).

Albania) (Preliminary Objection) [1948] ICJ Rep 15, 27; *Case Concerning Certain Questions of Mutual Assistance in Criminal Matters (Djibouti v France)* (Judgment) [2008] ICJ Rep 177, paras 60–64.

24 See only Schreuer (n 17) Art 25 paras 481–498 with further references.

25 cf Kendra (n 5) 593.

a) Approaches which focus on the wording

Especially older arbitral decisions place a heavy emphasis on the wording of the IIAs' arbitration clause in approaching the present question, almost to the exclusion of other considerations. This line of cases distinguishes different typical formulations in IIAs to determine jurisdiction for counterclaims.[26]

IIAs hardly ever contain wording that expressly affirms jurisdiction for counterclaims or names both parties as having the right to file a claim. Such rare examples can be found in Art 28 (9) COMESA Investment Agreement[27] or Art 11 (2) Germany-Poland BIT.[28] Much more common are other formulations. One typical category of arbitration clauses expresses that it is the foreign investor who can file an investment arbitration claim, and only the foreign investor. It does so by explicitly naming 'the foreign investor' as the actor entrusted to file an investment claim. Alternatively, but with the same result, there are clauses which allow claims based on the violation of an investor right. *Roussalis v Romania* represents an investment arbitration case that illustrates these constellations. The Tribunal encountered an arbitration clause in Art 9 Greece-Romania BIT[29] with the wording:

---

26 For an overview of typical formulations in IIAs see Veenstra-Kjos (n 1) 15–23; Douglas, *International* (n 17) paras 443–446.

27 Art 28 (9) Investment Agreement for the COMESA Common Investment Area (adopted 23 May 2007) ‹https://investmentpolicy.unctad.org/international-investment-agreements/treaty-files/3092/download› accessed 7 December 2021 (COMESA Investment Agreement): 'A Member State against whom a claim is brought by a COMESA investor under this Article may assert as a defence, counterclaim, right of set off or other similar claim, that the COMESA investor bringing the claim has not fulfilled its obligations under this Agreement, including the obligations to comply with all applicable domestic measures or that it has not taken all reasonable steps to mitigate possible damages.'

28 Art 11 (2) Germany-Poland BIT (adopted 10 November 1989, entered into force 24 February 1991, date of termination 18 October 2019) ‹https://investmentpolicy.unctad.org/international-investment-agreements/treaty-files/1393/download› accessed 7 December 2021 (Germany-Poland BIT): 'If a dispute under paragraph 2 of Article 4 or under Article 5 has not been settled within six months after it has been raised by one of the parties to the dispute, either of the parties to the dispute shall be entitled to appeal to an international arbitral tribunal.'

29 Greece-Romania BIT (adopted 23 May 1997, entered into force 11 June 1998) ‹https://edit.wti.org/document/show/f236f60e-3166-4763-a8bc-00bee9e4fc18› accessed 7 December 2021 (Greece-Romania BIT).

> [...] If such [investment] disputes cannot be settled within six months from the date either party requested amicable settlement, the investor concerned may submit the dispute either to the competent courts of the Contracting Party in the territory of which the investment has been made or to international arbitration. [...]

The Tribunal highlighted that the provision's language only left it to the investor to file an investment arbitration claim, and thus conversely excluded the filing of a counterclaim.[30] In addition, because the BIT did not contain any investor obligations, there was no basis for a counterclaim under the applicable substantive law of the arbitration.[31] Important recent IIAs embody such language restricted to the person or rights of the investor such as Art X.17 CETA or Art 3.1 (2) (b) and (e) EU-Singapore Investment Protection Agreement.[32]

Other arbitration clauses do not contain such textual restrictions. A good example is Art 17 OIC Agreement, the basis of the proceedings in *Al-Warraq v Indonesia*:

> [...] a) If the two parties to the dispute do not reach an agreement as a result of their resort to conciliation, or if the conciliator is unable to issue his report within the prescribed period, or if the two parties do not accept the solutions proposed therein, then each party has the right to resort to the Arbitration Tribunal for a final decision on the dispute.

---

30 *Roussalis v Romania*, Award (n 16) para 869; similarly *Rusoro Mining Limited v The Bolivarian Republic of Venezuela*, ICSID Case No. ARB(AF)/12/5, Award (22 August 2016) paras 623–628.

31 ibid 871; cf Martin Jarrett, Sergio Puig and Steven R Ratner, 'Towards Greater Investor Accountability: Indirect Actions, Direct Actions by States and Direct Actions by Individuals' (2021) Journal of International Dispute Settlement 1, 15, advance article version ‹https://doi.org/10.1093/jnlids/idab035› accessed 7 December 2021 on the problem that there must be a substantive obligation that the state must be able to base its claim on.

32 Comprehensive Economic and Trade Agreement (adopted 30 October 2016) ‹https://investmentpolicy.unctad.org/international-investment-agreements/treaty-files/3593/download› accessed 7 December 2021 (CETA); EU-Singapore Investment Protection Agreement (adopted 15 October 2018) ‹https://investmentpolicy.unctad.org/international-investment-agreements/treaty-files/5714/download› accessed 7 December 2021 (EU-Singapore IPA).

One can find similar clauses for example in Art 9 BLEU-Burundi BIT[33] which was applied in *Goetz v Burundi (Goetz II)*,[34] and Art 11 Ukraine-Germany BIT[35] invoked in *Inmaris v Ukraine*,[36] both proceedings involving a counterclaim by the host state. These Tribunals relied solely on the wording of these provisions in determining if the IIA in question generally provided for jurisdiction for counterclaims.[37]

Overall, to focus on the IIA's wording represents a restrictive approach to counterclaims because there are many IIAs with wording that points against such jurisdiction.

b) Jurisdiction for counterclaims 'ipso-facto'

The opposite approach affirms investment tribunals' jurisdiction to hear counterclaims on teleological grounds without giving regard to the specific wording of IIAs' arbitration clauses. *Reisman* in his dissenting declaration in *Roussalis v Romania* suggested this method. The fact alone that state parties had agreed in an IIA to apply the ICSID Convention was sufficient to establish jurisdiction for counterclaims – given that Art 46 ICSID Convention allows for counterclaims and is incorporated into the arbitration agreement. *Reisman* argued that counterclaims do not only operate to the detriment of the investor. They also provide states with the advantage of not having to pursue their counterargument through

---

33 Convention entre l'Union Économique Belgo-Luxembourgeoise et la République du Burundi Concernant l'Encouragement et la Protection Réciproques des Investissements (adopted 13 April 1989, entered into force 12 September 1993) ‹https://www.investorstatelawguide.com/documents/documents/BIT-0137%20-%20Belgium-Luxembourg-Burundi%20BIT%20(1989)%20[french].pdf› accessed 7 December 2021 (Belgium-Luxembourg Economic Union-Burundi BIT).

34 *Goetz v Burundi (Goetz II)* (n 12).

35 Ukraine-Germany BIT (adopted 15 February 1993, entered into force 29 June 1996) ‹https://investmentpolicy.unctad.org/international-investment-agreements/treaty-files/1442/download› accessed 7 December 2021 (Ukraine-Germany BIT).

36 *Inmaris Perestroika Sailing Maritime Services GmbH and Others v Ukraine*, ICSID Case No. ARB/08/8, Award (1 March 2012) paras 431–432.

37 *Saluka Investments BV v The Czech Republic*, Decision on Jurisdiction over the Czech Republic's Counterclaim (UNCITRAL, 7 May 2004) para 39; *Sergei Paushok, CJSC Golden East Company, CJSC Vostokneftegaz Company v The Government of Mongolia*, Award on Jurisdiction and Liability (UNCITRAL, 28 April 2011) para 689; *Roussalis v Romania*, Award (n 16) paras 868–875; *Inmaris v Ukraine*, Award (n 36) para 432; see also Rivas (n 8) 804–808.

additional domestic measures or proceedings. Then, states would face a potential new investment claim against these new measures. It would make sense for both disputing parties to deal with the dispute in full before the arbitral tribunal to save time and avoid unnecessary transaction costs.[38] This teleological argumentation was explicitly affirmed by the Tribunal in *Goetz v Burundi (Goetz II)* in distinction to *Roussalis v Romania*.[39] Therefore, *Goetz v Burundi (Goetz II)* represents a lenient approach to the jurisdictional requirements of counterclaims.

c) A holistic interpretive approach

It is suggested that an adequate solution lies in between these two approaches. To interpret the arbitration agreement that embodies the IIAs' arbitration clause, it is necessary to resort to international rules of treaty interpretation enshrined in Art 31 and 32 VCLT. These rules call for a holistic interpretation of the IIA, taking into account wording, context and *telos* among other factors.[40]

One should affirm jurisdiction for counterclaims in an often-encountered constellation: The arbitration clause's wording is neutral as to its personal scope and the IIA incorporates the ICSID Convention or the UNCITRAL Arbitration Rules. In line with *Reisman*, referring to a set of rules that allows for counterclaims is a contextual argument that they are a default option available in the interest of arbitral economy.[41] In interpreting an arbitration clause, however, this argument should not be absolute. Other textual and contextual aspects should be considered as well.[42]

---

38 *Syridion Roussalis v Romania*, ICSID Case No. ARB/06/1, Declaration of Arbitrator Reisman (28 November 2011).

39 *Goetz v Burundi (Goetz II)* (n 12) paras 279–280; cf *Oxus Gold v Republic of Uzbekistan*, Award (UNCITRAL, 17 December 2015) paras 947–948 which left this controversy open.

40 Similarly Atanasova, Martínez Benoit and Ostransky (n 2) 371; Scherer, Bruce and Reschke (n 3) 419–424 construed as a question of consent.

41 Indeed, from the beginning, the ICSID Convention was conceived to offer equal access to investors and states and welcomed the possibility of counterclaims, see only Vohryzek-Griest (n 9) 87–89. See also *David Aven et al. v The Republic of Costa Rica*, Case No. UNCT/15/3, Final Award (UNCITRAL, 18 September 2018) para 741 which affirmed jurisdiction for a counterclaim inter alia for the reason that this has 'practical advantages on procedural economy and efficiency'.

42 In this regard correct Atanasova, Martínez Benoit and Ostransky (n 2) 367; Dudas (n 19) 392–393.

Similarly, the wording of the arbitration clause should not by itself be exclusively decisive.[43] Even if it names only the investor as the person to file an investment claim, counterclaims can still be possible. One could well understand such wording as only deciding which party was allowed to file the *primary* claim while leaving open the possibility for a subsequent counterclaim.[44] Indeed, this was the approach of the UNCITRAL Tribunal in *Aven v Costa Rica* which affirmed jurisdiction for a counterclaim despite Art 10.28 CAFTA-DR[45] defining 'claimant' as 'an investor of a Party that is a party to an investment dispute with another Party'.[46] In the same vein, the recent awards in *Al-Warraq v Indonesia* and *Urbaser v Argentina* only highlighted the broad language of the respective arbitration clauses to affirm their jurisdiction as one argument among others.[47]

An important contextual argument in favour of jurisdiction for counterclaims is the presence of direct obligations. If an IIA provides for both rights and obligations, it is reasonable to assume that arbitration should likewise encompass both. Indeed, this was an important argument that the Tribunal in *Al-Warraq v Indonesia* used to affirm its jurisdiction for a counterclaim based on Art 9 OIC Agreement.[48]

Another contextual argument is the mentioning of counterclaims in IIA provisions other than the arbitration clause. For example, US FTAs with Korea, Colombia and Peru as well as US BITs with Rwanda and Uruguay contain a clause that

---

43 Supported by Thomé (n 19) 677; for an approach that appears to primarily centre on the wording of the arbitration clause see Barnali Choudhury, 'Investor Obligations for Human Rights' (2020) 35(1–2) ICSID Review 82, 95; Jarrett, Puig and Ratner (n 31) 15–16.

44 Similarly Atanasova, Martínez Benoit and Ostransky (n 2) 376–377; see also Veenstra-Kjos (n 1) 21–22 who argues that only if both the personal and the substantive scope has been limited to the state and its obligations, counterclaims should be excluded. The contrary position underlines that a counterclaim is nothing other than a claim, see for example Bjorklund (n 13) 468.

45 Dominican Republic-Central America FTA (adopted 5 August 2004, entered into force 1 March 2006) ‹https://investmentpolicy.unctad.org/international-investment-agreements/treaty-files/2482/download› accessed 7 December 2021 (CAFTA-DR).

46 *Aven v Costa Rica* (n 41) paras 731, 738–740.

47 *Hesham Talaat M. Al-Warraq v The Republic of Indonesia*, Final Award (UNCITRAL, 15 December 2014) paras 660–661; *Urbaser v Argentina*, Award (n 18) paras 1143–1144.

48 *Al-Warraq v Indonesia*, Final Award (n 47) paras 662–663.

> [a] respondent may not assert as a defence, counterclaim, right of set-off, or for any other reason that the claimant has received or will receive indemnification or other compensation for all or part of the alleged damages pursuant to an insurance or guarantee contract.

It implies that in all other cases, there is jurisdiction for counterclaims.[49] This holds true even though these IIAs contain arbitration clauses with restrictive wording. They mention only the right to file an investment claim for a breach of an investor right, an investment authorisation or an investment agreement in the arbitration clause.[50] But if this wording would categorically rule out counterclaims, their mentioning in other provisions would be without meaning.[51] Even more clearly, the Trans-Pacific Partnership (TPP) that was eventually abandoned by the US quite explicitly provided in its Art 9.19 (2) that '[…] the respondent may make a counterclaim in connection with the factual and legal basis of the claim or rely on a claim for the purpose of a set off against the claimant.' Interestingly, the Comprehensive and Progressive Agreement for Trans-Pacific Partnership (CPTPP) builds on the TPP's text by reference. Yet, it precisely suspends this paragraph on counterclaims from entering into effect.[52]

---

49 Art 11.20 (9) US-Korea FTA (adopted 30 June 2007, entered into force 15 March 2012) ‹https://www.iisd.org/toolkits/sustainability-toolkit-for-trade-negotiators/wp-content/uploads/2016/09/US-Korea.pdf› accessed 7 December 2021 (US-Korea FTA); Art 10.20 (7) US-Colombia Trade Promotion Agreement (adopted 22 November 2006, entered into force 15 May 2012) ‹https://investmentpolicy.unctad.org/international-investment-agreements/treaty-files/2737/download› accessed 7 December 2021 (US-Colombia FTA); Art 10.20 (7) US-Peru Trade Promotion Agreement (adopted 12 April 2006, entered into force 1 February 2009) ‹https://investmentpolicy.unctad.org/international-investment-agreements/treaty-files/2721/download› accessed 7 December 2021 (US-Peru FTA); Art 28 (7) US-Rwanda BIT (adopted 19 February 2008, entered into force 1 January 2012) ‹https://investmentpolicy.unctad.org/international-investment-agreements/treaty-files/2241/download› accessed 7 December 2021 (US-Rwanda BIT); Art 28 (7) US-Uruguay BIT (adopted 4 November 2005, entered into force 31 October 2006) ‹https://investmentpolicy.unctad.org/international-investment-agreements/treaty-files/2380/download› accessed 7 December 2021 (US-Uruguay BIT); Rivas (n 8) 814. The presented contextual argument is supported by Clodfelter and Tsutieva (n 10) para 17.48.

50 Art 11.16 (1) (a) US-Korea FTA; Art 10.16 (1) (a) US-Colombia FTA; Art 10.16 (1) (a) US-Peru FTA; Art 24 (1) (a) US-Rwanda BIT; Art 24 (1) (a) US-Uruguay BIT.

51 Left open by Rivas (n 8) 815–816.

52 See Art 9.19 (2) Transpacific Partnership (adopted 4 February 2016) ‹https://investmentpolicy.unctad.org/international-investment-agreements/treaty-files/3573/download› accessed 7 December 2021 compared with Annex No. 2 (b) (ii) Comprehensive and Progressive Agreement for Trans-Pacific Partnership (adopted 8

3. Jurisdiction ratione materiae for public interest-related matters

The investment tribunal must also have jurisdiction *ratione materiae* for the public interest matters that form the basis of the counterclaim.[53] If IIAs enshrine direct obligations as discussed above,[54] this requirement is easily met.

Nevertheless, there are voices that are reluctant to accept an investment tribunal's jurisdiction *ratione materiae* for counterclaims related to the public interest. The underlying concern appears to be that the protecting of human rights, the environment and labour standards or the combatting of corruption is not the task of an *investment* tribunal (close to the doctrine of *forum non conveniens*). It lied outside of its jurisdiction as a matter of principle.[55]

These concerns are not compelling in their generality. One may rebut that, on the contrary, international investment tribunals regularly engage with matters of public interest as they interpret investor rights. This has been one of the prime reasons for the right to regulate debate of the last years. Rather, if a tribunal has jurisdiction on matters of the public interest depends on the interpretation of the specific arbitration agreement.[56] One

---

March 2018, entered into force 30 December 2018) ‹https://investmentpolicy.unctad.org/international-investment-agreements/treaty-files/5672/download› accessed 7 December 2021. For a comparative analysis of Asian IIAs see Trisha Mitra and Rahul Donde, 'Claims and Counterclaims Under Asian Multilateral Investment Treaties' in Leïla Choukroune (ed), *Judging the State in International Trade and Investment Law* (Springer Singapore 2016) 116–124.

53 Ursula Kriebaum, 'Foreign Investments & Human Rights: The Actors and Their Different Roles' (2013) 10(1–17) Transnational Dispute Management on the example of human rights.

54 See Chapter 3.

55 See for example Jorge E Viñuales, *Foreign Investment and the Environment in International Law* (Cambridge University Press 2012) 91 who takes a sceptical stance related to independent environmental heads of claims by investors against host states.

56 Supported by Tarcisio Gazzini and Yannick Radi, 'Foreign Investment with a Human Face – with Special Reference to Rights of Indigenous Peoples' in Rainer Hofmann and Christian J Tams (eds), *International Investment Law and Its Others* (Nomos 2012) 93–94; Vid Prislan, 'Non-Investment Obligations in Investment Treaty Arbitration: Towards a Greater Role for States?' in Freya Baetens (ed), *Investment Law Within International Law: Integrationist Perspectives* (Cambridge University Press 2013) 455–457; Eric de Brabandere, 'Human Rights and International Investment Law' in Markus Krajewski and Rhea Hoffmann (eds), *Research Handbook on Foreign Direct Investment* (Edward Elgar Publishing 2019) 627–629

may recall the important finding of the Tribunal in *AAPL v Sri Lanka* that international investment law

> [...] is not a self-contained closed legal system limited to provide for substantive material rules of direct applicability, but it has to be envisaged within a wider juridical context in which rules from other sources are integrated through implied incorporation methods, or by direct reference to certain supplementary rules, whether of international law character or of domestic law nature.[57]

4. Jurisdiction ratione materiae for domestic public law

Furthermore, the Tribunal in *Paushok v Mongolia* accepted an additional, jurisdictional objection. It rejected jurisdiction to hear counterclaims based on the host state's domestic public law. The decision relates to the category of internationalised domestic investor obligations discussed above in Chapter 3.VI. Its reasoning is not convincing.

In this case, Mongolia filed a counterclaim based on domestic tax law. The Tribunal found that this was a matter exclusively for Mongolian domestic courts to decide. Affirming jurisdiction would allow to enforce Mongolia's domestic public law extraterritorially. The Tribunal considered this to be contrary to the 'universally accepted rule that public law may not be extraterritorially enforced'.[58] It borrowed these words from the Iran-US Claims Tribunal's award in *Computer Sciences* which had rejected a counterclaim based on tax law obligations for the same reason.[59]

This argument is hard to sustain. The rule that the Tribunal finds to be universally accepted does not exist in international law. It is of course true that sovereign equality and the principle of non-intervention enshrined in Art 2 (1) and (7) of the UN-Charter prohibit a state from enforcing its

---

who, however, emphasises the jurisdictional limitations; Amado, Kern and Rodriguez (n 19) 109–113.

57 *Asian Agricultural Products Ltd. v Republic of Sri Lanka*, ICSID Case No. ARB/87/3, Final Award (27 June 1990) para 21; see also *Limited Liability Company AMTO v Ukraine*, SCC Case No 080/2005, Final Award (26 March 2008) para 118 which – methodologically correctly – interpreted the applicable Energy Charter Treaty and found that it does not contain any obligations of the investor which could form the basis of the counterclaim raised, hence rejecting its jurisdiction.

58 *Paushok v Mongolia* (n 37) para 695.

59 *Computer Sciences Corporation v The Government of the Islamic Republic of Iran and Others* (Award) (1986) 10 Iran-USCTR 269, paras 55–56.

law in the territory of another sovereign state. However, the other state is free to consent to such an extraterritorial enforcement.[60] Thus, if two states agree in an IIA to allow for counterclaims based on the respective host state's domestic law, this entails the mutual consent to accept the resulting awards – without regard to any prerogative of domestic courts.

What is more, the ICSID Convention and the 2010 UNCITRAL Arbitration Rules do not restrict counterclaims only to violations of a contract to which the investor is a party. This is a decisive difference to the Iran-US Claims Tribunal: Art II.1 of the Declaration concerning the Settlement of Claims of the Algiers Accords allows for counterclaims only if they 'arise out of the same contract, transaction or occurrence that constitute the subject matter of that national's claim'.[61] Therefore, one cannot transfer the Iran-US Claims Tribunal's jurisprudence to investment arbitration as the Tribunal did in *Paushok v Mongolia*.[62]

Recent investment tribunals have not followed this problematic argumentation. On the contrary, as discussed above, the Tribunals in *Perenco v Ecuador* and *Burlington v Ecuador* have been very active in interpreting and applying domestic administrative and constitutional law.[63] This confirms that there are no fundamental obstacles against applying domestic law in counterclaims.

---

60 cf on the intervention by invitation in the *ius ad bellum* Georg Nolte, *Eingreifen auf Einladung: Zur völkerrechtlichen Zulässigkeit des Einsatzes fremder Truppen im internen Konflikt auf Einladung der Regierung* (Springer 1999); on international police cooperation see the analysis by Carsten Bormann, *Transnationale Informationsgewinnung durch Nachrichtendienste und Polizei: Eine Untersuchung von Zulässigkeit und Verwertbarkeit* (Peter Lang GmbH Internationaler Verlag der Wissenschaften 2016); on the European arrest warrant system see Frank Schorkopf, 'European Arrest Warrant' in Anne Peters (ed), *Max Planck Encyclopedia of Public International Law* (January 2009). In the same vein Xuan Shao, 'Environmental and Human Rights Counterclaims in International Investment Arbtiration: at the Crossroads of Domestic and International Law' (2021) 24(1) Journal of International Economic Law 157, 170–171.

61 Declaration of the Government of the Democratic and Popular Republic of Algeria concerning the Settlement of Claims by the Government of the United States of America and the Government of the Islamic Republic of Iran, Algiers Accords (19 January 1981) ‹https://iusct.com/wp-content/uploads/2021/02/1-General-Declaration_.pdf› accessed 7 December 2021 (Algiers Accords).

62 Atanasova, Martínez Benoit and Ostransky (n 2) 385.

63 See Chapter 3.VI.2.

5. Direct relation to the primary claim's subject matter

Lastly, the counterclaim must arise directly out of the same dispute's subject matter. This requirement, best understood as an admissibility criterion,[64] reflects the purpose of counterclaims to promote arbitral economy and efficiency. A tribunal should discuss matters that belong together in the same proceedings to avoid unnecessary duplications. It appears that this requirement has substantially evolved in the practice of investment tribunals from a very restrictive to a much more lenient stance.

The earlier restrictive approach is present, for example, in the award in *Saluka v Czech Republic*. Here, the UNCITRAL Tribunal rejected a counterclaim that the investor had violated Czech domestic law. It required that claims and counterclaims constituted an 'indivisible whole',[65] building on the investment contract case of *Klöckner v Cameroon*.[66] Essentially, it demanded them to be grounded in the same legal instrument. Because the investor's primary claim was based on a contract and the Czech Republic's counterclaim on general Czech law, the Tribunal rejected to find a sufficient nexus. Instead, it indicated that it was up to Czech domestic courts to decide on this matter.[67]

Similarly, the UNCITRAL Tribunal in *Paushok v Mongolia* also rejected jurisdiction for the counterclaim based on general Mongolian domestic law. It pointed to Art 19 (3) of the UNCITRAL Arbitration Rules, requiring the counterclaim to arise out of an investment contract or other contract to which the investor was a party.[68]

Yet, both decisions must be appreciated in the light of the then still applicable UNCITRAL Arbitration Rules of 1976 which stipulated in Art 19 (3):

> In his statement of defence, or at a later stage in the arbitral proceedings if the arbitral tribunal decides that the delay was justified under the circumstances, the respondent may make a counter-claim arising

---

64 See the discussion by Atanasova, Martínez Benoit and Ostransky (n 2) 379–380; similarly Veenstra-Kjos (n 1) 30.

65 *Saluka v Czech Republic*, Decision on Jurisdiction over the Czech Republic's Counterclaim (n 37) para 79.

66 *Klöckner Industrie-Anlagen GmbH, Klöckner Belge S.A. et Klöckner Handelsmaatschappij v République unie du Cameroun et Sté camerounaise des engrais (SOCAME)*, ICSID Case No. ARB/81/2, Sentence (21 October 1983) 17.

67 *Saluka v Czech Republic*, Decision on Jurisdiction over the Czech Republic's Counterclaim (n 37) paras 61–80.

68 *Paushok v Mongolia* (n 37) para 694.

out of the same contract or rely on a claim arising out of the same contract for the purpose of a set-off.

Precisely this formulation was changed to a more lenient wording in the 2010 UNCITRAL Arbitration Rules which now stipulate in Art 21 (3):

> In its statement of defence, or at a later stage in the arbitral proceedings if the arbitral tribunal decides that the delay was justified under the circumstances, the respondent may make a counterclaim or rely on a claim for the purpose of a set-off provided that the arbitral tribunal has jurisdiction over it.[69]

Indeed, more recently, tribunals did not give weight to the different legal bases of the primary claim and counterclaim. Essentially, they demanded that they relate to the same investment activity. For example, the ICSID Tribunal in *Goetz v Burundi (Goetz II)* found the close proximity of the underlying facts of both claims to be decisive.[70] In the same vein, the ICSID Tribunal in *Burlington v Ecuador* only briefly remarked that 'the counterclaims arise directly out of the subject-matter of the dispute, namely Burlington's investment in Blocks 7 and 21'.[71] The ICSID Tribunal in *Urbaser v Argentina* explicitly held that a factual connection of principal claim and counterclaim would be sufficient to affirm jurisdiction, while taking legal aspects into account as an addition.[72] The UNCITRAL Tribunal in *Al-Warraq v Indonesia* applied the same test under the revised 2010 UNCITRAL Arbitration Rules. It only dismissed the counterclaim because the host state had not filed a counterclaim against the complainant but against a third person.[73]

Therefore, one may conclude that there is a trend in recent investment arbitration towards interpreting the requirement of connectedness leniently. It is sufficient that claim and counterclaim relate to the same investment determined mainly by the facts of the case.[74]

---

69 See further Clodfelter and Tsutieva (n 10) paras 17.88–17.93.

70 *Goetz v Burundi (Goetz II)* (n 12) para 285.

71 *Burlington v Ecuador*, Decision on Counterclaims (n 15) para 62.

72 *Urbaser v Argentina*, Award (n 18) para 1151.

73 *Al-Warraq v Indonesia*, Final Award (n 47) paras 667–669.

74 Supported by Veenstra-Kjos (n 1) 44–46; James Crawford, 'Treaty and Contract in Investment Arbitration' (2008) 24(3) Arbitration International 351, 366; Douglas, 'Enforcement' (n 1) 431–433; Clodfelter and Tsutieva (n 10) para 17.36; Shahrizal M Zin, 'Reappraising Access to Justice in ISDS: A Critical Review on State Recourse to Counterclaim' in Alan M Anderson and Ben Beaumont (eds), *The Investor-State Dispute Settlement System: Reform, Replace or Status Quo?*

III. Counterclaims' relevance for extraterritorial enforcement

The tendency towards more lenient jurisdiction and admissibility requirements for counterclaims may lead to more successful awards against foreign investors in the near future following *Perenco v Ecuador* and *Burlington v Ecuador*. What is the consequence of a successful counterclaim? Why would host states aim to pursue this avenue in addition or instead of domestic enforcement through courts and executive agencies?

At first glance, one may see the filing of counterclaims as a litigation strategy. The host state can proactively defend itself against the investor's claim, turning the parties' traditional roles in investment arbitrations around. However, the potential repercussions of counterclaims go much further.

The host state can benefit from investment arbitration's international enforcement regime against the investor in the same manner that investors profited from it in the past.[75] States do not even face the hurdle of state immunity – the last resort for the state to defend itself against the enforcement of an arbitral award.[76] From the perspective of the host state, there are a number of potential advantages over domestic enforcement. They depend on the political situation and the state of its legal system. For example, the host state may simply face legal constrains under domestic law in acting against the foreign investor that it does not encounter with regard to counterclaims. Furthermore, the state may be unable to effectively enforce a domestic obligation, for example because of a lack of economic, police or political resources, or corruption in its institutions.[77]

(Wolters Kluwer 2020) 244–245; Ted Gleason, 'Examining Host-State Counterclaims for Environmental Damage in Investor-State Dispute Settlement from Human Rights and Transnational Public Policy Perspectives' (2021) 21(3) International Environmental Agreements 427, 431; more cautiously Atanasova, Martínez Benoit and Ostransky (n 2) 387; Thomé (n 19) 679; Shao (n 60) 169–172.

75 Bjorklund (n 13) 464; Viñuales, 'Investment' (n 18) para 17; Patrick Abel, 'Counterclaims Based on International Human Rights Obligations of Investors in International Investment Arbitration: Fallacies and Potentials of the 2016 ICSID Urbaser v. Argentina Award' [2018] Brill Open Law 1, 24.

76 cf Art 55 ICSID Convention.

77 Mehmet Toral and Thomas Schultz, 'The State, a Perpetual Respondent in Investment Arbitration? Some Unorthodox Considerations' in Michael A Waibel (ed), *The Backlash Against Investment Arbitration: Perceptions and Reality* (Wolters Kluwer Law & Business 2010) 600–601; Mitra and Donde (n 52) 109–110; Jarrett, Puig and Ratner (n 31) 17–18; Molly Anning, 'Counterclaims Admissibility in

What is more, counterclaims allow for extraterritorial enforcement. The investor may have significant assets in third countries. Due to its territorial confines, these are usually out of reach for the host state. However, as illustrated, awards rendered through counterclaims are part of the far-reaching enforcement networks of the New York and the ICSID Conventions.[78] They are quite easily enforceable in third states, in particular far more easily than judgments of foreign domestic courts. This means that counterclaims extend the host state's reach beyond its territory.[79] This is particularly remarkable if the award is grounded in the application of domestic obligations, because these are then enforced in a third state.[80] Notwithstanding, one should not forget that only the investor who is party to the arbitral proceedings is the person against whom enforcement can take place. Generally, one cannot enforce an award against assets of other separate companies or persons belonging to an investor's corporate group. This can effectively limit the reach of such awards given the sometimes-intricate corporate structures of multinational enterprises.

IV. Obstacles to primary claims by host states against foreign investors

Even appreciating the promising features of counterclaims as a tool for international enforcement, they remain a reactive means. *Per definitionem*, host states can only file them after the investor has initiated the primary claim. In this light, requirements for counterclaims function as gatekeepers for international enforcement of direct obligations. In contrast, in other procedural contexts, they only promote procedural efficiency. This Section will inquire how, if at all, the state may actively enforce direct obligations through *primary* investment claims against the foreign investor.

It will show that there is little basis for such primary claims in investment law's present state. The necessary consent of the disputing parties generally prevents host states from filing a primary claim (1.) if the state did not reach consent through indirect means (2.). While technically possible, establishing a legal fiction of consent by the investor may often

---

Investment Arbitration' in Julien Chaisse, Leïla Choukroune and Sufian Jusoh (eds), *Handbook of International Investment Law and Policy* (Springer 2021) 1285.

78 See Chapter 3.VI.3.c); see also Jarrett, Puig and Ratner (n 31) 18.

79 Laborde (n 19) 99 pointing to further strategic arguments in the comparison to domestic enforcement means; Toral and Schultz (n 77) 600–601; Anning (n 77) 1285; Shao (n 60) 173.

80 cf the concerns of some investment tribunals above in Chapter 4.II.4.

preclude the award from being enforceable in the system of the New York and ICSID Conventions (3.). There may be greater possibilities for primary claims before international investment *courts* – yet, again to the price of losing access to the mentioned enforcement systems (4.).

1. Lacking investor consent

Interestingly, there have been a few instances in which a host state or one of its public entities filed a primary investment *contract* claim against the foreign investor. They remained without success for various particular reasons of less interest for the present analysis.[81] The central obstacle to such primary claims is the requirement of consent.

81 In the 1976 case of *Gabon v Société Serete S.A.* ICSID Case No. ARB/76/1, Order Taking Note of the Discontinuance Issued by the Tribunal (27 February 1978), Gabon filed an investment arbitration claim against the foreign investor for a breach of a construction contract which was then settled and discontinued, see Toral and Schultz (n 77) 589; Mitra and Donde (n 52) 111. – In 1998 the state enterprise Tanzania Electricity Supply Company filed an investment arbitration contract claim against a foreign investor concerning a dispute over a power production agreement. Apparently, the state-owned enterprise favoured international arbitration over domestic courts which it considered to suffer from corruption and be partial to the foreign investor. It was then the investor who brought a claim to domestic Tanzanian courts. Eventually, the parties consented to bring the matter before an ICSID Tribunal, but the case was discontinued later, see *Tanzania Electric Supply Company Limited v Independent Power Tanzania Limited*, ICSID Case No. ARB/98/8, Final Award (12 July 2001) paras 10–13; Toral and Schultz (n 77) 591–595; Mitra and Donde (n 52) 111. – In 2007 the Indonesian Province of East Kalimantan filed an investment arbitration contract claim against a foreign investor (*Government of the Province of East Kalimantan v PT Kaltim Prima Coal and Others*). It abstained from resorting to measures under domestic law because it was in a political conflict with the central Indonesian government. The ICSID Tribunal explicitly held that it 'finds nothing in the ICSID Convention [which] prevents a State or its subdivisions or agencies from appearing as claimant in an arbitration based on a contract. The question might receive a different response if the basis for jurisdiction were an investment treaty which, in principle, reserves the right to bring an arbitration to investors and does not grant substantive protections to States.', see *Government of the Province of East Kalimantan v PT Kaltim Prima Coal and Others*, ICSID Case No. ARB/07/3, Award on Jurisdiction (28 December 2009) para 174. However, the ICSID Tribunal dismissed the case for the reason that the Province did not validly represent the state of Indonesia and had neither been designated to ICSID by Indonesia as a constituent subdivision or agency under Art 25 (1) ICSID Convention, see *Government of the Province of East Kalimantan v PT Kaltim Prima Coal and Others*

As seen, the arbitration clause in an IIA embodies the host state's offer to arbitrate to investors. If the investor does not file a claim first, there is no arbitration agreement. In turn, the filing of a primary claim by the host state against the investor must be understood as an offer to arbitrate. The investor does not need to accept it. Without such an arbitration agreement, international investment tribunals have no jurisdiction. Therefore, it seems that there is a structural obstacle against the filing of a primary investment arbitration claim by the host state if the investor does not voluntarily consent.[82]

2. Indirect ways of acquiring investors' consent

An elegant way of inducing the investors' consent is to use options outside of investment law. After all, investors can declare their consent to investment arbitration in other ways than the filing of an investment claim against the host state. For example, host states may require the investor to declare consent to investment arbitration *in abstracto* and in advance by making it a condition under domestic law for admitting the investment to the host state.[83] They could also offer positive incentives for such a declaration such as financial support. Then, this declaration by the investor would be the offer to the host state to file a primary claim. The host state would accept this offer by filing such an arbitral claim against the investor with reference to the investor's declaration. Hence, a consensus of the disputing parties would materialise in reversed roles compared to how primary claims filed by investors against the host state are usually understood to bring about such a consensus.[84]

3. Legal fictions of investor consent

But are there ways to establish jurisdiction of an investment tribunal even against the will of the investor and to realise a form of compulsory

---

(n 81) paras 177–202; Toral and Schultz (n 77) 595–600; Mitra and Donde (n 52) 111.

82 cf the assessment by Friedman and Popova (n 8) 153–160.

83 Schreuer (n 17) Art 25 para 455; Amado, Kern and Rodriguez (n 19) 82–84.

84 On how the consent of the disputing parties is construed in the standard cases of claims by the investor against the host state see already Chapter 4.II.1.

jurisdiction in this regard? One could think of establishing the investor's consent as a legal fiction or irrebuttable presumption through IIAs. States indeed lay down forms of legal fictions or irrebuttable presumptions for *their* consent to investment arbitration in IIAs. For example, they have agreed on clauses which state that the IIA qualifies for jurisdiction under the ICSID Convention.[85] Similarly, states have stipulated in IIAs that the taking up of an investment by a foreign investor establishes consent to investment arbitration and satisfies the requirements of the ICSID and New York Conventions.[86] Following these techniques, an IIA could, for example, presume investors' consent to host states' primary claims because they are conducting an investment in the host state.

Such an approach would quite harshly depart from the consensual model of investment arbitration. However, there is nothing in international law that bars such an irrebuttable presumption or legal fiction from operating.[87] Some scholars object by pointing to consent as the elementary basis of international dispute settlement as it was for example applicable for proceedings before the ICJ.[88] Yet, the requirement of consent applies only to states, vested in the principle of sovereignty and sovereign equality enshrined in Art 2 (1) UN-Charter.[89] In international law, there is no

---

85 For example: '1. Each Party consents to the submission of a claim to arbitration under this Section in accordance with this Agreement. 2. The consent under paragraph 1 and the submission of a claim to arbitration under this Section shall satisfy the requirements of: (a) Chapter II (Jurisdiction of the Centre) of the ICSID Convention and the ICSID Additional Facility Rules for written consent of the parties to the dispute; and (b) Article II of the New York Convention for an "agreement in writing."', Art 11.17 US-Korea FTA; similarly Art 8.25 Comprehensive Economic and Trade Agreement (adopted 30 October 2016) ‹https://investmentpolicy.unctad.org/international-investment-agreements/treaty-files/3593/download› accessed 7 December 2021 (CETA).

86 cf Amado, Kern and Rodriguez (n 19) 91–92.

87 But see the contrary position for example by Nigel Blackaby and others, *Redfern and Hunter on International Arbitration* (6th edn, Oxford University Press, Wolters Kluwer Law & Business 2015) para 2.01.

88 Atanasova, Martínez Benoit and Ostransky (n 2) 365.

89 Note the reasoning of the PCIJ in *Status of Eastern Carelia* (Advisory Opinion) [1923] PCIJ Rep Series B No 5, 27: 'This rule [the requirement of consent], moreover, only accepts and applies a principle which is a fundamental principle of international law, namely, the principle of the independence of States. It is well established in international law that no State can, without its consent, be compelled to submit its disputes with other States either to mediation or to arbitration, or to any other kind of pacific settlement.' What is more, the principle of consent is not as absolute in practice as sometimes believed, see Alain Pellet, 'Judicial Settlement of International Disputes' in Anne Peters (ed), *Max Planck Ency-*

similar ground for rejecting jurisdiction of an international tribunal over private actors. To the contrary, international criminal tribunals serve as a prime example of how states create compulsory jurisdiction without non-state actors' consent.[90] Rather, to create such a compulsory forum is an exertion of states' sovereign power – doing together what they regularly do alone by creating compulsory jurisdiction of domestic courts.

A different question is if it would still be adequate to consider an investment tribunal based on an investor's fictitious consent to conduct *investment arbitration*. The different methods of international dispute settlement such as adjudication, arbitration, mediation, conciliation and others are archetypes. Their properties can be combined in practice to create hybrid forms.[91] Even an investment tribunal based on the investor's fictitious consent could, for example, leave the selection of arbiters to the disputing parties. This is often considered a characteristic of arbitration in contrast to adjudication. In addition, one may argue that already today states one-sidedly dictate the procedure and applicable law in investment arbitration:

---

clopedia of Public International Law (July 2013) paras 7–24; Patrick Abel, 'Negative Zuständigkeitskonflikte internationaler Gerichte durch Subsidiaritätsklauseln: Zur Bedeutung des Maritime Delimitation in the Indian Ocean-Urteils des IGH für die internationale Streitbeilegung' (2018) 78(2) Zeitschrift für ausländisches öffentliches Recht und Völkerrecht 339, 370.

90 See for example Art 12 Rome Statute of the International Criminal Court (adopted 17 July 1998, entered into force 1 July 2002) 2187 UNTS 3 (Rome Statute). See also the Sea-Bed Disputes Chamber of the International Tribunal for the Law of the Sea which has compulsory jurisdiction for disputes by states or the Authority against a contractor operating in the Area as defined in Art 187 (c), (d), (e) United Nations Convention on the Law of the Sea (adopted 10 December 1982, entered into force 16 November 1994) 1833 UNTS 396 (UNCLOS). There, one may argue that consent is provided by the contractors through the concluding of the respective contract for activities on the Area. But, firstly, this is not presupposed by the Convention, and secondly does Art 187 (d) even accord jurisdiction for disputes with a 'prospective contractor'. See also Art 20 (2) Annex VI of the Convention, the Statute of the International Tribunal for the Law of the Sea, which stipulates: 'The Tribunal shall be open to entities other than States Parties in any case expressly provided for in Part XI [such as Art 187] or in any case submitted pursuant to any other agreement conferring jurisdiction on the Tribunal which is accepted by all the parties to that case.'

91 For example supported by John G Merrills, *International Dispute Settlement* (6th edn, Cambridge University Press 2017) 307; Bernardo Sepúlveda-Amor, 'Opening Remarks' in Laurence Boisson de Chazournes, Marcelo G Kohen and Jorge E Viñuales (eds), *Diplomatic and Judicial Means of Dispute Settlement* (Martinus Nijhoff Publishers 2013) 8–10.

through the IIA and standardised rules such as the ICSID Convention and UNCITRAL Arbitration Rules.

More specific obstacles could follow from Art 25 ICSID Convention which many consider to impose objective jurisdictional requirements independent of the arbitral agreement between the disputing parties.[92] Indeed, the Tribunal in *AMT v Zaire* expressly held that '[...] two States cannot, by virtue of Article 25 of the Convention, compel any of their nationals to appear before the Centre; this is a power that the Convention has not granted to the States.'[93] But the Tribunal dealt only with the general question if the existence of an IIA with an ICSID arbitration clause was sufficient to provide jurisdiction. It solely pointed out that, in addition to the IIA arbitration clause, consent by the disputing parties is required. It did not address the separate question of whether such consent can validly be grounded in an irrebuttable presumption or in a legal fiction.[94]

Yet another question is that of the enforcement of such awards against investors. It is submitted that their enforcement could take place in the home and the host state, on the basis that *they* are bound to accept the fiction as part of their mutual obligations under the IIA. It is a different matter if third states would have to recognise and enforce such an award. The said international obligation in the IIA has only an *inter-se* binding effect between its state parties.[95] There is a high danger that third states which are party to the New York Convention could refuse to recognise and enforce such an investment award. They could argue that the arbitration agreement was invalid, or that the decision was beyond the scope of the submission to arbitration, or that the arbitral tribunal was not properly constituted (Art V (a), (c) or (d) New York Convention). Under the ICSID Convention, such a rejection would presuppose a successful annulment under Art 52 ICSID Convention.[96]

All in all, it is technically possible for states to replace the actual consent of a foreign investor by a legal fiction.[97] However, it remains doubtful

---

92 Schreuer (n 17) Art 25 paras 5–8.

93 *American Manufacturing & Trading, Inc. v Republic of Zaire*, ICSID Case No. ARB/93/1, Award (21 February 1997) para 5.18.

94 A contrary position appears to be presented by Schreuer (n 17) Art 25 paras 451–452 who, however, comments on the different question if an arbitration clause in an IIA alone suffices to qualify for an ICSID Tribunal's jurisdiction.

95 On *pacta tertiis* see already Chapter 2.III.

96 The same concerns share Amado, Kern and Rodriguez (n 19) 93, n 29.

97 See also the elaborate procedural suggestions *de lege ferenda* to include in one way or another third private parties in investment arbitraiton by ibid, 19–69.

whether an investment tribunal would find this to be a sufficient consensual basis for its jurisdiction. Third states are likely to challenge that such an award operates within the New York Convention system or subject to the ICSID Convention.

4. Primary claims before international investment courts?

Thinking about investment arbitration based on fictitious investor consent leads to the question if not other models or institutions of international dispute settlement fit primary claims of host states better. In contrast to arbitral tribunals, courts are the fora that give less control to the parties over the proceedings. Their jurisdiction is generally predefined in their constituent treaty.[98]

Even beyond providing the floor for primary claims by states, the setting of a court could possibly also allow third persons the right to bring claims against the foreign investor.[99] Especially in the case that direct obligations protect human rights or workers' rights, third parties' interests are directly at stake.

As of today, there are no international investment courts. Recently, there have been suggestions to create such an institution, for example by UNCTAD and the IISD in 2015 and 2016 respectively.[100] Currently, the EU pursues this goal in the investment protection chapters of its FTAs and in separate investment agreements: For example, Art 3.38–3.59 EU-Viet-

98 On the differences between courts and arbitral tribunals Pellet (n 89) paras 53–63.

99 A concept that may find inspiration in the model of the Court of Justice of the EU and access of individuals to claim violations of fundamental freedoms, though mostly only indirectly through domestic courts, see on this comparison in the context of labour rights Patrick Abel, 'Comparative Conclusions on Arbitral Dispute Settlement in Trade-Labour Matters Under US FTAs' in Henner Gött (ed), *Labour Standards in International Economic Law* (Springer International Publishing 2018) 179–181; in the same direction Ernst-Ulrich Petersmann, *Multilevel Constitutionalism for Multilevel Governance of Public Goods: Methodology Problems in International Law* (Bloomsbury Publishing 2017) 303–304; analysed as one potential model for including more symmetry into international investment arbitration by Amado, Kern and Rodriguez (n 19) 19–23.

100 Joerg Weber and Catharine Titi, 'UNCTAD's Roadmap for IIA Reform of Investment Dispute Settlement' (2015) 21(4) New Zealand Business Law Quarterly 319; IISD, *Investment-Related Dispute Settlement: Towards an Inclusive Multilateral Approach* (2017).

nam Investment Protection Agreement[101] and Art 8.18–8.45 CETA contain respective provisions on an international investment court – but these norms have not yet come into force at the time of writing.[102] However, even in the above-mentioned EU FTAs, consent by the disputing parties – including the investor – is still required.[103] They focus on reforming other features such as the replacing of party-elected arbiters by pre-determined judges.[104] The 2017 IISD reflections on possible future multilateral investment dispute settlement procedures go further. They consider that states could create a forum with broad compulsory jurisdiction for investment disputes that also allows for claims by stakeholders.[105]

However, even if a different model of an international investment court would abandon the requirement of consent by the foreign investor, its judgments would not qualify for the ICSID Conventions' recognition and enforcement system and would stand the risk that domestic courts would

---

101 EU-Vietnam Investment Protection Agreement (adopted 30 June 2019) ‹https://investmentpolicy.unctad.org/international-investment-agreements/treaty-files/5868/download› accessed 7 December 2021 (EU-Vietnam IPA), a mixed-agreement complementing the EU-Vietnam FTA (adopted 30 June 2019, entered into force 1 August 2020) ‹https://policy.trade.ec.europa.eu/eu-trade-relationships-country-and-region/countries-and-regions/vietnam/eu-vietnam-agreement/texts-agreements_en› accessed 7 December 2021 (EU-Vietnam FTA) as an EU-only agreement.

102 In the long run the EU aims at creating a Multilateral Investment Court to which different single IIAs can relate and be connected with another, see Council of the European Union 'Negotiating Directives for a Convention Establishing a Multilateral Court for the Settlement of Investment Disputes' 12981/17 ADD 1 (1 March 2018); generally on the Multilateral Investment Court see Rob Howse, 'Designing a Multilateral Investment Court: Issues and Options' (2017) 36(1) Yearbook of European Law 209; Marc Bungenberg and August Reinisch, *Draft Statute of the Multilateral Investment Court* (Nomos 2021). If this project will be realised remains to be seen, especially in light of rather restrictive judgments of the European Court of Justice on the EU's competence in international investment law and investment arbitration, see Opinion C-2/15 *Free Trade Agreement between the European Union and the Republic of Singapore* [2017] ECLI:EU:C:2017:376 paras 78–110, 285–293; on intra-EU investment arbitration see Case C-284/16 *Slovak Republic v Achmea BV* [2018] ECLI:EU:C:2018:158 paras 31–60.

103 Art 3.36 EU-Vietnam IPA and Art 8.25 CETA.

104 Howse (n 102) 221.

105 IISD, *Dispute Settlement* (n 100) 5–6; from the literature see the proposal by George K Foster, 'Investors, States, and Stakeholders: Power Asymmetries in International Investment and the Stabilizing Potential of Investment Treaties' (2013) 17(2) Lewis & Clark Law Review 361, 398–408.

reject recognition and enforcement under the New York Convention.[106] Both presuppose a (foreign) arbitral award and do not apply to court judgments. The departing from the arbitration model would come at the price of losing one of the most appealing features of investment law: its highly effective international enforcement system.

106 Marc Bungenberg and August Reinisch, *From Bilateral Arbitral Tribunals and Investment Courts to a Multilateral Investment Court* (2nd edn, Springer 2020) paras 495–540, 642–650.

Chapter 5.
Interim Conclusion: The Dawn of Direct Obligations

All in all, Part I has shown that direct obligations have recently emerged in international investment law – not only as important possible reform suggestions but already in first instances in investment law practice. These obligations are legally binding and directly applicable to foreign investors as a matter of international law. Investors owe them to the respective host state. They relate to the protection of different facets of the public interest such as human rights, workers' labour rights, environmental protection and anti-corruption. And states are capable of internationally enforcing them through arbitral counterclaims under many IIAs. While especially African states have recently included direct obligations into new IIAs and model instruments,[1] the analysis has shown that this trend is not limited to the African continent.

It is remarkable that investment law is subject to such a development as a field that used to be famous for its asymmetry: the awarding of rights without obligations. It has shared this feature with other branches of international law which only exceptionally provide for obligations directly applicable to non-state actors.

In the substantive dimension, the analysis has shown that investment law even allows to discern a nascent doctrine of direct obligations. Varying techniques for their creation, drawing on different normative sources exist, and each comes with its own advantages and shortcomings. As of today,

---

1 On African reform efforts of investment law which contain direct foreign obligations towards the public interest see Meg Kinnear and Paul J Le Cannu, 'Concluding Remarks: ICSID and African States Leading International Investment Law Reform' (2019) 34(2) ICSID Review 542, 544 with a general comment on the features of African investment law reforms; Makane M Mbengue, 'Africa's Voice in the Formation, Shaping and Redesign of International Investment Law' (2019) 34(2) ICSID Review 455, 465–466 on direct obligations as an 'overarching objective' to balance 'investors' rights and obligations' as part of a broader domestic, bilateral and regional reform effort of 'Africa as a rule maker' (462) of investment law; Priscila Pereira de Andrade and Nitish Monebhurrun, 'Mapping Investors' Environmental Commitments and Obligations' in Jean Ho and Mavluda Sattorova (eds), *Investors' International Law* (Hart 2021) 277–278 on African IIAs as 'avant-gardist examples' for direct environmental investor obligations.

the most promising and easiest method is to employ domestic obligations. IIAs and investment arbitration can internationalise and turn them into norms that are detached from their domestic origins.

Procedurally, states have given arbitral counterclaims, an old instrument of investment arbitration, a new purpose: to examine if investors wrongfully violated public goods or individual rights of others. Even though counterclaims have always been available, it appears that states and scholars have become conscious of their potential only in the last years. The jurisdiction and admissibility requirements are relatively lenient, allowing for counterclaims in a significant number of current IIAs. While they remain reactive enforcement tools which presuppose a prior primary claim by the investor, they empower the host state to enforce against assets of the investor outside of its territory.

Of course, the encountered new practice is still little in quantity vis-à-vis the more than 3000 existing IIAs and compared to the many investment arbitration proceedings conducted so far. Most states remain reluctant to include direct investor obligations in IIAs. Notwithstanding, the findings reflect dynamics indicative of a new qualitative approach that one should not underestimate[2] – possibly even signaling the dawn of direct obligations.

2 For a more sceptical position see Karsten Nowrot, 'How to Include Environmental Protection, Human Rights and Sustainability in International Investment Law?' (2014) 15(3/4) Journal of World Investment & Trade 612, 636; Markus Krajewski, 'A Nightmare or a Noble Dream? Establishing Investor Obligations Through Treaty-Making and Treaty-Application' (2020) 5(1) Business and Human Rights Journal 105, 114, 120–121.

Part II
Indirect Obligations

Part I has concluded that, recently, first IIAs and arbitral awards have brought about direct obligations in investment law. Part II will widen the perspective and elaborate on a different type of obligation, one that is even more established: indirect international investor obligations.

In many instances, tribunals have made investor *rights* contingent on compliance with standards of conduct. As will be seen, many of these standards address how investors behave towards the public interest. If investors violate these standards, they forfeit investment protection. This way of setting standards for investor behaviour is understood here as an indirect obligation.

The term 'indirect obligation' has, thus far, not been established as a term of art in investment law practice and scholarship. This book introduces it as a means of expressing that there exists an established pattern in arbitral jurisprudence: to condition investment protection on proper investor behaviour with concrete standards of conduct. First, Part II will explain the concept of 'indirect obligations' in more detail (Chapter 6). Then, by studying IIAs, arbitral awards and scholarly writing, it will trace the many different indirect obligations that exist throughout investment law doctrine today (Chapter 7). Finally, some more general conclusions on indirect obligations will be drawn (Chapter 8).

Chapter 6.
Indirect Obligations as a Concept

Chapter 6 will elaborate on the concept of 'indirect obligation'. It lays the groundwork for the in-depth study of indirect obligations in arbitral jurisprudence which will be conducted in the subsequent Chapter 7.

This Chapter will start by defining indirect obligations more precisely and presenting an example which will be used recurrently throughout the Chapter (I.). Indirect obligations' distinctive feature is that they are partially compulsory norms: a violation thereof will lead to the loss of an investor right as a sanction. As such, they are more binding than CSR norms but, in a way, less binding than direct obligations (II.). They turn public interest-friendly behaviour into a self-interest of the investor (III.). In doing so, they operate on the level of international law – thus independently from the host state's domestic legal system (IV.). The mentioned sanction for breaching an indirect obligation can be loss of procedural or of substantive investor rights (V.). Interestingly, standards of conduct can function as a direct and indirect obligation simultaneously (VI.). The analytical potential of the new concept of indirect obligations is to offer better insights into the changing role of the investor in investment law than alternative approaches can provide (VI.). The term reveals that investment law increasingly expects a certain behaviour from the investors, in contrast to its historical focus on merely awarding rights to them (VIII.). Part II, therefore, introduces the concept of indirect obligations as a new theoretical category to capture a dynamic reinterpretation of the field (IX.).

I. Definition

Indirect investor obligations[1] are norms which stipulate a standard of conduct. Yet, the host state cannot force investors to obey. Instead, they

1 The meaning of the term 'indirect international investor obligation' differs from the use of this notion in the literature, for example by Karsten Nowrot, 'Obligations of Investors' in Marc Bungenberg and others (eds), *International Investment Law* (Nomos 2015) paras 18–21 and by Stefanie Schacherer, *Sustainable Development in EU Foreign Investment Law* (Brill 2021) 271. Barnali Choudhury, 'Investor

can choose to comply. There is no obligation to pay compensation to the host state in case of a breach. However, non-compliance will have negative consequences, depriving investors of substantial or procedural protection under an IIA in full or in part.

For example, one could imagine an IIA clause with the following content:

> If the investor does not comply with the duty to respect human rights as enshrined in the ICCPR, the right to protection against expropriation granted in this treaty does not apply.

This clause would address a situation like the injection of toxin into ground water causing local casualties – a violation of the right to life enshrined in Art 6 (1) ICCPR. Here, by virtue of the IIA clause, ICCPR norms (usually only imposed on states) operate as indirect investor obligations. The state cannot demand from the investor to comply with the ICCPR. There is nothing in the text that indicates that a violation should have any other consequences than the one mentioned: deprival of protection against expropriation under the IIA.

II. Partially compulsory norms

Such an indirect obligation differs from direct obligations studied in Part I. Direct obligations are self-standing. In contrast, indirect obligations are intertwined with an investor right, in the aforementioned hypothetical example the protection against expropriation. While direct obligations are compulsory, investors have the freedom not to comply with an indirect obligation – if they are ready to accept that they lose the corresponding investor right.

However, this does not mean that indirect obligations are voluntary, non-binding norms. They do have legal effect because they change the

---

Obligations for Human Rights' (2020) 35(1–2) ICSID Review 82 employs the term 'investor obligations' taking account of direct and indirect obligations within the meaning of this study, but without distinguishing between these two categories as suggested here. A concept fairly similar to the one proposed here is identified by Tillmann R Braun, *Ausprägungen der Globalisierung: Der Investor als partielles Subjekt im Internationalen Investitionsrecht: Qualität und Grenzen dieser Wirkungseinheit* (Nomos 2012) 193 and by George K Foster, 'Investors, States, and Stakeholders: Power Asymmetries in International Investment and the Stabilizing Potential of Investment Treaties' (2013) 17(2) Lewis & Clark Law Review 361, 403.

investor's legal position under an IIA. Importantly, the consequence of losing an investor right does not depend on the investor's will but occurs automatically. In other words, in the above-mentioned example, the investor cannot choose not to comply with the ICCPR *and* keep protection against expropriation at the same time. A breach of an indirect obligation thus leads to a legal sanction. For this reason, one can understand it to exert a partially compulsory effect of lower intensity compared to direct obligations.[2] Furthermore, often foreign investors will not have a choice if they wish to preserve investment protection. Corporate law may require them to make use of all available legal protection to safeguard their shareholders' interests, including IIAs[3] – hence forcing them to fulfil the indirect obligations. Indeed, practically speaking, the automatic loss of investment protection may harm investors more than the prospect of being liable for not complying with direct obligations.[4]

The partly compulsory effect operates indirectly by using investor rights as leverage – which is the reason for naming these norms *indirect* obligations. In this regard, indirect obligations express a behavioural expectation[5] and set an according legal standard of conduct. Similarly, the IISD noted in its 2018 expert meeting on integrating obligations into IIAs:

> Throughout the two-day meeting, the meaning of 'investor obligations' was repeatedly brought up and debated by participants. It was noted that, in a broad sense, provisions laying out conditions relating to the behaviour of an investor could be seen as an investor obligation.[6]

---

2 Quite similar is the assessment of such implied norms as '[…] behavioural expectations being incumbent upon investors on the basis of the principle of good faith, a violation of which does not give rise to compensation, but "merely" results in a legal disadvantage with the investor forfeiting the protection under the respective investment agreement' by Nowrot (n 1) para 31.

3 The presence and reach of such an obligation of course varies according to the applicable domestic law and the corporate structure of the investor. On the variety of such corporate models see for example Peter Muchlinski, *Multinational Enterprises and the Law* (2nd edn, Oxford University Press 2007) 52–77.

4 More details on the steering potential of investor obligations will be provided in Chapter 10.

5 Similarly Nowrot (n 1) para 31.

6 IISD, *Integrating Investor Obligations and Corporate Accountability Provisions in Trade and Investment Agreements: Report of the Expert Meeting Held in Versoix, Switzerland, January 11–12, 2018* (2018) 18.

The binding character of indirect obligations becomes even clearer if one compares them to CSR norms. The latter are truly voluntary, in the sense that there is no legal sanction or consequence in case of non-compliance. If investors do not live up to the UN Guiding Principles on Business and Human Rights, the CSR norm by itself does not alter their legal position.[7] They may only be subject to non-legal sanctions such as reputational loss or increasing consumer pressure. In contrast and as seen above, indirect obligations entail a negative legal consequence which justifies categorising them as a form of *obligation*.

III. Turning the public interest into a self-interest

Indirect obligations' partially compulsory character leads to the question of their purpose. On the one hand, one can understand them as norms that serve their addressees' own interest. This is because of their effect on investor rights. If investors do not comply, they impair their own legal position. In this sense, they comply for their own sake.

However, this does not mean that indirect obligations cannot serve the public interest at the same time. Legal norms often pursue more than one purpose. It depends on indirect obligations' *content* if they also protect the public interest.

In the hypothetical example at the beginning of this Chapter, the ICCPR-clause will motivate investors to comply with the ICCPR in their own interest not to lose protection against expropriation. However, at the same time, the clause serves the public interest, too. It assumes that investors will comply because they may want to avoid the sanction of losing protection.

Therefore, indirect obligations can, at least incidentally, aim to protect the public interest. Not by demanding public interest-friendly behaviour and threatening enforcement like direct obligations do but instead by turning such behaviour into a self-interest of the investor. They take advantage of the leverage that investor rights offer and the striving of investors for lowering their investment risk.

7 A different question is whether a certain legal norm may define its content by reference to CSR standards. In this case, the legal effect follows from the legal norm only.

IV. International character

It is of importance for the analysis that, just as direct obligations, indirect obligations operate on the level of international law. This follows from the fact that they relate to international rights. They cause the investor to partly or completely lose such an international right, e.g. the protection against expropriation. Therefore, indirect obligations necessarily share these rights' status of international norms.

In the above-mentioned example, the ICCPR clause is of international character. Its source is the respective IIA, an international treaty. And it curtails the right to protection against expropriation, an international right of the investor in case of non-compliance with the ICCPR.

Notwithstanding, as will be proven in Chapter 7 in detail, indirect obligations also allow for an interplay with domestic law. In this respect, they are similar to direct obligations in light of the findings in Part I. For example, one could alter the above-mentioned IIA clause as follows:

> If the investor does not comply with the duty to respect human rights as enshrined in the host state's constitution, the right to protection against expropriation granted in this treaty does not apply.

Again, this indirect obligation would operate on the level of international law for the same reasons described in the previous paragraph: it forms part of a clause of an international treaty and has effect on an international right. Only the standard of conduct's *content* is defined by reference to domestic law. Potentially, this allows indirect obligations to build on the many obligations in domestic legal systems which protect the public interest.

V. Loss of procedural or substantive rights

Violating an indirect obligation can cause the loss of a substantive or a procedural investor right. The former has already been introduced. But investors can also forfeit their procedural right to file a claim before an investment tribunal. To give another example, a respective IIA clause could state as follows:

> If the investor does not comply with the duty to respect human rights as enshrined in the ICCPR, any arbitral claim filed within the terms of this agreement against the host state is inadmissible.

This type of indirect obligation changes the investor's legal position, too. After violating the ICCPR, the investor forfeits the right to file an arbitration claim – an important procedural right given in the IIA's arbitration clause which grants access to an international dispute settlement procedure. The analysis will, thus, include negative consequences on both substantive and procedural investor rights.

VI. Norms with dual character

Indirect obligations do not preclude that a certain standard of conduct may simultaneously operate as a direct obligation. Standards can have a dual character in this regard. In such a case, violating them accrues both types of negative legal consequences: The host state can enforce the standard and claim compensation as a matter of international law. And the investor automatically loses an investor right in part or in total.

One can illustrate this by altering the above-mentioned hypothetical IIA clause to the following:

> (1) The investor must comply with the duty to respect human rights as enshrined in the ICCPR. In case of non-compliance, the host state can file an investment arbitration claim against the investor and demand compensation.
>
> (2) In addition, if the investor does not comply with the duty to respect human rights as enshrined in the ICCPR, the right to protection against expropriation granted in this treaty does not apply.

Paragraph one imposes a direct, paragraph two an indirect obligation on the investor. Yet, both obligations define their content by the same standard: the duty to respect ICCPR rights. Thus, this example shows that the identical standard can have a dual character. Imposing direct and indirect obligations on investors at the same time is a way of addressing their conduct towards the public interest in a particularly restrictive way.

VII. Analytical potential

Introducing the concept of indirect obligations follows from the assessment that, as will be seen, it best describes and models the encountered legal practice. It is not the only possible way of conceptualising clauses such as the ones used in the presented hypothetical examples. Alternatively, one could understand such clauses as requirements or conditions of investor rights. In this view, in the example given above, the protection against expropriation would simply have another requirement: compliance with ICCPR rights. Another alternative, as for example elaborated by *Jarrett*, is to conceive aspects of the practice analysed in this Part as a *defence* against investment claims.[8] For *Jarret*, the function of defences is to eliminate or reduce state liability.[9] This function indeed covers an important part of the analysis in Part II. Where the concepts of indirect obligations and defences of state obligations overlap, they are simply two sides of the same coin.[10] However, indirect obligations as understood here are broader in scope than *Jarrett's* understanding of defences. For example, indirect obligations do not only relate to the question of liability but also to reasons for defeating a tribunal's jurisdiction[11] and can encompass investor misconduct that is not in a causal relationship to the state's breach of an investor right.[12]

By turning away from the focus on the state's breach of investor rights, the concept of indirect obligations offers additional and different insights into how investment law is changing – and what this change means for investors. The notion of 'obligation' expresses that something is actively expected from its addressee. If one is subject to an obligation, that person's actions are under scrutiny. It reflects that compliance is at the investor's

---

8 Martin Jarrett, *Contributory Fault and Investor Misconduct in Investment Arbitration* (Cambridge University Press 2019).

9 ibid, 22.

10 This is supported for example by Jean-Michel Marcoux and Andrew Newcombe, 'Bear Creek Mining Corporation v Republic of Peru: Two Sides of a "Social License" to Operate' (2018) 33(3) ICSID Review 653, 658 on the example of a 'social license' that investors may require to operate their investment. In their view, investment law may cover it as a responsibility of the state to monitor foreign investors' attempt to seek consent for the investment from local communities; but one could also understand it as an obligation imposed on the investors. The authors consider these two constructions to be 'two sides of the same coin', but only the latter allowed for a 'meaningful application' of the concept of social license.

11 Such defeats of jurisdiction, similarly to reasons for finding a claim inadmissible, are excluded from the term 'defence' in Jarrett (n 8) 40–41.

12 Fundamental to *Jarrett's* study is acknowledging the multitude of causes for a state's breach of investor rights and specifying that the legal elements of contributory fault should distinguish between investor conduct directly causal for this breach – so called mismanagement – and investor conduct only indirectly causal for this breach – so called investment reprisal, see ibid, 160–161 and his theory on causation in 53–77.

disposal: obligations express behavioural expectations.[13] In contrast, 'conditions', 'requirements' or 'defences' have a much more neutral connotation. They do not necessarily relate to personal behaviour – for example, that the sun is shining surely is a condition for enjoying the beach. They can also relate to all sorts of objective circumstances, for example distress due to a natural catastrophe by which we may evaluate the *state's* conduct in a new light.[14] The category of 'indirect obligations' is more specific in this regard. It better emphasises a new active role of the foreign investor vis-à-vis the public interest. In the broader picture, it sheds light on a recent development that is at the heart of this book: how investment law increasingly examines not only the state's but also the investor's misconduct.

Conversely, it is clear that not every circumstance related to the investor's conduct can constitute an indirect obligation in a manner that is conceptually meaningful. Eventually, every investor right requires the investor to act in some way to fulfil its requirements. For example, the protection against expropriation requires the investor to have assets. Without assets, there is nothing the host state can expropriate. Yet, there is no analytical advantage in understanding the requirement of 'having assets' as an indirect obligation. It does not serve as a relevant standard for how the investor is expected to behave in the host state's society.

Rather, indirect obligations as they are understood here are only those norms which set a certain standard as to how investors must behave towards the public interest. It must be possible to formulate that if investors harm the public interest by doing X, the consequence is that they partly or completely lose investor right Y.

By shedding light on this linkage between a public interest standard and a legal consequence, the concept of indirect obligations allows to compare them to direct obligations more easily and clearly. As especially Part III will show, direct and indirect obligations form part of a common development. They also share normative features. For example, both raise the question of how to determine the attributable conduct. In the above-mentioned example: under which circumstances is the investor responsible for polluting the ground water? Is intent required? Is negligence sufficient? This assessment is relevant irrespectively of the consequences of breaching the obligation – be it that investors have to pay compensation (in case of a

---

13 cf n 5.

14 This covers some cases of defences which contain an 'external legal element' compared to a state's investment obligation as understood by Jarrett (n 8) 17.

direct obligation) or that they lose their investment protection (in case of an indirect obligation).

Interestingly, in some domestic jurisdictions, the category of indirect obligations is established as a legal subtype of obligations in private law, especially in insurance law.[15] There, insurance terms are the equivalent to what has been defined here as indirect obligations. For example, theft insurances for bikes may require the locking of the bike if left in public. Car insurances may call for regular inspections and reparations. Health insurances may prohibit particularly dangerous activities such as bungee jumping. In all these cases, the consequence of not complying with these rules is the loss of insurance protection. In contrast to this domestic terminology, no branch of international law has so far invented a similar concept. Yet, the analogy to domestic insurance law is helpful to point out the analytical potential of indirect obligations. After all, investor rights enshrined in IIAs serve a similar function as a form of international insurance for investors in a foreign domestic legal system.

The insurance terms in domestic jurisdictions mainly serve to safeguard the insured's own interest: a bike that is locked is less likely to be stolen. There, these terms serve to distribute risks between private parties. In contrast, investment law is a branch of public law.[16] Tribunals which apply investor rights often review state regulation and engage in the balancing of investors' interests with public goods and third-party rights. By intertwining indirect obligations with investor rights, they share this public law character. Consequently, they have ground to express how investors should behave towards public goods and other individuals – in other words, to define their role in a society.

VIII. Lacking tradition

This makes indirect obligations interesting to study as a matter of international law. As seen above, in contrast to domestic jurisdictions in which there are plenty of obligations directly applicable to private actors, interna-

---

15 For example, in the German jurisdiction, it is established to consider these types of norms as a specific form of an obligation, called 'Obliegenheit', see the fundamental study by Reimer Schmidt, *Die Obliegenheiten: Studien auf dem Gebiet des Rechtszwanges im Zivilrecht unter besonderer Berücksichtigung des Privatversicherungsrechts* (Karlsruhe 1953).

16 See for example the in-depth analysis by Gus van Harten, *Investment Treaty Arbitration and Public Law* (Oxford University Press 2007).

tional law only rarely directly addresses their actions.[17] This is not solely the case for direct obligations which have emerged only recently as laid out in Part I. In addition, in the history of international investment law, there exists no tradition of addressing the investors' misconduct regarding investor rights, even in an indirect way.

Before international investment law existed, only the home state could protect the investor of its nationality against the host state through diplomatic protection. Every state was (and continues to be) bound by the customary law of aliens which constitutes a minimum standard of treatment. Traditionally, it was construed as being purely inter-state in nature: If a host state violated the law of aliens, it infringed on an international right of the home state in the person of its national. In other words, the state fully mediatised the national – it was the only bearer of the international right of aliens.[18] Because of this inter-state character, diplomatic protection did not consider the national's misconduct as a relevant point to determine protection. Within the inter-state logic, this makes sense: individuals like an investor cannot impair the sovereign right of their state of nationality through their actions.[19]

---

17 cf the studies by John H Knox, 'Horizontal Human Rights Law' (2008) 102(1) American Journal of International Law 1, 18 who identifies that international human rights law sometimes does specify conduct expected from private actors. But these norms are much rarer than ones that provide discretion to the state how to enact and enforce its duty to protect human rights.

18 *The Mavrommatis Palestine Concessions (Greece v Britain)* (Objection to the Jurisdiction of the Court) [1924] PCIJ Rep Series A No 2, 12; confirmed by *Case Concerning the Barcelona Traction, Light and Power Company, Limited (Belgium v Spain) (Second Phase)* (Judgment) [1970] ICJ Rep 3, para 78. To also understand rights underlying diplomatic protection as individual rights is a rather new development, see *LaGrand Case (Germany v USA)* (Judgment) [2001] ICJ Rep 466, para 77; *Case Concerning Avena and Other Mexican Nationals (Mexico v United States of America)* (Judgment) [2004] ICJ Rep 12, para 40 on Art 36 (1) Vienna Convention on Consular Relations (adopted 24 April 1963, entered into force 19 March 1967) 596 UNTS 261 (VCCR).

19 The requirements of diplomatic protection that at first glance appear to consider the national's conduct do not allow for a different conclusion: The requirement that the national has to exhaust the host state's local remedies serves to give the host state a chance to remedy a violation towards the home state through internal institutions and processes, see *Interhandel Case (Switzerland v USA)* (Preliminary Objections) [1959] ICJ Rep 6, 27. The doctrine of clean hands relates to the claiming state's misconduct and is not established in relation to an improper behaviour of the national. The ILC has rejected to exclude diplomatic protection in such constellations precisely because the national cannot thereby impair a right of the sovereign home state, see ILC 'Sixth Report on Diplomatic Protection, by

Precisely because of diplomatic protection's inter-state nature, states invented investment law in the late 1950s. Yet, within investment law's original logic, investor misconduct towards the public interest was of no concern: The process of decolonisation had started, and tensions between developing and developed states were increasing. The international community failed to agree on a comprehensive international economic treaty, the Havana Charter. Many states feared that general political controversies would impair the exertion of diplomatic protection on behalf of their investors.[20] In this contentious political climate, IIAs were an attempt to depoliticise the protection of foreign investors.[21] These treaties should exclusively focus on granting rights to the investors. They served to attract foreign investment on the premise that any increase of the investment volume would benefit the host state's development.[22] As a consequence, their sole purpose was to protect investors and discipline host states accordingly.

Mr. John Dugard, Special Rapporteur' UN Doc A/CN.4/546 (11 August 2004), para 8. Only the principle of contributory negligence allows to examine the impact of the national's conduct on the damage caused to the home state, see Art 39 of the ILC Articles on State Responsibility, UNGA 'Responsibility of States for Internationally Wrongful Acts' UN Doc A/RES/56/83 (12 December 2001), that to determine reparation, 'account shall be taken of the contribution to the injury by wilful or negligent action or omission of the injured state *or any person or entity in relation to whom reparation is sought*' (emphasis added). However, it is a standard of causation and thus originally did not serve to scrutinise the investor's behaviour towards the public interest, see Brigitte Bollecker-Stern, *Le préjudice dans la théorie de la responsabilité internationale* (Editions A. Pedone 1973) 316.

20 Similarly, the then existing bilateral treaties of friendship, navigation and commerce (FCN-treaties) between various states had a comprehensive scope. Hence, they could not alleviate the concern that questions of general politics could burden the protection of foreign investors, see Andreas L Paulus, 'Treaties of Friendship, Commerce and Navigation' in Anne Peters (ed), *Max Planck Encyclopedia of Public International Law* (March 2011) paras 7–16; John F Coyle, 'The Treaty of Friendship, Commerce, and Navigation in the Modern Era' (2013) 51(2) Columbia Journal of Transnational Law 302, 311–316; their highly political character is well-evidenced by two famous contentious proceedings of the ICJ on the use of force that build on FCN-treaties, namely *Case Concerning Military and Paramilitary Activities in and against Nicaragua (Nicaragua v United States of America)* (Jurisdiction of the Court and Admissibility of the Application) [1984] ICJ Rep 392, paras 77–83; *Case Concerning Oil Platforms (Islamic Republic of Iran v United States of America)* (Preliminary Objection) [1996] ICJ Rep 803, paras 17–54.

21 See Ibrahim F Shihata, 'Towards a Greater Depoliticization of Investment Disputes: The Roles of ICSID and MIGA' (1986) 1(1) ICSID Review 1, 1–12, 24–25.

22 See above Chapter 1.II.2 and for a further analysis on how this telos is changing Chapter 9.III.

Even the recent debate on the right to regulate did not bring about much awareness to the investor's misconduct. Rather at stake were the host state's actions and its remaining leeway to protect the public interest.

IX. A new doctrinal category in a developing field

Against this background, Part II must be understood as attempting to read a changing interpretation of investor rights in a new light. The concept of indirect obligations is not (yet) established in investment law. As will be shown, there is an ongoing process of reinterpreting investor rights so as to give regard to investor misconduct.

In contrast to this book, tribunals do not have to decide if a certain feature of an investor right qualifies as an indirect obligation – and forms part of an overarching development. They simply must solve the dispute at hand. The tribunals' decisions predominantly revolve around specific legal issues. Consequently, the subsequent Chapter that studies investment practice will encounter a field which is doctrinally underdeveloped in this regard. In the same vein, already in 2006, *Muchlinski* pointed out that the FET right

> [...] has been discussed primarily as a measure for determining the obligations of host countries towards investors and investments. In this process the role, if any, that the conduct of the investor may play in the evolution and application of the standard has not been examined in much detail.[23]

Nevertheless, the study will show that practice has already established indirect obligations in different ways – even though, as will be seen, tribunals and scholars have not defined them as such and rarely have pointed out that they establish a separate doctrinal category.

Yet, the analysis will also reveal that, at times, tribunals have shown a notable, new awareness of the investor's misconduct but without strictly and automatically depriving investors of protection in case of the breach of a certain standard of conduct. In these cases, investor misconduct is only one balancing criterion amongst other considerations. Consequently, one cannot, yet, understand them as bringing about an indirect obligation.

23 Peter Muchlinski, '"Caveat Investor"? The Relevance of the Conduct of the Investor Under the Fair and Equitable Treatment Standard' (2006) 55(3) International & Comparative Law Quarterly 527, 527–528.

The IISD has described such instances as an '[i]nterpretation approach: the fact of non-compliance will be taken into consideration when a tribunal interprets the treaty.'[24]

Nevertheless, they are worth being taken into account because they indicate indirect obligations in imperfect forms. They reflect a desire to make investor rights dependent on such proper conduct as a preliminary step to indirect obligations. Therefore, as Part II will prove, they contribute to the ongoing dynamics in investment law.

24 IISD (n 6) 18.

Chapter 7.
Indirect Obligations in Investment Law Practice

The concept of indirect obligations has been laid out in Chapter 6. Chapter 7 will now show that they already exist in many forms in investment law practice. To that end, it will analyse relevant IIAs, investment arbitration awards and scholarly writing.

As seen, 'indirect obligations' are not yet established as a term in investment law. Consequently, this Chapter will first focus on identifying arbitral jurisprudence and IIAs which examine investors' conduct in some way – instead of only concentrating on a potential wrongdoing by the host state. Then, it will assess if the manner in which tribunals and IIAs examined such conduct functionally amounts to an indirect obligation: the automatic deprival of protection. In doing so, it will distinguish such instances from cases in which investor misconduct only constitutes a balancing criterion – hence not giving rise to such a stringent sanction.

The analysis will follow three doctrinal categories. First, it will address jurisdiction and admissibility requirements in international investment arbitration. They bring about indirect obligations which foreclose access to arbitration in case of a breach (I.). Second, substantive investment law entails indirect obligations that deprive investors of an investor right (II.). Third, rules on compensation also imply indirect obligations. A violation thereof partly curtails a substantive investor right because the investor receives less compensation (III.). Lastly, the Chapter will separately address the role played by the clean hands doctrine. Despite the suggestion that the doctrine may function in a manner that would give rise to indirect obligations, it is submitted that the doctrine is, in fact, redundant (IV.).

I. Arbitration's jurisdiction and admissibility requirements

The analysis will begin by shedding light on indirect obligations related to the right to file an arbitration claim. Here, the sanction for non-compliance is that any claim by the investor is inadmissible or leads the tribunal to lack jurisdiction. Hence, investors forfeit the international right to an international adjudicatory procedure. They lose a right that the host state otherwise grants in the respective IIA's arbitration clause.

This section will identify three indirect obligations. There exists jurisprudence according to which tribunals only have jurisdiction under the ICSID Convention if the investment at stake contributes to the host state's development. This implies an indirect obligation with an indeterminate standard of conduct (1.). More elaborate indirect obligations are implied by the wide-spread jurisdiction requirements to comply with the host state's domestic law (2.) and with international law (3.).

1. Contribution to the host state's development

Building on the award in *Salini Costruttori S.P.A. and Italstrade S.P.A. v Morocco*, ICSID tribunals have developed the jurisdiction requirement that the investor must contribute to the host state's development (a). This requirement implies an indirect obligation (b). However, the content of the obligation itself, is relatively indeterminate. It vaguely requires the investor to positively affect the national economy and, as some tribunals have indicated, the host state's social and cultural environment (c). Overall, therefore, this jurisprudence constitutes an example of an indirect obligation which is yet to be further concretised.

a) The Salini jurisprudence

The requirement to contribute to the host state's development draws on Art 25 (1) ICSID Convention. The provision stipulates: 'The jurisdiction of the Centre shall extend to any legal dispute arising directly out of an investment [...]'.

States have the freedom to define which rules shall govern investment arbitration proceedings. Often, they determine in an IIA that the respective rules should follow those of the ICSID Convention. If the states choose to do so, the prepondering arbitral jurisprudence understands Art 25 (1) ICSID Convention as constituting an objective jurisdiction requirement – irrespective of and in addition to the IIA's other terms.[1] The ICSID award

1 The so-called objective or double-barrelled test, supported by *Consortium R.F.C.C. v Kingdom of Morocco*, ICSID Case No. ARB/00/6, Decision on Jurisdiction (16 July 2001) para 60; *Joy Mining Machinery Limited v Arab Republic of Egypt*, ICSID Case No. ARB/03/11, Award on Jurisdiction (6 August 2004) para 50; *Helnan International Hotels A/S v Arab Republic of Egypt*, ICSID Case No. ARB/05/19, Decision

in *Salini Costruttori S.P.A. and Italstrade S.P.A. v Morocco* for the first time understood this clause to require foreign investments to make a 'contribution to the economic development of the host State of the investment'.[2]

---

of the Tribunal on Objection to Jurisdiction (17 October 2006) para 77; *Víctor Pey Casado and President Allende Foundation v Republic of Chile*, ICSID Case No. ARB/98/2, Award (8 May 2008) para 232; *RSM Production Corporation v Grenada*, ICSID Case No. ARB/05/14, Award (13 March 2009) paras 235–238; *Bureau Veritas, Inspection, Valuation, Assessment and Control, BIVAC B.V. v The Republic of Paraguay*, ICSID Case No. ARB/07/9, Decision of the Tribunal on Objections to Jurisdiction (29 May 2009) para 78; *Malaysian Historical Salvors SDN, BHD v The Government of Malaysia*, ICSID Case No. ARB/05/10, Award on Jurisdiction (17 May 2007) paras 65–68; *Saba Fakes v Republic of Turkey*, ICSID Case No. ARB/07/20, Award (14 July 2010) para 108; *Global Trading Resource Corp. and Globex International, Inc. v Ukraine*, ICSID Case No. ARB/09/11, Award (1 December 2010) paras 44–45; see also *Ceskoslovenska Obchodni Banka, A.S. v The Slovak Republic*, ICSID Case No. ARB/97/4, Decision of the Tribunal on Objections to Jurisdiction (24 May 1999) para 68 and *Saba Fakes v Turkey* (n 1) para 108 which both *in abstracto* confirm the objective nature of Art 25 (1) ICSID Convention but consider the specific consent of the Parties to be an important element in interpreting the provision, thereby blurring a clear distinction between an objective and a subjective approach. From the literature in favour of the objective approach see Jan A Bischoff and Richard Happ, 'The Scope of Application of International Investment Agreements' in Marc Bungenberg and others (eds), *International Investment Law* (Nomos 2015) para 31; Christoph Schreuer, *The ICSID Convention: A Commentary* (2nd edn, Cambridge University Press 2009) paras 122–123. The contrary subjective approach argues that Art 25 (1) ICSID Convention does not bring about any restrictions other than those agreed upon by the Parties in the relevant IIA. This view is supported for example by *Fraport AG Frankfurt Airport Services Worldwide v The Republic of Philippines (Fraport I)*, ICSID Case No. ARB/03/25, Award (16 August 2007) para 305; *Biwater Gauff (Tanzania) Ltd v United Republic of Tanzania*, ICSID Case No. ARB/05/22, Award (24 July 2008) paras 312–318; *Pantechniki S.A. Contractors & Engineers (Greece) v Republic of Albania*, ICSID Case No. ARB/07/21, Award (30 July 2009) paras 41–47; *Malaysian Historical Salvors SDN BHD v The Government of Malaysia*, ICSID Case No. ARB/05/10, Decision on the Application for Annulment (16 April 2009) paras 62–74. In addition, some tribunals do not undertake a separate analysis of Art 25 (1) ICSID Convention and thus appear to follow the subjective approach, see for example *PSEG Global Inc. The North American Coal Corporation, and Konya Ilgin Elektrik Üretim ve Ticaret Limited Sirketi v Republic of Turkey*, ICSID Case No. ARB/02/5, Decision on Jurisdiction (4 June 2004) paras 79–105, however, see *MHS v Malaysia*, Award on Jurisdiction (n 1) paras 119–122 arguing that in *PSEG v Turkey* the *Salini*-test was so clearly fulfilled that a separate analysis was not warranted.

2 *Salini Costruttori S.P.A. and Italstrade S.P.A. v Kingdom of Morocco*, ICSID Case No. ARB/00/4, Decision on Jurisdiction (23 July 2001) para 52; in the same direction already *Ceskoslovenska v The Slovak Republic*, Decision of the Tribunal on Objections to Jurisdiction (n 1) para 64 in 1999.

The main argument is a teleological one: States had created ICSID to foster development by attracting foreign investment, willing to grant protection only if investors actually contributed to that end. This argument is supported by the ICSID Convention's preamble. In its first paragraph it explicitly highlights the 'need for international cooperation for economic development, and the role of private international investment therein'.[3] Other tribunals have followed the same approach[4] although it remains controversial.[5]

---

3 Similarly, the Report of the Executive Directors of the IBRD on ICSID reveals that the Convention's object and purpose is to 'strengthen the partnership between countries in the cause of economic development', see IBRD 'Report of the Executive Directors on the Convention of the Settlement of Investment Disputes Between States and Nationals of Other States' ICSID/15/Rev.1, 35–49 (18 March 1965) para 9.

4 *Mr. Patrick Mitchell v Democratic Republic of the Congo*, ICSID Case No. ARB/99/7, Decision on the Stay of Enforcement of the Award (9 February 2004) paras 28–31; *Jan de Nul N.V. and Dreging International N.V. v Arab Republic of Egypt*, ICSID Case No. ARB/04/13, Decision on Jurisdiction (16 June 2006) para 91; *Saipem S.p.A. v The People's Republic of Bangladesh*, ICSID Case No. ARB/05/07, Decision on Jurisdiction and Recommendation on Provisional Measures (21 March 2007) para 99; *Ioannis Kardassopoulos v The Republic of Georgia*, ICSID Case No. ARB/05/18, Decision on Jurisdiction (6 July 2007) para 116; *Helnan International Hotels v Egypt* (n 1) para 77; *Malaysian Historical Salvors SDN BHD v The Government of Malaysia*, ICSID Case No. ARB/05/10, Dissenting Opinion of Judge Mohamed Shahabuddeen (19 February 2009) paras 17–18; *Millicom International Operations B.V. and Sentel GSM S.A. v The Republic of Senegal*, ICSID Case No. ARB/08/20, Decision on Jurisdiction of the Arbitral Tribunal (16 July 2010) para 80, finding all four criteria to be fulfilled without commenting on the relevance of each of them; sceptical on the future relevance are Antonio Parra, 'The Convention and Centre for Settlement of Investment Disputes' (2014) 374 Recueil des Cours 313, 342; Emmanuel Gaillard and Yas Banifatemi, 'The Long March Towards a Jurisprudence Constante on the Notion of Investment: Salini v. Morocco, ICSID Case No. ARB/00/4' in Mairée Uran Bidegain and others (eds), *Building International Investment Law: The First 50 Years of ICSID* (ICSID, Wolters Kluwer 2016) 119.

5 Other tribunals have rejected the criterion, for example because it was impossible to ascertain that a contribution to the host state's development was a consequence, not a requirement of investment, see *Saba Fakes v Turkey* (n 1) para 111; *Alpha Projektholding GmbH v Ukraine*, ICSID Case No. ARB/07/16, Award (8 November 2010) para 312; *Quiborax S.A., Non Metallic Minerals S.A. and Allan Fosk Kaplún v Plurinational State of Bolivia*, ICSID Case No. ARB/06/2, Decision on Jurisdiction (27 September 2012) para 220; *Electrabel S.A. v Republic of Hungary*, ICSID Case No. ARB/07/19, Decision on Jurisdiction, Applicable Law and Liability (30 November 2012) para 5.43; *KT Asia Investment Group B.V. v Republic of Kazakhstan*, ICSID Case No. ARB/09/8, Award (17 October 2013) para 171.

b) Contribution to development as an indirect obligation

The requirement to contribute to the host state's development implies an indirect obligation as defined in Chapter 6. It entails the behavioural expectation that investors must contribute to the host state's development. If they do not act accordingly, they suffer the sanction of being precluded from filing an ICSID arbitration claim. They lose their procedural protection against any adverse host state action.

It is also an indirect obligation that relates to the public interest because it considers how the investment benefits society. For example, in the *Salini* award, the claimants constructed a part of a highway between the Moroccan cities Rabat and Fès. The Tribunal affirmed the contribution to Morocco's development because the construction of infrastructure was a public task. To build a highway served the public. Besides, the transfer of construction expertise to Morocco was also beneficial.[6]

This shows that the requirement tests the foreign investment's role and value for society. In turn, investors must make sure that they contribute to the host state's development to safeguard their right to file an ICSID claim. Incidentally, this may serve the public interest as investors might behave more public interest-friendly for their own sake.

Furthermore, the criterion also operates on the level of international law. The right to file an ICSID claim against the host state follows from the IIA's arbitration clause. Thus, the *Salini* requirement potentially holds a negative consequence with regard to an international right. What is more, the standard of 'contribution to development' itself is international in character. It follows from Art 25 (1) ICSID Convention, an international treaty.

c) Vague content of the obligation

However, the content of this indirect obligation is relatively indeterminate. As seen, the Tribunal in the *Salini* award only laid out why the investment at hand contributed to Morocco's development. It did not

6 *Salini v Morocco* (n 2) para 57; but see the critical remark that the award actually showed a very limited effective transfer of know-how by Farouk Yala, 'The Notion of "Investment" in ICSID Case Law: A Drifting Jurisdictional Requirement? Some "Un-Conventional" Thoughts on Salini, SGS and Mihaly' (2005) 22(2) Journal of International Arbitration 105, 111.

develop an abstract test to assess the investment – in other words, what conduct exactly is to be expected from the investor to meet the jurisdiction threshold. Other awards following *Salini* also remained ambiguous in this regard. Some added that the contribution must be 'significant'[7] – apparently setting a form of minimum threshold.

Yet, one can discern lines of cases that, at least to some extent, outline a material scope of expected conduct: some hold that investors must have a general positive impact on the host state's national economy (1), while others also indicate that other forms of the public interest might be relevant as well (2).

(1) The economy as a public good

The *Salini* award already explicitly required a 'contribution to the *economic* development'.[8] Similarly, the Tribunal in *GEA v Ukraine* confirmed that the claimant contributed to Ukraine's development

> [...] in the form of over one million metric tons of diesel and naphtha, catalysts and other materials, delivered to Ukraine as part of a broad economic operation, as well as the contribution of the Claimant's know-how on logistics, marketing, and the mobilisation of repairs and services.[9]

In the same vein, the Tribunal in *Toto Costruzioni Generali SpA v Lebanon* considered that the construction of a part of a highway between Beirut and Damascus advanced 'Lebanon's position as a transit country for goods from and to Middle East countries'[10] and thus contributed to Lebanon's economy.

The Tribunal in *Malaysian Historical Salvors v Malaysia* took a rather strict approach and construed the requirement to be met only in case of the investment having an impact on the economy and to be rejected when the economy is not affected. The claimant performed marine salvage services to Malaysia for a ship sunken off Malaysia's coast to enable Malaysia

7 See for example *Joy Mining Machinery v Egypt* (n 1) para 53; *MHS v Malaysia*, Award on Jurisdiction (n 1) para 138.

8 *Salini v Morocco* (n 2) para 52 (emphasis added).

9 *GEA Group Aktiengesellschaft v Ukraine*, ICSID Case No. ARB/08/16, Award (31 March 2011) para 52.

10 *Toto Costruzioni Generali S.P.A. v Republic of Lebanon*, ICSID Case No. ARB/07/12, Decision on Jurisdiction (11 September 2009) para 86 lit d).

to recover Chinese porcelain. The Tribunal rejected its jurisdiction. It argued that the benefits of the claimant's activities were merely cultural and historical in nature, lacking any economic impact.[11]

All these awards indicate that the investor's conduct must, in some way, be beneficial to the host state's economy. This line of argument conforms with the concept of an indirect obligation: A strong national economy constitutes a public good. Thus, the requirement expresses that foreign investments should not only serve the investor's financial interests but rather, they should overall strengthen national economy to the benefit of everyone. However, in the cases mentioned above, the Tribunals appear to have applied a rather broad test. Apparently, it suffices that the investment *in general* – as identifiable from the investment strategy – brings about economic advantages to the community.

(2) Other forms of the public interest

Furthermore, there are indications that the investor also should contribute to other forms of the public interest to establish ICSID jurisdiction.

Schreuer finds it possible to integrate considerations of 'development of human potential, political and social development and the protection of the local and the global environment.'[12] Similarly, others propose to read the concept of sustainable development into the notion of 'development'.[13]

---

11 *MHS v Malaysia*, Award on Jurisdiction (n 1) paras 113, 138. Later, the Ad-Hoc Committee in *MHS v Malaysia*, Decision on the Application for Annulment (n 1) paras 77–81 annulled the award, rejecting the requirement of contribution to the host state's development altogether.

12 Schreuer, *ICSID* (n 1) Art 25 para 74. Such an interpretation is also supported by Martin Endicott, 'The Definition of Investment in ICSID Arbitration: Development Lessons for the WTO?' in Marie-Claire Cordonier Segger and Markus W Gehring (eds), *Sustainable Development in World Trade Law* (Kluwer Law International 2005) 390–391; Marek Jeżweski, 'Development Considerations in Defining Investment' in Marie-Claire Cordonier Segger, Markus W Gehring and Andrew P Newcombe (eds), *Sustainable Development in World Investment Law* (Kluwer Law International 2011) 216; for a contrary view see Sven L E Johannsen, *Der Investitionsbegriff nach Art. 25 Abs. 1 der ICSID-Konvention* (Martin-Luther-Universität Halle-Wittenberg Institut für Wirtschaftsrecht 2009) 21–22.

13 Supported for example by Diane A Desierto, 'Development as an International Right: Investment in the New Trade-Based IIAs' (2011) 3(2) Trade, Law and Development 296, 298; Diane A Desierto, 'Deciding International Investment

In this direction, the Tribunal in *RSM Production Corporation v Grenada* required 'a contribution to the economic and *social* development of the host state'.[14] This indicates that the investment must do more than benefit the respective national economy. For example, one could imagine that strengthening employment could qualify as a social contribution. However, when the Tribunal applied its definition to the facts of the case, it emphasised the economic impact without elaborating on the social dimension. It held that the oil exploration at stake 'was in Grenada's public interest to ascertain whether the country had commercially viable resources in offshore petroleum.'[15]

In *Víctor Pey Casado and President Allene Foundation v Republic of Chile*, the Tribunal considered other forms of the public interest more explicitly. The claimant was the publisher and owner of the newspaper 'El Clarín'. After Pinochet came into power, the government confiscated the newspaper.[16] The Tribunal affirmed that the investment contributed without doubt to Chile's economic, social and cultural progression ('[...] contribuyó sin duda alguna al progreso económico, social y cultural del país'[17]). This decision vaguely expressed that it was relevant, in the Tribunal's view, how the investor's conduct affected social and cultural conditions in Chile. It remained unclear if this contribution was an alternative requirement in relation to a support of the national economy – or if ICSID

Agreement Applicability: The Development Argument in Investment' in Freya Baetens (ed), *Investment Law Within International Law: Integrationist Perspectives* (Cambridge University Press 2013) 253; Jeżweski (n 12) 235; for a sceptical perspective see Stephan W Schill, 'Investitionsschutzrecht als Entwicklungsvölkerrecht' (2012) 72(2) Zeitschrift für ausländisches öffentliches Recht und Völkerrecht 261, 287 who argues that the host state has sufficient means to exclude unwanted investments through its domestic law; Julian Scheu, *Systematische Berücksichtigung von Menschenrechten in Investitionsschiedsverfahren* (Nomos 2017) 303 who considers that qualitative elements of an investment such as duration and risk lead to a presumption that the investment is favourable for the host state's development. Generally on the concept of sustainable development see only UNGA 'Rio Declaration on Environment and Development' UN Doc A/CONF.151/26 (Vol. I) (12 August 1992); Ulrich Beyerlin, 'Sustainable Development' in Anne Peters (ed), *Max Planck Encyclopedia of Public International Law* (October 2013) para 11.

14 *RSM v Grenada* (n 1) para 240 (emphasis added).

15 ibid 245 (emphasis added).

16 *Víctor Pey Casado and President Allende Foundation v Chile* (n 1) paras 56–80.

17 ibid 234. This finding is notable even though the Tribunal rejected the *Salini* requirement and considered it to be fulfilled only as a subsidiary argument.

tribunals only had jurisdiction if investors in some form also promoted the host state's society and culture.

2. Compliance with host state's domestic law before admission

A more concrete indirect obligation follows from the jurisdiction requirement that investors must comply with the host state's domestic law.

The requirement is established in arbitral jurisprudence even without explicit basis in the applicable IIA (a). It implies an indirect obligation. If investors do not comply, they lose the right to file an investment arbitration claim (b). This indirect obligation's content can potentially relate to the protection of all forms of the public interest – depending on the purpose of the respective domestic provision. Yet, investment law doctrine modifies the underlying domestic norm by adding certain qualifications (c).

a) Compliance as a jurisdiction requirement

There are explicit and implicit bases for the requirement of compliance with domestic law – sometimes also coined the 'legality requirement'. Many IIAs contain a clause which define that only investments which comply with the host state's domestic law receive protection.[18] This type of clause determines not only the substantive scope of investor rights but also serves as a basis for tribunals to accept or reject jurisdiction for arbitral claims. Even without an explicit clause, the majority of tribunals interpret IIAs as implying such a requirement. The main argument is a teleological interpretation of IIAs: States would not intend to provide investment protection for investments which contravene their domestic law.[19]

---

18 For other clauses that require compliance with host state law see for example on market access Rudolf Dolzer and Christoph Schreuer, *Principles of International Investment Law* (2nd edn, Oxford University Press 2012) 88–90.

19 See *Salini v Morocco* (n 2) para 46; see also *Plama Consortium Limited v Republic of Bulgaria*, ICSID Case No. ARB/03/24, Award (27 August 2008) paras 138–139; *SAUR International S.A. v Republic of Argentina*, ICSID Case No. ARB/04/4, Decision on Jurisdiction and Liability (6 June 2012) para 308; *Mamidoil Jetoil Greek Petroleum Products Societe S.A. v Republic of Albania*, ICSID Case No. ARB/11/24, Award (30 March 2015) paras 293, 359–360. There is also a historical argument based on the *travaux préparatoires*, see *Inceysa Vallisoletana, S.L. v Republic of El*

In applying the legality requirement, most tribunals make a temporal distinction. Only compliance until the investment is admitted to and established in the host state is a question of jurisdiction.[20] In contrast, non-compliance after admission is a matter for the merits.[21] Only few tribunals have rejected such a temporal differentiation.[22] Consequently, this Section will only address legality at the time of admission.

Salvador, ICSID Case No. ARB/03/26, Award (2 August 2006) paras 192–195 and the consideration that the legality requirement follows from the need for objective protection of the international investment protection system or is even a general principle of law, see *Gustav FW Hamester GmbH & Co KG v Republic of Ghana*, ICSID Case No. ARB/07/24, Award (18 June 2010) paras 123–124; furthermore, it was considered to follow from Art 25 (1) ICSID Convention by *Phoenix Action, Ltd. v The Czech Republic*, ICSID Case No. ARB/06/5, Award (15 April 2009) para 113; for a contrary result that rejects a requirement of legality because the applicable IIA's wording indicated that there had to be an express basis for such a requirement which was absent in the treaty at hand see *Bear Creek Mining Corporation v Republic of Perú*, ICSID Case No. ARB/14/21, Award (30 November 2017) paras 319–322, 335. The Tribunal in *Blusun S.A, Jean-Pierre Lecorcier and Michael Stein v Italian Republic*, ICSID Case No. ARB/14/3, Award (27 December 2016) para 264 deduced the legality requirement from the principle of international public order – a position which does seem to conflate the levels of domestic and international law.

20 *Fraport v Philippines (Fraport I)*, Award (n 1) paras 334–340, 401; *Inceysa v El Salvador* (n 19) paras 142–145; *Saba Fakes v Turkey* (n 1) paras 112–114; Stephan W Schill, 'Illegal Investments in Investment Treaty Arbitration' (2012) 11(2) The Law & Practice of International Courts and Tribunals 281, 307–308; Nathalie Bernasconi-Osterwalder, 'Inclusion of Investor Obligations and Corporate Accountability Provisions in Investment Agreements' in Julien Chaisse, Leïla Choukroune and Sufian Jusoh (eds), *Handbook of International Investment Law and Policy* (Springer 2021) 473; see also the overview by Katharina Diel-Gligor and Rudolf Hennecke, 'Investment in Accordance with the Law' in Marc Bungenberg and others (eds), *International Investment Law* (Nomos 2015) paras 11–15.

21 It belongs to the requirements of investor rights according to *Hamester v Ghana* (n 19) para 129 or to the quantum phase as found by *Yukos Universal Limited (Isle of Man) v The Russian Federation*, PCA Case No. AA 227, Final Award (18 July 2014) paras 1354–1355; for a criticism see for example Patrick Dumberry, 'State of Confusion: The Doctrine of "Clean Hands" in Investment Arbitration After the Yukos Award' (2016) 17(2) Journal of World Investment & Trade 229, 242–245.

22 For example *Vladimir Berschader and Moïse Berschader v The Russian Federation*, SCC Case No 080/2004, Award (21 April 2006) para 111 which regarded compliance with domestic law at the time of the investment's admission as a question of the merits of the case; *Mamidoil v Albania* (n 19) paras 289–290 which dealt with domestic law compliance both on the stage of jurisdiction and on the merits. For an analysis of this question see Ursula Kriebaum, 'Investment Arbitration –

b) Compliance as an established indirect obligation

The legality requirement constitutes an indirect obligation. Domestic rules serve as the implied standard of conduct. If investors violate a domestic rule before the investment is admitted to the host state, the tribunal will reject its jurisdiction, depriving the investors of their right to file an arbitral claim. Many domestic rules set public interest standards. By referring to these norms, the legality requirement incites public interest-friendly behaviour: Investors will avoid violating any such rules – and thus harming the public interest – in order to qualify for investment arbitration. Similarly, UNCTAD understands the legality requirement as a policy option to bring about investor obligations and responsibilities as a way to '[e]stablish sanctions' in order to 'promote compliance by investors with domestic [...] norms'.[23]

For example, in *Fraport v Philippines (Fraport I)*, the respondent argued that the investor had circumvented domestic law at the investment's admission. It contended that the investor did not fulfil the constitutional requirement under which foreign investors may only hold up to 40 percent of shares of a Philippian company. To undermine this rule, the investor had concluded covert strawmen agreements in violation of a Philippian Anti Dummy Law.[24] The Tribunal affirmed that '[r]espect for the integrity of the law of the host state is also a critical part of development and a concern of international investment law'.[25] It dismissed a violation only

---

Illegal Investments' in Christian Klausegger and others (eds), *Austrian Yearbook on International Arbitration* (Stämpfli Verlag 2010) 330–334; Schill, 'Illegal' (n 20) 288–291.

23 UNCTAD 'Investment Policy Framework for Sustainable Development' UNCTAD/DIAE/PCB/2015/5 (2015), 109; see also Barnali Choudhury, 'Investor Obligations for Human Rights' (2020) 35(1–2) ICSID Review 82, 96–97 who considers this jurisdictional requirement an entry point for human rights obligations of investors.

24 *Fraport v Philippines (Fraport I)*, Award (n 1) paras 281–287; Schill, 'Illegal' (n 20) 287.

25 *Fraport v Philippines (Fraport I)*, Award (n 1) para 402. The award was later annulled because of a serious departure from a fundamental rule of procedure pursuant to Art 52 (1) (d) ICSID Convention because the claimant was not given sufficient opportunity to be heard in the proceedings. Yet, the Ad-hoc Committee did not find an annulment ground in the way the Tribunal had dealt with the criterion of compliance with domestic law, see *Fraport AG Frankfurt Airport Services Worldwide v Republic of Philippines*, ICSID Case No. ARB/03/25, Decision on the Application for Annulment of Fraport AG Frankfurt Airport Services

because any such adverse conduct by the investor could not be proven. This shows that the Tribunal understood the Anti Dummy obligation as a means to protect the Philippian rule of law. Investors should abide by the rule that imposes a maximum of shares held. Strawmen agreements attempt to circumvent this rule through non-transparent legal constructions and thus stand in conflict with the rule of law. Therefore, foreclosing a non-compliant investor from investment arbitration qualifies as a sanction for misconduct towards the rule of law – which forms a public good and part of the public interest. The Tribunal was aware of this public interest dimension as it highlighted the concern for the 'integrity' of Philippian law. Other tribunals and scholars have also affirmed the purpose to protect the public interest regarding the obligation to comply with domestic law.[26]

Interestingly, tribunals and scholars are particularly aware of this requirement's sanctioning character when it comes to domestic anti-corruption obligations. It is highly controversial if jurisdiction should be foreclosed if the host state was complicit in the corruption. There is a strong view that investors should not be able to resort to an arbitral tribunal in this case either. Proponents argue that they should suffer the negative consequence for their misconduct.[27] They hope that investors will pre-emp-

Worldwide (23 December 2010) paras 112, 244–245; Schill, 'Illegal' (n 20) 298–299 and fn 56.

26 *Plama v Bulgaria*, Award (n 19) paras 139, 143; *Fraport v Philippines (Fraport I)*, Award (n 1) para 402; *Alasdair Ross Anderson et al v Republic of Costa Rica*, ICSID Case No. ARB(AF)/07/3, Award (19 May 2010) para 53; Jarrod Hepburn, *Domestic Law in International Investment Arbitration* (Oxford University Press 2017) 157.

27 In favour of such an approach are for example *Fraport v Philippines (Fraport I)*, Award (n 1) para 346; *Railroad Development Corporation (RDC) v Republic of Guatemala*, ICSID Case No. ARB/07/23, Second Decision on Objections to Jurisdiction (18 May 2010) para 146; Hepburn (n 26) 157–158; see also Christina Knahr, 'Investments "In Accordance with Host State Law"' (2007) 4(5) Transnational Dispute Management 1, 16–17 who, however, does not connect this requirement with the furthering of the host state's rule of law. Notwithstanding, most tribunals held that the state's complicity exculpates the investor's breach and reopens access to investment arbitration, see *Swembalt AB, Sweden v The Republic of Latvia*, Decision (UNCITRAL, 23 October 2000) paras 33–34; *Tecnicas Medioambientales Tecmed S.A. v The United Mexican States*, ICSID Case No. ARB (AF)/00/2, Award (29 May 2003) para 149; *Tokios Tokelės v Ukraine*, ICSID Case No. ARB/02/18, Decision on Jurisdiction (29 April 2004) para 86; *ADC Affiliate Limited and ADC & ADMC Management Limited v The Republic of Hungary*, ICSID Case No. ARB/03/16, Award (2 October 2006) paras 456, 474; *Ioannis Kardassopoulos v Georgia* (n 4) paras 190–194; *Fraport v Philippines (Fraport I)*,

tively abstain from corruption, deterred by this eventual consequence on their investment protection. This effect of imposing a sanction precisely reflects the character of an indirect obligation.

This indirect obligation is of an international legal character for two reasons. First, the legality requirement follows from an interpretation of the IIA and its arbitration clause – hence, from an international treaty. And second, its violation has an effect on the international procedural right to file an investment arbitration claim.

Considering domestic and international law, the respective domestic obligation operates in two different manners. It, of course, remains an enforceable, directly applicable rule in the domestic legal system. In the above-mentioned example, the Philippines can enforce the respective Anti Dummy Law through domestic institutions and processes against the investor. At the same time, the obligation forms part of the jurisdiction requirements of investment arbitration – hence, appears on the level of international law in this regard. As a matter of international investment arbitration, investors are free to choose whether to comply but if they do not comply, they suffer the consequence of losing access to investment arbitration. Therefore, the legality requirement is an example of the dual character of the same rule as a (domestic) direct and an (international) indirect obligation as pointed out in Chapter 6.VI.

Award (n 1) para 346; *Desert Line Projects LLC v The Republic of Yemen*, ICSID Case No. ARB/05/17, Award (6 February 2008) para 120; *Inmaris Perestroika Sailing Maritime Services GmbH and Others v Ukraine*, ICSID Case No. ARB/08/8, Decision on Jurisdiction (8 March 2010) para 140; *RDC v Guatemala* (n 27) paras 139–147; *Alpha Projektholding v Ukraine* (n 5) para 302; *Quiborax v Bolivia*, Decision on Jurisdiction (n 5) para 257; Kriebaum, 'Investment' (n 22) 325–329; Schill, 'Illegal' (n 20) 303. Generally on corruption and investment law see the overview by Ralph A Lorz and Manuel Busch, 'Investment in Accordance with the Law – Specifically Corruption' in Marc Bungenberg and others (eds), *International Investment Law* (Nomos 2015) para 26; for in-depth analyses on the consequences of corruption see for example Andrea J Menaker, 'The Determinative Impact of Fraud and Corruption on Investment Arbitrations' (2010) 25(1) ICSID Review 67, 75; Stephan Wilske, 'Sanctions for Unethical and Illegal Behavior in International Arbitration: A Double-Edged Sword?' (2010) 3 Contemporary Asia Arbitration Journal 211, 220; Tamar Meshel, 'Use and Misuse of the Corruption Defence in International Investment Arbitration' (2013) 30(3) Journal of International Arbitration 267, 272–274, 279–281; Yarik Kryvoi, 'Economic Crimes in International Investment Law' (2018) 67(3) International & Comparative Law Quarterly 577.

c) Content of the obligation

Indirect obligations implied by the legality requirement have a well-defined content. Domestic rules spell out the expected behaviour for establishing jurisdiction. Tribunals and investors can resort to domestic jurisprudence to concretise the meaning of domestic law. So far, most tribunals and scholars concentrated on cases of fraud, corruption and misrepresentation by the investor.[28] However, in principle, it is possible that the indirect obligation can cover domestic obligations which protect very different facets of the public interest: for example, domestic human rights, labour standard or environmental obligations.[29] In the same vein,

---

28 See the detailed study on corruption as a defence against investment claims by Alexander Bothe, *Die 'Corruption Defence' des Gaststaats in internationalen Investitionsschiedsverfahren* (Nomos 2021); see also Martin Jarrett, Sergio Puig and Steven R Ratner, 'Towards Greater Investor Accountability: Indirect Actions, Direct Actions by States and Direct Actions by Individuals' (2021) Journal of International Dispute Settlement 1, 6, advance article version ‹https://doi.org/10.1093/jnlids/idab035› accessed 7 December 2021.

29 See Christoph Schreuer and Ursula Kriebaum, 'From Individual to Community Interest in International Investment Law' in Ulrich Fastenrath and others (eds), *From Bilateralism to Community Interest: Essays in Honour of Judge Bruno Simma* (Oxford University Press 2011) 1095 who argue that applying host state law allows tribunals to take account of environmental concerns and human rights; Patrick Dumberry and Gabrielle Dumas-Aubin, 'When and How Allegations of Human Rights Violations Can Be Raised in Investor-State Arbitration' (2012) 13 Journal of World Investment & Trade 349, 365 advocating that tribunals should consider breaches against domestic human rights as a matter of admissibility; Christian Tietje, *Individualrechte im Menschenrechts- und Investitionsschutzbereich – Kohärenz von Staaten- und Unternehmensverantwortung?* (Martin-Luther-Universität Halle-Wittenberg 2012) 19 who claims that tribunals must consider corporate human rights breaches in the tradition of the jurisprudence on the abuse of investor rights; Diane A Desierto, 'Conflict of Treaties, Interpretation, and Decision-Making on Human Rights and Investment During Economic Crises' (2013) 10(1) Transnational Dispute Management 1, 80–81 who argues that through the host state's law, an ICESCR-sensitive interpretation of IIAs could be possible; Dominik Kneer, *Investitionsschutz und Menschenrechte: Eine Untersuchung zum Einfluss menschenrechtlicher Standards auf die Investitionssicherung* (Nomos 2013) 146–147 who considers that breaches of domestic human rights could make investment claims inadmissible; specifically on environmental protection see Jorge E Viñuales, *Foreign Investment and the Environment in International Law* (Cambridge University Press 2012) 96–100 who considers arbitral case-law on domestic environmental law as a possible preliminary objection against investment claims; Jeff Sullivan and Valeriya Kirsey, 'Environmental Policies: A Shield or a Sword in Investment Arbitration?' (2017) 18(1) Journal of World Investment & Trade 100,

Cremades suggested in his Dissenting Opinion in *Fraport v Philippines (Fraport I)* that ownership prohibitions under domestic environmental law could constitute relevant domestic obligations.[30] Due to this potential, UNCTAD understands the legality requirement as an approach for a more sustainable investment law.[31]

Notwithstanding, any reference to domestic law must be subject to some limits. Investment law cannot blindly adopt domestic law as the relevant standard. Otherwise, it would be in the host state's hands alone to decide on the investor's access to arbitration – circumventing the customary principle that a state cannot invoke its national law to justify breaches of international law.[32] This is reflected in arbitral jurisprudence. Tribunals add certain qualifications to the requirement to comply with domestic law. For example, tribunals have limited the requirement to rules which specifically regulate the admission of foreign investment.[33] Others have required a certain minimum intensity regarding the violation.[34] Again, a

---

118–129 on the requirements for breaches of domestic environmental law to lead to an inadmissibility of investment claims.

30 *Fraport AG Frankfurt Airport Services Worldwide v The Republic of Philippines (Fraport I)*, ICSID Case No. ARB/03/25, Dissenting Opinion of Mr Bernardo Cremades (16 August 2007) paras 10–12.

31 UNCTAD 'IPFSD' (n 23) 109.

32 Enshrined in Art 27 VCLT and Art 32 of the ILC Articles on the Responsibility of States for Internationally Wrongful Acts; also supported by Jarrett, Puig and Ratner (n 28) 9; see in detail Hepburn (n 26) 15, 193–197.

33 For example, this view excluded regulation on the telecommunication sector and competition law from the scope of the legality requirement because it did not exclusively regulate the admission of foreign investors but more generally the economy, see *Saba Fakes v Turkey* (n 1) paras 119–120; on this view see further *Inceysa v El Salvador* (n 19) paras 249–257; *Fraport v Philippines (Fraport I)*, Dissenting Opinion of Mr Bernardo Cremades (n 30) para 12; Hepburn (n 26) 148; *Álvarez y Marín Corporación S.A. and Others v República de Panamá*, ICSID Case No. ARB/15/14, Laudo (12 October 2018) para 149. However, the majority of tribunals consider all types of obligations covered, see for example *Fraport v Philippines (Fraport I)*, Award (n 1) paras 339–343, 401–403; *Plama v Bulgaria*, Award (n 19) paras 133–135; *Anderson v Costa Rica* (n 26) paras 51–59; *Hamester v Ghana* (n 19) paras 129–135; Cameron A Miles, 'Corruption, Jurisdiction and Admissibility in International Investment Claims' (2012) 3(2) Journal of International Dispute Settlement 329, 346–347; Hepburn (n 26) 148–151.

34 For the exclusion of *de minimis*-violations see *Tokios Tokelės v Ukraine* (n 27) para 85; *Alpha Projektholding v Ukraine* (n 5) para 297; see further Schill, 'Illegal' (n 20) 293; for a requirement that the investor must have violated a fundamental domestic legal principle see *Consorzio Groupement L.E.S.I.-DIPENTA v People's Democratic Republic of Algeria*, ICSID Case No. ARB/03/08, Award (10 January

number of tribunals have excluded violations in good faith or without negligence.[35] What is more, if investors contend that the domestic obligation in question violates an investor right, the tribunal must deal with the alleged violation at the merits stage. Only then it can inquire if the state itself has violated the IIA through said domestic obligation.[36]

For example, the investor could claim that the admission requirement to obtain an environmental permit violates the right to FET. In this case, tribunals cannot reject jurisdiction on the grounds that the investor did not comply with this domestic admission requirement. Otherwise, the host state could arbitrarily shield itself against a potentially legitimate claim. Instead, the tribunal has to decide on the permit requirement at the merits stage.

These reservations show that the indirect obligation to comply with domestic law sets an autonomous standard in international law. It modifies the domestic obligation on which it builds. These modifications embody a rudimentary balancing between the investors' interests and the public interest pursued by the domestic rule.[37]

The recent ICSID award in *Cortec v Kenya* confirms how the legality requirement connects to the protection of the public interest and sets an autonomous international standard building on domestic law. The claimants were engaged in a mining project at Mrima Hill in Kenya which

---

2005) para II.24 (iii); *L.E.S.I. S.p.A. and ASTALDI S.p.A. v People's Democratic Republic of Algeria*, ICSID Case No. ARB/05/3, Decision (12 July 2006) para 83 (iii); *Desert Line Projects v Yemen* (n 27) para 104; *Rumeli Telekom A.S. and Telsim Mobil Telekomikasyon Hizmetleri A.S. v Republic of Kazakhstan*, ICSID Case No. ARB/05/16, Award (29 July 2008) para 319; for a requirement that the violated norm must be relevant in the domestic legal system and that the breach was intentional, see *Álvarez y Marín Corporación v Panamá* (n 33) paras 151–154.

35 For the exclusion of good faith violations see *Fraport v Philippines (Fraport I)*, Award (n 1) paras 396–398, 401, 403; similarly *Desert Line Projects v Yemen* (n 27) paras 116–117; see further Kriebaum, 'Investment' (n 22) 307, 324; for a contrary approach see *Anderson v Costa Rica* (n 26) para 52 where the Tribunal declared the investor's knowledge or intentions irrelevant for the question of compliance with host state law. For the requirement of actions against due diligence see *Anderson v Costa Rica* (n 26) paras 52, 58.

36 *Mr. Franck Charles Arif v Republic of Moldova*, ICSID Case No. ARB/11/23, Award (8 April 2013) paras 375–376; *Yukos v Russia*, Final Award (n 21) para 1355.

37 Similarly Stephanie B Leinhardt, 'Some Thoughts on Foreign Investors' Responsibilities to Respect Human Rights' (2013) 10(1) Transnational Dispute Management 1, 19–20; Diane A Desierto, *Public Policy in International Economic Law: The ICESCR in Trade, Finance, and Investment* (Oxford University Press 2015) 324–325.

the government had given special protected status as a forest reserve, nature reserve and national monument.[38] The Tribunal denied jurisdiction because the claimants had not complied with regulation on the forest and nature reserve and had failed to obtain an environmental impact assessment license before establishing the investment.[39] To reach this verdict, the Tribunal did not simply apply Kenyan law. Rather, building on the ICSID award in *Kim v Uzbekistan*[40] the tribunal made the denying of investment protection dependent on whether this was a 'proportional response' to breaching a domestic law resulting 'in a compromise of a correspondingly significant interest of the Host State'.[41] Importantly for the present context, the proportionality test consists of three steps. The second requires the Tribunal to 'assess the seriousness of the investor's conduct', including the investor's intent, exercise of due diligence and subsequent conduct.[42]

Applying this test, the Tribunal in *Cortec v Kenya* considered that it was 'difficult to overstate the importance of environmental protection in areas, such as Mrima Hill, of special vulnerability'. The Kenyan environmental regulations were 'of fundamental importance in an environmentally vulnerable area faced with a project to remove and at least partially process 130 million tonnes of Mrima Hill.'[43] It held that the claimants had 'showed serious disrespect for the fundamental public policies of the host country in relation to the environment and resource development.'[44] This shows that the Tribunal *autonomously* evaluated the domestic environmental rules and measured the investors' mining activities against the importance of environmental protection, applying a (rather vague) international proportionality test. It is important to point out that the referenced award of *Kim v Uzbekistan* dealt with alleged corruption by the investors, a category much better established in investment jurisprudence[45] – transferred

38 *Cortec Mining Kenya Limited, Cortec (PTY) Limited and Stirling Capital Limited v Republic of Kenya*, ICSID Case No. ARB/15/29, Award (22 October 2018) paras 1, 5.

39 ibid 365.

40 *Vladislav Kim and Others v Republic of Uzbekistan*, ICSID Case No. ARB/13/6, Decision on Jurisdiction (8 March 2017) paras 404–409.

41 ibid 413; *Cortec Mining v Kenya* (n 38) para 315.

42 *Kim v Uzbekistan* (n 40) para 407.

43 *Cortec Mining v Kenya* (n 38) paras 345–346.

44 ibid 349.

45 cf Choudhury, 'Investor' (n 23) 96–99 on the distinction between jurisdiction, requiring compliance with domestic law, and admissibility which may be rejected if the claim itself is defective in case of corruption or fraud.

in *Cortec v Kenya* to environmental issues. It appears possible to generalise this line of argument and to apply it, for example, to domestic human rights obligations.[46]

3. Compliance with international law

At times, tribunals also require investors to comply with certain rules of international law as a precondition for the admissibility of investor claims or for the respective tribunal's jurisdiction. This jurisprudence implies indirect obligations as well.

In the following Section, the analysis will demonstrate three different approaches to such indirect obligations in investment practice. Recently, states have introduced clauses into new IIAs that explicitly demand such compliance (a). Furthermore, one can find them – in less determinate forms – in arbitral jurisprudence as tribunals have required investors to comply with the *ordre public international* (b) and fundamental rules of human rights protection (c).

a) New IIA clauses with indirect obligations

New IIAs make arbitral tribunal's jurisdiction expressly dependent on compliance with international law. These clauses illustrate very clearly the presence of a new indirect obligation with the purpose to protect the rule of law.

For example, Art 13.4 of the India Model BIT stipulates:

> An investor may not submit a claim to arbitration under this Chapter if the investment has been made through fraudulent misrepresentation, concealment, corruption, money laundering or conduct amounting to an abuse of process or similar illegal mechanisms.

Art 13.4 must be understood to impose an *international* standard of conduct. The norm does not refer to domestic law. What is more, Art 11 enshrines a separate obligation to comply with domestic law – hence, Art 13.4 would have been superfluous if it solely built on domestic law. Thus, it establishes an autonomous rule that tribunals will have to concretise further. In this regard, the IIA's clause is no different compared to

46 ibid, 97.

domestic laws which use general terms to comprehensively cover different situations.

Furthermore, the clause does not constitute a direct obligation because it does not stipulate that the host state can demand compliant behaviour. Instead, it only accords the negative consequence that the investor loses the right to submit a claim to arbitration – hence, establishing an indirect obligation.

In a very interesting, complex manner, Art 18 (1) ECOWAS Investment Rules establishes an indirect obligation by stipulating:

> Where it is established by a court of competent jurisdiction of the host State that an investor has breached Article 13 of this Supplementary Act, the investor shall not be entitled to initiate any dispute settlement process established under this Supplementary Act. A host or home State may raise this as an objection to jurisdiction in any dispute under this Supplementary Act.

Art 13 ECOWAS Investment Rules determines:

> Investors and their investments shall prior to the establishment of an investment or afterwards, refrain from involving themselves in corrupt practices as defined in Article 30 of this supplementary Act.

In turn, Art 30 ECOWAS Investment Rules provides:

> Member States shall consider as criminal the following offences and investigate, prosecute and punish the said offences with appropriate sanctions
> (a) the offering [...] of any pecuniary or other nature [...] to any public official of the host State [...] in order that the official [...] act[s] or refrain[s] from acting in relation to the [...] investment [...].

Art 30 imposes an international obligation on the IIA's state parties to combat corruption. Art 13 is an example of a direct obligation created by diverting this state obligation to investors as discussed above in Chapter 3.II.2. To recall, it is a technique of creating an obligation directly applicable to the investor by referring to the content of a state's obligation. Here, Art 13 orders the investor to refrain from the very acts of corruption the member states are obliged to prosecute by Art 30. On this basis, member states can demand compliance and demand compensation from the investor in case of a breach as a matter of international law.

Art 18 builds on this net of obligations. It draws on the same behavioural standard, the anti-corruption norm. In case of a breach that has been established by a court of competent jurisdiction of the host state, it accords another, different sanction: The investor can no longer initiate any dispute settlement envisaged in the ECOWAS Investment Rules. Consequently, the (diverted) anti-corruption standard also operates as an indirect obligation taking away the investor's right to file a claim.

This indirect obligation is purely international in character: The anti-corruption standard itself is part of international law as seen. The obligation's source is an international treaty: the ECOWAS Investment Rules. And the sanction therein affects the right to initiate dispute settlement procedures. Even though Art 33 also envisages national courts as relevant fora in this context, it includes access to the ECOWAS Court of Justice in case of doubt – hereby allowing for an international dispute settlement procedure.

Therefore, the ECOWAS Investment Rules illustrate well how investment practice can combine direct and indirect obligations. Here, one anti-corruption standard defines the content of three obligations: the international obligation of the ECOWAS member states, a direct and an indirect obligation of investors. It demonstrates how the same norm can have a dual (or even, if the state is included: threefold) character as part of different types of obligations. By this combination, the ECOWAS Investment Rules aim at combatting and sanctioning corruption by investors in a particularly comprehensive manner.

b) Ordre public international as an indirect obligation

Apart from these new IIAs, indirect obligations to comply with international law as a jurisdiction or admissibility requirement also exist in arbitral jurisprudence. They are much more established than the relatively few IIA clauses presented above – yet, they are also less determinate in content. This section will address the indirect obligation to comply with the *ordre public international.*

The *ordre public international* or transnational public policy is a term borrowed from private international law and commercial arbitration. The ILA defined it as a concept 'of universal application, comprising fundamental rules of natural law, principles of universal justice, *jus cogens* in public international law, and the general principles of morality accepted by what are referred to as "civilized nations"'.[47] Although this definition resembles the concept of *ius cogens*, the two must be distinguished from each other. An important exemplary rule that most consider enjoying the status of *ordre public international* but not of *ius cogens* is the prohibition of corruption.[48] While it remains controversial if the concept should be applied to investment treaty arbitration and if it is even recognised in commercial arbitration,[49] investment tribunals have relied on the concept in investment treaty arbitration.

Investment tribunals have rejected jurisdiction for investor claims if the investor violated norms covered by the *ordre public international*. Claims that stand against the international consensus that the principle embodies should not be entertained. Sometimes, tribunals also cite the principle of good faith in addition.[50]

These norms operate as indirect obligations: In the words of the Tribunal in *World Duty Free v Kenya*, they constitute 'norms of conduct'[51]. In

47 Audley Sheppard, 'Interim ILA Report on Public Policy as a Bar to Enforcement of International Arbitral Awards' (2003) 19(2) Arbitration International 217, 220; Eric de Brabandere, 'The (Ir)Relevance of Transnational Public Policy in Investment Treaty Arbitration – a Reply to Jean-Michel Marcoux' (2020) 21(6) Journal of World Investment & Trade 847, 852. The concept must be distinguished from the *ordre public* in the domestic law of conflict. There, it is a principle by which a state bars the application of foreign domestic law and the recognition and enforcement of foreign arbitral awards due to prepondering public interest concerns. Sometimes, the term 'international *ordre public*' is used for rules which harmonise this domestic *ordre public* between different states, for example under Art V (2) New York Convention and Art 36 UNCITRAL 'Model Law on International Commercial Arbitration 1985 (With Amendments as Adopted in 2006)' UN Doc A/40/17, Annex I and UN Doc A/61/17, Annex I. On this distinction see Régis Bismuth, 'Customary Principles Regarding Public Contracts Concluded with Foreigners' in Mathias Audit and Stephan W Schill (eds), *Transnational Law of Public Contracts* (Bruylant 2016) 331; see generally on the concept *of ordre public* Martin Gebauer, 'Ordre Public (Public Policy)' in Anne Peters (ed), *Max Planck Encyclopedia of Public International Law* (May 2007) paras 1–3.

48 Bismuth (n 47) 330.

49 For a criticism that the principle is not fully established in commercial arbitration and that it should not apply to investment treaty arbitration because it is superfluous, given that investment treaties are based on public international law (rather than private autonomy) and the legality requirement already covers all the relevant constellations, see Brabandere, 'Transnational' (n 47) 852–865.

50 *Plama v Bulgaria*, Award (n 19) paras 143–144.

51 *World Duty Free Company Limited v Republic of Kenya*, ICSID Case No. ARB/00/7, Award (4 October 2006) para 139; cf Jorge E. Viñuales, 'Investor Diligence in Investment Arbitration: Sources and Arguments' (2017) 32(2) ICSID Review 346,

case of a breach, tribunals accord a sanction to the investor's procedural right to file an investment claim. So far, investment tribunals have only applied this obligation in relation to anti-corruption and anti-fraud rules. This indirect obligation addresses how the investor's conduct affects the host state's rule of law.

For example, in *Plama Consortium v Bulgaria*, the ICSID Tribunal found that the investor had fraudulently misrepresented its shareholders. It held that this conduct violated not only Bulgarian law but also the *ordre public international*.[52] The Tribunal stated that this violation foreclosed the investor from *substantive* protection under the ECT.[53] However, it also appeared to accord a procedural consequence. The Tribunal found that 'a contract obtained by wrongful means should not be enforced by a tribunal'[54] and that it 'cannot lend its support to Claimant's request'.[55] This points to an inadmissibility of the 'improper' claim.

Interestingly, the Tribunal was aware that this sanction incidentally serves the public interest. To support its argument, it invoked the purpose of the applicable ECT to further the host state's rule of law by holding:

> In accordance with the introductory note to the ECT '[t]he fundamental aim of the Energy Charter Treaty is to strengthen the rule of law on energy issues [...]'. Consequently, the ECT should be interpreted in a manner consistent with the aim of encouraging respect for the rule of law.[56]

However, the content of this indirect obligation is relatively indeterminate. It is unclear which other facets of the public interest it may cover.[57] The award in *Inceysa v El Salvador* illustrates this well. It defined the international public policy rather vaguely as 'a series of fundamental principles that constitute the very essence of the State'.[58] There is no jurisprudence if basic standards of environmental protection would qualify as such fundamental principles, for example. Even the existing practice on fraud and

---

360 who considers this constellation to be an 'entry point' for norms on 'investor diligence'.

52 *Plama v Bulgaria*, Award (n 19) paras 141–142.

53 ibid 139.

54 ibid 143.

55 ibid 146.

56 ibid 139.

57 Choudhury, 'Investor' (n 23) 99 suggests that breaches of human rights could be considered contrary to international public policy.

58 *Inceysa v El Salvador* (n 19) para 245.

corruption does not elaborate on what conduct tribunals require from investors in abstract. Instead, they decide if the investor committed fraud in the specific circumstances of the case.[59] The open character of the *ordre public international* has led to scholarly suggestions that the concept could serve 'as a vehicle to impose human rights obligations in international investment arbitration'.[60]

An interesting attempt to concretise this indirect obligation can be found in *World Duty Free v Kenya*.[61] The Tribunal attempted to define more closely how the *ordre public international* protects the rule of law against corruption. To that end, it referred to state practice by arguing that 'most, if not all, countries penalise bribery'.[62] It went even further and considered international anti-bribery conventions such as the 1996 Inter-American Convention against Corruption,[63] the 1997 OECD Anti-Bribery Convention, the 1999 Criminal Law Convention on Corruption,[64] the 1999 Civil Law Convention on Corruption,[65] the 2003 Additional Protocol to the Criminal Law Convention on Corruption,[66] the 2003 African Union Convention on Preventing and Combating Corruption[67] and the 2003 UN Convention against Corruption. It also cited the non-binding

59 See also for example *Phoenix v Czech Republic* (n 19) paras 111–113.

60 Jean-Michel Marcoux, 'Transnational Public Policy as a Vehicle to Impose Human Rights Obligations in International Investment Arbitration' (2020) 21(6) Journal of World Investment & Trade 809; opposed by Brabandere, 'Transnational' (n 47).

61 While it is an investment contract arbitration that in the relevant part elaborates on the merits of the claim, it was however used as authority by the investment treaty arbitration award in *Plama Consortium v Bulgaria* for questions of jurisdiction and admissibility, see *Plama v Bulgaria*, Award (n 19) para 142 and Schill, 'Illegal' (n 20) 317.

62 *World Duty Free v Kenya* (n 51) para 142.

63 Inter-American Convention against Corruption (adopted 29 March 1996, entered into force 6 March 1997) 35 ILM 724 (Inter-American Anti-Corruption Convention).

64 Criminal Law Convention on Corruption (adopted 27 January 1999, entered into force 1 July 2002) 2216 UNTS 225 (Criminal Law Convention on Corruption).

65 Civil Law Convention on Corruption (adopted 4 November 1999, entered into force 1 November 2003) 2246 UNTS 3 (Civil Law Convention on Corruption).

66 Additional Protocol to the Criminal Law Convention on Corruption (adopted 15 May 2003, entered into force 1 February 2005) 2466 UNTS 168 (Criminal Law Convention on Corruption AP).

67 African Union Convention on Preventing and Combating Corruption (adopted 11 July 2003, entered into force 5 August 2006) 2860 UNTS 113 (AU Anti-Corruption Convention).

1996 UN General Assembly Declaration against Corruption and Bribery in International Commercial Transactions.[68]

Interestingly, then, the Tribunal explicitly held that these conventions only bind their state parties.[69] Notwithstanding, it continued by finding that the conventions

> [...] have shown [States'] common will to fight corruption, not only through national legislation, as they did before, but also through international cooperation. In doing so, States not only reached a new stage in the fight against corruption, but also solidly confirmed their prior condemnation of it.[70]

It seems that the Tribunal found it possible to define the indirect obligation's content by reference to international obligations of states. Apparently, the anti-bribery conventions evidenced a universal consensus which also applied to investors. This technique resembles the diverting of state obligations to direct obligations encountered in Chapter 3.II – with the difference that, here, the Tribunal turned them into an indirect obligation.

c) Fundamental rules of human rights protection as indirect obligations

Fundamental rules of human rights protection form the standard for another indirect obligation. Tribunals have found that if investors breach them, they have no jurisdiction.

The Tribunal in *Phoenix v Czech Republic* referred to this argument in an *obiter dictum*. In the process of establishing its jurisdiction, the Tribunal elaborated that both the ICSID Convention and the BIT at stake were subject to international law. For this reason, they had to be interpreted according to Art 31 VCLT. It held that this included the giving of due regard to general principles of law. To support this finding, it pointed to the WTO Appellate Body's report in *US—Gasoline* in which the Appellate Body found that the GATT 'is not to be read in clinical isolation from pu-

68 UNGA 'United Nations Declaration Against Corruption and Bribery in International Commercial Transactions' UN Doc A/RES/51/191 (21 February 1997); the Tribunal cited the above-mentioned treaties and this declaration in *World Duty Free v Kenya* (n 51) paras 143–145.

69 *World Duty Free v Kenya* (n 51) para 146.

70 ibid.

blic international law'[71], a passage that the Tribunal quoted in its award.[72] The Tribunal went on to find that the ICSID Convention and the BIT

> [...] cannot be read and interpreted in isolation from public international law, and its general principles. To take an extreme example, nobody would suggest that ICSID protection should be granted to investments made in violation of the most fundamental rules of protection of human rights, like investments in pursuance of torture or genocide or in support of slavery or trafficking of human organs.[73]

The Tribunal precisely described the functioning of an indirect obligation. It did not hold that the respondent could enforce these human rights norms against investors through investment arbitration. Instead, it elaborated on a sanction for non-compliance within investment arbitration: that tribunals could not grant ICSID protection. Consequently, violation of these international human rights norms has a negative consequence on investors' right to file an ICSID claim.

On the one hand, the award partly lays down a concrete standard of conduct. The listed examples of fundamental human rights violations are well-established prohibitions. Other international instruments concretise them, such as the Convention on the Prevention and Punishment of the Crime of Genocide[74]. On the other hand, aside from these examples, the notion of 'fundamental rules of protection of human rights' is fairly indeterminate. Notably, it does not seem possible to equate it with *ius cogens*. This follows from the presented example of trafficking of human organs. It is not accepted to have the status of *ius cogens* which reflects that, seemingly, the Tribunal did not have a reference to *ius cogens* in mind.

In contrast, the Tribunal's award in *EDF et al. v Argentina* favours such a resort to *ius cogens* as it affirmed that '[i]t is common ground that the Tribunal should be sensitive to international *jus cogens* norms, including

71 WTO, *United States—Standards for Reformulated and Conventional Gasoline* (29 April 1996) WT/DS2/AB/R.

72 *Phoenix v Czech Republic* (n 19) paras 74–77.

73 ibid 78.

74 Convention on the Prevention and Punishment of the Crime of Genocide (adopted 9 December 1948, entered into force 12 January 1951) 78 UNTS 278 (Genocide Convention).

basic principles of human rights'.[75] However, there, the Tribunal did not elaborate on the consequences of such sensitivity.

4. Interim conclusion

Section I has shown that indirect obligations are established in investment practice within investment arbitration's jurisdiction and admissibility requirements. They follow from explicit IIA clauses and from arbitral jurisprudence. Fitting the concept of indirect obligations, they imply standards of conduct and sanction non-compliance by forfeiting investor's procedural right to file an arbitral claim. The content of these standards draws on international and domestic law. Yet, they vary in how determinate they formulate the expected behaviour. For example, the requirement to contribute to the host state's development is particularly vague. In contrast, compliance with the host state's domestic law draws on concrete norms because, for example, aside from being part of the black letter law, domestic courts in most cases will have clarified their meaning.

The encountered indirect obligations examined the investor's conduct towards very different facets of the public interest. They included, for example, human rights, the rule of law, the host state's economy as well as a favourable social and cultural environment. Where domestic law defines indirect obligations' content, they can potentially cover any aspect of the public interest.

As these indirect obligations operate on the level of jurisdiction and a claim's admissibility, their sanction is relatively strong. They already hinder the tribunal from addressing the substantive matter of a dispute at the merits stage. It is apparent that the encountered indirect obligations appear to address this issue by requiring a *qualified* violation: either the indirect obligation relates to a fundamental rule,[76] or the breach must

---

75 *EDF International S.A. SAUR International S.A. and León Participaciones Argentinas S.A. v Argentine Republic*, ICSID Case No. ARB/03/23, Award (11 June 2012) para 909.

76 Most clearly indicated by the requirements to comply with the international *ordre public* and fundamental human rights, see Chapter 7.I.3.b) and Chapter 7.I.3.c); cf Matthew A.J. Levine, 'Emerging Practice on Investor Diligence: Jurisdiction, Admissibility, Merits' in Julien Chaisse, Leïla Choukroune and Sufian Jusoh (eds), *Handbook of International Investment Law and Policy* (Springer 2021) 1087–1088.

exceed a certain intensity,[77] or it has to constitute a *prima facie* violation.[78] It, thus, appears that the encountered indirect obligations serve to filter graver forms of investor misconduct towards the public interest. In doing so, they incidentally serve the public interest, because there is an incentive for investors to comply for their own stake. Otherwise, they will not even be heard with their substantive arguments before an arbitral tribunal.

II. Substantive requirements of investor rights

After studying jurisdiction and admissibility requirements, the analysis will now turn to investor rights' substantive requirements. This Section will show that, increasingly, tribunals and IIAs include standards for the investor's conduct in the analysis of investor rights. In most instances, tribunals have considered misconduct towards the public interest only as a balancing criterion amongst others – hence without giving rise to an indirect obligation as understood here. However, this development is notable, too. It is evidence of a tendency to make investor rights dependent on proper investor behaviour, contributing to an overall trend towards indirect obligations. What is more, in some important cases, indirect obligations can be seen to have already emerged.

This Section will present these findings alongside the different approaches that have been used to address investors' misconduct.

It will start with approaches which only consider investor misconduct as a balancing criterion: by a changing understanding of what constitutes legitimate expectations of investors (1.), through the principle of proportionality (2.) and by interpreting investor rights in the light of soft law (3.). In the next step, the analysis will turn to cases in which indirect obligations have already arisen. Namely, indirect obligations can appear in rare instances in which tribunals interpret investor rights in the light of host states' international obligations (4.). Finally, the requirement to comply with the host state's domestic law after the investment's admission implies broadly established indirect obligations already today (5.).

77 See for example the qualifications for a breach of domestic law elaborated in Chapter 7.I.2.c).

78 For example, because the requirement of contribution to the host state's development only considers the strategic field and character of the investment, not concrete actions, see Chapter 7.I.1.c).

Excluded from this Section's scope are rules on compensation which will find separate attention in the subsequent Section III.

1. Investors' legitimate expectations

One could consider the notion of investors' 'legitimate expectations' as a possible basis for an indirect obligation. It forms part of important rights such as the right to FET. Because, by its nature, the criterion entails the taking of the investor's perspective,[79] it deserves specific attention.

This section will first lay out in which regard legitimate expectations form an established requirement especially of the right to FET and the protection against expropriation (a). Still, so far, investment practice has not applied it in a manner implying an indirect obligation as understood here. A standard of conduct that automatically deprives the investor of an investor right in case of a breach is missing. Instead, tribunals have used it to consider investors' misconduct towards the public interest as only one amongst other balancing criteria (b). Yet, there is an increasing tendency to give the criterion a more concrete content – hence, intimating a potential development of indirect obligations in the future (c).

---

79 cf *Urbaser S.A. and Consorcio de Aguas Bilbao Bizkaia, Bilbao Biskaia Ur Partzuergoa v The Argentine Republic*, ICSID Case No. ARB/07/26, Award (8 December 2016) para 615: 'The next step is therefore to determine the scope of events, acts or omissions on part of the host State that are not triggering an investor's right for protection under the fair and equitable treatment standard and that it has to expect to be faced with. This is why the interpretation of this standard is usually focusing on the legitimate expectations of the investor [...]. While the Tribunal understands Respondent's objection that Article IV of the BIT does not allow an extensive interpretation covering the "legitimate expectations" of the investor, the argument is simply subject to the understanding and meaning of the term "legitimate."'

a) Relevant requirements of investor rights

Most IIAs consider if the investor has legitimate expectations as part of the right to FET[80] and the protection against indirect expropriation.[81]

The right to FET developed out of the customary minimum standard of treatment of aliens. The correct definition of this right is highly controversial.[82] For example, the UNCITRAL Tribunal in *Saluka v Czech Republic* found state action that is 'manifestly inconsistent, non-transparent, unreasonable (i.e. unrelated to some rational policy) or discriminatory (i.e. based on unjustifiable distinctions)'[83] to violate the right to FET. The protection against (direct) expropriation originally limited the host state's capacity to transfer control of investors' property to itself. But many IIAs and tribunals have acknowledged that investors also receive protection against

80 See for example *Saluka Investments BV v The Czech Republic*, Partial Award (UNCITRAL, 17 March 2006) para 302; Fulvio M Palombino, *Fair and Equitable Treatment and the Fabric of General Principles* (T.M.C. Asser Press 2018) 85–119.

81 See for example *Metalclad Corporation v The United Mexican States*, ICSID Case No. ARB(AF)/97/1, Award (30 August 2000) para 103; *Tecmed v Mexico* (n 27) para 149; Ursula Kriebaum, 'Expropriation' in Marc Bungenberg and others (eds), *International Investment Law* (Nomos 2015) paras 174–186; from the international treaty practice see for example the definition of indirect expropriation in Annex 8-A of Comprehensive Economic and Trade Agreement (adopted 30 October 2016) ‹https://investmentpolicy.unctad.org/international-investment-agreements/treaty-files/3593/download› accessed 7 December 2021 (CETA) which stipulates in no 2 (c) as one criterion: 'the extent to which a measure or series of measures interferes with distinct, reasonable investment-backed expectations'.

82 For a comprehensive analysis of the right to FET see for example Christoph Schreuer, 'Fair and Equitable Treatment in Arbitral Practice' (2005) 6(3) Journal of World Investment & Trade 357; see also the monographs by Mārtiņš Paparinskis, *The International Minimum Standard and Fair and Equitable Treatment* (Oxford University Press 2013); Palombino (n 80); Teerawat Wongkaew, *Protection of Legitimate Expectations in Investment Treaty Arbitration* (Cambridge University Press 2019).

83 *Saluka v Czech Republic*, Partial Award (n 80) para 309. For an alternative, expansive definition, see *Tecmed v Mexico* (n 27) para 154 which interpreted the right to FET as demanding from the state to act 'in a consistent manner, free from ambiguity and totally transparently in its relationship with the foreign investor'; cf the definition of the customary minimum standard for the treatment of aliens in *L.F.H. Neer and Pauline Neer (U.S.A.) v United Mexican States* (Decision) (1926) 4 Reports of International Arbitral Awards 60, 65 which held that a 'treatment of an alien, in order to constitute an international delinquency, should amount to an outrage, to bad faith, to wilful neglect of duty, or to an insufficiency of governmental action so far short of international standards that every reasonable and impartial man would readily recognize its insufficiency.'

indirect expropriations. These are measures by the host state that have an effect tantamount to a direct expropriation by devaluating the investment's worth.[84]

The right to FET and the protection against indirect expropriation are both rather indeterminate in scope. Considering investors' legitimate expectations is a way of giving these rights a more defined content. IIAs of the newest generation even explicitly mention legitimate expectations as a criterion limiting these rights.[85] The teleological argument is that investors only deserve these rights if they could legitimately expect no interference by the state. IIAs protect investors' trust in a stable legislative framework and business environment at the time of the investment. Drastic, unpredictable changes which seriously affect the investment can constitute a breach of these rights.[86]

b) Consideration of investor misconduct

Tribunals have considered the investor's misconduct in assessing if the investor's expectations to be protected against the host state are *legitimate*. One can identify that tribunals are increasingly willing to take account of the way the investor behaves towards the public interest.

---

84 See generally on expropriation Dolzer and Schreuer (n 18) 98–129 with further references. The details are highly controversial, see for example Dolzer and Schreuer (n 18) 120–123; Jeswald W Salacuse, *The Law of Investment Treaties* (3rd edn, Oxford University Press 2021) 395–423; for an in-depth analysis see for example Sebastián López Escarcena, *Indirect Expropriation in International Law* (Edward Elgar Publishing 2014); from the case law see in particular *Philip Morris Brands Sàrl, Philip Morris Products S.A. and Abal Hermanos S.A. v Oriental Republic of Uruguay*, ICSID Case No. ARB/10/7, Award (8 July 2016) paras 287–307.

85 See for example Art 8.10 CETA which mentions the legitimate expectations of investors that accrue from a specific representation that the host state made to them.

86 For more details on legitimate expectations as an argument in the analysis of the right to FET see for example *CMS Gas Transmission Company v The Argentine Republic*, ICSID Case No. ARB/01/8, Decision of the Ad Hoc Committee on the Application for Annulment of the Argentine Republic (25 September 2007) paras 274–276; *LG&E Energy Corp. LG&E Capital Corp. and LG&E International, Inc. v Argentine Republic*, ICSID Case No. ARB/02/1, Decision on Liability (3 October 2006) paras 124–133; Schreuer, *ICSID* (n 1) Art 42 para 132; on indirect expropriation see *Tecmed v Mexico* (n 27) para 149; *Azurix Corp. v The Argentine Republic*, ICSID Case No. ARB/01/12, Award (14 July 2006) paras 316–322; Dolzer and Schreuer (n 18) 115–117.

This was not always the case. Originally, tribunals have understood the criterion as a way of distributing risks between the state and the investor. For example, the Tribunal in *Maffezzini v Spain* pointedly held that 'BITs are not an insurance against business risk'[87] – a definition that appears to examine the investor's economic decisions. This way of arguing follows a private law paradigm. It is disinclined to assess the investor's role in the host state's society more holistically.

Yet, the normative value judgment to determine what is 'legitimate' is free to consider the investor's conduct towards the public interest. In *Muchlinski*'s words: '[t]he fairness of such regulatory conduct towards investors cannot be judged without also assessing the conduct of investors towards the community on behalf of which the State may act.'[88]

Some tribunals, for example the UNCITRAL award in *Methanex v USA*, have interpreted investor rights in this manner. The claimant in this case produced methanol. A Californian ban on methanol-based fuel additives negatively affected its investment. The Tribunal rejected that the Californian ban constituted an expropriation or a violation of the right to FET. It argued *inter alia* that California was known for its environmentally-friendly policy. The investor decided to enter the market despite knowing this fact. Thus, in the absence of specific representations, the foreign investor had to bear the risk that followed from the Californian regulatory environment.[89] The Tribunal in *Unglaube v Costa Rica*, interpreting the right to FET, observed that the claimants, engaging in tourism services

87 *Emilio Agustín Maffezini v The Kingdom of Spain*, ICSID Case No. ARB/97/7, Award (13 November 2000) para 64; see also Jorge E Viñuales, 'The Environmental Regulation of Foreign Investment Schemes Under International Law' in Pierre-Marie Dupuy and Jorge E Viñuales (eds), *Harnessing Foreign Investment to Promote Environmental Protection: Incentives and Safeguards* (Cambridge University Press 2013) 299 who elaborates on arbitral tribunals which have interpreted the right FET as allocating regulatory (rather than economic) risks between investors and the host state.

88 Peter Muchlinski, '"Caveat Investor"? The Relevance of the Conduct of the Investor Under the Fair and Equitable Treatment Standard' (2006) 55(3) International & Comparative Law Quarterly 527, 534; this necessity to analyse investors' conduct is affirmed for example by Kneer (n 29) 280; Roland Kläger, '"Fair and Equitable Treatment" and Sustainable Development' in Marie-Claire Cordonier Segger, Markus W Gehring and Andrew P Newcombe (eds), *Sustainable Development in World Investment Law* (Kluwer Law International 2011) 255; specifically on environmental protection see Viñuales, 'Environmental' (n 87) 297–301.

89 *Methanex Corporation v United States of America*, Final Award of the Tribunal on Jurisdiction and Merits (UNCITRAL, 3 August 2005) Part IV Chapter D paras 9–10.

in an environmentally sensitive area, 'were, of course, required, as part of their due diligence, to become familiar with Costa Rican law and procedure.'[90] The use of the term 'due diligence' very openly expresses behavioural expectations towards the investors as to environmental protection.[91] Other tribunals have concretised the notion of legitimate expectations in a similar manner[92] in spite of remaining criticism.[93]

Herein, the tribunals departed from an exclusive focus on the host state's measure. Instead, they considered the interests at stake through the investor's eyes. Implicitly, they gave weight to the fact that investors must, to a certain degree, conform with public interest policy established in the host state. In the example of *Methanex v USA*, the Tribunal subtly expressed that the claimant must take Californian societal preferences as they are. By investing in an environmentally-friendly state, the claimant had to conform with these policies to some degree. Therefore, this provides evidence that investment law expects proper conduct towards public goods and individual rights of others – here, as defined by Californian policy.

c) A lacking character as an indirect obligation

However, this observation also shows that the notion of legitimate expectations does not imply an indirect obligation. They do not pronounce a

---

90 *Marion Unglaube and Reinhard Unglaube v Republic of Costa Rica*, ICSID Case No. ARB/08/1, ARB/09/20, Award (16 May 2012) para 258.

91 Jorge E Viñuales, 'Foreign Investment and the Environment in International Law: Current Trends' in Kate Miles (ed), *Research Handbook on Environment and Investment Law* (Edward Elgar Publishing 2019) 30 identifies 'a mindset more attuned to the current understanding of environmental protection needs' herein.

92 See for example *S.D. Myers, Inc. v Government of Canada*, Partial Award (UNCITRAL, 13 November 2000) para 263; *Saluka v Czech Republic*, Partial Award (n 80) para 305; *Charanne and Construction Investments v The Kingdom of Spain*, SCC Case No V 062/2012, Award (21 January 2016) para 505; supported by Ioana Knoll-Tudor, 'The Fair and Equitable Treatment Standard and Human Rights Norms' in Pierre-Marie Dupuy, Ernst-Ulrich Petersmann and Francesco Francioni (eds), *Human Rights in International Investment Law and Arbitration* (Oxford University Press 2009) 326; Viñuales, 'Diligence' (n 51) 362–363; further on the relevance of the police powers doctrine Viñuales, 'Environmental' (n 87) 301–304.

93 Some criticise this jurisprudence because it relied too exclusively on the host state's regulatory intentions in assessing the police powers doctrine. See for example *Methanex v USA* (n 89) Part IV Chapter D para 7; see also Kriebaum, 'Expropriation' (n 81) paras 155–161 with further references.

certain standard of conduct. There is no automatic sanction in the form of forfeiting an investor right. Instead, legitimate expectations only constitute a requirement to consider the investor's misconduct as a balancing criterion amongst others. Vaguely, tribunals give an undefined weight to these actions. For example, in *Methanex v USA*, it remains elusive up to which point the tribunal would have expected the investor to integrate into the Californian environmentally-friendly regulatory framework.

Nevertheless, the criterion of legitimate expectations increasingly forms a focal point for interpreting investor rights mindful of the investors' conduct. Seemingly, there exists a need to worsen investors' positions under an IIA when they impair the public interest. This reinterpretation points in the same direction as indirect obligations: to make investment protection in some way dependent on proper investor behaviour.

Apart from scholarly suggestions,[94] the award in *Urbaser v Argentina* strongly indicates such tendencies. The claimant undertook water and sewage services in Argentina and contended that Argentina violated the right to FET. Further details of the case have been laid out above.[95] The Tribunal elaborated in detail on the interpretation of the right to FET in Art IV of the Spain-Argentina BIT. It is worth quoting the Tribunal's reasoning at length:

> The investor's expectations, and their importance in the particular case, are usually measured on the basis of the contractual commitments undertaken. However, these contractual rights should not be considered in isolation. They are placed in a legal frame-work embracing the rights and obligations of the host State and of its authorities, subject to the protections provided in the BIT. […]
>
> Moreover, the host State is bound by obligations under international and constitutional laws. Therefore, the host State is legitimately expected to act in furtherance of rules of law of a fundamental character. The scope of such rules is broad. […]

---

94 See for example Muchlinski (n 88) 550–551 who argues that investors must be aware of the regulatory environment and must foresee any likely regulatory change; Stephan W Schill, Christian J Tams and Rainer Hofmann, 'International Investment Law and Development: Friends or Foes?' in Christian J Tams, Rainer Hofmann and Stephan W Schill (eds), *International Investment Law and Development: Bridging the Gap* (Edward Elgar Publishing 2015) 26 who observe that 'in a rudimentary manner […] expectations of foreign investors need to be considered relative to the state of development of the host country.'

95 See Chapter 3.I.2.

> This means that the investor's interests are not to be identified as separate and distinct from the legal framework into which they have been placed upon entering into the investment. […] In the instant case, this obligation relates to the Government's responsibilities under the Federal Constitution to ensure the population's health and access to water and to take all measures required to that effect. […] When measures had been taken that have as their purpose and effect to implement such fundamental rights protected under the Constitution, they cannot hurt the fair and equitable treatment standard because their occurrence must have been deemed to be accepted by the investor when entering into the investment and the Concession Contract. In short, they were expected to be part of the investment's legal framework.[96]

It is striking how the Tribunal intertwined the investor's legitimate expectations with domestic and international obligations of the host state. It explicitly highlighted the investor's decision to invest in a state which is subject to certain obligations to protect the public interest – here, to ensure the right to health and access to water. The Tribunal almost appeared to extend these obligations to the investor by highlighting that it 'accepted' them.

Yet, it still only considered the investor's conduct as one balancing aspect among others in the analysis. For example, it also examined the host state's intentions and actions more closely.[97] This shows that the investor did not automatically forfeit the right to FET as a strict legal consequence of impairing the right to water. However, the award evidences an attempt to connect the definition of legitimate expectations with legal norms. Herein, it at least foreshadows a concept of the right to FET that could imply an indirect obligation in the future.

One can also identify a desire for giving weight to investors' misconduct in the most recent generation of IIAs. For example, Art X.11 CETA stipulates that one must assess the question whether a certain measure constitutes an expropriation on a case-by-case basis. To that end, one must *inter alia* consider '2. […] the extent to which the measure or series of measures interferes with *distinct, reasonable* investment-backed expectations; […]'

96 *Urbaser v Argentina*, Award (n 79) paras 619, 621–622.

97 Patrick Abel, 'Counterclaims Based on International Human Rights Obligations of Investors in International Investment Arbitration: Fallacies and Potentials of the 2016 ICSID Urbaser v. Argentina Award' [2018] Brill Open Law 1, paras 624–625.

(emphasis added). What is more, the qualifying criterion of 'reasonableness' was even read into IIAs that do not contain such explicit language by investment tribunals.[98] To determine what is distinct and reasonable, the CETA Investment Court could develop a standard of conduct. If sufficiently determinate, it could constitute an indirect obligation by defining certain investor misconduct as always being unreasonable – hence depriving the investor of the right to protection against expropriation.

2. Proportionality

Furthermore, investment tribunals have examined how the investor behaves towards the public interest through the proportionality principle. It is established as a requirement especially of the right to FET and the protection against expropriation (a). Tribunals have increasingly applied it in a manner that considers investors' misconduct as a balancing criterion in the analysis. This includes, for example, their impact on human rights and the environment (b). However, the principle does not give rise to an indirect obligation. It does not establish an automatism between the breach of a certain standard of conduct and the loss of an investor right. Similar to the changing role of legitimate expectations, it is part of broader dynamics: to make investor rights dependent on proper investor conduct (c).

a) The proportionality principle in investment law

The principle of proportionality is established in various areas of international law.[99] In its most advanced form, it entails four sub-principles: The state must pursue a legitimate goal. The means applied must be suitable to achieve this goal. Furthermore, they must be necessary in the sense that there cannot be a less intrusive but equally effective alternative available.

98 For example in *Waste Management, Inc. v United Mexican States*, ICSID Case No. ARB(AF)/00/3, Award (30 April 2004) para 98; *Duke Energy Electroquil Partners & Electroquil S.A. v Republic of Ecuador*, ICSID Case No. ARB/04/19, Award (18 August 2008) para 340; *Plama v Bulgaria*, Award (n 19) para 219; *Chemtura Corporation v Government of Canada*, Award (UNCITRAL, 2 August 2010) para 149.

99 Some even consider it a general principle of law, for example Emily Crawford, 'Proportionality' in Anne Peters (ed), *Max Planck Encyclopedia of Public International Law* (May 2011) para 1.

Finally, the measure must be appropriate to the objective sought and to the right interfered with (proportionality *stricto sensu*).[100] The last element requires a weighing and balancing of all interests and rights involved on a case-by-case basis.

Many investment tribunals have applied the principle especially as part of the right to FET and the protection against indirect expropriation.[101] This means, to determine if the host state breached these rights, they have balanced the investor's economic interests against the rights and interests the host state pursued. Only where the state acted disproportionately, they affirmed a violation. Sometimes, the principle is also an element of clauses which exclude certain types of foreign investment from the IIA's scope of protection (so called exception clauses) and which safeguard the host state's right to regulate (right to regulate clauses). Both constitute new types of clauses which feature in the most recent generation of IIAs.[102]

---

100 Supported i.e. by ibid, paras 1–2. Not every branch of international law applies all of these steps, cf Thomas Cottier and others, 'The Principle of Proportionality in International Law: Foundations and Variations' (2017) 18(4) Journal of World Investment & Trade 628, 630.

101 Sometimes this jurisprudence is also coined the police powers-doctrine. Essentially, it entails a weighing and balancing between all interests affected by the host state measure and thus constitutes a form of proportionality test, see *Tecmed v Mexico* (n 27) para 119; *Saluka v Czech Republic*, Partial Award (n 80) para 306; *Azurix v Argentina* (n 86) paras 311–312; *LG&E v Argentina*, Decision on Liability (n 86) para 194; *BG Group Plc. v Republic of Argentina*, Final Award (UNCITRAL, 24 December 2007) para 298; *Biwater Gauff v Tanzania* (n 1) paras 503, 515, 519; *Occidental Petroleum Corporation and Occidental Exploration and Production Company v Republic of Ecuador*, ICSID Case No. ARB/06/11, Award (5 October 2012) paras 404–409; Kriebaum, 'Expropriation' (n 81) para 173; Cottier and others (n 100) 657–659. The application of the principle of proportionality is for example supported by Benedict Kingsbury and Stephan W Schill, 'Public Law Concepts to Balance Investors' Rights with State Regulatory Actions in the Public Interest – the Concept of Proportionality' in Stephan W Schill (ed), *International Investment Law and Comparative Public Law* (Oxford University Press 2010) 75–85; Andreas Kulick, *Global Public Interest in International Investment Law* (Cambridge University Press 2012) 225–341. For the alternative approach of the 'sole effects' doctrine which only considers the host state's impact on the investment to the exclusion of other criteria, see for example *Siemens A.G. v The Argentine Republic*, ICSID Case No. ARB/02/8, Award (6 February 2007) para 270; and the contrary approach of only requiring that the host state followed a legitimate purpose, see *Methanex v USA* (n 89) Part IV, Chapter D, para 7; see also Kriebaum, 'Expropriation' (n 81) paras 132, 155–161 with further references.

102 For an analysis of the proportionality principle as part of these new clauses see Jasper Krommendijk and John Morijn, '"Proportional" by What Measure(s)?

b) Consideration of investor misconduct

Increasingly, tribunals have applied the principle of proportionality to consider investor misconduct.

A good example is the ICSID award in *Tecmed v Mexico*. There, the Tribunal considered if the investor had adversely affected the environment. The investor contended that Mexico had violated the right to FET and the protection against expropriation by refusing to extend a permit. This permit served to operate a landfill of hazardous industrial waste.[103] In examining if Mexico had indirectly expropriated the investment, the Tribunal engaged in a proportionality analysis. It did so by explicitly building on jurisprudence of the European Court of Human Rights on the human right to property.[104]

To that end, it cited a passage of the ECtHR's judgment in *James and Others v UK* in which the Court required 'a reasonable relationship of proportionality between the means employed and the aim sought to be realized […] The requisite balance will not be found if the person concerned has had to bear "an individual and excessive burden"'.[105]

Balancing Investor Interests and Human Rights by Way of Applying the Proportionality Principle in Investor-State Arbitration' in Pierre-Marie Dupuy, Ernst-Ulrich Petersmann and Francesco Francioni (eds), *Human Rights in International Investment Law and Arbitration* (Oxford University Press 2009) 437–438; Gebhard Bücheler, *Proportionality in Investor-State Arbitration* (Oxford University Press 2015) 211–252; Cottier and others (n 100) 662–665; on the role of proportionality as part of the defence of necessity under customary international law that is not pursued here any further see Bücheler (n 102) 253–300.

103 *Tecmed v Mexico* (n 27) para 41.

104 The human right to property is enshrined in Art 1 of Protocol 1 to the European Convention for the Protection of Human Rights and Fundamental Freedoms (adopted 20 March 1952, entered into force 18 May 1954) ETS 9 (ECHR Protocol No 1). The Tribunal referred to specific case law on the principle of proportionality, see *Tecmed v Mexico* (n 27) para 122 citing *Case of Mellacher and Others v Austria* App no 10522/83, 11011/84, 11070/84, ECHR Series A no 169 (European Court of Human Rights, 19 December 1989) para 48; *Case of Pressos Compania Naviera S.A. and Others v Belgium* App no 17849/91, ECHR Series A no 332 (European Court of Human Rights, 20 November 1995) para 38; *Case of Matos e Silva, Lda. and Others v Portugal* App no 15777/89, ECHR 1996-IV (European Court of Human Rights, 16 September 1996) paras 90–92.

105 *Tecmed v Mexico* (n 27) para 122 citing *Case of James and Others v The United Kingdom* App no 8793/79, ECHR Series A no 98 (European Court of Human Rights, 21 February 1986) para 50.

This passage calls for examining the investors' conduct – if they had to bear an excessive burden. Indeed, the Tribunal considered how the investor had affected the environment and the rights of others. It held that the findings

> [...] do not suggest that the violations [of the permit conditions by the investor] compromise public health, impair ecological balance or protection of the environment, or that they may be the reason for a genuine social crisis. [...] [The investor's] operation of the Landfill never compromised the ecological balance, the protection of the environment or the health of the people [...][106]

This award shows that because the proportionality principle is about balancing all interests affected in a concrete case, the investor's conduct towards the public interest can form an important part of this analysis. Consequently, misconduct may be an attenuating balancing factor. For example, in the case of *Tecmed v Mexico*, the Tribunal not only examined how the investor affected the right to health but it also took account of the investment's environmental impact.

c) A lacking character as an indirect obligation

Some have argued that the proportionality principle could fulfil a function which resembles an indirect obligation as understood here. For example, in their studies on public law analogies, *Kingsbury* and *Schill* criticised 'that investment treaties only impose substantive obligations on host states, without matching these investors' rights with investors' obligations'[107]. They considered that the principle of proportionality could alleviate this lack of obligations.[108]

However, in the way the proportionality principle is construed, it cannot operate as an indirect obligation as understood here. As seen, the principle takes account of the investor's misconduct as one balancing criterion among others. The tribunal still has to weigh this misconduct against many other aspects of the case: for example, the gravity of the state's misconduct, the purpose of the state's measure and how likely that measure is to improve the public interest. Necessarily, the analytical result

---

106 *Tecmed v Mexico* (n 27) paras 124, 148.
107 Kingsbury and Schill (n 101) 76.
108 ibid.

for the same misconduct varies from case to case. For example, in one case environmental pollution caused by investors may be grave enough to justify disqualifying them from protection. In other cases, the state's misconduct may be of greater weight, and investors may receive protection despite causing pollution.

Consequently, the principle neither formulates a defined standard of conduct, nor does it automatically apply the sanction of a loss of an investor right. For example, in *Tecmed v Mexico*, it is not possible to identify a norm that, in case of the investor's non-compliance, would have automatically led the Tribunal to consider the state's behaviour to be proportional, with the result of a complete loss of protection. Rather, misconduct only 'tips the scales' of the proportionality test to the disadvantage of the investor.

Nevertheless, the very fact that tribunals apply the principle so as to consider the investor's misconduct is a remarkable development in itself – especially appreciating that its application had been contested at least for some time by a number of tribunals.[109] It brings about a change of perspective from the host state's to the investor's actions. Similar to the findings in the previous Section on legitimate expectations, it involves appreciating the investor's role in the society – hence to express behavioural expectations that the investor should treat public goods and rights of others in a positive way. Therein, it departs from a private or commercial law paradigm which would rather frame the analysis as the delineating of risks between the two parties. As seen, the recent generation of IIAs explicitly includes the proportionality principle in the treaty texts, fuelling this development even further.

3. Interpreting rights in the light of soft law

Furthermore, a number of investment tribunals have measured the investor's conduct against soft law as they applied an investor right (a). At least, these awards indicate that conformity with soft law can form a balancing criterion in determining an investor right (b). However, one would go too far to construe an indirect obligation out of soft law without explicit basis in the IIA. Therefore, the existing practice is better understood as contributing to the already-encountered dynamics in the last Sections: to

109 For alternative approaches to interpret investor rights without entailing a proportionality analysis see n 101.

give legal relevance to investors' misconduct within the analysis of investor rights (c).

a) Soft law as interpretive standards

Two arbitral awards serve as best examples of how soft law can constitute a potential basis of indirect obligations in investment practice.

The first is the 1992 ICSID award in *SPP v Egypt*, an investment contract arbitration. The claimants had concluded a contract with Egypt to build tourist facilities at the Pyramids area near Cairo and Ras El Hekma ('Pyramids Oasis'). Later, Egypt cancelled the project and declared the lands *d'utilité publique*.[110] The claimant contended that this cancellation violated Egyptian law which was applicable in the arbitration proceedings. However, Egypt argued that the cancellation was necessary to abide by the UNESCO World Heritage Convention.[111] Its Art 4 and 5 contain an international obligation of state parties to endeavour to protect cultural property.[112] The Tribunal rejected Egypt's argument. It found it decisive that at the time of the cancellation the pyramid fields had not yet been included on the World Heritage List.

The World Heritage List contains property which the states themselves consider as forming part of cultural or natural heritage in the meaning of Art 1 and 2 of the UNESCO Convention. Importantly, it has no legally binding nature. It is non-exhaustive and has only a declaratory effect.[113] What is more, Art 6 (1) stipulates that the status of world heritage is 'without prejudice to property right provided by national legislation'. Consequently, one can consider the including of certain property on the World Heritage List as non-binding soft law.

---

110 *Southern Pacific Properties (Middle East) Limited v Arab Republic of Egypt*, ICSID Case No. ARB/84/3, Award on the Merits (20 May 1992) paras 42–65.

111 Convention Concerning the Protection of the World Cultural and Natural Heritage (adopted 16 November 1972, entered into force 17 December 1975) 1037 UNTS 151 (World Heritage Convention).

112 On the content of this obligation see Ulrich Fastenrath, 'Das UNESCO-Übereinkommen zum Schutz des Kultur- und Naturerbes der Welt und seine Wirkungen im deutschen Recht' (2016) 54(4) Archiv des Völkerrechts 382, 396–398.

113 ibid, 394–395.

However, the Tribunal found that such listing of the Pyramids Oasis would have changed the investor's legal position.[114] After a successful listing, 'a hypothetical continuation of the Claimants' activities interfering with antiquities in the area could be considered as unlawful from the international point of view'.[115] Because of this emphasis on international law, this passage of the contract arbitration award is of relevance for treaty arbitrations, too.

Similarly, the ICSID Tribunal in *Urbaser v Argentina* considered non-legal norms as part of its inquiry into whether Argentina had breached the right to FET. As shown above, the Tribunal considered if the investor had legitimate expectations and to that end examined Argentina's domestic and international obligations.[116] However, additionally it found that the 'fair and equitable treatment standard is not focused exclusively on interests and expectations of a legal nature. It does also include the actual social and economic environment of the host State'.[117] The Tribunal then concretised these non-legal considerations as including the 'universal basic human right' to guarantee basic water supply.[118] Herein, the Tribunal appears to engage in a teleological interpretation, making use of legally non-binding norms to define the FET right's content. Indeed, already the ordinary meaning of 'fair and equitable treatment' suggests that not only strict legal standards may be of interpretive relevance.

b) Consideration of investor misconduct

Both awards at the very least considered if the investor's conduct was in line with non-legal norms as a balancing criterion. As seen, in *SPP v Egypt*, the Tribunal explicitly addressed that if the investor continued to 'interfere' with protected antiquities, the company would act unlawful and lose contractual protection. In *Urbaser v Argentina*, the investor had to

---

114 cf Lahra Liberti, 'The Relevance of Non-Investment Treaty Obligations in Assessing Compensation' in Pierre-Marie Dupuy, Ernst-Ulrich Petersmann and Francesco Francioni (eds), *Human Rights in International Investment Law and Arbitration* (Oxford University Press 2009) 562 pointing out the Tribunal's reasoning that a listing would have had significant consequences on the quantum of compensation.

115 *Southern Pacific Properties v Egypt* (n 110) para 154.

116 See Chapter 7.II.1.c).

117 *Urbaser v Argentina*, Award (n 79) para 623.

118 ibid 624.

align with actual societal and economic expectations. Had it not, it appears it would have worsened its legal position in the overall balancing test that the FET right entailed.

Interestingly, the tribunals gave no regard to the fact that these norms had no legal force. They still found them relevant for taking account of the investor's conduct. The awards demonstrate a desire to make investment protection to some extent dependent on conforming with these relatively vague norms. Arguably, other tribunals could rely to that end on more determinate soft law standards such as the proliferating CSR norms. Scholars have suggested that compliance with these standards could influence investor rights' interpretation as a balancing criterion.[119]

c) Soft law as a potential indirect obligation

One step further, one could consider if soft law can give rise to an indirect obligation. For example, one could argue that *legitimate* expectations of investors only arise if they comply with applicable CSR norms. Indeed,

---

119 See Kneer (n 29) 286 who argues that if investors have voluntarily set CSR standards, this influences how tribunals should assess their legitimate expectations as such investors must foresee that the host state might want to take similar action, however without distinguishing between a voluntary investor and a binding state approach; Leinhardt (n 37) 23–24 claims that the interpretation of legitimate expectations should also account for the moral responsibilities of investors for human rights which should not go beyond what international instruments such as the ICESCR require – however, she does not take into account that investors are not addressees of international human rights treaties; Nitish Monebhurrun, 'Mapping the Duties of Private Companies in International Investment Law' (2017) 14(2) Brazilian Journal of International Law 50, 59–61 understands CSR norms in an IIA as a means to 'enlighten' the understanding of investor rights; Catherine Kessedjian, 'Rebalancing Investors' Rights and Obligations' (2021) 22(5–6) Journal of World Investment & Trade 645, 647–649 argues that human rights and CSR norms constitute basic principles of the international community that judges and arbitrators should apply to 'complement hard law norms […], when needed, to find an adequate solution for the particular case and context at stake'; Prabhash Ranjan, 'Investor Obligations in Investment Treaties: Missing Text or a Matter of Application?' in Jean Ho and Mavluda Sattorova (eds), *Investors' International Law* (Hart 2021) 141 for whom CSR may 'reframe' the purpose of IIAs; Barnali Choudhury, 'The Role of Soft Law Corporate Responsibilities in Defining Investor Obligations in International Investment Agreements' in Jean Ho and Mavluda Sattorova (eds), *Investors' International Law* (Hart 2021) 165–168.

it has been suggested that investors could forfeit an investor right if they breached certain soft law standards.[120]

The award in *SPP v Egypt* appears to favour such an approach. It seemed ready to accept that the investor would have forfeited its right if the company had interfered with property listed in the non-binding World Heritage List. One could understand this as an indirect obligation. If investors violate a non-binding norm – here: interfering with certain property listed as protected world heritage – they lose investment protection. However, it is likely that the Tribunal mistakenly understood the World Heritage List to be legally binding. Its reasoning that the investor's actions could be 'unlawful from the international point of view', quoted above, points to such a misunderstanding.

Moreover, it is submitted that construing soft law as indirect obligations would go too far. As demonstrated in Chapter 6.II, indirect obligations constitute partly compulsory norms: they accord a sanction in the form of a loss of an investor right. In contrast, compliance with soft law is entirely voluntary. It rests on cooperation and on businesses complying with it due to consumer pressure. Without a respective explicit clause in the IIA, the interpretation of investor rights alone cannot overcome this lack of compulsory effect. Therefore, as a matter of law, it appears more compelling to consider violations of soft law as a mere balancing criterion.

Nevertheless, the presented awards and discussions are again evidence of changing dynamics in investment law. These dynamics point towards investor rights as being in some way dependent on good investor behaviour towards the public interest – here, in the form of soft law that aims to

---

120 See for example Roland Kläger, 'Revising Treatment Standards – Fair and Equitable Treatment in Light of Sustainable Development' in Steffen Hindelang and Markus Krajewski (eds), *Shifting Paradigms in International Investment Law: More Balanced, Less Isolated, Increasingly Diversified* (Oxford University Press 2016) 76 who considers 'the investor's conduct including the observance of universally recognized standards' such as the ILO 'Tripartite Declaration of Principles Concerning Multinational Enterprises and Social Policy' adopted by the Governing Body of the International Labour Office at its 204th Session (Geneva, November 1977) and amended at its 279th (November 2000), 295th (March 2006) and 329th (March 2017) Sessions, (1978) 17 ILM 422 (16 November 1977) ‹www.ilo.org/wcmsp5/groups/public/---ed_emp/---emp_ent/---multi/documents/publication/wcms_094386.pdf› accessed 7 December 2021, the UN Human Rights Council 'Guiding Principles on Business and Human Rights Implementing the United Nations "Protect, Respect and Remedy" Framework' UN Doc HRC/RES/17/4 (2011) and CSR standards to be 'relevant in determining' a breach of the right to FET.

protect public goods such as cultural heritage and individual rights of others.

4. Interpreting rights in the light of other host state obligations

The analysis will now turn to the use of norms which do not lack a compulsory effect: international obligations of states. By interaction with them, investment law can, already today, bring about indirect obligations under certain specific circumstances.

In the last years, tribunals and scholars have increasingly interpreted investor rights in the light of public interest obligations of the states, for example under international human rights treaties (a). By and large, such interpretation only allows to consider investor misconduct as a balancing criterion without giving rise to an indirect obligation. Yet, the increasing tendency to do so is, again, notable (b). What is more, if the host state's obligation is sufficiently specific, reading investor rights in its light does bring about an indirect obligation (c).

a) Art 31 (1) and (3) (c) VCLT

Most relevant for the present purpose are the methods of contextual interpretation and systemic interpretation of an IIA in the light of other treaties as stipulated in Art 31 (1) and (3) (c) VCLT, respectively. They allow to resort to other obligations of states which protect the public interest.

Contextual interpretation means that investor rights should be understood in a manner consistent with other provisions of the same IIA.[121] More and more, IIAs contain clauses which relate to the public interest. Here one may think of IIAs with preambular language mentioning the public interest. At the time of writing, UNCTAD lists 60 IIAs that refer to sustainable development, 188 IIAs that include 'social investment aspects (e.g. human rights, labour, health, CSR, poverty reduction)' and 121 IIAs

121 See generally on contextual interpretation of IIAs August Reinisch, 'The Interpretation of International Investment Agreements' in Marc Bungenberg and others (eds), *International Investment Law* (Nomos 2015) paras 28–39.

that mention environmental aspects in their preamble and are currently in force.[122]

In addition, the recent generation of IIAs increasingly contains provisions on the protection of the public interest.[123] For example, these IIAs prohibit the lowering of public interest standards. In this regard, the 2012 US Model BIT stipulates in Art 12 (2) that the 'Parties recognize that it is inappropriate to encourage investment by weakening or reducing the protections afforded in domestic environmental laws'.[124] Such a clause was also present in NAFTA's investment protection chapter in Art 1114 (2) which states that '[t]he Parties recognize that it is inappropriate to encourage investment by relaxing domestic health, safety or environmental measures. [...]'. Equally relevant are exception or right to regulate clauses of newer IIAs. They exclude investment protection under certain circumstances if the state protects the public interest.[125] For example, the investment chapter of

122 UNCTAD 'IIA Mapping Project' ‹https://investmentpolicy.unctad.org/international-investment-agreements/iia-mapping› accessed 7 December 2021; see also more specifically related to sustainable development Tarcisio Gazzini, 'Bilateral Investment Treaties and Sustainable Development' (2014) 15(5–6) Journal of World Investment & Trade 929, 941–944; Karsten Nowrot, 'How to Include Environmental Protection, Human Rights and Sustainability in International Investment Law?' (2014) 15(3/4) Journal of World Investment & Trade 612, 630; related to human rights see Ursula Kriebaum, 'Human Rights of the Population of the Host State in International Investment Arbitration' (2009) 10(5) Journal of World Investment & Trade 653, 662.

123 Bruno Simma, 'Foreign Investment Arbitration: A Place for Human Rights?' (2011) 60(3) International & Comparative Law Quarterly 573, 581; specifically on modern expropriation clauses see Lukas Stifter and August Reinisch, 'Expropriation in the Light of the UNCTAD Investment Policy Framework for Sustainable Development' in Steffen Hindelang and Markus Krajewski (eds), *Shifting Paradigms in International Investment Law: More Balanced, Less Isolated, Increasingly Diversified* (Oxford University Press 2016) 90–96.

124 On the origins, rationale and diffusion of such clauses see Mary E Footer, 'Bits and Pieces: Social and Environmental Protection in the Regulation of Foreign Investment' (2009) 18(1) Michigan State Journal of International Law 33, 43–44; Gazzini (n 122) 944–946.

125 See for example Caroline Henckels, 'Protecting Regulatory Autonomy Through Greater Precision in Investment Treaties: The TPP, CETA, and TTIP' (2016) 19(1) Journal of International Economic Law 27 who explains how more specific language in the recent generation of IIAs contributes to strengthening host states' right to regulate.

the USMCA[126] – which replaced NAFTA – states in Art 10.11: 'Nothing in this Chapter shall be construed to prevent a Party from adopting, maintaining, or enforcing any measure otherwise consistent with this Chapter that it considers appropriate to ensure that investment activity in its territory is undertaken in a manner sensitive to environmental concerns.' Indeed, FTAs often even contain entire chapters on the public interest: one may take the EU's sustainable development chapters as an example. They may be read into the FTA's investment chapters that contain investor rights.[127]

Systemic interpretation means that IIAs should be understood to be consistent with the state parties' other international obligations. Art 31 (3) (c) VCLT provides that in interpreting a treaty, account shall be taken of '[a]ny relevant rules of international law applicable in the relations between the parties'. Thus, one has to read common international obligations of the IIA's state parties to protect the public interest into investor rights. This could, for example, include international human rights or environmental protection treaties. The interpretation of investment law in

126 Agreement between the United States of America, the United Mexican States, and Canada (adopted 30 November 2018, revised 10 December 2019 by the Protocol of Amendment, entered into force 1 July 2020) (USMCA).

127 See the USMCA's chapters 23 and 24 on labor and environment and the separate Agreement on Environmental Cooperation among the Governments of Canada, the United Mexican States, and the United States of America (adopted 30 November 2018, entered into force 1 July 2020) (ECA) which replace and build on NAFTA's two side agreements on the protection of the environment (North American Agreement on Environmental Cooperation (adopted 14 September 1993, entered into force 1 January 1994, date of termination 1 July 2020) (NAAEC)) and labour standards (North American Agreement on Labor Cooperation (adopted 14 September 1993, entered into force 1 July 1994, date of termination 1 July 2020) (NAALC)) and the labour and environmental protection chapters in later US FTAs. For a comparative analysis of these US labour and environmental protection provisions see Patrick Abel, 'Comparative Conclusions on Arbitral Dispute Settlement in Trade-Labour Matters Under US FTAs' in Henner Gött (ed), *Labour Standards in International Economic Law* (Springer International Publishing 2018) 153–184. See also the sustainable development chapters in EU FTAs, for example in CETA and the EU-South Korea Free Trade Agreement (EU-Korea FTA); for a contextualisation of these EU provisions see Frank Hoffmeister, 'The Contribution of EU Trade Agreements to the Development of International Investment Law' in Steffen Hindelang and Markus Krajewski (eds), *Shifting Paradigms in International Investment Law: More Balanced, Less Isolated, Increasingly Diversified* (Oxford University Press 2016) 361–363.

light of other international treaties is often also suggested as a means to strengthen host states' right to regulate.[128]

b) Consideration of investor misconduct

Some have suggested to use these interpretive methods in a manner which would qualify as an indirect obligation as understood here. However, it will be shown that in many cases, such interpretation does not bring about indirect obligations.

For example, NGOs have proposed such an approach in *amicus curiae* briefs in *Biwater Gauff v Tanzania*. The claimant conducted water and sewage services in Dar es Salaam. After running into financial difficulties, the company could not provide and extend the population's access to water as contractually promised. Eventually, Tanzania terminated the contract. Therein, the claimant saw a violation of the UK-Tanzania-BIT.[129] The *amici* argued that Tanzania did not violate the BIT. In their view, the investor violated its responsibility under the human right to water and under concepts of sustainable development.[130] As summarised by the Tribunal,

> [t]he *Amici* submit that human rights and sustainable development issues are factors that condition the nature and extent of the investor's responsibilities, and the balance of rights and obligations as between the investor and the host State. They conclude that foreign corporations engaged in projects intimately related to human rights and the capacity to achieve sustainable development (such as the project here), have the highest level of responsibility to meet their duties and obligations as foreign investors, before seeking the protection of international law. This is precisely because such investments necessarily carry with them very serious risks to the population at large.[131]

Following this concept, human rights would constitute an indirect obligation: if investors violate them, they are deprived of protection under the BIT. The same would be true for sustainable development – however, with a rather indeterminate standard of conduct.

---

128 See Chapter 3 n 57.

129 *Biwater Gauff v Tanzania* (n 1) paras 95–228.

130 ibid 378–380.

131 ibid 380.

In the same vein scholars have suggested that investor rights do not protect against a measure that the host state takes to fulfil its international obligations. Following this interpretation, consequently, an investor right could not protect investors who infringe on, for example, international human rights.[132]

However, it is suggested that such interpretation does not bring about indirect obligations in most cases. One has to bear in mind that states enjoy certain discretion in how they fulfil most of their international obligations.[133] This means that international law often only prescribes a certain result a state must achieve while leaving the means to the policy preferences of the state. Or it even only requires from the state a certain conduct, that is, to exercise best efforts in striving for a result. Often, there are many different ways a state can live up to these international obliga-

---

132 In this vein Muchlinski (n 88) 535 who only generally refers to 'binding conventions'; Moshe Hirsch, 'Interactions Between Investment and Non-Investment Obligations' in Peter Muchlinski, Frederico Ortino and Christoph Schreuer (eds), *The Oxford Handbook of International Investment Law* (Oxford University Press 2008) 176–177 with a sound emphasis on the point in time in which the relevant international obligation is in force; Kriebaum, 'Human' (n 122) 669 who claims that '[t]here can be no legitimate expectations that are contrary to human rights law'; Knoll-Tudor (n 92) 341 who argues that FET is about a balance at giving the host state and the investor each what is due, which must include assessing the investors' behaviour, for example if they breach international labour standards; Bruno Simma and Theodore Kill, 'Harmonizing Investment Protection and International Human Rights: First Steps Towards a Methodology' in Christina Binder and others (eds), *International Investment Law for the 21st Century: Essays in Honour of Christoph Schreuer* (Oxford University Press 2009) 705 contending that any legitimate expectations must include 'an expectation that the State would honour its international human rights obligations'; Kneer (n 29) 282, 289 bringing forward that human rights violations by investors exclude their investment protection or reduce compensation; Filip Balcerzak, *Investor – State Arbitration and Human Rights* (Brill Nijhoff 2017) 173 agreeing with *Kill*, *Kriebaum* and *Simma* that investors must expect the host state to enforce human rights law; see also the more specific proposal by Simma (n 123) 594–596 that investors should conduct a human rights audit that also takes into account the international human rights obligations of the host state and that this impact assessment could inform the definition of 'legitimate expectations'.

133 See only Olivier D Schutter, *International Human Rights Law: Cases, Materials, Commentary* (2nd edn, Cambridge University Press 2014) 441–462; Anne Peters, *Beyond Human Rights: The Legal Status of the Individual in International Law* (Cambridge University Press 2016) 69; for an in depth-analysis of the often-relevant concept of due diligence, see Joanna Kulesza, *Due Diligence in International Law* (Brill Nijhoff 2016) 18–114.

tions. For example, international human rights provide a comprehensive system in which the state must balance the different colliding interests. In many cases, there are alternative ways it can live up to its obligations.[134] In the above-mentioned case of *Biwater Gauff v Tanzania*, the human right to water could, for example, envisage both the state and the underfinanced investor to provide the water services. In other words: it is focussed on a certain result, not the means to that end. Just as other international treaties, human rights usually do not specify how the host state should treat the investor.[135]

This is well illustrated by the *Philip Morris v Uruguay* award. Uruguay had prescribed plain packaging for tobacco products. The claimant contended that Uruguay had violated the right to FET. Yet, the Tribunal denied that Uruguay had acted arbitrarily. It observed that Uruguay had enacted said regulation to comply with its obligations under the WHO Framework Convention on Tobacco Control.[136] Its Art 2 obliges state parties to protect the population against health, social, environmental and economic consequences of tobacco consumption and exposure to tobacco smoke. Observing that the Convention imposed rather general obligations, the Tribunal affirmed that Uruguay had a 'margin of appreciation' under the IIA 'at least' in the context of regulating public health.[137]

Conversely, reading international obligations of states into investor rights does not allow to discern a specific standard of conduct. It only crystallises through the host state's policy decisions.[138] In other words,

---

134 cf Simma (n 123) 591–592 on the complex task of harmonising human rights and investment law obligations in a concrete case.

135 John H Knox, 'Horizontal Human Rights Law' (2008) 102(1) American Journal of International Law 1, 18.

136 WHO Framework Convention on Tobacco Control (adopted 21 May 2003, entered into force 27 February 2005) 2302 UNTS 166 (WHO Framework Convention on Tobacco Control).

137 *Philip Morris v Uruguay* (n 84) para 399; from the literature see the discussion about the transfer of the margin of appreciation-doctrine to international investment law by Barnali Choudhury, 'Recapturing Public Power: Is Investment Arbitration's Engagement of the Public Interest Contributing to the Democratic Deficit?' (2008) 41(3) Vanderbilt Journal of Transnational Law 775, 823–827.

138 On the example of investment-labour linkages, see Henner Gött and Till P Holterhus, 'Mainstreaming Investment-Labour Linkage Through "Mega-Regional" Trade Agreements' in Henner Gött (ed), *Labour Standards in International Economic Law* (Springer International Publishing 2018) 244–252; cf the methodological remarks on norm conflicts by Jörg Kammerhofer, 'The Theory of Norm Conflict Solutions in International Investment Law' in Marie-Claire Cordonier Segger, Markus W Gehring and Andrew P Newcombe (eds), *Sus-*

there is nothing that prescribes that investors must do X in order to receive and keep the respective investor right. Human rights (or other treaties) could also have allowed them to do Y if the host state had taken Y as an alternative domestic policy.[139] The same is true for public interest provisions in the same IIA and according contextual interpretation of investor rights. Most of them give states the same discretion.

Rather, the presented methods of interpretation merely allow consideration of the investor's misconduct as one balancing criterion within the analysis of an investor right. This is a noteworthy development by itself. In the past, tribunals have sometimes categorically refused to interpret investor rights in the light of other international treaties which protect the public interest.[140] Or they gave wide deference to the host state in this regard.[141]

There are indications that tribunals are increasingly more willing to consider investor misconduct. As a consequence of the right to regulate-debate, arbitral tribunals affirm the interpretive relevance of other international treaties more and more – although the concrete interpretive impact is not always clear.[142] For example, in the above-mentioned case of *Biwater Gauff v Tanzania*, the Tribunal considered the *amicus curiae* briefs as follows:

tainable Development in World Investment Law (Kluwer Law International 2011) 89–91; Balcerzak (n 132) 152–153.

139 For positions which too quickly and too generally exclude FET protection when the host state fulfils its international human rights obligations, see Knoll-Tudor (n 92) 341; Kneer (n 29) 288–289; Julian Scheu, 'Trust Building, Balancing, and Sanctioning: Three Pillars of a Systematic Approach to Human Rights in International Investment Law and Arbitration' (2017) 48(2) Georgetown Journal of International Law 449, 497; cf also the methodological problem of applying international obligations of states to non-state actors rightly raised by Nowrot (n 122) 637.

140 On international environmental law see *Compañía del Desarrollo de Santa Elena, S.A. v The Republic of Costa Rica*, ICSID Case No. ARB/96/1, Final Award (17 February 2000) paras 71–72.

141 Regarding indigenous peoples' rights see *Glamis Gold, Ltd. v The United States of America*, Award (UNCITRAL, 8 June 2009) para 24; *Grand River Enterprises Six Nations, Ltd. and Others v United States of America*, Award (UNCITRAL, 12 January 2011) paras 137–145; for a discussion of these cases see for example Laurence B de Chazournes and Brian McGarry, 'What Roles Can Constitutional Law Play in Investment Arbitration?' (2014) 15(5–6) Journal of World Investment & Trade 862, 872–875.

142 In this direction point for example Kriebaum, 'Human' (n 122) 676 who argues that how much weight an investment tribunal may give to human rights depends on the design of the applicable treaty; Eric de Brabandere, *Investment Treaty Arbitration as Public International Law: Procedural Aspects and Implications*

> [T]he Arbitral Tribunal has also taken into account the submissions of the Petitioners [...] which emphasise countervailing factors such as the responsibility of foreign investors, both in terms of prior due diligence as well as subsequent conduct; the limit to legitimate expectations in circumstances where an investor itself takes on risks in entering a particular investment environment; and the relevance of the parties' respective rights and obligations as set out in any relevant investment agreement (here the Lease Contract).[143]

It is notable that the tribunal used the term 'obligations' also when referring to the investor. Building on the submission by the *amici* that investors had responsibilities towards the public interest, the Tribunal affirmed that it gave weight to the investor's conduct as a countervailing factor. However, it remains unclear how these 'obligations' affected the Tribunal's decision.[144] Yet, it serves as an example of an award that generally affirms the analytical relevance of the investor's misconduct towards the public interest. Apparently, the Tribunal in *Suez v Argentina* had the same in mind when it observed that obligations under international investment and human rights law are not 'inconsistent, contradictory, or mutually exclusive'[145].

(Cambridge University Press 2015) 129 who considers that human rights are relatively absent in arbitral decisions even though tribunals have relied on the jurisprudence of the ECtHR to determine a breach of investor rights; Vivian Kube and Ernst-Ulrich Petersmann, 'Human Rights Law in International Investment Arbitration' (2016) 11(1) Asian Journal of WTO & International Health Law and Policy 65, 93 who observe that 'the occasional references by arbitrators to human rights for interpretative guidance [...] do not follow a transparent, legal methodology'; sceptical Marc Jacob, 'Faith Betrayed: International Investment Law and Human Rights' in Rainer Hofmann and Christian J Tams (eds), *International Investment Law and Its Others* (Nomos 2012) 45–46 finding that 'human rights arguments have to date not fared particularly well in the practice of investment tribunals.'

143 *Biwater Gauff v Tanzania* (n 1) para 601.

144 Kriebaum, 'Human' (n 122) 676.

145 *Suez, Sociedad General de Aguas de Barcelona S.A. and Vivendi Universal S.A. v The Argentine Republic*, ICSID Case No. ARB/03/19, Decision on Liability (30 July 2010) para 262.

c) Specific state obligations as indirect obligations

Exceptionally, contextual and systemic interpretation can imply an indirect obligation. To do so, the relevant public interest obligation of the state that should be read into an investor right must be sufficiently specific so as not to leave the state any discretion how to fulfil its obligation. Such strict obligations exist in rare instances. Without such discretion, these obligations specify what the host state must do towards private actors.[146]

For example, several international labour standards[147] qualify as sufficiently specific in this regard. To name but one, ILO Convention No 105[148] requires parties to abolish forced labour. If the state encounters an investor which engages in forced labour, it is clear what it must do: prohibit said practice. The state has no discretion in that regard. Only the actual enforcement of the obligation is left to the state.

If the IIA's state parties are also parties to the ILO Convention, one must read the Convention into investor rights through systemic interpretation according to Art 31 (3) (c) VCLT. In some cases, contextual interpretation may also apply to the same end. For example, in Art 23.3 CETA, the parties reaffirm their commitments under the ILO Declaration on Fundamental Principles and Rights at Work and ILO Conventions.

Then, the prohibition of forced labour serves as a determinate standard of conduct. If investors breach it, systemic and contextual interpretation

146 Knox (n 135) 2 has illustrated this with the model of a norm pyramid for human rights: Most human rights obligations only generally require the state to protect human rights against violations by other private actors, constituting the road floor of the pyramid. Domestic policy decisions must specify and enforce them. Higher located in the pyramid are a smaller number of private duties that human rights specify as actions necessary to protect human rights in this regard, only leaving their enforcement to governments. These are the obligations of interest here. Finally, there are very few human rights obligations which international law specifies and enforces itself – the top of the pyramid: those forming part of international criminal law. These belong to this book's category of direct obligations. See also more generally Bruno Simma and Andreas L Paulus, 'The Responsibility of Individuals for Human Rights Abuses in Internal Conflicts: A Positivist View' (1999) 93(2) American Journal of International Law 302, 313.

147 For a general call to consider labour standards see Reingard Zimmer, 'Implications of CETA and TTIP on Social Standards' in Henner Gött (ed), *Labour Standards in International Economic Law* (Springer International Publishing 2018) 218.

148 ILO Convention (No 105) concerning the Abolition of Forced Labour (adopted 25 June 1957, entered into force 17 January 1959) 320 UNTS 291 (ILO Convention No 105).

requires that they forfeit their investor rights against state measures which build on this prohibition. This consequence is automatic, because the state has no discretion in how it addresses investors who engage in forced labour. The ILO Convention specifies that it is prohibited. Nevertheless, the IIA does not integrate it as a direct obligation: the state cannot claim compliance with the prohibition through the IIA and demand compensation. Instead, it deprives investors of the rights that it would otherwise award. Thus, in this case, the presented methods of interpretation imply an indirect obligation.

Practice gave rise to a case in which such an indirect obligation would have applied if the case had not been discontinued. In *Foresti v South Africa*, investors filed a claim against South Africa which enacted mineral ownership laws to eliminate the consequences of apartheid.[149] The Convention on the Elimination of All Forms of Racial Discrimination[150] prohibits apartheid and does not leave states any discretion to that end. Hence, the Tribunal would have had to read South Africa's obligation into the applicable IIA's non-discrimination right. If the investor's mineral ownership followed from the apartheid regime, the investor would not have qualified for protection.[151] This implies an indirect obligation – if investors engage in apartheid in breach of the named prohibition, they forfeit the right to non-discrimination.

Moreover, indeed any IIA that contains substantive direct obligations as discussed in Part I, allows for such contextual interpretation of investor rights. Consistency requires that an investor who violates such direct obligations cannot be protected for the same conduct by an investor right.[152] This means that such direct obligations operate at the same time as indirect obligations.[153] They serve as a good example of the possibility that the

---

149 *Piero Foresti and Others v The Republic of South Africa*, ICSID Case No. ARB(AF)/07/1, Award (4 August 2010) paras 54–58, 79–82.

150 International Convention on the Suppression and Punishment of the Crime of Apartheid (adopted 30 November 1973, entered into force 18 July 1976) 1015 UNTS 243 (Anti-Apartheid Convention).

151 Similarly Simma (n 123) 585–586.

152 Supported for example by Anne-Juliette Bonzon, 'Balance Between Investment Protection and Sustainable Development in BITs' (2014) 15(5–6) Journal of World Investment & Trade 809, 822.

153 See *Hesham Talaat M. Al-Warraq v The Republic of Indonesia*, Final Award (UNCITRAL, 15 December 2014) paras 631–648, 663 in which the international obligation of investors under Art 9 Agreement on Promotion, Protection and Guarantee of Investments among Member States of the Organisation of the Islamic Conference (adopted 5 June 1981, entered into force 23 September 1986)

same norm has a dual character as both a direct and an indirect obligation. For example, if the IIA contains a direct investor obligation prohibiting corruption, this has consequences for any investor right in the same IIA. Consistency requires that the same fraudulent conduct which violates said direct obligation cannot be protected under, for example, the right to FET.

It is notable that this type of indirect obligation has a narrower scope than the ones encountered as part of admissibility and jurisdiction requirements in the previous Section. They do not generally deprive investors of all protection in case of a breach. Instead, investors only lose protection against those state measures which serve to protect the same type of public interest as the indirect obligation. In the above-mentioned example, investors only lose protection against state measures that serve to enforce the ILO Convention. They continue to be protected against all other types of state measures. For example, they could still invoke investor rights against anti-corruption measures by the host state. In contrast, the indirect obligations encountered in Section I categorically deprived investors of access to investment arbitration.

5. Compliance with host state's domestic law after admission

Finally, the requirement to comply with the host state's domestic law forms an established indirect obligation.

Tribunals consider that investors who violate domestic law after having been admitted to the host state do not qualify for substantive investment protection under certain conditions (a). One can construe this requirement as an indirect obligation: if investors do not comply, they are deprived of substantive protection by IIAs' investor rights (b). The requirement can relate to very different facets of the public interest (c).

‹https://investmentpolicy.unctad.org/international-investment-agreements/treaty-files/2399/download› accessed 7 December 2021 (OIC Investment Agreement) features both as grounds to reject international investor obligation and as the basis for a counterclaim, hence in the indirect and the direct dimension. Futhermore, if the international community would eventually decide to conclude an international treaty with directly applicable human rights obligations (see above Chapter 1.III.1), of course these obligations could be read into an IIA pursuant to Art 31 (3) (c) VCLT, see Peter Muchlinski, 'The Impact of a Business and Human Rights Treaty on Investment Law and Arbitration' in Surya Deva and David Bilchitz (eds), *Building a Treaty on Business and Human Rights: Context and Contours* (Cambridge University Press 2017) 362–370.

a) Compliance as a substantive requirement

Breaches of domestic law must take place after the admission of the investment to become a matter for the merits phase in an arbitration. Before the admission, compliance with domestic law already conditions investment tribunals' jurisdiction – bringing about an indirect obligation which affects the procedural right to file an investment claim as shown in Chapter 7.I.2. In contrast, the requirement studied here is one that has a consequence for the investor's substantive international right. It demands that the investor complies with domestic law throughout the entire performance of the investment.[154]

Again, this requirement can follow from explicit IIA clauses or as an implicit part of any investor right's personal scope – of defining what constitutes a 'foreign investment' in the meaning of the IIA. For example, as will be seen, the Tribunal in *Al-Warraq v Indonesia* applied Art 9 of the applicable OIC Agreement to that end. The provision stipulates:

> The investor shall be bound by the laws and regulations in force in the host state and shall refrain from all acts that may disturb public order or morals or that may be prejudicial to the public interest. He is also to refrain from exercising restrictive practices and from trying to achieve gains through unlawful means.

The Tribunal identified fraudulent behaviour by the investor which violated this clause.[155] The Tribunal thus concluded:

> […] that the Claimant failed to uphold the Indonesian laws and regulations. […] The Claimant having breached the local laws and put the public interest at risk, he has deprived himself of the protection afforded by the OIC Agreement.[156]

---

154 See n 20 and 21.

155 *Al-Warraq v Indonesia*, Final Award (n 153) paras 631–645.

156 ibid 645. Even though the Tribunal referred to the claim's inadmissibility due to the clean hands doctrine in the subsequent paragraphs, it is submitted that the Tribunal in reality engaged in an interpretation and application of the substantive investor rights. Up until paragraph 645, the Tribunal interpreted the investor rights in the light of Art 9 OIC Investment Agreement – hence, it understood the personal scope of its rights as covering only investors that complied with this clause. It appears that the subsequent argument based on the clean hands doctrine only served to support and strengthen this argument. It has no autonomous relevance to the case. Chapter 7.IV will explain in more detail why invoking the clean hands doctrine is generally superfluous.

Even without any such explicit clause, the Tribunal in *Plama v Bulgaria* has denied substantive protection for a breach of domestic anti-corruption laws[157] – supported for example by the Tribunals in *World Duty Free v Kenya*[158] and *Yukos v Russia*.[159]

b) Compliance as an established indirect obligation

For similar reasons as its jurisdictional counterpart, the requirement implies an indirect obligation. If investors breach domestic law throughout the investment after it has been admitted, they are subject to a sanction as the IIA deprives them of substantive protection.

It is fair to say that this indirect obligation is particularly far-reaching. The investor has to observe it throughout the entire performance of the investment. This means that investment law takes account of the investor's conduct over, potentially, many years. It institutes a constant threat of sanctioning non-compliance with the depriving of substantive protection.

c) Content of the obligation

From the quoted reasoning in *Plama v Bulgaria*, it is explicitly apparent that the Tribunal measured the investor's behaviour against its impact on the public interest – here, the Indonesian rule of law. This shows that tribunals applying domestic anti-corruption laws, at least incidentally, serve this public good.

Other tribunals have applied domestic laws that protect different aspects of the public interest. For example, the ICSID Tribunal in *Maffezzini v Spain* applied Spanish domestic regulation on environmental protection. The claimant in this case was an Argentinian entrepreneur investing in the chemicals industry. The Tribunal held that Spanish law required an environmental impact assessment ('EIA'). It pointed out that international law increasingly demanded such an assessment, too. It then held that the claimant had not adequately conducted the EIA because he wanted to minimise his costs. Thus, Spain could not be responsible for interfering with

157 *Plama v Bulgaria*, Award (n 19) para 139.
158 *World Duty Free v Kenya* (n 51) para 157.
159 *Yukos v Russia*, Final Award (n 21) para 1349.

the investment based on domestic environmental law.[160] In the same vein, the ICSID Tribunal in *World Duty Free v Kenya*, an investment contract arbitration, declared the investment contract void due to corruption by the investor that *inter alia* violated the host state's domestic law.[161]

Furthermore, the Tribunal in *Quiborax v Bolivia* considered domestic labour and environmental regulation. The claimants engaged in the mining of the Bolivian Gran Slaar de Uyuni basin, an environmentally sensitive dry salt lake area. They claimed that Bolivia violated the Bolivia-Chile BIT[162] by annulling the mining concessions.[163] The respondent raised the defence that investment law did not protect the investors because they breached domestic industrial safety, environment and labour laws. The Tribunal dismissed the argument – but only for the reason that the violations were 'minor breaches of law',[164] and that 'Bolivia has not established that a lack of environmental licences would warrant the termination of the concessions.'[165]

Both awards indicate the potentially broad scope of public goods and individual rights that the indirect obligation to comply with the host state's domestic law can protect. The award in *Quiborax v Bolivia* also shows that tribunals require qualified breaches of domestic law. The respective jurisprudence on compliance with domestic host state law at the time of admission for establishing tribunals' jurisdiction applies here, too. To recall: tribunals have demanded *inter alia* that the breach reaches a certain intensity, that the investor acted negligently or in bad faith.[166] It is submitted that such qualifications are necessary: it would be disproportionate if minor breaches of domestic law could cause the drastic consequence of entirely depriving the investor of investment protection. Therefore, the indirect obligation's standard of conduct does not purely incorporate the domestic obligation but internationalises it through these qualifications.

---

160 *Maffezini v Spain*, Award (n 87) paras 65–71.

161 *World Duty Free v Kenya* (n 51) para 157.

162 Bolivia-Chile BIT (adopted 22 September 1994, entered into force 21 July 1999, date of termination 11 April 2020) ‹https://investmentpolicy.unctad.org/international-investment-agreements/treaty-files/448/download› accessed 7 December 2021 (Bolivia-Chile BIT).

163 *Quiborax S.A. and Non Metallic Minerals S.A. v Plurinational State of Bolivia*, ICSID Case No. ARB/06/2, Award (16 September 2015) paras 7–35.

164 ibid 219.

165 ibid 220.

166 See Chapter 7.I.2.c).

Another parallel is that non-compliance with domestic law after admission to the investment can deprive investors of investment protection entirely. This means that if investors breach domestic law that protects public good X, they may also lose investment protection against state measures that protect the entirely different public good Y. A nexus between the state's regulatory intentions and the scope of the domestic law that the investors breached is not necessary.

6. Interim conclusion

This Section has shown a development to make substantive investor rights dependent on the investor's conduct towards the public interest. Investor rights are not only about delineating the business risk undertaken by the investor anymore. Instead, investment law is increasingly also about appreciating investors' role in society, their impact on public goods and individual rights.

Tribunals have considered very different facets of the public interest to be relevant, including cultural heritage, human rights, environmental protection and the rule of law. Some of the approaches presented took account of the investor's actions only as one balancing criterion amongst others. This means that investor misconduct 'tips the scale' to the disfavour of the investor when the tribunal interprets an investor right and applies it to the facts of the case. They do not constitute indirect obligations, but serve similar functions in a less stringent, automatic way. Other doctrinal methods have already brought about indirect obligations – especially the requirement to comply with the host state's domestic law. They sanction non-compliance with a standard of conduct with the loss of investment protection.

III. Rules on compensation

The requirements of investor rights represent one side of how indirect obligations come about in substantive investment law. Of similar importance are the rules on compensation for damages caused to foreign investors by the host state. If the host state violates an investor right, it must pay compensation following customary law of state responsibility.[167] Also, the state must pay compensation to legally expropriate an investment.[168] This Section will show that these rules, too, imply indirect obligations. These are constellations in which tribunals partly or even completely reduce the amount of compensation because the investor infringed the public interest.

This Section will examine two focal points for possible indirect obligations: Tribunals may adopt a qualitative instead of a quantitative methodology for calculating compensation or they may employ the principle of contributory negligence. As for the former, recent IIAs contain rules with indirect obligations to that end. A few arbitral awards appeared to have

167 However, one could doubt that Art 36 ILC Articles on State Responsibility – which reflects customary law – is applicable to international investment law: Art 33 ILC Articles on State Responsibility declares the chapter on consequences for breaches of international law to be applicable only to obligations of states owed to other states or to the international community without codifying in that regard the responsibility of a state towards any person or entity other than a state. However, arbitral jurisprudence and scholars regularly resort to Art 36 ILC Articles on State Responsibility and on the relevant PCIJ's decision in *Chorzów Factory* for determining compensation for breaches of investment law given that IIAs usually do not provide any rules on the determination of the amount of compensation owed for violations of obligations, see for example *LG&E Energy Corp. LG&E Capital Corp. and LG&E International, Inc. v Argentine Republic*, ICSID Case No. ARB/02/1, Award (25 July 2007) paras 29–32; *BG Group v Argentina* (n 101) paras 422–428; *National Grid PLC v The Argentine Republic*, Award (UNCITRAL, 3 November 2008) para 269; Sergey Ripinsky and Kevin Williams, *Damages in International Investment Law* (British Institute of International and Comparative Law 2008) 28–32; Salacuse (n 84) 555–558. Thus, the practice of investment tribunals can be understood to reflect that investment law has always entailed rules on the consequences of a breach identical to the respective inter-state law, or as a convergence of these rules crystallizing with the creation of the ILC Articles, or even as evidence of the state-centred model of international investment obligations as inter-state in their substantive nature. Irrespective of the doctrinal explanation, the applicability of the rule reflected in Art 36 ILC Articles on State Responsibility to breaches of international investment obligations is well-established, see Helmut P Aust, 'Investment Protection and Sustainable Development: What Role for the Law of State Responsibility?' in Steffen Hindelang and Markus Krajewski (eds), *Shifting Paradigms in International Investment Law: More Balanced, Less Isolated, Increasingly Diversified* (Oxford University Press 2016) 210–213 and the various possible explanations presented by Martins Paparinskis, 'Investment Treaty Arbitration and the (New) Law of State Responsibility' (2013) 24(2) European Journal of International Law 617, 635–640.

168 Dolzer and Schreuer (n 18) 100.

considered investor misconduct in calculating compensation, too – but only as a balancing criterion (1.). With regard to the latter, tribunals have applied the principle of contributory negligence in a manner that brings about indirect obligations to protect different public goods and individual rights (2.).

1. Qualitative methodology of calculating compensation

A qualitative methodology of calculating compensation may bring about indirect obligations. This Section will first explain the rules on calculation (a). Then, it will study new IIAs which contain rules that one could understand as indirect obligations. They define investor misconduct towards the public interest as a relevant criterion for the calculation (b). Apart from these new treaties, arbitral jurisprudence does not allow to discern such indirect obligations so far. Instead, some tribunals have considered investor misconduct as a vague balancing criterion that has some relevance for calculating compensation (c).

a) Rules on calculation

If an investment tribunal has determined that the state violated an investor right, it grants compensation to the investor for damages caused by this violation. This requires the tribunal to calculate the compensation. The determining of the right calculation methodology is complex, technical and often heatedly discussed by the disputing parties. Investment tribunals enjoy substantial discretion in choosing the method and, indeed, exercise this discretion in different ways.[169] Generally, these methods aim to adequately value the economic worth of the investment before the state's interference, or the loss of profit. They include, for example, market or sales comparisons, income- or asset-based valuation approaches.[170] Thus,

---

169 Ripinsky and Williams (n 167) 192; Jimmy S Hansen, '"Missing Links" in Investment Arbitration: Quantification of Damages to Foreign Shareholders' (2013) 14(3) Journal of World Investment & Trade 434, 446; regarding NAFTA see for example *Myers v Canada* (n 92) para 309.

170 See the in-depth analysis by Irmgard Marboe, *Calculation of Compensation and Damages in International Investment Law* (2nd edn, Oxford University Press 2017) paras 4.73–5.273.

rules on calculating compensation are usually about the most adequate *quantitative* assessment of the investment.[171]

b) Indirect obligations in new IIA clauses

However, new IIA clauses have included a *qualitative* element into these rules. They consider the investor's conduct towards the public interest as an attenuating factor. This means that if the investor adversely affects the public interest, the result of the calculation is a lower compensation.

There are new clauses which explicitly require tribunals to look into the investor's conduct[172] – without explicitly addressing its impact on the public interest. For example, Art 12 (2) of the Draft Pan African Investment Code stipulates:

> Where appropriate, the assessment of adequate compensation shall be based on an equitable balance between the public interest and interest of the investor affected, having regard to all relevant circumstances and taking account of: the current and past use of the property, the history of its acquisition, the extent of previous profit made by the foreign investor through the investment, and the duration of the investment.

Similarly, Art 6 SADC Model BIT Template proposes as the third IIA design option the following clause:

> [...] fair and adequate compensation shall be based on an equitable balance between the public interest and interest of those affected, having regard for all relevant circumstances and taking into account the current and past use of the property, the history of its acquisition, the fair market value of the property, the purpose of the expropriation, the extent of previous profit made by the foreign investor through the investment, and the duration of the investment.

---

171 See Toni Marzal, 'Quantum (In)Justice: Rethinking the Calculation of Compensation and Damages in ISDS' (2021) 22(2) Journal of World Investment & Trade 249, 254–279 on the evolution of quantitative calculation methods with a criticism that tribunals conceive quantum assessment as a 'fact-finding operation' and exclude 'considerations of equity, fairness or policy' (255).

172 Similar to the findings in the previous Chapters, it is by such wording in new IIA clauses that a change of perspective from the state as the entity to be disciplined to the investor is brought about.

Both clauses require the arbitral tribunal to strike a balance between private and public interests in determining the compensable damage. The listed balancing criteria also require the examining of the investor's conduct. How investors made 'use' of their property is a perspective that potentially allows to consider how their conduct affected the public interest – especially as the tribunal should consider 'all relevant circumstances'. Here, investor misconduct appears as a balancing criterion in the calculation exercise.

A more explicit reference to the public interest is offered by the 2015 India Model BIT. Its Art 5 covers the protection against expropriation and prescribes that

> […] compensation shall be adequate and be at least equivalent to the fair market value of the expropriated investment […]. Valuation criteria shall include going concern value, asset value including declared tax value of tangible property, and other criteria, as appropriate, to determine fair market value.

This Article must be read together with Art 26 which is a provision on the award of an investment tribunal. It further concretises which criteria are relevant for determining the amount of compensation. It stipulates in its paragraph 3 that '[…] [f]or the calculation of monetary damages, the Tribunal shall also reduce the damages to take into account any restitution of property or repeal or modification of the measure, or other mitigating factors.[4] [sic]' Footnote 4 spells out that

> [m]itigating factors can include, current and past use of the investment, the history of its acquisition and purpose, compensation received by the investor from other sources, any unremedied harm or damage that the investor has caused to the environment or local community or other relevant considerations regarding the need to balance public interest and the interests of the investor.

It is remarkable how explicitly this footnote requires to consider how the investor affected the public interest. It specifically requires a tribunal to look into 'unremedied harm' the investor 'caused' to public goods such as the environment and individual rights of the local community. Potentially, it relates to other aspects of the public interest too, given that it also points to 'other relevant considerations'.

In doing so, one could argue that the India Model BIT brings about an indirect obligation. If the investor harms the public interest, the BIT accords a legal sanction in the form of a lower amount of compensation.

Consequently, investors partly forfeit their investor right – it is devaluated. Admittedly, this indirect obligation remains vague in its content.[173] The BIT is silent on what exactly constitutes an 'unremedied harm' to a relevant public interest. Nor does the BIT specify by how much the tribunal shall reduce the amount of compensation. Hence, alternatively, one could read the clause as merely defining investor misconduct as a relevant balancing criterion.[174] The tribunal should apply it when it makes use of its discretion to calculate compensation. Even then, the clause marks a remarkable change from a purely quantitative calculation method.

Clearer is the existence of an indirect obligation in the ECOWAS Investment Rules. Its Art 18 stipulates in the here relevant parts:

> (2) Where an investor is alleged by a host Member State [...] to have failed to comply with its obligation relating to preestablishment impact assessment, the tribunal [...] shall consider whether this breach [..] is materially relevant to the issues before it, and if so, what mitigating or offsetting effects this may have on the merits of a claim or on any damages awarded in the event of such award.
>
> [...]
>
> (4) Where a persistent failure to comply with Article 14 or 15 is raised by a host Member State defendant [...], the tribunal [...] shall consider whether this breach [...] is materially relevant to the issues before it, and if so, what mitigating or offsetting effects this may have on the merits of a claim or on any damages awarded in the event of such award.

Paragraph 2 refers to the pre-establishment social and environmental impact assessment obligations that Art 12 imposes on investors. Art 14 and 15 impose post-establishment investor obligations such as the obligation to 'uphold human rights in the workplace and the community in which they are located'.

By referring to these concrete standards of conduct, Art 18 construes an indirect obligation: in case the investor breaches them, the BIT accords the

173 Notwithstanding, other indirect obligations that the analysis identified were at times vague in their scope too, see for example Chapter 7.I.1. That the standard of conduct is indeterminate does not appear to be a fundamental argument against affirming that a clause brings about an indirect obligation.

174 Similar to other identified instances in which substantive requirements of investor rights consider investor misconduct towards the public interest as a balancing criterion amongst others, see for example Chapter 7.II.2.

legal sanction of reducing compensation. The provision even sets different requirements for such an indirect obligation depending on the relevant standard of conduct. Whereas breaches of pre-establishment obligations *per se* qualify for a reduction of damages, post-establishment obligations presuppose a 'persistent failure to comply' – hence, recurring violations.

Yet, one could contest the character of an indirect obligation because the tribunal only 'may' apply a mitigating or offsetting effect. Therefore, it appears that the tribunal remains free to reduce the amount of compensation. Then, there would not be an automatic sanction in case of non-compliance. However, it seems adequate to consider Art 18 to be, at the very least, close to forming an indirect obligation. The provided criteria are fairly specific. It is unlikely that a tribunal would simply disregard them in exercising its discretion.

Surprisingly, the 2019 Netherlands Model BIT is particularly clear in instructing arbitral tribunals to take account of investor misbehaviour. Its Art 23 stipulates:

> Without prejudice to national administrative or criminal law procedures, a Tribunal, in deciding on the amount of compensation, is expected to take into account non-compliance by the investor with its commitments under the UN Guiding Principles on Business and Human Rights, and the OECD Guidelines for Multinational Enterprises.

It is remarkable that this provision builds on international CSR norms against which investors' behaviour can be tested. Notwithstanding that these norms are legally non-binding, Art 23 provides them with legal effect as tribunals could modify the calculation method by evaluating investors' behaviour towards human rights. Nonetheless, Art 23 is somewhat ambiguous in only 'expecting' – rather than 'requiring' – tribunals to take into account the investors behaviour. It seems that this expression serves to respect the discretion that the arbitrators have in deciding on the calculation methodology. As an 'expectation' is more than a simple 'suggestion', one may understand this provision as generally requiring tribunals to take account of investors' non-compliance with the listed CSR instruments while leaving tribunals leeway to disregard this criterion in exceptional circumstances.

c) Consideration of investor misconduct in arbitral awards

In contrast to these new IIA clauses, indirect obligations have not followed from calculation methods for compensation in arbitral practice. However, at least to some extent, tribunals have considered the investor's conduct towards the public interest as a relevant analytical criterion for the calculation of compensation. Herein, the tribunals show a tendency to a more qualitative calculation method – intimating the approaches of the presented new IIA clauses.

Tribunals did so by considering investors' role in society to be relevant for valuing the investment. In this direction, some tribunals expected the investor to assess the political risks in the host state[175] – indicating in vague terms that investors should conduct an impact assessment before investing.

For example, in *AMT v Zaire*, the ICSID Tribunal reduced the compensable damage caused by violent acts of Zairian soldiers. It argued that the investor had invested in Zaire knowing that it suffered from political turmoil,[176] stating that

> [...] the Tribunal will opt for a method that is most plausible and realistic in the circumstances of the case, while rejecting all other methods of assessment which would serve unjustly to enrich an investor who, rightly or wrongly, has chosen to invest in a country such as Zaire, believing that by so doing the investor is constructing a castle in Spain or a Swiss chalet in Germany without any risk, political or even economic or financial or any risk whatsoever.[177]

Conversely, the Tribunal seems to have expected the investor to assess the general political situation of the host state before investing. The investor failed to do so in this case: the company did not take account of the rule of law situation in Zaire. For this reason, the investment was valued to be of less worth – and hence the investor received less compensation.

Similarly, the award in *Lemire v Ukraine* rejected a favourable calculation method the investor had suggested. It held that the method must 'reflect country risk, i.e. the fact that the same company, situated in the US or

---

175 Maria Gritsenko, 'Relevance of the Host State's Development Status in Investment Treaty Arbitration' in Freya Baetens (ed), *Investment Law Within International Law: Integrationist Perspectives* (Cambridge University Press 2013) 349–351.

176 *American Manufacturing & Trading, Inc. v Republic of Zaire*, ICSID Case No. ARB/93/1, Award (21 February 1997) paras 7.13–7.15; Gritsenko (n 175) 350.

177 *American Manufacturing & Trading v Zaire* (n 176) para 7.15.

in Ukraine, is subject to different political and regulatory risks'.[178] Then, the Tribunal continued to assess whether the compensation the investor claimed was 'a fair reflection of the actual loss, reasonably proportional to the investment'.[179] To answer this question, it closely inquired into the claimant's actions. It stated *inter alia* that '[h]e had the courage to venture into a transitional State',[180] was an investor 'who [took] considerable risks'[181] and 'has devoted a significant proportion of his career to the [investment project] in Ukraine, and he brought and implemented a new conception of commercial radio which was entirely new in this ex-USSR environment.'[182]

For the present purpose it is notable that the Tribunal undertook a form of proportionality analysis when it assessed the due compensation. It engaged in a qualitative weighing and balancing in calculating the compensation. The result should reflect the societal conditions the investor encountered in the host state.[183] But it also seems that the investor's actions and his impact on society were relevant for the calculation as well.

Even clearer in addressing investors' conduct towards the public interest is the ICSID award in *Bear Creek v Peru.* This Tribunal also refused to apply a calculation method the investor had suggested. Said method would have compensated the investor for profits it could have gained had the project been carried out. Yet, the investor had not proven that a hypothetical purchaser of the project would have obtained the necessary social license. It referred to the well-known resistance by local indigenous communities.[184]

Herein, the Tribunal took account of how the project affected indigenous peoples. Because the project interfered with their rights, the Tribunal considered the investment to be of less value. It is an indirect way of sanctioning a public interest-adverse investment: To engage in a project which infringes on indigenous peoples' rights from the outset reduces the

---

178 *Joseph Charles Lemire v Ukraine*, ICSID Case No. ARB/06/18, Award (28 March 2011) para 280; Gritsenko (n 175) 351.

179 *Lemire v Ukraine*, Award (n 178) para 304.

180 ibid 303.

181 ibid.

182 ibid 305.

183 cf Gritsenko (n 175) 351 who identifies that the investor has been treated favourably in the choice of calculation methodology because he was considered a 'path breaker' for necessary investment in the risky environment of Ukraine.

184 *Bear Creek v Peru*, Award (n 19) paras 595–604.

amount of compensation achievable – because potential profits cannot be claimed.

The ICSID award in *Unglaube v Costa Rica* is perhaps the clearest example for considering investor conduct towards the public interest in the calculation method. The German claimants were engaged in the tourism sector in Costa Rica. To that end they owned land close to the beach Playa Grande. This beach was also an environmentally sensitive nesting area for leatherback turtles.[185] Costa Rica intended to expropriate the claimants to protect this nesting habitat and did so after several attempts, yet without compensation.[186] The Tribunal found a breach against the protection against expropriation under the Germany-Costa Rica BIT. In determining its methodology to calculate damages, the Tribunal explicitly took into account that the area was environmentally sensitive and could only be used subject to certain limitations:

> If, as Claimants' expert has suggested, it is appropriate, in determining fair market value, to identify the highest and best use of this particular property, it seems plain to the Tribunal that that can only be the highest and best use subject to all pertinent legal, physical, and economic constraints. In this case, it obviously should refer not to high density usage – appropriate to a large city or factory area – but rather to a usage appropriate to the environmentally-sensitive surroundings – including residential home construction, with a density comparable to that permitted by the guidelines set forth in the 1992 Agreement.[187]

This included that the property could, according to national standards, only be used for example with a maximum density of 20 persons per hectare, a maximum building height of two floors and a minimum setback from the street of 7 meters.[188] This means that to the extent the claimants did not use their property environmentally-friendly, they partially lose compensation as the tribunal would not recognize that use to reflect a 'fair market value'. Here, national environmental standards translate to an international calculation method for damages.[189] The award is remarkable in light of the Tribunal's findings in *CDSE v Costa Rica* twelve years before. It also dealt with tourism in an environmentally sensitive area in Costa Rica

185 *Unglaube v Costa Rica* (n 90) paras 37–39.
186 ibid 192–223.
187 ibid 309.
188 ibid 310.
189 Supported by Viñuales, 'Foreign' (n 91) 30.

and rejected that the environmental purpose of the governmental taking could have any impact on the calculation of damages.[190]

Overall, all these awards indicate a more qualitative calculation method that takes account of the investor's behaviour towards the public interest:[191] Investors have to assess the host state's general political environment before investing and, in doing so, becoming part of the host state's society. Their decision to invest in the respective state must be reflected in the amount of compensation.

This jurisprudence does not bring about an indirect obligation because there is no automatic sanction for breaching a defined standard of conduct. Instead, the investor's behaviour constitutes a balancing criterion in the calculation method.

This is supported by the ILC commentary on Art 36 of the ILC Articles on State Responsibility. This article addresses the compensation that states owe when committing an internationally wrongful act. The commentary states:

> As to the appropriate heads of compensable damage and the principles of assessment to be applied in quantification, these will vary, depending upon the content of particular primary obligations, *an evaluation of the respective behaviour of the parties* and, more generally, a concern to reach an equitable and acceptable outcome.[192]

---

190 *Santa Elena v Costa Rica* (n 140) para 71.

191 It is also a scholarly suggestion, see for example Diane A Desierto, 'ICESCR Minimum Core Obligations and Investment: Recasting the Non-Expropriation Compensation Model During Financial Crises' (2012) 44(3) George Washington International Law Review 473, 519 suggesting that the value of an investment should be considered lower if the investor suffered losses because the host state had to enact social protection measures – in reaction to certain behaviour by the respective investor – in a systemic economic crisis to comply with ICESCR minimum core obligations.

192 ILC 'Articles on Responsibility of States for Internationally Wrongful Acts, with Commentaries' (2001) II(2) Yearbook of the International Law Commission, 31 (53rd session of the International Law Commission, 23 April-1 June and 2 July 2001), 100 (emphasis added); see also Desierto, *Public* (n 37) 353 who underlines that 'compensation must be *equitably* determined from the perspective of both the injuring party and the injured party' (emphasis in the original).

2. Contributory negligence

Furthermore, investment practice has given rise to indirect obligations as part of the principle of contributory negligence. If investors negligently contribute to the damages that the host state has caused, the Tribunal reduces the amount of compensation (a). Tribunals have established standards of conduct for such negligence which relate to the public interest. If investors breach them, they partly lose compensation they would otherwise have received. This meets the definition of an indirect obligation. Four arbitral awards stand out as particularly good examples: The award in *MTD v Chile* applied an environmental indirect obligation (b); the award in *Yukos v Russia*, where the Tribunal reduced the investor's compensation for violating the Russian rule of law through corruption (c); the award in *Copper Mesa v Ecuador* implied an indirect human rights obligation (d); and the award in *Bear Creek v Peru*, which concerned the indirect obligation related to the protection of indigenous peoples' rights (e).

a) Foundations of contributory negligence

Contributory negligence is a general principle of law.[193] It is reflected in Art 39 of the ILC Articles on State Responsibility. The provision stipulates that for determining reparation, 'account shall be taken of the contribution to the injury by wilful or negligent action or omission of the injured state *or any person or entity in relation to whom reparation is sought.*' (emphasis added). The principle applies in investment law, too. It requires that investors' conduct is (at least in part) causal for the damages that they suffered from the host state's wrongful act.[194] To the extent investors caused the damage themselves, they do not receive compensation. Tribunals may reduce the amount even down to zero if investors alone caused the damage.

193 *Case Concerning Elettronica Sicula S.p.A. (ELSI) (USA v Italy)* (Judgment) [1989] ICJ Rep 15, paras 78, 100–101; *LaGrand Case (Germany v USA)* (Judgment) [2001] ICJ Rep 466, para 116; Borzu Sabahi, *Compensation and Restitution in Investor-State Arbitration: Principles and Practice* (Oxford University Press 2011) 175–176.

194 Brigitte Bollecker-Stern, *Le préjudice dans la théorie de la responsabilité internationale* (Editions A. Pedone 1973) 316; on this nexus between investor and state misconduct see also Jarrett, Puig and Ratner (n 28) 10.

As a first step, the tribunal will enquire who acted in a certain case, for example, who polluted the groundwater. But causation is not only a question of fact. It is well-established that one must complement the analysis with a normative assessment that involves value judgments.[195] Typical questions concern whether certain damages were foreseeable or if they follow sufficiently directly from the state's action.[196]

Investor rights inform this normative analysis. Their scope of protection and purpose guide tribunals in determining which damages the state must compensate. For example, the purpose of the right to FET is to protect investors against unforeseeable legislative changes. Thus, which damages, caused to the detriment of the investor, were foreseeable will also depend on how the tribunal interprets the right to FET. Many tribunals exclude those damages which accrue from risks that investors must bear as part of their business decision to invest; since, originally, distribution of risks was the central criterion for determining causation.[197]

b) MTD v Chile and the environment

Tribunals have drawn on indirect obligations in applying the principle of contributory negligence. They did so by including the investor's misconduct towards the public interest as a normative criterion for causation of

---

195 Martin Jarrett, *Contributory Fault and Investor Misconduct in Investment Arbitration* (Cambridge University Press 2019) 25.

196 The normative character of causation is explicitly pointed out in ILC 'Draft Articles on the Responsibility of International Organizations, with Commentaries' ‹http://legal.un.org/ilc/texts/instruments/english/commentaries/9_11_2011.pdf› accessed 7 December 2021, Art 31 para 10 with further references; see also André Hauriou, 'Les Dommages Indirects Dans Les Arbitrages Internationaux' (1924) 31 Revue Générale de Droit International Public 203, 209; Jarrett (n 195) 45. The proximity or foreseeability of damage was for example debated in *Trail Smelter Case (United States/Canada)* (Award) (1938 and 1941) 3 RIAA 1905, 1931 which rejected to award damages in respect to companies because they were 'too indirect and remote' as to be considered to be caused by the Trail Smelter fumes; see also Sabahi (n 193) 172.

197 See the general teleological remark by *Maffezini v Spain*, Award (n 87) para 64; more specifically on the role of risk distribution in compensation rules in international investment law see Sabahi (n 193) 120; Marboe (n 170) para 4.110; in the same vein on the international law of state responsibility see ILC 'Articles on State Responsibility with Commentaries' (n 192) 103–104.

damages. A good example portraying such an indirect obligation towards the environment is the award in *MTD v Chile*.

In this case, the claimants pursued the construction of a self-sufficient satellite city in Pirque, Chile. Yet, the Chilean authorities had zoned the pertinent area for agriculture. To realise the project, they needed to rezone the area. Due to lacking coordination between governmental agencies, Chile authorised the investment before the necessary rezoning permit had been issued. Eventually, the competent Chilean authorities rejected the rezoning permit.[198] In reaction, the claimant contended that Chile violated the obligations to MFN treatment, FET as well as expropriation and that the state breached investment contracts.[199]

The Tribunal found that Chile had violated the right to FET.[200] However, it only awarded the claimant compensation for fifty percent of the damages caused.[201] It held that 'BITs are not an insurance against business risk'[202] and that the claimants had 'failed to protect themselves against business risks inherent to their investment in Chile'.[203] It argued that a prudent businessman would have undertaken:

- to carry out at least a rudimentary inquiry on the agricultural land's quality and its role in the environmental health of the region;[204] furthermore, to verify the validity of the landowner's and the financing bank's land valuation and assumption of the region's development and re-zoning;[205]
- to seek contractual protections against losses arising from difficulties in obtaining governmental authorisations,[206] in particular, to bring about the 'issuance of the required development permits' before concluding a promissory contract on the investment;[207]
- not to proceed to enter into a promissory contract to conduct an investment without knowledge of Chile's laws despite warnings from

198 *MTD Equity Sdn. Bhd. and MTD Chile S.A. v Republic of Chile*, ICSID Case No. ARB/01/7, Award (25 May 2004) paras 39–85, 166, 253.

199 ibid 105.

200 ibid 166, 253.

201 ibid 243.

202 ibid 177; citing *Maffezini v Spain*, Award (n 87) para 69, however, the correct reference being para 64.

203 *MTD v Chile*, Award (n 198) para 253.

204 ibid 169.

205 ibid 170, 172–178.

206 ibid 170, 178.

207 ibid 178.

government officials and without additional professional advice on risks associated with the investment.[208]

The principle of contributory negligence as applied by the Tribunal implies an indirect obligation. The standards of conduct relate to the investment's environmental impact. One can read these passages as requiring a rudimentary form of an environmental impact assessment prior to initiating the investment. Because the investors breached this standard, the Tribunal accorded a sanction: the partial loss of their investment protection by fifty percent. Notably, the Tribunal explicitly understood its findings as a means for the investor to 'bear responsibility'[209] – a term which is usually employed in the context of legal obligations.

This indirect obligation is more flexible concerning the sanction applied than the obligations encountered in the analysis of admissibility and jurisdiction requirements in Chapter 7.I and the substantive requirements of investor rights in Chapter 7.II. Instead of the alternatives of granting full or no protection, the rules on contributory negligence allow for depriving the investor of an investor right only in part in case of breaching an indirect obligation. In the example of *MTD v Chile*, the Tribunal saw equal contributions by the host state and the investor, and thus sanctioned the investor by a reduction of fifty percent.

Problematic about this award is that the underlying standard of conduct remains relatively unclear in scope. What is more, the Tribunal's reasoning in other passages emphasises that the claimant mainly violated its own interests. For example, it also remarked that the claimant had not sufficiently protected itself in the contract with the host state against a possible rejection of the rezoning.[210] In the same vein, the Annulment Committee noted that the claimant had been subject to 'a failure to safeguard its own interests rather than a breach of any duty owed to the host State.'[211] Nevertheless, the award is an instance in which the indirect obligation at least incidentally served the public interest. Indeed, Chapter 6.III has pointed out that it is precisely a feature of indirect obligations to build on investors' self-interest: They turn public interest-friendly behaviour into an own interest of the investor. The award in *MTD v Chile* illustrates this effect well.

---

208 ibid 170.

209 ibid 242.

210 ibid 178.

211 *MTD Equity Sdn. Bhd. and MTD Chile S.A. v Republic of Chile*, ICSID Case No. ARB/01/7, Decision on Annulment (21 March 2007) para 101.

c) Yukos v Russia and the rule of law

Another good example of an indirect obligation is the award in *Yukos v Russia* relating to the Russian rule of law.

The claimants had invested in oil, gas and petroleum production in Russia.[212] They claimed that Russia had caused the investment's insolvency and illegally nationalised their assets.[213] In their view, Russia took these measures to harass them because they supported the political opposition. By this, Russia had violated the right to FET and the protection against illegal expropriation.[214] Russia countered that the claimants had engaged in tax fraud.[215]

The PCA Tribunal in its 2014 award affirmed that Russia had violated the investors' rights.[216] Yet, it also found that the claimants had contributed to the damage. Some of their tax avoidance arrangements had formed a valid basis for the government's measures.[217] Observing that the governmental reaction was disproportionate, it reduced the damages awarded to Yukos by 25 percent: from roughly USD 67 billion to USD 50 billion.[218]

The award is another instance in which a tribunal tested an investor's conduct against a public interest standard. Here, the Tribunal examined if the investors engaged in tax fraud. To that end, it studied if the investor had fraudulently abused loopholes in Russian tax law on low-tax regions to avoid taxation. As a sanction for this fraudulent conduct, it devalued the claimants' rights by 25 percent. This constitutes an indirect obligation as defined above.

In its reasoning, the Tribunal itself appears aware that it is applying an obligation to the investors. It held:

> [A]n award of damages may be reduced if the victim of the wrongful act of the respondent State also committed a fault which contributed to the prejudice it suffered and for which the trier of facts, in the exercise of its discretion, considers the claiming party should bear some responsibility. In the view of the Tribunal, Claimants should pay

212 *Yukos v Russia*, Final Award (n 21) paras 71–72.

213 Borzu Sabahi and Diora Ziyaeva, 'Yukos v. Russian Federation: Observations on the Tribunal's Ruling on Damages' (2015) 13(5) Oil, Gas & Energy Law 1, 2–3.

214 *Yukos v Russia*, Final Award (n 21) paras 81–105.

215 ibid 84–86, 96.

216 ibid 1575–1585.

217 ibid 1610–1621.

218 ibid 1634–1637, 1827.

> a price for Yukos' abuse of the low-tax regions by some of its trading entities.[219]

The Tribunal's use of terminology in this passage is revealing: the investors were at 'fault' and hence had to bear some 'responsibility'. It also very explicitly underlined the sanctioning character by considering that the claimants had to 'pay a price'. However, it rejected to foreclose the investors completely from protection.[220] Instead, it distributed the responsibilities between the claimants and the respondent by weighing how grave their respective misconduct was.[221]

By applying the principle of contributory negligence, the Tribunal construed an investor obligation towards the Russian rule of law. Fraudulent behaviour is a form of abusing a state's legislative framework and thus undermines the rule of law. The respondent itself highlighted this connection in its submissions.[222] Herein lies the incidental protection of the rule of law by the principle of contributory negligence.

d) Copper Mesa v Ecuador and human rights

A human rights-related application of the principle of contributory negligence features in the *Copper Mesa v Ecuador* award. Ecuador had granted the claimant mining concessions at Junín, Chaucha and Telimbela and revoked or terminated these later.[223] The claimant argued that this violated the Canada-Ecuador-BIT[224]. After finding that Ecuador had indeed violated this treaty, the Tribunal reduced the compensation awarded to the claimant as regards the Junín concessions by 30 percent due to contributory negligence.[225]

In the Junín area, a large part of the population, mostly farmers, rejected any mining activities because they would be directly and adversely

---

219 ibid 1633–1634.

220 ibid 1343–1374.

221 ibid 1635–1637.

222 ibid 109.

223 *Copper Mesa Mining Corporation v The Republic of Ecuador*, PCA Case No. 2012–2, Award (15 March 2016) paras 1.8–1.9.

224 Canada-Ecuador BIT (adopted 9 April 1996, entered into force 6 June 1997, date of termination 19 May 2018) ‹https://investmentpolicy.unctad.org/international-investment-agreements/treaty-files/609/download› accessed 7 December 2021 (Canada-Ecuador BIT).

225 *Copper Mesa v Ecuador* (n 223) para 7.32.

affected, forming an anti-mining opposition in an area with weak police presence.[226] Already before establishing the investment, potentially violent tensions between the claimant and local anti-miners became apparent.[227] These tensions exacerbated with recurring violence and protests taking place,[228] eventually blocking access to the operation of the Junín concessions by anti-miners.[229] The claimant then decided to employ armed security guards. The Tribunal found that the claimants had indeed organised 'armed men in uniform using tear gas canisters and firing weapons at local villagers and officials' and had thus 'acquired, irrevocably, a malign reputation for intimidation, threats, deception, mendacity and violence amongst members of the local communities', leading to a 'reckless escalation of violence'.[230]

Applying Art 39 of the ILC Articles on State Responsibility, the Tribunal found that the 'Claimant's injury was caused both by the Respondent's unlawful expropriation and also by the Claimant's own contributory negligent acts and omissions and unclean hands', leaving open if this was a matter of causation, contributory fault or unclean hands.[231] The Tribunal found negligence on behalf of the claimant with the following reasoning:

> In short, a foreign investor, by its local agents, whatever the illegal provocations by local residents in the form of road-blocks, violence, arson and other impediments, should not resort to recruiting and using armed men, firing guns and spraying mace at civilians, not as an accidental or isolated incident but as part of premeditated, disguised and well-funded plans to take the law into its own hands. [...]
>
> In the Tribunal's view, the evidence establishes that several of the Claimant's senior personnel in Quito were guilty of directing violent acts committed on its behalf, in violation of Ecuadorian criminal law. Their resort to subterfuge and mendacity aggravated those acts. The consequences could have led to serious injury and loss of life. [...][232]

Applying the concepts suggested by this chapter, one can read this decision as implying an indirect human rights obligation of the claimant. The

226 ibid 4.10–4.12.
227 ibid 4.95–4.97.
228 ibid 4.157.
229 ibid 4.214.
230 ibid 4.265.
231 ibid 6.97.
232 ibid 6.99–6.100.

Tribunal uses terms associated with the human right to life, for example that the claimant could have caused significant injury and loss of life. Even though the Tribunal notes that the claimant violated Ecuadorian criminal law, the analysis does not actually apply and analyse a domestic norm. Rather, the Tribunal appears to evaluate the conduct of the claimant autonomously, building on its discretion in determining contributory negligence, causation or clean hands as principles of international law. Some have criticised that the Tribunal did not invoke human rights norms.[233] Indeed, the Tribunal appears to adopt a pragmatic – rather than idealist – approach to the violence caused by the claimant. It is precisely this rather 'hidden' way of addressing investor misconduct towards the public interest that is typical for the pattern of indirect obligations in arbitral jurisprudence.

e) Bear Creek v Peru and indigenous peoples

In *Bear Creek v Peru*, contributory negligence gave rise to an indirect obligation related to indigenous peoples.

In this case, the claimant had received a governmental decree by Peru to operate a mine in Santa Ana close to the Bolivian border. Local indigenous communities protested against the prospective enterprise, even leading to violent outbreaks. The government reacted by prohibiting mining activities in the area through a second decree. It effectively denied Bear Creek the possibility of operating the mine as envisaged in the first decree.[234] In this light, the claimant filed ICSID proceedings against Peru on the basis of the Peru-Canada-FTA.[235] Peru defended itself by arguing that the claimant had acted in contributory negligence by not reaching out and engaging sufficiently with the affected local communities (the concept of a 'social license'). Through this omission, the company had caused the unrests that led the state to prohibit all mining activities.[236]

---

233 Choudhury, 'Investor' (n 23) 100 considers the Tribunal's approach to 'underemphasize the overarching importance of human rights' as it 'equates human rights breaches with investor negligence such as abusing low tax regions'.

234 *Bear Creek v Peru*, Award (n 19) paras 119–216.

235 Canada-Peru FTA (adopted 29 May 2008, entered into force 1 August 2009) ‹https://investmentpolicy.unctad.org/international-investment-agreements/treaty-files/2568/download› accessed 7 December 2021 (Canada-Peru FTA).

236 *Bear Creek v Peru*, Award (n 19) paras 560–564.

(1) The Tribunal's award

The Tribunal rejected this argument – however, only based on the lack of proof. It investigated the investor's conduct and considered its outreach activities. These included projects such as job programmes for neighbouring communities. In doing so, the Tribunal generally acknowledged that it had to assess if the 'Claimant took the appropriate and necessary steps to engage all of the relevant and likely to be affected communities'.[237] It concluded that Peru had failed to prove any alleged negligence on the part of the investor.[238] Instead, it took the social unrests as the reason to change the methodology of compensation calculation as discussed above.[239]

The award is notable because the Tribunal accepted as a matter of principle that the investor's actions towards indigenous communities were relevant.[240] It examined the claimant's social activities when determining possible contributory negligence – conversely implying that it measured the conduct against a certain standard. It explicitly found it possible that misconduct could have caused a reduction of compensation. This reflects the linkage between a standard of conduct and a sanction characteristic for an indirect obligation.

Interestingly, the Tribunal elaborated further on the conduct it expected from the investor. It did not only investigate the company's obligations under domestic Peruvian law to obtain a so-called social license. It also commented that

> [e]ven though the concept of '*social license*' is not clearly defined in international law, all relevant international instruments are clear that consultations with indigenous communities are to be made with the purpose of obtaining consent from all the relevant communities [...][241]

237 ibid 406.

238 ibid 565–569.

239 See Chapter 7.III.1.c).

240 This is noteworthy in light of other tribunals who have rejected to consider the attempt of investors to engage with the local population as part of a possible contributory negligence test; for such a strict approach see for example *South American Silver Limited (Bermuda) v The Plurinational State of Bolivia*, PCA Case No. 2013-15, Award (22 November 2018) para 875.

241 *Bear Creek v Peru*, Award (n 19) para 406.

Consequently, it cited Art 32 of the UNDRIP.[242] UNDRIP represents soft law which is at least in parts considered to reflect binding international obligations of states.[243] Therefore, the Tribunal appears to apply these standards within the principle of contributory negligence. In short, one could understand the Tribunal to mean that the investor must comply with UNDRIP. Otherwise, if the state acted to protect indigenous communities and violated an investor right, any compensation awarded would be reduced. This shows how the indirect obligation relates to the protection of the public interest – here, the rights of indigenous peoples.

(2) Sands' Partial Dissenting Opinion

Arbitrator *Sands* went even further in his Partial Dissenting Opinion. He concluded that Peru had sufficiently established Bear Creek's contributory negligence. In his assessment, he relied on the rights of local indigenous communities under national and international law. To that end, he cited ILO Convention No 169, the Indigenous and Tribal Peoples Convention which Peru had concluded in 1994, referring to two articles of the Convention:[244] Art 13 (1), the obligation to

> respect the special importance for the cultures and spiritual values of the peoples concerned of their relationship with the lands or territories, or both as applicable, which they occupy or otherwise use, and in particular the collective aspects of this relationship.

He also cited Art 15 which stipulates that

> [t]he rights of the peoples concerned to the natural resources pertaining to their lands shall be specifically safeguarded. These rights inclu-

242 UNGA 'United Nations Declaration on the Rights of Indigenous Peoples' UN Doc A/RES/61/295 (13 September 2007).

243 For further analysis, especially on UNDRIP's character as customary international law, see Martin Scheinin and Mattias Åhrén, 'Relationship to Human Rights, and Related International Instruments' in Jessie Hohmann and Marc Weller (eds), *The UN Declaration on the Rights of Indigenous Peoples: A Commentary* (Oxford University Press 2018) 64–85.

244 ILO Convention (No 169) Concerning Indigenous and Tribal Peoples in Independent Countries (adopted 27 June 1989, entered into force 5 September 1991) 1650 UNTS 383; *Bear Creek Mining Corporation v Republic of Perú*, ICSID Case No. ARB/14/21, Partial Dissenting Opinion by Professor Philippe Sands QC (12 September 2017) paras 10–13.

de the right of these peoples to participate in the use, management and conservation of these resources.

While *Sands* acknowledged that these international obligations address states, not private actors, he pointed out that this 'does not, however, mean that it is without significance or legal effects for them.'[245] To the contrary, he considered them relevant to define the standard of contributory negligence. He offered four doctrinal arguments to that end:

1. Art 837 of the Canada-Peru FTA defines international law as one of the applicable rules to the arbitration, which includes the ILO Convention.[246]
2. Peruvian law incorporated the ILO Convention which is thus applicable as domestic law to the investor.[247]
3. The parties to the dispute agreed that the ILO Convention was applicable to the case and to the conduct of the investor.[248]
4. *Sands* also seems to suggest that the ILO Convention itself may have a limited direct effect on private parties as a matter of international law. He cites the ICSID award in *Urbaser v Argentina*, discussed above,[249] with its statement that human rights 'are complemented by an obligation on all parts, public and private parties, not to engage in activity aimed at destroying such rights.'[250]

He concluded that the investor had failed to meet these obligations by not involving all the potentially affected communities, 'offering jobs only to some and engaging in consultations which were uneven and insufficient across the totality of communities.'[251] In consequence, he suggested to reduce the compensable damage by fifty percent and also advocated for the splitting of proceeding costs by the parties.[252]

This partial dissenting opinion most explicitly describes the existence of an indirect obligation. *Sands* defines a concrete standard of contributory negligence by building on ILO Convention No 169. He is even explicit about the doctrinal reasons for including the Convention. On this basis,

---

245 ibid 10.
246 ibid 11.
247 ibid 9, 12.
248 ibid.
249 See Chapter 3.I.2.
250 *Bear Creek v Peru*, Partial Dissenting Opinion by Professor Philippe Sands QC (n 244) para 10 citing *Urbaser v Argentina*, Award (n 79) para 1199.
251 *Bear Creek v Peru*, Partial Dissenting Opinion by Professor Philippe Sands QC (n 244) para 33.
252 ibid 39–40.

he expresses that the investor had to follow a certain standard of conduct. Because the investor's actions were insufficient, a sanction of fifty percent less compensation was in order. The reference to the ILO Convention also shows that contributory negligence serves to further the public interest: the investor was expected to contribute to it.

3. Interim conclusion

Section III has proven that the rules on compensation imply indirect obligations. Even after having found that the state violated an investor right, tribunals used the amount of compensation as leverage: If investors violated the public interest, they received less compensation than the tribunal would have granted otherwise.

The analysis especially found indirect obligations as part of the principle of contributory negligence. Tribunals have interpreted such 'negligence' as standards of conduct towards the public interest with which the investors must comply. The definition of what amounts to 'negligence' does not necessarily require or imply a breach of an obligation directly applicable to investors. It may thus serve to give legal effect to norms that otherwise for example only bind states.[253] The analysis found such obligations towards the environment, the rule of law, human rights and indigenous peoples. This indirect obligation sanctions investors by reducing compensation if the breach contributed to the same damages that the state has caused by interfering with the investors.

Because tribunals can choose to reduce this amount only in part, rules on compensation allow for nuanced sanctions. The tribunal can reflect the gravity of the conduct in comparison to the state's wrongdoing in the percentage of reduction. In short: it can impose gradual sanctions.

---

253 Supported for example by Markus Krajewski, 'A Nightmare or a Noble Dream? Establishing Investor Obligations Through Treaty-Making and Treaty-Application' (2020) 5(1) Business and Human Rights Journal 105, 125–126; Viñuales, 'Diligence' (n 51) 366; Farouk El-Hosseny and Patrick Devine, 'Contributory Fault Under International Law: A Gateway for Human Rights in ISDS?' (2020) 35(1–2) ICSID Review 105, 128; Kryvoi (n 27) 601–603 by implication.

IV. The clean hands doctrine

So far, Chapter 7 proceeded along systematic categories: jurisdiction and admissibility of arbitral claims, requirements of investor rights, rules on compensation. However, tribunals and scholars have also discussed the clean hands doctrine in a manner that could imply indirect obligations. Tribunals have applied it both as a question of admissibility and in the merits phase. Therefore, the doctrine will be discussed in this Section separately. It will show that the doctrine does not give rise to indirect obligations and that it is redundant altogether.

This Section will first explain the clean hands doctrine and how its very existence remains controversial in international law (1.). Then, it will show that arbitral tribunals and scholars have applied it in investment law in a manner that would imply an indirect obligation not to commit fraud or corruption (2.). However, it is suggested that these cases only relate to doctrinal requirements that have already been studied in the last Sections. The use of the clean hands doctrine is superfluous; hence, it does not play a role in bringing about indirect obligations (3.).

1. The clean hands doctrine as a general principle of law

The clean hands doctrine is said to go back to Roman law principles that are today linked to the doctrine of estoppel.[254] It also has a long tradition in the law of equity in common law legal systems. The US Supreme Court in *Precision Instrument Mfg. Co. v Automotive Co.* in 1945 instructively held that '[i]t is a self-imposed ordinance that closes the doors of a court of equity to one tainted with inequitableness or bad faith relative to the matter in which he seeks relief, however improper may have been the behaviour of the defendant.'[255] In other words, the clean hands doctrine precludes claimants from protection if they act with fault in the same context as the respondent.[256]

---

254 For example, the principles *ex dolo malo non oritur actio, nullus commodum capere potest de iniuria sua propria* and *ex iniuria ius non oritur*, see Stephen M Schwebel, 'Clean Hands, Principle' in Anne Peters (ed), *Max Planck Encyclopedia of Public International Law* (March 2013) para 1.

255 *Precision Instrument Mfg. Co. v Automotive Co.* (1945) 324 U.S. 806 (US Supreme Court) 814.

256 cf for the common law doctrine Ori J Herstein, 'A Normative Theory of the Clean Hands Defense' (2011) 17(3) Legal Theory 171, 173–174.

Whether the clean hands doctrine is established as a general principle of law in international law remains controversial. Preponderantly, its existence is rejected.[257] ILC Special Rapporteur *Crawford* in his Second Report on State Responsibility considered the arbitral practice to be divided. There were only a few, older cases related to specific circumstances in the law of diplomatic protection. Thus, he rejected its existence as a general principle of law.[258] Similarly, while admitting that the principle has been invoked in inter-state relations, Special Rapporteur *Dugard* in his Sixth Report on Diplomatic Protection found that 'the evidence in favour of the clean hands doctrine is inconclusive' in the law of diplomatic protection and its authority 'is uncertain and of ancient vintage, dating mainly from the mid-nineteenth century'.[259] The ICJ, too, is yet to accept it.[260] Only the dissenting opinions of Judges *Schwebel* in *Nicaragua v USA* and *van den Wyngaert* in the *Arrest Warrant Case* argued in favour of applying

---

257 The lack of authority for a clean hands doctrine was masterfully laid out in detail by Jean J Salmon, 'Des «Mains Propres» comme condition de recevabilité des réclamations internationales' (1964) 10 Annuaire Français de Droit International 225, 232–266; similarly Charles Rousseau, *Droit international public*, vol V Les rapports conflictuels (Sirey 1983) 172; Aleksandr Shapovalov, 'Should a Requirement of "Clean Hands" Be a Prerequisite to the Exercise of Diplomatic Protection? Human Rights Implications of the International Law Commission's Debate' (2005) 20(4) American University International Law Review 829, 861–866; but see the affirmation of the principle on a general basis by Bin Cheng, *General Principles of Law as Applied by International Courts and Tribunals* (Stevens & Sons Limited 1953) 155–158; Gerald Fitzmaurice, 'The General Principles of International Law, Considered from the Standpoint of the Rule of Law' (1957) 92 Recueil des Cours 1, 119, however without any further arguments.

258 ILC 'Second Report on State Responsibility, by Mr. James Crawford, Special Rapporteur' UN Doc A/CN.4/498 and Add.1 – 4 (17 March, 1 and 30 April, 19 July 1999), paras 334–336; see also ILC 'Articles on State Responsibility with Commentaries' (n 192) Art 19 para 9.

259 ILC 'Sixth Report on Diplomatic Protection, by Mr. John Dugard, Special Rapporteur' UN Doc A/CN.4/546 (11 August 2004), paras 6, 18.

260 The ICJ has only cited the supposedly related maxim *ex iuria ius non oritu* and estoppel in *Case Concerning the Gabčikovo-Nagymaros Project (Hungary v Slovakia)* (Judgment) [1997] ICJ Rep 7, para 133. Furthermore, there are individual and dissenting opinions which affirm the existence of related principles such as the *exceptio non adimpleti contractus*, see *The Diversion of Water From the Meuse (Netherlands v Belgium)* (Individual Opinion By Mr. Hudson) [1937] PCIJ Rep Series A/B No 70, 77; *The Diversion of Water From the Meuse (Netherlands v Belgium)* (Dissenting Opinion of M. Anzilotti) [1937] PCIJ Rep Series A/B No 70, 50; but see the contrary position by *Application of the Interim Accord of 13 December 1995 (the former Yugoslav Republic of Macedonia v Greece)* (Separate Opinion of Judge Simma) [2011] ICJ Rep 695, paras 19–20.

it.[261] In 2007, the Arbitral Tribunal constituted under Annex VII of the UN Convention on the Law of the Sea even held in *Guyana v Suriname* that '[n]o generally accepted definition of the clean hands doctrine has been elaborated in international law'.[262] Recently, in *Certain Iranian Assets*, the ICJ has explicitly left open if the clean hands doctrine exists in international law.[263]

2. Clean hands as a suggested indirect obligation

Nevertheless, the clean hands doctrine has been applied by a number of arbitral tribunals and suggested by scholars as a means to deprive investors of protection. These cases related to investors who engaged in corruption or fraud. In this view, the clean hands doctrine constitutes an indirect obligation: if investors present their case with unclean hands, they lose investment protection – even though it sometimes remains unclear if the obligation operates on the procedural level of access to investment arbitration or as a matter of receiving substantive investor rights. To prevent this loss of rights, investors have to comply with domestic anti-fraud and anti-corruption laws – similar to the study's findings in Chapter 7.I.2 and Chapter 7.II.5.

For example, in *Hamester v Ghana*, the respondent raised the defence that there was no 'investment' in accordance with Ghanaian law[264] as required by Art 10 of the Ghana-Germany BIT.[265] Ghana argued that the claimant had committed fraud and hence was to be disqualified from investment protection. Even though this argument conforms with the

---

261 *Case Concerning Military and Paramilitary Activities in and against Nicaragua (Nicaragua v United States of America)* (Dissenting Opinion of Judge Schwebel) [1986] ICJ Rep 259, para 268; *Case Concerning the Arrest Warrant of 11 April 2000 (Democratic Republic of the Congo v Belgium)* (Dissenting Opinion of Judge van den Wyngaert) [2002] ICJ Rep 137, para 35.

262 *Award in the Arbitration Regarding the Delimitation of the Maritime Boundary Between Guyana and Suriname (Guyana v Suriname)* (Award) (2007) 30 RIAA 1, para 418.

263 *Certain Iranian Assets (Islamic Republic of Iran v United States of America)* (Preliminary Objections) [2019] ICJ Rep 7, para 122.

264 *Hamester v Ghana* (n 19) para 81.

265 Ghana-Germany BIT (adopted 24 February 1995, entered into force 23 November 1998) ‹https://investmentpolicy.unctad.org/international-investment-agreements/treaty-files/1328/download› accessed 7 December 2021 (Ghana-Germany BIT).

requirement to comply with domestic law as discussed above,[266] the Tribunal dealt with it differently as follows:

> [T]he Tribunal will examine whether, on the facts of the case, there could have been international responsibility on the part of the [Respondent] towards Hamester for the different claims raised as to the [Joint Venture Agreement]'s performance. It is only if any of the acts complained of raises or could have raised an international responsibility of the [Respondent], that it then becomes relevant to analyse in detail the investor's behaviour and the accusations of fraud, in order to determine whether the investor has claimed with clean hands, and whether this could have consequences on any relief.[267]

The Tribunal did not have to go into any more detail because it already denied the respondent's responsibility.[268] Nevertheless, it is notable that the Tribunal seemed ready to apply the clean hands doctrine to examine the investor's alleged fraud. It found it possible that wrongful conduct could lead to 'consequences on any relief' – precisely implying an effect tantamount to an indirect obligation as understood here. Different from other tribunals as presented above,[269] the Tribunal does not rely on a self-standing requirement under the applicable IIA to comply with domestic law. Instead, it is the clean hands doctrine as a general principle of law which appears to bring about the indirect obligation.

Similarly, the Tribunal in *Fraport v Philippines (Fraport II)* understood other arbitral awards which required investors to comply with the host state's domestic law as authority for the clean hands doctrine. It held:

> Investment treaty cases confirm that [...] treaties do not afford protection to illegal investments either based on clauses of the treaties, as in the present case according to the above analysis, or, absent an express provision in the treaty, based on rules of international law, such as the 'clean hands' doctrine or doctrines to the same effect. One of the first cases having ruled on this issue, *Inceysa v. El Salvador*, has held that 'because Inceysa's investment was made in a manner that was clearly illegal, it is not included in the scope of consent expressed by Spain and the Republic of El Salvador in the BIT and, consequently,

266 See Chapter 7.I.2 and Chapter 7.II.5.
267 *Hamester v Ghana* (n 19) para 317.
268 ibid 350.
269 See Chapter 7.I.2 and Chapter 7.II.5.

> the disputes arising from it are not subject to the jurisdiction of the Centre.'[270]

On the one hand, the Tribunal affirmed the existence of the legality requirement – and hence, the indirect obligation that breaching domestic law deprives investors of international investment protection. On the other hand, it appeared to understand it as flowing from the clean hands doctrine. However, the quoted passage from *Inceysa v El Salvador* is at odds with such an interpretation: it does not mention the clean hands doctrine but interprets the scope of the disputing parties' consent to arbitrate. There, the Tribunal only started 'from the premise that the consent of the parties was [...] given in good faith'.[271] The role of the clean hands doctrine in this interpretive exercise remains unclear.

Another example of a tribunal that has applied the clean hands doctrine is the award in *Al Warraq v Indonesia*. It has already been discussed above as one that applies the requirement to comply with domestic law.[272] But the Tribunal also referred to the clean hands doctrine in its reasoning after having found that the investor had violated Indonesian laws:

> In this regard, the Tribunal is of the view that the doctrine of 'clean hands' renders the Claimant's claim inadmissible. [...] As mentioned above, it is established the Claimant has breached Article 9 of the OIC Agreement by failing to uphold the Indonesian laws and regulations and in acting in a manner prejudicial to the public interest. The Claimant's actions were also prejudicial to the public interest. The Tribunal finds that the Claimant's conduct falls within the scope of application of the 'clean hands' doctrine, and therefore cannot benefit from the protection afforded by the OIC Agreement. The Tribunal concludes that, although it has been established that the Claimant did not receive fair and equitable treatment, as set out in paragraphs 555 to 603 above however, by virtue of Article 9 of the OIC Agreement the Claimant is prevented from pursuing his claim for fair and equitable treatment.[273]

Here, the Tribunal appears to combine different approaches to indirect obligations. On the one hand, it relied on interpreting an explicit clause

270 *Fraport AG Frankfurt Airport Services Worldwide v The Republic of the Philippines (Fraport II)*, ICSID Case No. ARB/11/12, Award (10 December 2014) para 328.

271 *Inceysa v El Salvador* (n 19) para 181.

272 See Chapter 7.II.5.

273 *Al-Warraq v Indonesia*, Final Award (n 153) paras 646–648.

in the OIC Agreement to require compliance with domestic law and the public interest. On the other hand, it also applied the clean hands doctrine to reach the result that the investor is deprived of protection. Notably, the Tribunal introduced the doctrine after having found a breach of the FET right – hence, in the analysis on the merits. But declaring the claim inadmissible should have prevented the Tribunal from entering this substantive analysis in the first place. Thus, it appears that the clean hands doctrine rather served as an auxiliary argument to support the preceding, ordinary interpretation of the OIC Agreement.

This line of cases has prompted some scholars to understand the clean hands doctrine as the central principle to examine the investors' misconduct – even where tribunals have actually applied explicit treaty clauses without mentioning the doctrine.[274] Others distinguish the clean hands doctrine and the requirement of legality while finding overlaps.[275] Again, others have read the doctrine into other requirements studied in this Chapter, for example into the principle of *ordre public international*.[276] Just as the presented cases, these scholars focus on fraud, corruption and misrepresentations by the investor – hence, on a certain facet of misconduct towards the public interest, namely the violation of the state's rule of law.

3. Redundancy of the clean hands doctrine

Notwithstanding these interpretations, it is suggested that the clean hands doctrine is redundant.

274 Rahim Moloo, 'A Comment on the Clean Hands Doctrine in International Law' (2011) 8(1) Transnational Dispute Management 1, 6–11; Dumberry, 'State' (n 21) 234.

275 Aloysius Llamzon, 'Yukos Universal Limited (Isle of Man) v the Russian Federation: The State of the "Unclean Hands" Doctrine in International Investment Law: Yukos as Both Omega and Alpha' (2015) 30(2) ICSID Review 315, 316–321, 325.

276 Andrea K Bjorklund and Lukas Vanhonnaeker, 'Yukos: The Clean Hands Doctrine Revisisted' (2015) 9(2) Diritti Umani e Diritto Internazionale 365, 374 on reading the *ordre public international* as an expression of the clean hands doctrine; Monebhurrun (n 119) 62–64 on understanding international public policy as well as IIA provisions which prohibit corrupt behavior as reflecting the clean hands doctrine; Patrick Dumberry, 'The Clean Hands Doctrine as a General Principle of International Law' (2020) 21(4) Journal of World Investment & Trade 489, 521 on reading the legality requirement as an expression of the clean hands doctrine.

It is important to distinguish that applying the clean hands doctrine means invoking an alleged general principle of law (Art 38 (1) (c) ICJ-Statute). A different matter is the interpretation of the IIA as an international treaty (Art 38 (1) (a) ICJ-Statute). They represent two different sources of international law.[277]

The above-mentioned Tribunals applied the clean hands doctrine too carelessly. From their reasoning, it appears that they engaged in ordinary treaty interpretation – hence, applied the IIA as the indirect obligations' relevant source. As seen, the Tribunals in *Inceysa v El Salvador* and *Al Warraq v Indonesia* both built on explicit treaty clauses to establish the legality requirement.[278] The clean hands doctrine does not add anything to the interpretive result that states do not wish to grant protection to investments that contravene with domestic law. It seems that tribunals referred to the doctrine as a supplementary, rhetorical argument to give additional authority to their findings.

The Tribunal in *Yukos v Russia* came to the same conclusion as presented here. It is worth to quote the Tribunal's reasoning at length:

> The Tribunal notes that there is support in the decisions of tribunals in investment treaty arbitrations for the notion that, even where the applicable investment treaty does not contain an express requirement of compliance with host State laws (as is the case with the ECT), an investment that is made in breach of the laws of the host State may either: (a) not qualify as an investment, thus depriving the tribunal of jurisdiction; or (b) be refused the benefit of the substantive protections of the investment treaty. [...]
>
> The Tribunal agrees with this proposition. In imposing obligations on States to treat investors in a fair and transparent fashion, investment treaties seek to encourage legal and bona fide investments. An investor who has obtained an investment in the host State only by acting in bad faith or in violation of the laws of the host state, has brought itself within the scope of application of the ECT through wrongful acts. Such an investor should not be allowed to benefit from the Treaty. [...]

---

277 Very clearly pointed out by Bjorklund and Vanhonnaeker (n 276) 365–369.

278 See also *South American Silver v Bolivia* (n 240) para 449 on how the Tribunal in *Al-Warraq v Indonesia*, while invoking the clean hands doctrine, also expressly referred to Art 9 OIC Investment Agreement which requires the investor to comply with domestic law.

> The Tribunal is not persuaded that there exists a 'general principle of law recognized by civilized nations' within the meaning of Article 38(1)(c) of the ICJ Statute that would bar an investor from making a claim before an arbitral tribunal under an investment treaty because it has so-called 'unclean hands' [...].
>
> [A]s Claimants point out, despite what appears to have been an extensive review of jurisprudence, Respondent has been unable to cite a single majority decision where an international court or arbitral tribunal has applied the principle of 'unclean hands' in an inter-State or investor-State dispute and concluded that, as a principle of international law, it operated as a bar to a claim.[279]

Here, the Tribunal strictly distinguished between a teleological interpretation of the ECT and the application of the clean hands doctrine as a general principle of law. It already found the legality requirement to be established by the first method – while denying the existence of the doctrine altogether. This reasoning is even more notable considering that one member of the Tribunal – *Schwebel* – had argued as an ICJ Judge in favour of the doctrine in the above-mentioned dissenting opinion in *Nicaragua v USA*.[280]

Recently, the PCA Tribunal in *South American Silver Limited* joined the *Yukos* Tribunal in rejecting that the clean hands doctrine exists as a general principle of law within the meaning of Art 38 (1) (c) ICJ Statute.[281] Also regarding investment arbitration decisions, it was of the view that other investment tribunals 'reached their respective conclusions based on the appropriate treaty provisions or the applicable national law'[282] rather than on the clean hands doctrine as a general principle of law.

Furthermore, while the doctrine may fit well for fraudulent investor behaviour, it is less the case for other infringements of the public interest such as human rights, the environment or workers' rights. The reason is that the principle, as seen, operates with regard to a relative legal relationship, here between the host state and the investor. It does not condemn just any form of unethical conduct but watches especially the *fairness* be-

---

279 *Yukos v Russia*, Final Award (n 21) paras 1349, 1352, 1358, 1362.

280 ibid 1357–1363 with reference to *Nicaragua Case*, Dissenting Opinion of Judge Schwebel (n 261) paras 268–272; see also Bjorklund and Vanhonnaeker (n 276) 368, 373.

281 *South American Silver v Bolivia* (n 240) paras 445–446.

282 ibid 448.

tween the parties.[283] Another often-mentioned purpose is to safeguard the tribunal's integrity as it should not assist in inequitable behaviour.[284] Deceitful conduct like fraud and corruption go to the heart of the fair relative relationship between the parties (*tu quoque*).[285] They may be considered to violate a tribunal's integrity. This is not the case for violations of the other above-mentioned public goods and individual rights. Therefore, the clean hands doctrine cannot convey the many different indirect obligations that Chapter 7 has encountered throughout the analysis.

Notwithstanding the above discussion, other general principles such as good faith and estoppel can, of course, play an important role in investment law's interpretation, including indirect obligations. But it appears more adequate to understand them as corrective and complementing criteria *within* indirect obligations that have been identified in this Part[286] – hence not as reflecting indirect obligations themselves.[287]

All in all, it is suggested that investment law should affirm the preponderating opinion in general international law and deny that the doctrine of clean hands constitutes an established general principle. The encountered discussions by tribunals and scholars do not represent its growing recognition within investment law. Rather, they reflect a general, increasing concern that investment law should examine the investors' misconduct.[288] The doctrine appears as a form of 'workaround' to introduce indirect obli-

283 Herstein (n 256) 171–172; Llamzon (n 275) 323.

284 *Precision Instrument Mfg. Co. v Automotive Co.* (n 255) 814; Llamzon (n 275) 324.

285 cf Llamzon (n 275) 324; another way of framing this particular legal nature is to depict it as relating to the reciprocal obligations of the parties, see Ori Pomson, 'The Clean Hands Doctrine in the Yukos Awards: A Response to Patrick Dumberry' (2017) 18(4) Journal of World Investment & Trade 712, 716–718.

286 A good example how considerations of equity and good faith should be applied within the interpretation of international investment law offers Muchlinski (n 88) 531–532.

287 cf for an explanation of the doctrine of estoppel as a mechanism 'which precludes assertion of an *existent* legal position' (emphasis added) see Andreas Kulick, 'About the Order of Cart and Horse, Among Other Things: Estoppel in the Jurisprudence of International Investment Arbitration Tribunals' (2016) 27(1) European Journal of International Law 107, 124–128.

288 That remains, for example, the opinion of Caroline Le Moullec, 'The Clean Hands Doctrine: A Tool for Accountability of Investor Conduct and Inadmissibility of Investment Claims' (2018) 84(1) Arbitration: The International Journal of Arbitration, Mediation and Dispute Management 13, 21, 36–37, who however welcomes a greater place for taking account of the investor's misconduct in international investment law; see also the observation that investment law is in the course of developing a 'social conscience' by Footer (n 124) 33 and

gations as an element originally alien to the field. Therefore, the invoking of the doctrine shows that investment law is in a transitory phase that is still doctrinally underdeveloped in how it addresses investors' misconduct.

---

that investors' conduct is increasingly seen more critically as put forward by Llamzon (n 275) 323.

Chapter 8.
Interim Conclusion: Established Indirect Obligations

Part II has shown that, already today, indirect obligations are quite broadly established in investment law. They constitute standards of conduct that investors are free to comply with – but if they choose not to do so, investment law accords a sanction in the form of a loss of right. This may be that the investment claim to an arbitral tribunal becomes inadmissible or will not suffice to establish the tribunal's jurisdiction. Alternatively, investors may be deprived of investor rights as a matter of substantive investment law. Or their investor right could be partly devaluated because they receive less compensation for a violation than they would otherwise have been granted.

The term 'indirect obligations' is not yet used in practice. Instead, Part II introduced it to reflect that tribunals have imposed standards of conduct towards the public interest on investors. These penetrate the entire investment law doctrine. Of course, tribunals only adjudicate on the case at hand, and concentrate on the concrete requirement in dispute. The term 'indirect obligations' sheds light on the fact that the high number of analysed awards constitutes a pattern. It serves to show that these single instances follow a common development which is to condition investment protection on proper investor behaviour.[1]

These indirect obligations relate to how the investor affects the public interest. Herein, investment law departs from an earlier, private or com-

---

1 The increasing application of investor obligations in investment arbitration is, as Jean-Michel Marcoux and Andrew Newcombe, 'Bear Creek Mining Corporation v Republic of Peru: Two Sides of a "Social License" to Operate' (2018) 33(3) ICSID Review 653, 658 have put it, 'the elephant in the room'; in the same vein Jorge E. Viñuales, 'Investor Diligence in Investment Arbitration: Sources and Arguments' (2017) 32(2) ICSID Review 346, 367; Matthew A.J. Levine, 'Emerging Practice on Investor Diligence: Jurisdiction, Admissibility, Merits' in Julien Chaisse, Leïla Choukroune and Sufian Jusoh (eds), *Handbook of International Investment Law and Policy* (Springer 2021) 1101; for a more sceptical perspective see Mavluda Sattorova, 'Investor Responsibilities from a Host State Perspective: Qualitative Data and Proposals for Treaty Reform' (2019) 113 AJIL Unbound 22, 24 who considers that the inconsistency of arbitral jurisprudence precludes that investor obligations become established by reinterpretation of IIAs and calls for creating new, reformed IIAs.

mercial law paradigm: investor rights are not only about delineating which business risk the investor must bear anymore – investors must also earn investment protection by fulfilling a certain role in the society through their actions.[2] Investment tribunals have examined investors' impact on a broad range of different public goods and individual rights, including human rights, the environment, labour standards, the host state's economy, cultural heritage and the rule of law.

Tribunals have applied different methods to construe indirect obligations. Some built on explicit IIA provisions, for example the requirement to comply with domestic law. But the majority found them also to be implicit in IIAs. Thus, it is ordinary treaty (re-)interpretation pursuant to Art 31 VCLT that brought about indirect obligations – supported by recent IIAs with new treaty designs. In contrast, the study found the clean hands-doctrine to be redundant to that end.

Part II has proven indirect obligations to be a useful concept. It reflects that there are international behavioural expectations towards the investor with a partially compulsory effect. This insight is important, because Part I has shown that direct obligations have only emerged recently and remain few in numbers. Similar to direct obligations, indirect obligations operate without requiring enforcement by the state as an intermediary. In fact, by definition states cannot enforce indirect obligations. But they do not need to either. Instead, indirect obligations apply the above-mentioned sanction automatically. If investors do not comply, they forfeit investment protection *ipso jure*. In this understanding, investors do not only face standards of conduct in the form of direct obligations discussed in Part I, but also (and on a much broader basis) in the form of indirect obligations.

The study was careful to distinguish these indirect obligations from other approaches of examining investors' misconduct. Sometimes, tribunals took account of such misconduct only as a balancing criterion amongst others within the analysis of an investor right. Then, misconduct only 'tips

2 For a different interpretation and suggestion on contributory misconduct of the investor see Martin Jarrett, *Contributory Fault and Investor Misconduct in Investment Arbitration* (Cambridge University Press 2019) 95–97, 162–163 who proposes that tribunals should apportion the contributions of investors and the state to the state's breach of an investor right based on the economic contributions or net income of the investor to the host state's economy (instead of punishing investors for their fault), which, arguably, rather follows a private law paradigm and ideas of unjustified enrichment – on the other hand, he considers post-establishment illegality to be based on an 'affront to state sovereignty' (126) which appears to be closer to the public law paradigm identified here.

the scales' against the investor. In contrast to indirect obligations, there is no automatic sanction – investors are just less likely to win their case. This approach is more flexible than indirect obligations because investment protection is not strictly contingent on pro-public interest behaviour. Nevertheless, these cases contribute to a broader trend of making investment law dependent on proper investor conduct. This development is dynamic, as the reinterpretation of existing investment law and reform proposals go hand in hand. Within this development, indirect obligations are the most stringent method of giving investor misconduct legal relevance.

Notwithstanding, these different indirect obligations lack coordination. Only rarely have tribunals addressed the question of whether a certain standard of conduct should rather condition admissibility or jurisdiction, substantive investor rights or determine the amount of compensation. Nor have they addressed the question of whether different aspects of the public interest should be treated differently. Indirect obligations remain chaotic.

For this reason, Part II concentrated on shedding light on the presence of indirect obligations in investment practice itself. To identify this presence is an important observation. As the subsequent Part III will show, they have an important role to play in rebalancing investment law and steering investors in a public interest-friendly way.

Part III
Common Implications

The previous Parts discussed how already today direct obligations have begun to emerge and how deeply indirect obligations are already established. These observations are important and perhaps even surprising. Most reform discussions on investment law centre around the right of states to regulate, assuming that the field focuses solely on international rights of investors. Parts I and II demonstrate that there is more to investment law. Part III will bring these insights together. It will show that direct and indirect obligations are facets of a common development. In doing so, it will identify three implications.

First, these investor obligations rebalance investment law from within. There has been a lot debate on how to change investment law so that it emphasises the public interest more strongly. Investor obligations represent such an approach. It is complementary to other reform strategies such as reinforcing states' right to regulate. Investor obligations' creation transforms the field into a *sustainable* investment law (Chapter 9).

Second, investor obligations extend the function of investment law which originally focused on protecting investors only. As investor obligations become established, IIAs can serve as an incentive-based instrument steering investors' behaviour on the international level. This can help alleviate regulatory problems that states face encountering transnational corporations (Chapter 10).

Third, investor obligations serve as a case study for the role of the individual in international law. Investors as natural or private legal persons are individuals in that sense. In this more general view, investor obligations outline a new concept of individual international responsibility. They form part of a Global Administrative Law and support the long-lasting trend of creating individual rights and duties in international law (Chapter 11).

Chapter 9.
The Internal Perspective: Rebalancing Investment Law

Investor obligations rebalance investment law from within. Direct and indirect obligations are parts of the same development towards a symmetrical investment law in which rights and obligations go hand in hand (I.). They constitute an approach of changing investment law's value preferences – emphasising the public interest more strongly and providing investors at least to some extent with a new, 'public' role (II.). In consequence, they change the field's character towards a 'sustainable investment law' (III.). In doing so, investor obligations represent a reform option complementary to the oft-suggested reinforcing of host states' right to regulate. At the same time, they interact with the latter – depending on the perspective, they simultaneously expand and limit the right to regulate (IV.).

I. One common development towards symmetry

Direct and indirect obligations encountered in Parts I and II form part of the same development: a change in investment law to complement investor rights with obligations.

To recall: originally, investment law provided neither for direct nor for indirect obligations.[1] As an asymmetrical branch of international law, one of its main characteristic has always been that states would award rights without imposing obligations.[2]

---

1 See the similar historical remarks for direct and indirect obligations in Chapter 2.V and Chapter 6.VIII.

2 *Hesham Talaat M. Al-Warraq v The Republic of Indonesia*, Final Award (UNCITRAL, 15 December 2014) para 659; Patrick Dumberry and Gabrielle Dumas-Aubin, 'A Few Pragmatic Observations on How BITs Should Be Modified to Incorporate Human Rights Obligations' (2014) 11(1) Transnational Dispute Management 1, 2–3.

Investor obligations depart from this asymmetry.[3] Direct obligations do so to the full extent. Outright, they produce symmetry as investors face rights and obligations. Indirect obligations have a similar effect: their standards of conduct express behavioural expectations towards the investor. Even though it is true that investors are free in choosing to comply, a breach neutralises the IIA's investor rights. Therefore, only by observing these standards, they qualify for investment protection in the first place. In this sense, investment law forms a 'package' which contains symmetrical rights and obligations.

For example, a hypothetical IIA may impose a direct obligation to comply with a certain ILO Convention, thus symmetrically awarding both rights and obligations. Within the logic of the IIA, a similar clause drafted as an indirect obligation is no different. Technically speaking, the IIA still only awards rights. But investors can only invoke these rights if they comply with the ILO Convention. Both effects are qualitatively new to investment law – even though direct obligations surely constitute the more advanced alternative.

What is more, direct and indirect obligations share a common feature as they both operate detached from the host state's domestic legal system. Many encountered obligations define their content without regard for domestic law. The techniques to create direct obligations resonate in the way tribunals construed indirect obligations: to refer to international obligations of states,[4] to CSR,[5] to the (few) directly applicable international obligations of private actors[6] or by defining an entirely new standard.[7] For

---

3 Supported by Jorge E. Viñuales, 'Investor Diligence in Investment Arbitration: Sources and Arguments' (2017) 32(2) ICSID Review 346, 367; Tomoko Ishikawa, 'Counterclaims and the Rule of Law in Investment Arbitration' (2019) 113 AJIL Unbound 33, 37 focussing on counterclaims; Barnali Choudhury, 'Investor Obligations for Human Rights' (2020) 35(1–2) ICSID Review 82, 100, 102–103 however without distinguishing between direct and indirect obligations within the meaning of this book; James J Nedumpara and Aditya Laddha, 'Human Rights and Environmental Counterclaims in Investment Treaty Arbitration' in Julien Chaisse, Leïla Choukroune and Sufian Jusoh (eds), Handbook of International Investment Law and Policy (Springer 2021) 1849 who consider counterclais to 'assume substantial relevance' and to 'remedy the inherent asymmetry' of investment arbitration.

4 See for example Chapter 3.II, Chapter 7.I.3 and Chapter 7.II.4.

5 See for example Chapter 3.III and Chapter 7.II.3; see also Choudhury (n 3) 101 who shares the assessment that investor obligations may 'harden' soft law human rights responsibilities of investors.

6 See for example Chapter 3.I and Chapter 7.I.3.

7 See for example Chapter 3.V and Chapter 7.I.1.

example, the analysis has encountered the approach to integrate already-existing international obligations of private actors as a direct obligation – the *Urbaser v Argentina* award[8] – and an indirect obligation – the *ordre public international* as understood by the *World Duty Free v Kenya* award.[9]

On the other hand, another common feature encountered was that the obligations have sometimes defined their content indeed by referring to domestic law[10] – this way taking advantage of the fact that domestic regulation offers many obligations already tailored to private actors, usually comprehensively covering the public interest. Moreover, both types of obligations internationalised these domestic norms in the course of referring to them – by explicitly requiring qualified violations, applying domestic law in harmony with international law and interpreting domestic law autonomously.[11]

Furthermore, direct and indirect obligations are both enforced internationally. States can file counterclaims for the former. And in case of the latter, while one could argue that states cannot enforce them at all as investors are free to comply, one could, however, understand the automatic sanction that they apply in case of a breach as a form of an 'enforcement'.

To illustrate this by the above-mentioned example: Counterclaims are the international means to enforce the ILO Convention in case of a direct obligation. If it was an indirect obligation, states would not be able to file a counterclaim. But the breach would deprive the investor of protection under the IIA. This sanction applies automatically and thus is, in this sense, 'self-enforced'. The difference between such indirect obligation and the direct obligations is more minor than it seems at first glance: In most cases, just like any investment claim, counterclaims will primarily serve to enforce compensation.[12] They thus emphasise the enforcing of the breach's

8 See Chapter 3.I.2.

9 See Chapter 7.I.3.b).

10 Compare for example the elevating of domestic investor obligations to direct substantive international investor obligations (Chapter 3.IV), the applying and internationalising of domestic investor obligations in investment arbitration (Chapter 3.VI) and the criterion of compliance with the host state's domestic law as a jurisdiction or admissibility criterion for investment arbitration claims by investors (Chapter 7.I.2).

11 See for example Chapter 3.VI.3.a), Chapter 7.I.2.c) and Chapter 7.II.5.c).

12 For analyses which similarly emphasise compensation see Andrea K Bjorklund, 'The Role of Counterclaims in Rebalancing Investment Law' (2013) 17(2) Lewis & Clark Law Review 461, 475–476; Thomas Kendra, 'State Counterclaims in Investment Arbitration – a New Lease of Life?' (2013) 29(4) Arbitration International 575, 599–600 and the focus on the risk of liability for environmental dam-

secondary consequences rather than compelling actual compliance with the ILO Convention.

Overall, this means that direct and indirect obligations are new instruments with which investment law directly addresses investors' misconduct – without the state as an intermediary. Instead of only disciplining states, investment law starts to discipline investors too; hence, investor obligations continue the trend towards a 'generalisation'[13] of investment law. One could say that the field is transitioning from an 'international investment *protection* law' to a more holistic 'international investment law'.

II. Rebalancing investment law from within

Together, direct and indirect obligations change the field's underlying value preferences by strengthening the public interest compared to the protection of the investors' economic interests (1.). They represent an approach of rebalancing investment law from within. They come about from reinterpreting investment law and creating new IIA designs, albeit in a rather chaotic development (2.). This development changes the investor's role into an actor entrusted with serving the society to a certain extent (3.).

---

age caused by the investor by James Harrison, 'Environmental Counterclaims in Investor-State Arbitration: Perenco Ecuador Ltd v Republic of Ecuador, ICSID Case No ARB/08/6, Interim Decision on the Environmental Counterclaim, 11 August 2015 (Peter Tomka, Neil Kaplan, J Christopher Thomas)' (2016) 17(3) Journal of World Investment & Trade 479, 487.

13 'Generalisation' is used in the title of the article by Peter-Tobias Stoll and Till P Holterhus, 'The "Generalization" of International Investment Law in Constitutional Perspective' in Steffen Hindelang and Markus Krajewski (eds), *Shifting Paradigms in International Investment Law: More Balanced, Less Isolated, Increasingly Diversified* (Oxford University Press 2016); see also Karsten Nowrot, 'How to Include Environmental Protection, Human Rights and Sustainability in International Investment Law?' (2014) 15(3/4) Journal of World Investment & Trade 612, 613 on how investment law as a specialised field that hardly received scholarly attention turned into an area of law in which the balance between investors' economic interests and the 'domestic steering capacity' of host states in a comprehensive sense is heatedly debated in the public and academia alike.

1. Strengthening the public interest

Turning investment law symmetrical strengthens the role of the public interest.

In the last years, many have criticised investment law for being biased towards investors. This observation was one of this study's starting points.[14] Critics alleged that tribunals interpreted investors rights overly broadly: Investors would enjoy too far-reaching protection that could shield them even against host states' legitimate regulatory concerns, and the high amounts of compensation they could receive amounted to unjust international privileges. In short: they claimed that investors' economic concerns trumped the public interest.

Investor obligations are suitable to address this criticism.[15] They offer a way to emphasise the public interest in IIAs. Already the mere presence of

---

14 See Chapter 1.II.3.

15 See the similar assessment on imposing human rights obligations through IIAs by George K Foster, 'Investors, States, and Stakeholders: Power Asymmetries in International Investment and the Stabilizing Potential of Investment Treaties' (2013) 17(2) Lewis & Clark Law Review 361, 405; Choudhury (n 3) 103. For suggestions to introduce or use investment arbitration counterclaims see Gustavo Laborde, 'The Case for Host State Claims in Investment Arbitration' (2010) 1(1) Journal of International Dispute Settlement 97, 97–98; Bjorklund (n 12) 475–477; José A Rivas, 'ICSID Treaty Counterclaims: Case Law and Treaty Evolution' in Jean E Kalicki and Anna Joubin-Bret (eds), *Reshaping the Investor-State Dispute Settlement System: Journeys for the 21st Century* (Brill 2015) 780; Stefan Dudas, 'Treaty Counterclaims Under the ICSID Convention' in Crina Baltag (ed), *ICSID Convention After 50 Years: Unsettled Issues* (Wolters Kluwer 2017) 405; Makane Moise Mbengue and Stefanie Schacherer, 'The Africanization of International Investment Law: The Pan-African Investment Code and the Reform of the International Investment Regime' (2017) 18(3) Journal of World Investment & Trade 414, 445; Mark A Clodfelter and Diana Tsutieva, 'Counterclaims in Investment Treaty Arbitration' in Catherine Yannaca-Small (ed), *Arbitration Under International Investment Agreements: A Guide to the Key Issues* (2nd edn, Oxford University Press 2018) para 17.02; UNCITRAL 'Possible Reform of Investor-State Dispute Settlement (ISDS), Multiple Proceedings and Counterclaims' (22 January 2020) UN Doc A/CN.9/WG.III/WP.193, para 33; with some critical reservations Ina C Popova and Fiona Poon, 'From Perpetual Respondent to Aspiring Counterclaimant? State Counterclaims in the New Wave of Investment Treaties' (2015) 2(2) BCDR International Arbitration Review 223, 244–245; Maxim Scherer, Stuart Bruce and Juliane Reschke, 'Environmental Counterclaims in Investment Treaty Arbitration' (2021) ICSID Review 36(2) 413, 434–435. Investor obligations may even contribute to alleviating distributive justice concerns as envisaged by Steven R Ratner, 'International Investment Law Through the Lens of Global Justice' (2017) 20(4) Journal of International Economic Law 747, 758.

obligations along rights contributes to that end. Such obligations change the overall architecture of an IIA because they express a value judgment that investors' protection has its limits. Contextual interpretation pursuant to Art 31 (1) VCLT requires tribunals to take this into account when applying other clauses of the IIA, including investor rights. Therefore, even when a concrete obligation is not at stake, they 'tip the scales' in an IIA towards the public interest.

Furthermore, naturally, the public interest is emphasised because IIAs formulate respective standards of conduct – and accord negative consequences in case of a breach. The findings in Parts I and II have shown that investor obligations tend to be comprehensive in their substantive scope: often, it has appeared possible to apply them to very different public goods and individual rights. This indicates that they could potentially operate as a form of general international regulation for all aspects of foreign investment activity.

Yet, investor obligations can also operate in a more specific manner. States can define the type of conduct that they consider detrimental. They can tailor the obligations to problems they have encountered with foreign investment in the past. For example, environmentally-friendly states may choose to predominantly include environmental investor obligations. In the same vein, arbitral jurisprudence on indirect obligations has quite often considered and sanctioned corruption by investors. Herein, the development of such obligations towards the rule of law reflects a regulatory need that has arisen in practice and to which tribunals have reacted.

At the same time, it is problematic that investor obligations often remain fairly indeterminate – this is especially true for indirect obligations. One may doubt that some of these obligations will actually bring about a rebalancing effect. For example, the indirect obligation that stems from the requirement to contribute to the host state's development does not yet

---

The integration of norms from other areas of international law into international investment law to 'temper investor rights' has been suggested by Kate Miles, *The Origins of International Investment Law: Empire, Environment and the Safeguarding of Capital* (Cambridge University Press 2013) 331. Generally on the prospect of including public interest considerations in IIAs, see Nowrot (n 13) 644. For a contrary position in the context of counterclaims see Xuan Shao, 'Environmental and Human Rights Counterclaims in International Investment Arbitration: at the Crossroads of Domestic and International Law' (2021) 24(1) Journal of International Economic Law 157, 160–165 who argues that only domestic law is a feasible basis for environmental obligations of investors.

set a defined standard of conduct.[16] Notwithstanding, a substantial number of investor obligations is already fairly determinate – for example those which build on domestic provisions.[17] And the general trend towards a stronger emphasis on the public interest is clear. This is underlined by the high number of identified investor obligations throughout the entire investment law doctrine.

2. Reinterpretation and new treaty designs

This rebalancing of investment law represents a way of changing investment law from within. It rests on two pillars:

First, states have introduced new IIA designs with innovative clauses. Recurrently, the analysis has found that especially developing countries like India, Brazil and African states engage in such novel treaty-making. The new clauses are highly diverse, encompassing direct and indirect obligations alike. Even where these new clauses have so far only appeared in model BITs, these may serve as negotiating positions with other states and can bring about more public interest-oriented IIAs – even if the respective state cannot completely convince the other party from its model.

Second, many investor obligations followed from reinterpreting existing IIAs.[18] Increasingly, tribunals have been reading indirect obligations into investment law. This constitutes an approach that allows to transform the many IIAs in force without the need for creating new treaties. It offers an alternative to states which otherwise would consider terminating IIAs they perceive to overly disfavour their side.[19]

---

16 See Chapter 7.I.1.c).

17 See in particular Chapter 7.I.2 and Chapter 7.II.5.

18 Some even consider that investment law practice is merely discovering features that have always existed. On the requirement to comply with domestic law as such a 'dormant' requirement see Panayotis M Protopsaltis, 'Compliance with the Laws of the Host Country in Bilateral Investment Treaties' (2015) 12(6) Transnational Dispute Management 1, 2–3; Jeff Sullivan and Valeriya Kirsey, 'Environmental Policies: A Shield or a Sword in Investment Arbitration?' (2017) 18(1) Journal of World Investment & Trade 100, 117.

19 This is what Stephan W Schill, 'The Sixth Path: Reforming Investment Law from Within' in Jean E Kalicki and Anna Joubin-Bret (eds), *Reshaping the Investor-State Dispute Settlement System: Journeys for the 21st Century* (Brill 2015) 624–625 calls the 'sixth path'; for example also suggested by Kendra (n 12) 600; in the same direction Miles (n 15) 383; for an overview of different reform approaches see

However, reinterpretation takes place on a case-by-case basis, and single awards with new interpretive approaches may constitute a trend only if encountered consistently and over a period of time. When adjudicating, tribunals are restricted by the facts of the given case and can only decide on the concrete dispute that has arisen. It follows that they can only reinterpret selectively and concentrate on the specific problem presented by the parties. As a result, much of the developments that especially Part II on indirect obligations has presented, constitutes a fairly chaotic, still ongoing process.[20] The different types of indirect obligations lack coordination. As seen, so far there is no overarching system that defines if and why certain misconduct is treated as a matter of jurisdiction and admissibility, substantive investor rights or rules on compensation.

3. A changing role of investors

This chaotic evolution is due to a gradual, ongoing change of how states and society perceive the role of investors in investment law. To include investor obligations in IIAs means changing this role profoundly.

As IIAs impose standards of conduct towards the public interest, they express the idea that investors have an active role to play in a host state's society.[21] Some standards expect them not to impair public goods and

---

the contributions in Andreas Kulick (ed), *Reassertion of Control over the Investment Treaty Regime* (Cambridge University Press 2017).

20 Generally on the dynamic character of investment law see José E Alvarez and others (eds), *The Evolving International Investment Regime: Expectations, Realities, Options* (Oxford University Press 2011); see also Stephan W Schill, 'Cross-Regime Harmonization Through Proportionality Analysis: The Case of International Investment Law, the Law of State Immunity and Human Rights' (2012) 27(1) ICSID Review 87, 90 on the dynamic relationship of different areas of international law; Steffen Hindelang and Markus Krajewski, 'Conclusion and Outlook: Whither International Investment Law?' 377–379 sketching dynamic paradigm shifts in international investment law.

21 See also Choudhury (n 3) 103 who considers introducing human rights investor obligations to better align international investment law with 'society's expectations for business, which is necessary for businesses' (including foreign investors') social licence to operate'; Nicolás M Perrone, 'The "Invisible" Local Communities: Foreign Investor Obligations, Inclusiveness, and the International Investment Regime' (2019) 113 AJIL Unbound 16, 16–17 who calls for an '*inclusive*, relational approach to foreign investment governance' (emphasis in the original). cf the identification of changes in tribunals' perspectives by Moshe Hirsch, 'Investment Tribunals and Human Rights Treaties: A Sociological Perspective' in

individual rights of others.[22] Many obligations may require the investor to go even further and promote the public interest.[23] In contrast, the originally envisaged role of foreign investors was different: Generally, IIAs assured them the right to be left alone by the state and to follow their own economic interests.

This fundamental change of role goes even deeper. In Part II, the study has revealed that some tribunals also take account of investor misconduct without establishing indirect obligations. Instead, they only consider it as a balancing factor – especially as part of investor rights' substantive requirements. These tribunals introduced the described new expectations in a more preliminary, cautious manner while following the same tendency as indirect and direct obligations.

Investment law's development is part and parcel of increasing demands towards corporations. The understanding that businesses can limit themselves to achieve profits is increasingly contested. On the UN level, the business and human rights discussions encourage, at the very least, a moral responsibility for individual rights and public goods.[24] Parts I and II have shown that investment law does not operate in a vacuum. Investor obligations can be understood as reflective of these international debates – especially as they often build on pre-existing international standards of conduct.

Consequently, investment law shifts the traditional divide between the public and the private. As originally envisaged, these ambits were clearly distributed: the host state represents the public sphere, the investor the private. As IIAs impose and enforce public interest obligations on investors, investors do enter, at least partly, the public sphere. In the process of doing so, they also become entrusted with safeguarding the public interest.

III. Sustainable investment law

Rebalancing investment law towards a partially public role for the investor has consequences for the field's overall character. This Section will show

---

Freya Baetens (ed), *Investment Law Within International Law: Integrationist Perspectives* (Cambridge University Press 2013) 100–103.

22 For example, the principle of contributory negligence sanctions investors who acted negligently towards the public interest, see Chapter 7.III.2.

23 For example, the requirement to contribute to the host state's development, see Chapter 7.I.1.

24 See Chapter 1.III.1.

that the encountered investor obligations turn it into a 'sustainable investment law'. To begin, it will shortly describe the concept of sustainable development (1.). It will then show that the shift towards sustainability is best understood against investment law's original purpose of increasing the volume of foreign investment (2.). Finally, it will demonstrate that introducing investor obligations changes this telos to only attract *quality* investment – in line with the concept of sustainable development (3.).

1. The concept of sustainable development

The concept of sustainable development was first introduced in the 1970s and has received increasingly stronger ground in international law from the late 1980s onwards.[25] It concerns the way societies and states should evolve. The UN define it as

> development that meets the needs of the present without compromising the ability of future generations to meet their own needs. [...] For sustainable development to be achieved, it is crucial to harmonize three core elements: economic growth, social inclusion and environmental protection. These elements are interconnected and all are crucial for the well-being of individuals and societies.[26]

---

25 See the overview by Ulrich Beyerlin, 'Sustainable Development' in Anne Peters (ed), *Max Planck Encyclopedia of Public International Law* (October 2013) paras 2–8; important milestones of how the concept crystallised in international law are the World Commission on Environment and Development, *Our Common Future* (Oxford University Press 1987), the UNGA 'Rio Declaration on Environment and Development' UN Doc A/CONF.151/26 (Vol. I) (12 August 1992) and UNGA 'Transforming Our World: The 2030 Agenda for Sustainable Development' UN Doc A/RES/70/1 (25 September 2015); see further Giorgio Sacerdoti, 'Investment Protection and Sustainable Development: Key Issues' in Steffen Hindelang and Markus Krajewski (eds), *Shifting Paradigms in International Investment Law: More Balanced, Less Isolated, Increasingly Diversified* (Oxford University Press 2016) 23–28.

26 ‹www.un.org/sustainabledevelopment/development-agenda/› accessed 7 December 2021 in the FAQ, 'What is sustainable development?'.

The UN have translated sustainable development into an Agenda which includes 17 goals and 169 targets that states strive to meet by 2030.[27] The UN Development Goals also address investment as follows:

> Goal 10. Reduce inequality within and among countries [...]
>
> 10.b Encourage official development assistance and financial flows, including foreign direct investment, to States where the need is greatest, in particular least developed countries, African countries, small island developing States and landlocked developing countries, in accordance with their national plans and programme. [...]
>
> Means of implementation and the Global Partnership [...]
>
> 67. Private business activity, investment and innovation are major drivers of productivity, inclusive economic growth and job creation. We acknowledge the diversity of the private sector, ranging from micro-enterprises to cooperatives to multinationals. We call upon all businesses to apply their creativity and innovation to solving sustainable development challenges. We will foster a dynamic and well-functioning business sector, while protecting labour rights and environmental and health standards in accordance with relevant international standards and agreements and other ongoing initiatives in this regard [...].[28]

The UN acknowledge that private investment forms an important means to achieve the Sustainable Development Goals, in particular to support developing countries. Foreign investors should take an active role to that end. Yet, the UN also highlight that investments have to operate in line with public goods and individual rights of others – reflecting the general approach of harmonising the three mentioned dimensions of sustainability.

27 Most prominently reflected in the 17 UN Sustainable Development Goals for 2030, see 'UNGA Res 70/1' (n 25).

28 UNGA 'Transforming Our World: The 2030 Agenda for Sustainable Development' UN A/RES/70/1 (21 October 2015), paras 10b and 67. They contain further, more specific references to investment for ending hunger through sustainable agriculture in para 2 and in the energy sector in para 7.a.

2. The original purpose to increase investment volume

To understand how the investor obligations identified in this book fit the idea of sustainable development, it is useful to recall investment law's original purpose: IIAs should focus on protecting investors in order to attract foreign investment to the state parties. In this vein, the ICSID Conventions' preamble states at the very beginning:

> Considering the need for international cooperation for economic development, and the role of private international investment therein; [...]

The 1965 Report of the Executive Directors on the ICSID Convention explicitly explains how the ICSID Convention may serve economic development:

> 9. In submitting the attached Convention to governments, the Executive Directors are prompted by the desire to strengthen the partnership between countries in the cause of economic development. The creation of an institution designed to facilitate the settlement of disputes between States and foreign investors can be a major step toward promoting an atmosphere of mutual confidence and thus stimulating *a larger flow* of private international capital into those countries which wish to attract it.[29]

In other words, by awarding international protection states have generally aimed to attract *any* foreign investment. Investment law has served to increase the total foreign investment volume. In this view, the host state benefits from a stronger economy and the home state from new markets for corporations of its nationality which may bring profits home. This original purpose does not provide for holistically intertwining the economy with the environment and society that the (later invented) concept of sustainable development promotes.

---

29 IBRD 'Report of the Executive Directors on the Convention of the Settlement of Investment Disputes Between States and Nationals of Other States' ICSID/15/Rev.1, 35–49 (18 March 1965), para 9 (emphasis added).

3. Towards attracting sustainable investment

Investment law with investor obligations transforms this original purpose into the furthering of *sustainable* development.

By imposing obligations, investment law practically limits its scope to those investors who behave in accordance with the public interest. In turn, only such well-behaved investors do not have to fear counterclaims or the loss of investment protection. It is a choice of quality over quantity: rather than increasing *any* foreign investment flow, it offers an incentive exclusively for investors who abide by the imposed standards of conduct. This means that instead of fostering any economic development, IIAs now promote only sustainable development.[30]

These findings of a turn to sustainability are in line with UNCTAD's observations which in 2015 proposed a more sustainable investment law. It outlined a reform concept to that end in its 2015 Investment Policy Framework for Sustainable Development.[31] Then, in 2017, UNCTAD identified that these reforms had indeed reached a 'phase 2' in practice.[32] It found

30 In the same vein Gudrun Monika Zagel, 'Achieving Sustainable Development Objectives in International Investment Law' in Julien Chaisse, Leïla Choukroune and Sufian Jusoh (eds), Handbook of International Investment Law and Policy (Springer 2021) 1955–1957; cf for a *de lege ferenda* perspective Howard Mann, 'Reconceptualizing International Investment Law: Its Role in Sustainable Development' (2013) 17(2) Lewis & Clark Law Review 521, 540–541 who proposes investor obligations as a solution for aligning investment law with sustainable development; similarly Graham Mayeda, 'Sustainable International Investment Agreements: Challenges and Solutions for Developing Countries' in Marie-Claire Cordonier Segger, Markus W Gehring and Andrew P Newcombe (eds), *Sustainable Development in World Investment Law* (Kluwer Law International 2011) 544; Choudhury (n 3) 102; Surya Deva, 'Conclusion: Investors' International Law: Beyond the Present' in Jean Ho and Mavluda Sattorova (eds), *Investors' International Law* (Hart 2021) 314–316. Such a shift has been demanded by stakeholders, see for example Howard Mann, 'Civil Society Perspectives: What Do Key Stakeholders Expect from the International Investment Regime?' in José E Alvarez and others (eds), *The Evolving International Investment Regime: Expectations, Realities, Options* (Oxford University Press 2011) 27.

31 UNCTAD 'Investment Policy Framework for Sustainable Development' UNCTAD/DIAE/PCB/2015/5 (2015).

32 UNCTAD, *World Investment Report: Investment and the Digital Economy* (United Nations Publications 2017) 126. In the same vein, others have observed that the still rather young international investment law system has matured from a phase of 'infancy' to ongoing 'adolescence', '[a]pproaching [...] adulthood', see Anthea Roberts, 'Clash of Paradigms: Actors and Analogies Shaping the Investment Treaty System' (2013) 107(1) American Journal of International Law 45, 75–93

that a 'sustainable development-oriented IIA reform has entered the mainstream of international investment policymaking'.[33] In UNCTAD's view, it complemented other approaches such as promoting and facilitating investment, reforming investment dispute settlement and reinforcing the right to regulate. As examples for such policy strategies it explicitly mentioned the ensuring of responsible investment.[34]

IV. Interactions with host states' right to regulate

UNCTAD's remarks lead the analysis to another starting point of this book: How do the encountered investor obligations relate to host states' right to regulate? Strengthening the latter has been at the heart of reform suggestions in the last years.

It is submitted that investor obligations are a complementary rebalancing approach (1.). However, as investor obligations become part of IIAs, they also interact with the right to regulate. Depending on the perspective taken, they can strengthen (2.) or limit (3.) it.

1. Complementary reform options

In their effort to rebalance investment law, investor obligations and the right to regulate serve the same purpose.

To recall the right to regulate-approach for a better comparison:[35] Proponents of a stronger right to regulate focus on the host state. They aim to limit investor rights' disciplining effect on states. As a result, the leeway of states to regulate for the public interest should increase. In particular, in doing so, they should face less investment claims. In order to provide clarity that the state can enact such legislation, they suggest different ways to reform investment law. On the one hand, IIAs should include new right

---

with reference to Brigitte Stern, 'The Future of International Investment Law: A Balance Between the Protection of Investors and the States' Capacity to Regulate' in José E Alvarez and others (eds), *The Evolving International Investment Regime: Expectations, Realities, Options* (Oxford University Press 2011) 175 who observes a '*crise de croissance*' in the backlash against international investment law.

33 UNCTAD, *World* (n 32) 126.

34 ibid; this observation is supported for example by Hindelang and Krajewski (n 20) 380–381.

35 See already Chapter 1.II.3.

to regulate clauses. They operate as justifications for a breach of an investor right or even as carve-out clauses. Often, they specify areas of the public interest in which the host state is free to regulate, for example human rights, environmental protection and social standards. On the other hand, one should foster the right to regulate by interpreting investor rights under existing IIAs more restrictively. To that end, especially systemic interpretation in accordance with other international treaties such as human rights pursuant to Art 31 (3) (c) VCLT is advised.[36]

The similarities of the right to regulate to the encountered investor obligations are apparent. Both approaches give greater weight to the public interest in the overall balance with investors' economic goals. The scope of relevant public goods and individual rights to be protected is equally comprehensive. They apply the same methods to reform investment law from within: creating new IIA clauses and reinterpreting existing investment law. Both find ground in recent arbitral jurisprudence. The main difference is, of course, that investor obligations focus on a different actor. In other words, they tackle the same concerns from a different angle. Thus, they represent a tool which may complement the strengthening of the right to regulate in rebalancing investment law.[37]

2. Strengthening the right to regulate

However, investor obligations and the right to regulate are not detached from one another. Instead, they interact. This Section will show that imposing investor obligations can expand host states' right to regulate.

First, if an IIA contains indirect investor obligations, the state's regulatory leeway automatically increases. This follows from the way indirect obligations operate. If investors breach them, they forfeit investment protection. They can no longer challenge the host state's actions by invoking investment law.[38]

---

36 On systemic interpretation see Chapter 3 n 57.

37 Similarly UNCTAD, *World* (n 32) 126; Hindelang and Krajewski (n 20) 380–381.

38 cf *Ioannis Kardassopoulos v The Republic of Georgia*, ICSID Case No. ARB/05/18, Decision on Jurisdiction (6 July 2007) para 182 which considers investors' actions to be a relevant point of analysis to determine if they enjoy investor rights: '"Protection of investments" under a BIT is obviously not without some limits. It does not extend, for instance, to an investor making an investment in breach of the local laws of the host State. [...] This [...] relates to the investor's actions in making the investment. It does not allow a State to preclude an investor

For example, an IIA could contain a clause which deprives investors of investment protection if they violate international anti-corruption standards. As seen, a corrupt investor suffers the sanction of losing protection. If the host state now enacts anti-corruption regulation, said investor cannot challenge this regulation anymore by invoking the IIA. In effect, the indirect obligation has increased the host state's right to regulate by freeing it from its international obligations under the IIA.

Second, direct obligations can similarly strengthen host states' right to regulate. This effect follows from the already-mentioned contextual interpretation of IIAs pursuant to Art 31 (1) VCLT:[39] Consistency requires that IIAs cannot simultaneously protect and prohibit the same conduct. This means that investors cannot invoke an investor right when behaving in a way which fails to meet the standard of conduct that direct obligations impose.

To illustrate this with the aforementioned example: Now, the IIA's clause prohibits corruption as a direct obligation. When the investor violates the anti-corruption obligation, the host state can claim compensation under the IIA. At the same time, the IIA allows the host state to take domestic measures against such behaviour. According to Art 31 (1) VCLT the IIA's investor rights have to be interpreted in a way consistent with the anti-corruption obligation. This means that the investor cannot invoke investor rights against the host state's domestic anti-corruption measures. Again, the host state's right to regulate is strengthened compared to an IIA without a direct investor obligation.

Admittedly, these observations only serve as general lines; investor obligations' expanding effect on the right to regulate has limits. The aforementioned examples assume that the investor's violation of such an obligation is clear, and that the host state reacted proportionately. If that is not the case, the assessment may change. In this vein, recurrently, the analysis in Parts I and II has found that investor obligations require a weighing and balancing of the affected interests in a certain dispute. To that end, the obligations often contained qualifications, for example, that the public interest affected must be of a fundamental nature. These qualifying

from seeking protection under the BIT on the ground that its own actions are illegal under its own laws.' (emphasis in the original); see also Ursula Kriebaum, 'Investment Arbitration – Illegal Investments' in Christian Klausegger and others (eds), *Austrian Yearbook on International Arbitration* (Stämpfli Verlag 2010) 310.

39 See Chapter 9.II.1 on the effect that contextual interpretation has on the overall architecture of an IIA if it contains investor obligations.

elements provide interpretive flexibility. Therefore, in the aforementioned example, one cannot simply say that the IIA provides states with a *carte blanche* to combat corruption.[40] Indeed, Art 31 (1) VCLT also requires that investor obligations be interpreted in a way consistent with investor rights. Consequently, even if an IIA does contain investor obligations, the IIA still continues to impose disciplines on the host state, related especially to the *manner* the state acts towards the investors.

For example, if the state in the above examples acted disproportionately against corrupt investors – by incarcerating them over an extended period of time without judicial review – it is quite certain that even a breach of anti-corruption investor obligations may not expand the state's right to regulate and enforce said regulation so broadly.

In case of an indirect obligation, the tribunal could find that its sanction does not apply and preserve the investor right. Indeed, this study has provided examples of arbitral jurisprudence in which investors who violated an indirect obligation did not forfeit investment protection if the host state itself committed a wrongdoing.[41] When considering direct obligations, the overall interpretive outcome may change. The tribunal may, for example, consider that both the state and the investor have violated their respective obligations under the IIA.

All in all, it is decisive that investor obligations 'tip the scales' within investment law in favour of the public interest.[42] This opens a regulatory space for the host state while remaining restrained especially in the *manner* in which it acts towards the investors.

3. Limiting the right to regulate

Having pointed out how investor obligations may strengthen host state's right to regulate, this Section will show that they can also limit the latter.

---

40 The concern that directly applicable international obligations provide states with such a *carte blanche* features as an argument against directly applicable international obligations in other fields, for example regarding international human rights see Christian Tomuschat, 'Grundpflichten des Individuums nach Völkerrecht' (1983) 21(3) Archiv des Völkerrechts 289, 311–312; Kofi Quashigah, 'Scope of Individual Duties in the African Charter' in Manisuli Ssenyonjo (ed), *The African Regional Human Rights System: 30 Years After the African Charter on Human and Peoples' Rights* (Martinus Nijhoff Publishers 2012) 121–123.

41 See Chapter 7.I.2.b).

42 See Chapter 9.II.1.

The reason is that investor obligations operate on the level of international law, detached from the host state's domestic legal system.

As seen, investor obligations express international standards of conduct for investors. After being agreed upon in an IIA, they cannot be unilaterally changed without abiding by regular treaty amendment procedures. As such, investor obligations represent a form of international regulation for foreign investment. For example, if states include a certain ILO Convention in an IIA as an investor obligation, the Convention becomes a common applicable labour standard. The states cannot unilaterally decide to allow for a lower standard without amending or terminating the treaty.

Furthermore, tribunals may interpret investor obligations autonomously and alter their meaning contrary to states' original expectations. The impairing effect on states' right to regulate is particularly visible where investor obligations draw on domestic law and internationalise it in the process. The awards in *Perenco v Ecuador* and *Burlington v Ecuador* show the different ways in which tribunals may understand even fundamental domestic rules such as constitutions.[43] This effect limits host states' right to regulate in the sense that they cannot oversee how exactly international obligations apply – compared to domestic obligations which are enforced by their courts and executive agencies.

In short, investor obligations also restrict states' sovereignty because states have jointly decided to follow common rules. To create international institutions such as investment tribunals always implies that they work autonomously. Their interpretation of investor obligations may evolve within the boundaries set by international treaty law,[44] 'transferring authority from the national to the international'.[45]

---

43 See Chapter 3.VI.2.

44 cf Patrick Abel, 'Menschenrechtsschutz durch Individualbeschwerdeverfahren: Ein regionaler Vergleich aus historischer, normativer und faktischer Perspektive' (2013) 51(3) Archiv des Völkerrechts 369, 370–392 on the dynamic role that regional human rights courts play; on the requirements for an evolutive interpretation in the law of treaties see *Dispute Regarding Navigational and Related Rights (Costa Rica v Nicaragua)* (Judgment) [2009] ICJ Rep 213, paras 63–71.

45 This expression is borrowed from Jacob K Cogan, 'The Regulatory Turn in International Law' (2011) 52(2) Harvard International Law Journal 321, 362–363.

Chapter 10.
The Regulatory Perspective: Steering Investors

The last Chapter has demonstrated how investor obligations rebalance IIAs by emphasising the public interest more strongly. In doing so, it has considered how investor obligations affect IIAs' original purpose to protect investors and attract foreign investment. This Chapter will show that investor obligations may also provide investment law with an entirely new function: to serve as an international regulatory instrument that steers investors' behaviour.

Considering that, originally, investment law only awarded investor rights, its use to regulate investment was never at stake. As investor obligations have emerged, they prompt an inquiry if IIAs could now serve such a purpose (I.). The Chapter presents two regulatory approaches that investor obligations could follow: 'command-and-control' and 'incentive-based' regulation (II.). It is submitted that investor obligations hardly ever serve the former function. They allow states to 'command and control' investors only reactively because the investor has to invoke investment protection first (III.). Instead, they constitute a promising incentive-based regulatory approach: Investor obligations use investor rights as leverage to induce compliance (IV.).

I. Considering international regulation of foreign investment

Chapter 10 takes a perspective that is unusual for investment law. It asks if IIAs could represent an international tool to steer foreign investors' behaviour.

The term 'regulation' has been employed in various ways. Generally, regulation aims to make sure that persons behave in a certain manner to meet a regulatory goal. Traditionally, regulation is understood as authoritative rule-making to control the behaviour of private actors, typically by the state in its domestic legal system.[1] Many international treaties serve to

1 For such an understanding see for example Jacob K Cogan, 'The Regulatory Turn in International Law' (2011) 52(2) Harvard International Law Journal 321, 324.

harmonise such rules or to provide minimum standards. For example, human rights treaties address how states should protect human rights against infringements by private parties such as investors. ILO Conventions define minimum labour standards in the relationship between employers and employees. Therefore, these international treaties embody obligations for states to regulate the behaviour of private actors. In contrast, originally IIAs did not serve this regulatory purpose. Instead, as seen,[2] they should discipline host states in their actions towards investors.

The findings of Parts I and II could change this assessment. As investor obligations have been established, IIAs may take over new functions beyond the attracting of (quality) foreign investment. In that, they could become more similar to treaties that engage in international regulation, such as human rights and labour protection treaties mentioned above.

This leads to a further question that Chapter 1 has presented: Could IIAs play a part in addressing the regulatory problems that states encounter vis-à-vis transnationally operating corporations? To recall,[3] their economic power challenges states' capacity to effectively regulate them within their territory. Foreign investors form a subgroup of these corporations. For example, investors' main assets may be located in third states and thus out of host states' reach. What is more, the host state may be unwilling to protect the public interest – or unable to do so due to organisational, financial, political or other deficits.[4]

II. Relevant regulatory strategies

Domestic and international regulatory approaches are plenty. States have adopted regulatory strategies that go beyond the above-mentioned authoritative rule making.[5] For the present purpose, the study will concentrate on contrasting two regulatory strategies which serve to classify investor obligations' potential best: 'command-and-control' (1.) and 'incentive-based' (2.) regulation.

---

2 See Chapter 9.I and Chapter 9.III.2.

3 See in more detail Chapter 1.III.1.

4 On the unwilling and the unable state see Anne Peters, *Beyond Human Rights: The Legal Status of the Individual in International Law* (Cambridge University Press 2016) 76.

5 For an in-depth analysis of different regulatory approaches see Peter Drahos (ed), *Regulatory Theory: Foundations and Applications* (Australian National University Press 2017).

1. Command-and-control

The term 'command-and-control' shall be understood as regulation that relies on law's authoritative character. It operates by prohibiting unwanted behaviour and actively responding, suppressing or punishing it when it occurs. In domestic legal systems, it relies on courts and executive agencies to investigate violations and enforce rules against the non-compliant person's will[6] – conforming with the traditional understanding of regulation mentioned above.

But command-and-control regulation also takes place on the international level. The most advanced example is that of international criminal law. These international norms are enforced against individual perpetrators before international tribunals such as the International Criminal Court. However, similar international command-and-control mechanisms against businesses are missing. As seen above, critics argue that non-binding CSR rules are not enough to compel businesses to comply with human rights.[7] It is one of the main reasons why a Working Group at the UN level is currently debating 'an international legally binding instrument to regulate, in international human rights law, the activities of transnational corporations and other business enterprises'.[8] However, regulatory gaps

---

6 This term builds for example on literature on international environmental protection governance, see for example Sanja Bogojević, 'Ending the Honeymoon: Deconstructing Emissions Trading Discourses' (2009) 21(3) Journal of Environmental Law 443, 460–461; see also the overview and comparison with other policy instrument terms in a regulatory theory-perspective by Neil Gunningham and Darren Sinclair, 'Smart Regulation' in Peter Drahos (ed), *Regulatory Theory: Foundations and Applications* (Australian National University Press 2017) 140; for a more general theoretical contextualisation of coercion in inter-state international law from the perspective of international relations see Beth A Simmons, 'International Law' in Walter Carlsnaes, Thomas Risse and Beth A Simmons (eds), *Handbook of International Relations* (2nd edn, Sage 2013) 366–367.

7 See Chapter 1.III.1.

8 See the original mandate in UN Human Rights Council 'Elaboration of an Internationally Legally Binding Instrument on Transnational Corporations and Other Business Enterprises with Respect to Human Rights' UN Doc A/HRC/RES/26/9 (14 July 2014), no 1; for a comprehensive scholarly analysis see Surya Deva and David Bilchitz (eds), *Building a Treaty on Business and Human Rights: Context and Contours* (Cambridge University Press 2017). However, it is important to note that the envisaged treaty should not only reflect command-and-control regulation but also contains cooperative elements, see for example UN Human Rights Council 'Elements for the Draft Legally Binding Instrument on Transnational Corporations and Other Business Enterprises with Respect to Human Rights' (29 September

exist for the protection of other individual rights and public goods too, and call for similar command-and-control approaches – for example international labour law.[9]

2. Incentives

'Incentive-based regulation' is a regulatory strategy which aims to achieve voluntary compliance. To that end, it offers advantages to the addressee and makes them contingent on a certain desired behaviour. In contrast to the command-and-control setting, it does not primarily rest on proscribing behaviour and investigating, as well as punishing, non-compliance. Instead, the threat of possible, enforceable sanctions stands in the background and can fuel the incentivising effect.[10]

Domestic legal systems have a long tradition of incentive-based policy strategies to steer foreign investment. One may name the granting of fiscal incentives like tax breaks and tariff reliefs or grants, aids and credits.[11] For example, in 2018, the UN Human Rights Council has proposed that states should condition export credits upon respect for human rights.[12]

2017) ‹www.ohchr.org/Documents/HRBodies/HRCouncil/WGTransCorp/Session3/LegallyBindingInstrumentTNCs_OBEs.pdf› accessed 7 December 2021, 12.

9 cf on labour standards Patrick Abel, 'Comparative Conclusions on Arbitral Dispute Settlement in Trade-Labour Matters Under US FTAs' in Henner Gött (ed), *Labour Standards in International Economic Law* (Springer International Publishing 2018) 164–180.

10 See for example the importance of the loss of advantages as a form of reciprocal self-enforcement of international law from the perspective of rationalist international relations, laid out by Simmons (n 6) 367–369; for an economic viewpoint see Eric A Posner and Alan O Sykes, *Economic Foundations of International Law* (Belknap Press of Harvard University Press 2013) 20–26 for an interpretation of international law as a mechanism of bargaining and incomplete contracting. Incentive-based regulation appears comparable to the so-called 'leverage regime' that is contrasted with the 'cessation regime' in the business and human rights discussions as for example distinguished by Radu Mares, 'Legalizing Human Rights Due Diligence and the Separation of Entities Principle' in Surya Deva and David Bilchitz (eds), *Building a Treaty on Business and Human Rights: Context and Contours* (Cambridge University Press 2017) 288–292.

11 Further details with examples of specific countries are presented by Peter Muchlinski, *Multinational Enterprises and the Law* (2nd edn, Oxford University Press 2007) 219–226.

12 UN Human Rights Council 'Report of the Working Group on the Issue of Human Rights and Transnational Corporations and Other Business Enterprises'

Here, it is the home state of a corporation which incentivises public interest-friendly behaviour abroad. In this example, investors have an interest to comply with human rights to receive export credits. If they do not meet the requirements, they are disqualified from obtaining them. In situations of non-compliance, the state may also demand export credits back – which constitutes the mentioned threat of a sanction.

Incentive-based regulation should be distinguished from policies which rest on pure cooperation. The latter do not offer defined advantages for compliance. Similarly, they exclude threatening legal sanctions. Instead, cooperation builds on common moral perceptions which should persuade private actors to act in accordance with the public interest. It assumes that the majority of persons are willing to behave, at least to a certain extent, altruistically.[13] For example, CSR norms largely follow this cooperative approach – possible consumer pressure is too diffused to qualify as a defined threat and is not of a legal character.[14] In contrast, incentive-based regulation relies on addressees' self-interest to gain advantages the state offers.

UN Doc A/HRC/38/48 (2 May 2018), paras 38–79. cf the general overview on conditionality by Cesare Pinelli, 'Conditionality' in Anne Peters (ed), *Max Planck Encyclopedia of Public International Law* (November 2013); on the conditionality practice of the EU, see Daniela Donno and Michael Neureiter, 'Can Human Rights Conditionality Reduce Repression? Examining the European Union's Economic Agreements' (2018) 13(3) The Review of International Organizations 335, 336–357; for the practice of the IMF see Randall W Stone, 'The Scope of IMF Conditionality' (2008) 62(4) International Organization 589, 591–617; on the potential impact on the public interest see Matthias Sant'ana, 'Risk Managers or Risk Promoters? The Impact of Export Credit and Investment Insurance Agencies on Human Development and Human Rights' in Johan F M Swinnen, Jan Wouters and Olivier D Schutter (eds), *Foreign Direct Investment and Human Development: The Law and Economics of International Investment Agreements* (Routledge 2013) 193–230.

13 In international relations, this approach is categorised as ideational, see for example Simmons (n 6) 369–372; specifically on the role of reputation see for example Mark J C Crescenzi, *Of Friends and Foes: Reputation and Learning in World Politics* (Oxford University Press 2018) 29–84. There are also other models, for example theory on so called value-driven behaviour, see Tom R Tyler, 'Value-Driven Behavior and the Law' in Francesco Parisi (ed), *The Oxford Handbook of Law and Economics*, vol I Methodology and Concepts (Oxford University Press 2017) 405–416. On the advantages of such a 'soft law'-approach from the relevant actors' perspectives see Kenneth W Abbott and Duncan Snidal, 'Hard and Soft Law in International Governance' (2000) 54(3) International Organization 421, 434–450.

14 See further Chapter 1.III.1 on international CSR norms.

III. IIAs as limited command-and-control regulation

This section will first consider if investor obligations can serve as a form of international command-and-control regulation. It is suggested that they qualify as such only to a very limited extent.

At first glance, their legally binding character appears to conform with the command-and-control setting (1.). However, states cannot initiate their enforcement. Rather, their sanctions come into effect only *reactively* after investors have themselves invoked an investor right. Thus, investor obligations are not well suited to actively respond to unwanted behaviour and punish investor misconduct (2.).

1. Binding international public interest standards

Investor obligations fit the command-and-control approach to the extent they bring about legally binding international standards.[15] One can illustrate this with a comparison to the business and human rights discussion. Many investor obligations realise core suggestions of the 2017 Elements for the Draft Legally Binding Instrument on Transnational Corporations and Other Business Enterprises with Respect to Human Rights of the related UNHRC Open-ended Intergovernmental Working Group. These draft elements included the proposal to create human rights obligations directly applicable to corporations – a property which the three subsequently discussed treaty drafts developed by the Working Group did not pursue any further.[16] From its proposals, investor obligations adopt for example the following:

- Corporations should comply with all applicable laws,[17]
  resonating in investor obligations to comply with domestic and international law;[18]

15 On the legally binding character of direct obligations see Chapter 2; on the partly compulsory character of indirect obligations see Chapter 6.II.

16 See above Chapter 1.III.1.

17 UNHRC 'Elements for the Draft Legally Binding Instrument on Transnational Corporations' (n 8) 6.

18 See for example Chapter 3.IV, Chapter 3.VI, Chapter 7.I.2, Chapter 7.I.3.

- businesses should abide by internationally recognised human rights, prevent human rights impacts of their activities and use their influence to help promote and ensure respect for human rights,[19]
  reflected in many investor obligations which build on international standards outside of investment law;[20]
- enterprises should be bound by human rights with a broad substantive scope, including the protection of labour rights, the environment and the combatting of corruption,[21]
  mirrored by the comprehensive and inclusive scope of investor obligations;[22]
- entrepreneurs should face legal liability for human rights abuses,[23]
  brought about by the investor obligations' legal consequences of a breach: compensation or loss of investor rights;[24]
- corporations should be responsible for human rights abuses beyond limitations by territorial jurisdiction,[25]
  features that investor obligations serve because they are international legal instruments as recurrently found.

2. Reactive enforcement

Nevertheless, it is suggested that by and large, investor obligations are not suitable as an international tool for command-and-control regulation. They operate too reactively. Their sanctions only become effective after the investor has invoked an investor right against the host state. As such, the state cannot actively apply investor obligations to respond to misconduct – a defining feature of command-and-control regulation. This holds true for both direct and indirect obligations.

---

19 UNHRC 'Elements for the Draft Legally Binding Instrument on Transnational Corporations' (n 8) 6.

20 See for example Chapter 3.I, Chapter 3.II, Chapter 7.I.3, Chapter 7.II.4.

21 UNHRC 'Elements for the Draft Legally Binding Instrument on Transnational Corporations' (n 8) 4–5.

22 See Chapter 9.II.1.

23 UNHRC 'Elements for the Draft Legally Binding Instrument on Transnational Corporations' (n 8) 8.

24 See Chapter 4.III and Chapter 6.V.

25 UNHRC 'Elements for the Draft Legally Binding Instrument on Transnational Corporations' (n 8) 5, 11.

In the case of direct obligations, states cannot *initiate* international enforcement. Counterclaims require a prior, primary arbitral claim by the investor against the host state. The host state can only sue the investor back. Therefore, IIAs do not provide states with the means to actively respond to misconduct.

Of course, states may enforce direct obligations domestically. One could argue that the element of 'command' remains international; direct obligations exist as a matter of substantive international law. They unconditionally call for a certain behaviour. It is only the enforcement – the element of 'control' – that takes place reactively through arbitral counterclaims. Domestic administrative agencies and courts do not face such a limitation. They can actively apply these substantive international obligations to investors. However, as the actual responding and punishing of non-compliance would take place on the domestic level, this would rather qualify as a domestic command-and-control approach. In particular, it cannot remedy regulatory problems encountered with transnationally operating investors – it remains confined to the state's territory and depends on the state to act. Thus, it is outside of this Chapter's scope concerned with truly *international* command-and-control regulation.

All the more, indirect obligations do not qualify to serve as command-and-control regulation. Already the fact that investors can choose whether to comply is alien to a command-and-control approach which rests on unconditional authority of the law. One could argue that such an authoritative character is present in the automatic sanction of depriving investors of rights – indirect obligations' partly compulsory nature.[26] However, also this sanction comes into effect only reactively. Investors will experience it only if they actually invoke an investor right. Again, indirect obligations do not qualify as means to actively coerce investors to behave in a certain way.

To illustrate these observations, one could revisit the above-mentioned example and imagine an IIA which contains an investor obligation to comply with a certain ILO Convention. As a direct obligation, the IIA does not provide the state with any international means to actively respond to an investor's violation of the Convention. The state must wait until the investor files an arbitral claim against it alleging violation of an investor right. Only then can the state react with a counterclaim and enforce the obligation. Similarly, if the obligation was indirect, investors could violate the ILO Convention without immediately experiencing a sanction. Only

26 On this aspect see Chapter 6.II.

later may they find that they cannot invoke an investor right against the state for that reason. That investor obligations fall short from fitting a command-and-control setting becomes clear if compared with international criminal law. Here, international criminal courts can actively try perpetrators for committing an international crime.

IV. IIAs as promising incentive-based regulation

Rather, it is suggested that investor obligations have promising potential as a form of international incentive-based regulation.

Investment protection has an economic value to investors due to its risk-reducing effect (1.). IIAs can hence operate as incentive or leverage for complying with investor obligations (2.). As a result, investor obligations may influence investors' behaviour (3.) even in situations in which states fail to do so through domestic means (4.). Even though it is currently hard to determine the concrete incentivising effect, the regulatory potential is remarkable (5.).

1. Investment protection's economic value

Substantive investor rights and the right to file an investment arbitration claim are of economic value to investors. They reduce the investment risk premium by providing the possibility of compensation against possible infringements by the host state. Especially in politically unstable environments, the risk can be substantial – up to a complete loss in case of a full expropriation. Thus, investor rights represent a form of international insurance against wrongdoing by the host state.[27] As seen, precisely with

---

27 Alan O Sykes, 'Public Versus Private Enforcement of International Economic Law: Standing and Remedy' (2005) 34(2) Journal of Legal Studies 631, 632–633; Joseph E Stiglitz, 'Regulating Multinational Corporations: Towards Principles of Cross-Border Legal Frameworks in a Globalized World Balancing Rights with Responsibilities' (2007–2008) 23(3) American University International Law Review 451, 465, 528–529; Posner and Sykes (n 10) 288–290; for a categorisation as 'liability rules' see Jonathan Bonnitcha, *Substantive Protection Under Investment Treaties: A Legal and Economic Analysis* (Cambridge University Press 2014) 58–62; see also the birds-eye perspective applying theory of law and economics by Alan O Sykes and Andrew Guzman, 'Economics of International Law' in Francesco

this motive in mind, states have devised investment law to attract foreign investment.[28]

What is more, investors rarely rely exclusively on their own assets. Most foreign investments receive loans, credits and insurances from the private[29] and public[30] sector. By reducing their investment risk through IIAs, investors may receive cheaper credits and insurances from other parties.[31] This may further increase the economic value of investment protection. This economic value is even additionally underlined by the existence of a market for third party-funding of investment claims.[32]

Parisi (ed), *The Oxford Handbook of Law and Economics*, vol III Public Law and Legal Institutions (Oxford University Press 2017) 461–462.

28 See Chapter 9.III.2.

29 On equity investments, loans and credits see Annie Dufey and Maryanne Grieg-Gran, 'The Linkages Between Project Finance and Sustainable Development' in Sheldon Leader (ed), *Global Project Finance, Human Rights and Sustainable Development* (Cambridge University Press 2011) 13, 16–18; on political risk insurance see Kaj Hobér and Joshua Fellenbaum, 'Political Risk Insurance and Financing of Foreign Direct Investment' in Marc Bungenberg and others (eds), *International Investment Law* (Nomos 2015) paras 64–69.

30 For example on the substantial quantitative and qualitative importance of public political risk insurance in comparison to the private counterpart see Clint Peinhardt and Todd Allee, 'Political Risk Insurance as Dispute Resolution' (2016) 7(1) Journal of International Dispute Settlement 205, 207; on political risk insurance by home states see Hobér and Fellenbaum (n 29) paras 39–63; on credits by the International Finance Corporation see Peter Woicke, 'Putting Human Rights Principles into Development Practice Through Finance: The Experience of the International Finance Corporation' in Philip Alston and Mary Robinson (eds), *Human Rights and Development: Towards Mutual Reinforcement* (Oxford University Press 2005) 335–351.

31 cf with the pivotal role that risk insurances play to promote foreign investment necessary for environmental protection in developing countries as observed by Swenja Surminski, 'The Role of Insurance Risk Transfer in Encouraging Climate Investment in Developing Countries' in Pierre-Marie Dupuy and Jorge E Viñuales (eds), *Harnessing Foreign Investment to Promote Environmental Protection: Incentives and Safeguards* (Cambridge University Press 2013) 238–251; on the general steering potential of investment insurance see Karsten Nowrot, 'Obligations of Investors' in Marc Bungenberg and others (eds), *International Investment Law* (Nomos 2015) para 28; on the high interest of investors in receiving money from the insurer see Peinhardt and Allee (n 30) 215.

32 Third parties fund claims in exchange for a portion of any compensation eventually awarded, see *EuroGas Inc. and Belmont Resources Inc. v Slovak Republic*, ICSID Case No. ARB/14/14, Procedural Order No. 3: Decision on the Parties' Request for Provisional Measures (23 June 2015) para 123 observing that third party-funding had become 'a common practice'.

In the same vein, the ICSID Tribunal in *Saipem v Bangladesh* affirmed that curtailing the right to file an investment claim can constitute expropriation. To accept the right as the object of expropriation means that it is worth to protect it similar to property, reflecting its economic value. In line with this assessment, the Tribunal referred in its reasoning to the ECtHR's jurisprudence on the right to property.[33]

2. Investment protection as obligations' leverage

Because of this economic value, investor rights represent leverage to incentivise compliance with investor obligations. Investor obligations condition the receiving of this economic value: If investors violate indirect obligations, they are deprived of protection and hence, of the IIA's value to them. The same is true for direct obligations: a potential counterclaim may offset or even exceed any worth that the investor rights otherwise offer.[34] The prospect of receiving investment protection can, thus, deter investors from breaching these obligations.

Considering the incentives more specifically, direct obligations may be considered to be 'sticks' – threatening a possible sanction in the background. Indirect obligations operate more as 'carrots' – as what the investor must do to receive the reward of investment protection. Generally,

---

33 *Saipem S.p.A. v The People's Republic of Bangladesh*, ICSID Case No. ARB/05/07, Decision on Jurisdiction and Recommendation on Provisional Measures (21 March 2007) para 130; *Saipem S.p.A. v The People's Republic of Bangladesh*, ICSID Case No. ARB/05/7, Award (30 June 2009) paras 128–130 with reference to the right to property as applied by *Case of Stran Greek Refineries and Stratis Andreadis v Greece* App no 13427/87, ECHR Series A no 301-B (European Court of Human Rights, 9 December 1994) paras 59–62; *Case of Brumărescu v Romania* App no 28342/95, ECHR 1999-VII 201 (European Court of Human Rights, 28 October 1999) paras 75–77 which related to a court's judgment.

34 James Harrison, 'Environmental Counterclaims in Investor-State Arbitration: Perenco Ecuador Ltd v Republic of Ecuador, ICSID Case No ARB/08/6, Interim Decision on the Environmental Counterclaim, 11 August 2015 (Peter Tomka, Neil Kaplan, J Christopher Thomas)' (2016) 17(3) Journal of World Investment & Trade 479, 487; too limited is the assessment by Jose D Amado, Jackson S Kern and Martin D Rodriguez, *Arbitrating the Conduct of International Investors* (Cambridge University Press 2018) 118 that counterclaims are limited in their usefulness because they only apply *ex post facto*.

scholars consider the use of 'carrots' and 'sticks' as equivalent incentives for behavioural change, given that they often overlap.[35]

3. Steering investors' behaviour

The steering potential of these incentives for public interest-friendly investor behaviour can be substantial. Investors never know if they will need investment protection in the future. For instance, unexpected changes of governmental policies can occur through, for example, a change of administration. Yet, many investor obligations require investors to comply throughout the entire span of the investment. Thus, there is a constant incentive to abide by them.

This observation rests on the economic assumption that investors take rational choices: that they 'engage in purposive, means-ends calculation in order to attain their goals – that is, they select actions so as to maximize their utility' based on 'relevant environmental constrains'.[36] Investors' main goal is to carry out the investment and gain profits. The environmental constrain they face is the alien legal system in which they operate and the insecurity concerning the host state's future behaviour. IIAs represent a means to reduce this risk and thus to further their goal. A strategical investor will compare the costs of fulfilling investor obligations with the gain to reduce the investment risk of unknown host state behaviour. Because the risk can be substantial, investors may select compliance with investor obligations to maximise the prospect of a successful investment.

One can illustrate this by the above-mentioned example of an IIA with the investor obligation to comply with the ILO Convention. Here, the

---

35 On distinguishing 'sticks' and 'carrots' and general remarks on their use in different situations see only Giuseppe Dari-Mattiacci and Gerrit de Geest, 'Carrots vs. Sticks' in Francesco Parisi (ed), *The Oxford Handbook of Law and Economics*, vol I Methodology and Concepts (Oxford University Press 2017) 440–464; but see Anne van Aaken and Betül Simsek, 'Rewarding in International Law' (2021) 115(2) American Journal of International Law 218–241 who especially draw on psychological literature and submit that rewards have certain advantages over penalties for governance mechanisms between states – a position which is not necessarily in conflict with the proposal submitted here which relates to an international compliance mechanism for private actors.

36 This basic idea of rational choice theory is for example presented in the context of international law by Alexander Thompson, 'Applying Rational Choice Theory to International Law: The Promise and Pitfalls' (2002) 31(1) Journal of Legal Studies 285, 287.

rational investor will weigh two different types of costs. On the one hand, the ILO Convention will prescribe a certain minimum standard which will increase labour costs. On the other hand, the IIA reduces the overall risk encountered in the host state's legal system – and may even compensate for a total loss of the investment. If investors perceive the investment environment as risky, they will opt for complying with the ILO standard. That is especially the case if available investment protection was decisive for them to invest in the host state in the first place.

This allows to carefully generalise the regulatory effect as follows: The less secure and stable the investor perceives the host state, the greater the role of IIAs and hence the incentivising effect.[37] Likewise, the more long-term an investment, the less calculable are the risks, and the more important becomes compliance. In the same vein, the stronger an international investment law instrument's design, the more one perceives it to reduce risks,[38] and hence the more leverage does it offer for investor obligations.

4. Compensating for the unwilling or unable host state

Importantly, investor obligations may steer investors in advance of any measure taken by the host state and without the need for a resulting investment arbitration. The described incentivising effect applies pre-emptively. Investors will conduct the mentioned means-ends calculation in advance in order to decide how they should arrange their investment. If they breach investor obligations first before adapting their conduct, it might be too late. They may already be deprived of protection or face a potential counterclaim. Thus, the incentives are unaffected by the fact that states can

---

37 This finds ground for example in the study by Cédric Dupont, Thomas Schultz and Merih Angin, 'Political Risk and Investment Arbitration: An Empirical Study' (2016) 7(1) Journal of International Dispute Settlement 136, 151 who observe that investment arbitration especially relates to the political risk of corruption and a lack of the rule of law in the host state.

38 See for example Jay Dixon and Paul A Haslam, 'Does the Quality of Investment Protection Affect FDI Flows to Developing Countries? Evidence from Latin America' (2016) 39(8) The World Economy 1080, 1100 who find that high protection treaties with broadly formulated international investor rights have a positive effect on foreign direct investment flows.

enforce investor obligations only reactively.[39] This is also beneficial for the host states because they can spare enforcement costs.[40]

To continue the above-mentioned example: To qualify for the IIA's protection, rational investors will pre-emptively comply with the ILO Convention. Only then will they actually reduce their investment risk. This incentive applies irrespectively of the state's domestic actions, precisely because IIAs serve to protect against unforeseeable future state conduct. Even if the state does not demand the investor to comply with the ILO standard, the incentive applies. If investors breach the Convention, they lose the possibility to invoke the IIA later. To reuse the comparison of IIAs as an insurance policy: Investors lose 'insurance coverage' by the IIA. Therefore, even if the host state is inactive, the IIA may still steer the investor to abide by the ILO Convention.

In consequence, with all due care, investor obligations may even compensate for host states unwilling or unable to protect the public interest. They exert the described incentives without requiring the host state to be active. It is sufficient that the state *could* file a counterclaim at later date, or that the investor may be deprived of investment protection automatically. Moreover, unwilling or unable states often constitute a relatively insecure and instable investment environment. Especially there, investors may fear that the state might turn against them at some point and threaten their investment. Therefore, the economic value of investment protection may be particularly high – and similarly so may be the incentive to comply with investor obligations, potentially filling the regulatory gap left by the home state to some extent.[41]

5. Limits and potentials

To be sure, the analysis can only outline a *potential* steering effect of investor obligations for the following reasons.

Currently, there is a lack of awareness. Because investor obligations have not yet been studied comprehensively, investors do not know that they

39 See Chapter 10.III.2.

40 On the relevance of such 'self-enforcement' in the ambit of international law's enforcement from a law and economics perspective, see Posner and Sykes (n 10) 27 who consider that such self-enforcement, while not achieving the '"first-best", [...] can often accomplish a great deal'.

41 cf Dupont, Schultz and Angin (n 37) 151.

may be subject to obligations in investment law. Hence, they cannot make an informed decision whether to comply.[42] A better understanding of investor obligations which this book aims to achieve is a requirement for their regulatory potential to unfold.

Furthermore, the incentive to comply with investor obligations relies on the economic value of investment protection. Yet, how much IIAs affect the decision to invest abroad remains controversial.[43] Earlier empirical studies indicated a low impact of IIAs on attracting foreign investment.[44] In contrast, more recent analyses do find significant correlations while pointing out differences between countries and investment sectors.[45] The value of investment protection may also depend on the specific investor. For example, an investment may have other strong insurances and forms of security, or plenty of assets. In such cases, fulfilling investor obligations may be more costly than forfeiting investment protection. What is more, it is problematic that many encountered investor obligations remain relatively indeterminate in their scope. Then, investors may not know how they should behave, which would curtail the described steering effect. And there is the concern if investment arbitration represents an adequate

---

42 cf that rational choice theory depends on the fact that the actor in question has relevant and accurate information available to make an informed decision, see for example the observations in the context of international law by Robert O Keohane, 'Rational Choice Theory and International Law: Insights and Limitations' (2002) 31(1) Journal of Legal Studies 307, 308–309.

43 See for example the critical study by Jason W Yackee, 'Do BITs "Work"? Empirical Evidence from France' (2016) 7(1) Journal of International Dispute Settlement 55, 58; Bonnitcha (n 27) 102–113; contrast it with the more positive overall assessment by Dixon and Haslam (n 38) 1082–1100; see also Sykes and Guzman (n 27) 461 who, in light of the variety of empirical studies, consider the matter unsettled.

44 See for example Hallward-Driemeier, 'Do Bilateral Investment Treaties Attract Foreign Direct Investment? Only a Bit … And They Could Bite' [2003] World Bank Policy Research Working Paper 3121, 18–23 ‹https://openknowledge.worldbank.org/handle/10986/18118› accessed 7 December 2021.

45 See for example Arjan Lejour and Maria Salfi, 'The Regional Impact of Bilateral Investment Treaties on Foreign Direct Investment' [2014] CPB Netherlands Bureau for Economic Policy Analysis Discussion Paper 298, 18–23; a good overview on the empirical studies and the methodological problems provide Eugene Beaulieu and Kelly O'Neill, 'The Economics of Foreign Direct Investment and International Investment Agreements' in John Anthony VanDuzer and Patrick Leblond (eds), *Promoting and Managing International Investment: Towards an Integrated Policy Approach* (Routledge 2020) 110–115.

forum for assessing investor obligations at all, for example in light of the often-limited expertise of arbitrators in these matters.[46]

It is also submitted that investor obligations cannot replace domestic regulation and strong host state institutions.[47] Incentive-based regulation can complement it and, to some degree, compensate its deficiencies as seen. But a single IIA of course cannot substitute the comprehensive regulatory environment for which the state with its institutions provides. In particular, there remains a need to actively respond to misconduct of investors.[48]

Nevertheless, the claim being made here is more fundamental: investor obligations may turn IIAs into an international tool for steering foreign investors' behaviour.[49] This is remarkable because originally investment law was not meant to regulate foreign investment at all. This Chapter's findings indicate that it may play a part in better regulating transnationally operating corporations in the future. Investor obligations may be clarified and become more transparent as investment law continues to change. And they may even alleviate situations in which the host state is unwilling or unable to do so domestically – a problem to which international solutions are greatly desired.

46 Markus Krajewski, 'A Nightmare or a Noble Dream? Establishing Investor Obligations Through Treaty-Making and Treaty-Application' (2020) 5(1) Business and Human Rights Journal 105, 127–129.

47 This is supported by empirical studies on the effect of IIAs, see for example Beaulieu and O'Neill (n 45) 114–115.

48 Similarly UNCTAD, *World Investment Report: Reforming International Investment Governance* (United Nations Publications 2015) 126.

49 cf Stephan Schill and Vladislav Djanic, 'International Investment Law and Community Interests' in Eyāl Benveniśtî and Georg Nolte (eds), *Community Interests Across International Law* (Oxford University Press 2018) 244 who argue that counterclaims against investors 'could provide an important additional mechanism to ensure that obligations that are of interest to the wider international community are complied with by foreign investors.'

Chapter 11.

The Theoretical Perspective: Individuals in International Law

Because foreign investors are natural or private legal persons, the encountered investor obligations prompt the question of how they relate to the role of the individual in international law more generally. Chapter 11 will outline how one could appreciate investor obligations from this, more theoretical, perspective. It will concentrate on a few general lines without claiming to be exhaustive in its interpretation.

Firstly, it will show that investor obligations bring about individual international responsibility – which international law does not provide for in other branches except for international criminal law (I.). One can understand this development as constituting a phenomenon of Global Administrative Law (II.). At the same time, one may also understand investor obligations as an example of how international law centres increasingly more on the individual instead than on the state as the decisive subject. This has been a long-standing development, especially fuelled by human rights and international criminal law. Investor obligations contribute to this trend – although in a more pragmatic, less value-based manner than for example human rights do (III.).

I. Construing international responsibility of foreign investors

As seen, direct and indirect obligations place legal consequences on investors who breach them. It is possible to understand this effect as a new form of individual international responsibility of foreign investors.

As a first step, this Section will briefly explain the concept of international responsibility as developed for states and in international criminal law (1.). Then, it will outline how one can conceptualise investor obligations to conform with the concept of responsibility (2.). Finally, it will highlight that investors' responsibility does not exclude that states are also responsible for the same public interest violation. Instead, implementing shared responsibility is possible (3.).

1. The concept of international responsibility

The concept of international responsibility is best established with regard to states. The ILC Articles on State Responsibility have codified the established customary law.[1] Therein, the ILC distinguishes between primary and secondary rules.[2] Primary rules are the substantive standards that states have to comply with. They follow from international treaties, customary law and general principles of law. Secondary rules regulate circumstances under which a primary rule is breached, for example rules on attribution of conduct[3] and circumstances precluding wrongfulness.[4] They also determine the consequences for such a breach, namely, cessation of the wrongful act, non-repetition and reparation.[5] Hence, 'international responsibility' means that a state faces the described consequences for an attributable breach of a primary rule.[6]

For example: A state may violate the prohibition of the use of force in Art 2 (4) UN-Charter. The prohibition itself is the primary rule. The ILC Articles contain the secondary rules which define if certain conduct is attributable to the state and hence qualify as relevant to determine the violation of Art 2 (4) UN-Charter. If a breach can be established, said

1 UNGA 'Responsibility of States for Internationally Wrongful Acts' UN Doc A/RES/56/83 (12 December 2001). The Articles do not address rules of international responsibility applicable to private actors. Yet, they indicate that such rules may exist as a separate normative category in Art 58 which states that the Articles 'are without prejudice to any question of the individual responsibility under international law of any person acting on behalf of a State', see Anne Peters, *Beyond Human Rights: The Legal Status of the Individual in International Law* (Cambridge University Press 2016) 152–153. On the international responsibility of international organisations that is not investigated here any further and which follows the same general lines as the responsibility of states see ILC 'Draft Articles on the Responsibility of International Organizations' (2011) ‹http://legal.un.org/ilc/texts/instruments/english/draft_articles/9_11_2011.pdf› accessed 7 December 2021.

2 On this terminology see ILC 'Report of the International Law Commission on the Work of Its Twenty-Second Session, 4 May-10 July 1970' UN Doc A/8010/Rev.1, 306; James Crawford, *State Responsibility: The General Part* (Cambridge University Press 2013) 64–66; Jean d'Aspremont and others, 'Sharing Responsibility Between Non-State Actors and States in International Law: Introduction' (2015) 62(1) Netherlands International Law Review 49, 51.

3 Art 4–11 UNGA 'Articles on State Responsibility' (n 1).

4 Art 20–27 ibid.

5 Art 28–39 ibid.

6 Art 1–3 ibid.

secondary rules require to cease the attack against the other state, prohibit its repetition and order reparation.

While the concept of international responsibility can also apply to individuals, it is much less established and fleshed out as a rule of international law in this regard.[7] The main reason for this is that directly applicable obligations exist only exceptionally.[8] By and large, there are thus no primary rules on which secondary rules for individuals could build on. International criminal law shows that where such primary rules exist, secondary rules are necessary to apply the primary rules properly. For example, the Rome Statute defines secondary rules on attribution such as on aiding and abetting,[9] and on consequences for breaches of international crimes: individual penalties, enforceable by domestic or international criminal courts.[10] Another, rather specific example from the international law of the sea are contracts that private corporations and the International Seabed Authority conclude for activities in the Area.[11] They are governed by international law[12] – thus create primary rules of that character directly applicable to contractors – and contain secondary rules, for example on consequences in case contractors breach the contract.[13]

---

7 Steven R Ratner, 'Corporations and Human Rights: A Theory of Legal Responsibility' (2001) 111(3) Yale Law Journal 443, 491–492 notes that '[i]nternational law approaches to individual responsibility have not benefited from the sort of systematic, academic examination provided by the International Law Commission with respect to state responsibility' despite that it does exist in international criminal law; Christian Tomuschat, 'The Responsibility of Other Entities: Private Individuals' in James Crawford, Alain Pellet and Simon Olleson (eds), *The Law of International Responsibility* (Oxford University Press 2010) 317 observes that 'international civil responsibility of private individuals […] is not a well-defined and generally accepted concept'; d'Aspremont and others (n 2) 53–54 consider international responsibility of non-state actors to be 'a thorny issue' for which, in a mainstream perspective, a 'tailored framework' does not exist.

8 See Chapter 2.IV.

9 Art 25 Rome Statute of the International Criminal Court (adopted 17 July 1998, entered into force 1 July 2002) 2187 UNTS 3 (Rome Statute).

10 Art 77–80 ibid.

11 Art 153 (3) United Nations Convention on the Law of the Sea (adopted 10 December 1982, entered into force 16 November 1994) 1833 UNTS 396 (UNCLOS).

12 Annex III, Art 21 (1) ibid.

13 See Annex III, Art 22 ibid on the 'responsibility or liability' of the contractor. For a discussion how these law of the sea rules indicate an individual international responsibility, see Markos Karavias, 'Corporations and Responsibility Under International Law' in Photini Pazartzis and Panos Merkouris (eds), *Permutations of Responsibility in International Law* (Brill Nijhoff 2019) 59–63.

To prepare for the analysis of investors' responsibility, it is useful to make the structural similarities of state and individual criminal responsibility visible, focusing on their most relevant aspects for the present purpose:

- Primary rules:
  - For states: Their international obligations as enshrined in treaties, customary law and general principles;
  - For individuals: International crimes as recognised in international treaties and customary law.
- Secondary rules, attribution:
  - For states: Mainly conduct by their organs, but also for example individual conduct effectively controlled by states (Art 4–11 ILC Articles on State Responsibility);
  - For individuals: Principles such as committing, ordering or aiding and abetting a crime (i.e. Art 25 Rome Statute).
- Secondary rules, consequences of breaches:
  - For states: Cessation of the breach, non-repetition, reparation, the latter consisting of restitution, compensation and satisfaction (Art 28–39 ILC Articles on State Responsibility);
  - For individuals: Individual penalties, including imprisonment and fines (Art 77–80 Rome Statute).

2. Individual investor responsibility

Investor obligations give rise to a concept of individual international responsibility along similar lines as described in the previous Section.

The obligations constitute the primary rules. They define the substantive standards of conduct towards the public interest that investors must follow. Functionally, they are similar to the international obligations of states and the prohibited crimes under international criminal law.

In a next step, core findings of this study can be understood as constituting secondary norms on the consequences of breaching investor obligations. One can interpret the different sanctions that direct and indirect investor obligations bring about as different forms of secondary rules. This means that one can model them within the frame of responsibility as follows:

- Primary rules: investor obligations;
- Secondary rules on consequences:

- In case of direct obligations: Cessation of the breach, non-repetition and compensation,
- In case of indirect obligations: Complete or partial deprivation of investor rights.

In this view, direct obligations accrue a responsibility similar to the one encountered by states – but with a strong emphasis on compensation as the primary relief sought in arbitral practice. Investors' individual responsibility is a corollary of establishing symmetrical IIAs. Just as states can be responsible for breaching investment law, so can investors.

If indirect obligations can be conceived as leading to international responsibility is less obvious. It is correct that indirect obligations only incidentally address the wrongful conduct of investors and do not embody the similar value judgment of 'right and wrong' as direct obligations do.[14] Yet, indirect obligations are no different in bringing about a legal consequence for a breach, but this legal consequence functions differently. Due to indirect obligations' partially compulsory nature,[15] states cannot demand the cessation of the breach, non-repetition and compensation. *These* secondary rules do not apply. Nevertheless, the study has shown that investors face legal consequences with regard to their rights by forfeiting investment protection. This sanction can be understood as a *different* applicable secondary rule as presented above.

It also appears adequate to frame both types of legal consequences in these terms of international responsibility: This reflects that direct and indirect obligations fulfil similar functions in rebalancing investment law and steering investors' behaviour – as demonstrated in Chapter 9 and Chapter 10. Because indirect obligations deprive investors of protection *automatically*, they may hold investors responsible even more effectively than direct obligations. What is more, tribunals have also understood indirect obligations as giving rise to investors' responsibility.[16] As seen, a certain standard can also operate as a direct and indirect obligation simultaneously,[17] which means that both types of secondary rules apply.

Because of these dual types of consequences, investor obligations follow different rules of responsibility than those which apply to states and to in-

---

14 This is why Jean Ho, 'The Creation of Elusive Investor Responsibility' (2019) 113 AJIL Unbound 10, 12–13 regards examples of what this book defines as indirect obligations as contributing to an 'elusive investor responsibility'.

15 See Chapter 6.II.

16 See for example Chapter 7 n 143, 209 and 219.

17 See Chapter 6.VI.

dividuals under international criminal law. Rather, investment law appears to bring about its very own regime of responsibility.[18] One could describe it as a new and specific form of international civil responsibility or liability of private actors.[19]

It makes sense that investor obligations build a stand-alone regime of responsibility. Secondary rules embody value judgments. Thus, one cannot simply transfer the rules of state or individual criminal responsibility to investor obligations. This can be illustrated through the example of rules on attribution of conduct to states. These rules draw the line between the private and the public sphere. By that, they recognise the autonomy of persons as acting on their own and as not being associated or identical with public authority.[20] This telos does not apply if one wishes to determine if a certain conduct should be attributed to the foreign investor or another private actor.[21] Similarly, an analogy to international criminal law does

---

18 For a different view that more categorically distinguishes what is coined as direct and indirect international investor obligations here, see Karsten Nowrot, 'Obligations of Investors' in Marc Bungenberg and others (eds), *International Investment Law* (Nomos 2015) para 31.

19 It is an individual international responsibility in a particular context – the international regulation of foreign investment – which fits well with the conceptualisation by Karavias (n 13) 65 that 'corporations as addressees [and] bearers of international responsibility' should be considered mindful of their functions in particular contexts; cf on civil international responsibility concepts Tomuschat, 'Responsibility' (n 7) 318–325 who translates the concepts of primary and secondary rules established in the law of state responsibility and examines if and how they apply to possible obligations of individuals in the law of international organisations, international criminal law and international treaties on nuclear energy and on environmental protection; Andrew Clapham, 'The Role of the Individual in International Law' (2010) 21(1) European Journal of International Law 25, 30 who proposes to recognise that individuals have 'civil law international obligations' with corresponding international responsibility; Peters (n 1) 152–164 who reflects on the 'international non-criminal responsibility of the individual', in particular analysing international nuclear and environmental liability treaties; d'Aspremont and others (n 2) 54 who consider the responsibility of non-state actors as an alternative model to the mainstream framework focused on state responsibility. See also the elaborate model of secondary rules for corporations suggested by Ratner (n 7) 497–511, 518–524.

20 ILC 'Articles on Responsibility of States for Internationally Wrongful Acts, with Commentaries' (2001) II(2) Yearbook of the International Law Commission, 31 (53rd session of the International Law Commission, 23 April-1 June and 2 July 2001), Chapter II para 2.

21 cf the critical remarks on analogies to rules of state responsibility by d'Aspremont and others (n 2) 58–59; more open to analogies in this regard Ratner (n 7) 495.

not appear to fit here either. The quite differentiated rules of attribution that are, for example, enshrined in the Rome Statute revolve around the question of personal guilt. They appear inadequate for investor obligations which are concerned with the role of economic actors in the host state's society.

This reflection on the concept of 'responsibility' allows for further insights. By and large, rules on attribution are a missing piece in the encountered practice that Parts I and II have studied. IIAs and tribunals rarely address the question of which conduct is attributable to investors to determine if they violated an investor obligation. Only some tribunals elaborated on aspects that could imply attribution. For example, some tribunals required investors to breach domestic law in bad faith or negligently[22] – which one could understand as a criterion of fault. Such rules on attribution need to be concretised further.

3. Shared responsibility between states and investors

Modelling a new form of investor responsibility also helps to understand how investor misconduct relates to the obligations of states.

In particular, it alleviates the concern that investor obligations could release states from their own obligations towards the public interest. Outside of investment law, scholars have been reluctant to accept international obligations directly applicable to private actors for this reason: Arguably, to the extent the private actor is bound, they would free the state from corresponding obligations or at least provide a basis for an abusive excuse and neglect of obligations.[23] Following this scholarly opinion, for example, a state which is party to a human rights treaty which contains environ-

---

22 See for example Chapter 7.I.2.c); see also Martin Jarrett, Sergio Puig and Steven R Ratner, 'Towards Greater Investor Accountability: Indirect Actions, Direct Actions by States and Direct Actions by Individuals' (2021) Journal of International Dispute Settlement 1, 20 who discuss if investors (*in personam* claims) or the investment (*in rem* claims) should be the respondent of counterclaims, effectively reflecting on the adequate rules of attribution.

23 For example, scholars rejected individual duties in human rights law because states could invoke them to justify their own violations of human rights, see for example Christian Tomuschat, 'Grundpflichten des Individuums nach Völkerrecht' (1983) 21(3) Archiv des Völkerrechts 289, 311–312; Kofi Quashigah, 'Scope of Individual Duties in the African Charter' in Manisuli Ssenyonjo (ed), *The African Regional Human Rights System: 30 Years After the African Charter on Human and Peoples' Rights* (Martinus Nijhoff Publishers 2012) 121–123.

mental obligations for private actors could blame these private actors for environmental pollution, and decide to abstain from acting itself.

However, investor obligations bring about investors' responsibility without foreclosing the host state's responsibility at the same time. States remain bound by their obligations to protect the public interest. Herein, investor obligations affirm the UN Guiding Principles on Business and Human Rights' main observation that states are the principal guardians of the public interest.[24]

The principle of shared responsibility allows for such harmonisation of investor and state obligations. It expresses that two subjects are separately responsible for the same harmful outcome. It follows the underlying idea that there is no reason why the duty of one subject to protect a certain right should excuse another subject for breaches of obligations in the same matter.[25] It has been applied in other areas of international law for sharing responsibilities of states and private actors.[26]

For example, an IIA could contain an investor obligation to respect the human rights of others under the ECHR. In this hypothetical scenario, investors would harm the local population's health by causing pollution. Subject to the IIA, investors would be internationally responsible for violating the right to physical integrity under Art 8 ECHR. At the same time, the host state has an own obligation under Art 8 ECHR to protect the local population. It failed to do so and thus is internationally responsible for this breach. Irrespective of the investor's misconduct, inhabitants could file a claim against the state before the ECtHR. Hence, investors and the state

---

24 UN Human Rights Council 'Guiding Principles on Business and Human Rights Implementing the United Nations "Protect, Respect and Remedy" Framework' UN Doc HRC/RES/17/4 (2011), 3–4.

25 Ratner (n 7) 493 with reference to Joseph Raz, *The Morality of Freedom* (Clarendon Press 1988) 182–186.

26 For example, the rules on activities in the Area under chapter XI of UNCLOS. In an advisory opinion of 2011, the International Tribunal for the Law of the Sea elaborated in detail on the responsibilities of states and private commercial operators in exploring and exploiting the deep seabed and their relation to another under this chapter, see *Responsibilities and Obligations of States Sponsoring Persons and Entities with Respect to Activities in the Area* (Advisory Opinion, 1 February 2011) ITLOS Rep 2011, paras 199–205 in which the Tribunal found 'parallel liability' of the private contractor's violation of rules applying to deep-seabed mining and the sponsoring state for its own violations that to a substantial extent consist in due diligence obligations towards the contractor's actions; see also d'Aspremont and others (n 2) 56–64 who consider the concept of shared responsibility as found in the law of the sea and identify recurring legal questions.

are subject to a shared international responsibility. In addition, the state could become responsible for breaching an investor right if it then reacts disproportionately against the polluting investors.

This example shows that the concept of investors' (potentially shared) international responsibility leads to adequate results.[27] Shared responsibility reflects that investors and host states face autonomous international obligations – with separate and specific legal consequences.

II. Responsibility as an aspect of Global Administrative Law

That investors face international responsibility through IIAs can be understood as an expression of Global Administrative Law. This Section will start by shortly explaining the main idea of this school of thought (1.). Then, it will show that investor obligations with their very different sources from domestic and international law can be understood to form part of a 'global administrative space' (2) and that they follow functions and principles of administrative law (3.).

1. The idea of Global Administrative Law

Global Administrative Law[28] is a theory which postulates that administration is no longer something exclusive to the state and its domestic legal

---

27 In the same vein see for example Arne Vandenbogaerde, *Towards Shared Accountability in International Human Rights Law* (Intersentia 2016) 273–274; for a contrary position see Maria Monnheimer, *Due Diligence Obligations in International Human Rights Law* (Cambridge University Press 2021) 37–38 on the danger that states could 'try shifting their responsibility to corporations and vice versa' and thus calls for clearly defining who bears 'primary responsibility' (37). However, shared responsibility as understood here does not allow for mutual exculpations. Rather, each subject retains its own international responsibility – for example, in case of states for not observing due diligence towards private actors – measured against the international standard of, for example, human rights.

28 The term is used here as defined by scholars of the New York University, see Benedict Kingsbury and others, 'Foreword: Global Governance as Administration – National and Transnational Approaches to Global and Administrative Law' (2005) 68(3 & 4) Law and Contemporary Problems 1. It has roots in earlier writings on international administrative law, for example by Lorenz von Stein, 'Einige Bemerkungen über das internationale Verwaltungsrecht' (1882) 6(2) Jahrbuch für Gesetzgebung, Verwaltung und Volkswirtschaft im Deutschen

system. Rather, it describes the existence of global governance. It is comprised by procedures and institutions which include actors other than the state and make rules that have a regulatory effect on potentially everyone's behaviour.[29] These rules would penetrate the traditional divide between national and international law – instead forming an overarching 'global administrative space'.[30]

An often-mentioned example of Global Administrative Law is rule-making by international institutions such as the International Organisation for Standardisation (ISO). As a private international organisation, it creates technical standards for products, services and systems. They are highly relevant even for sensitive areas such as food safety which used to be the regulatory prerogative of states. These standards have a strong impact on every-day products and are, for example, taken up by national legislation – even though states did not create them. The interaction of ISO standards and national legislation constitutes a global administrative space.[31]

Global Administrative Law studies these institutions and processes. One of its core findings is that these increasingly follow principles of (classic state) administrative law. In turn, global rule-making and its outcome are also tested against principles encountered in domestic public law,

---

Reich 395; Paul S Reinsch, 'International Administrative Law and National Sovereignty' (1909) 3(1) American Journal of International Law 1; Philip C Jessup, *Transnational Law* (Yale University Press 1956); for an analysis of the various streams of Global Administrative Law scholarship see Lorenzo Casini, 'Global Administrative Law Scholarship' in Sabino Cassese (ed), *Research Handbook on Global Administrative Law* (Edward Elgar Publishing 2016).

29 On private rule-making see for example Jürgen Friedrich, 'Legal Challenges of Non-Binding Instruments: The Case of the FAO Code of Conduct for Responsible Fisheries' in Armin v Bogdandy and others (eds), *The Exercise of Public Authority by International Institutions: Advancing International Institutional Law* (Springer 2010) in the context of the FAO; Fabrizio Cafaggi, 'Transnational Private Regulation: Regulating Global Private Regulators' in Sabino Cassese (ed), *Research Handbook on Global Administrative Law* (Edward Elgar Publishing 2016).

30 Kingsbury and others (n 28) 3; Benedict Kingsbury, 'The Concept of "Law" in Global Administrative Law' (2009) 20(1) European Journal of International Law 23, 24; see also more generally the overview by Sabino Cassese and Elisa D'Alterio, 'Introduction: The Development of Global Administrative Law' in Sabino Cassese (ed), *Research Handbook on Global Administrative Law* (Edward Elgar Publishing 2016) 3–9.

31 On ISO as an example of Global Administrative Law see Benedict Kingsbury, Nico Krisch and Richard B Stewart, 'The Emergence of Global Administrative Law' (2005) 68(3) Law and Contemporary Problems 15, 22–24.

for example, the principles of legality, proportionality and transparency.[32] These may serve as 'legal tools capable of taming and framing global governance.'[33] In the above-mentioned example, one could study if the ISO observes principles such as proportionality, and hold the ISO accountable if it, for example, acts disproportionately.

Even without appreciating investor obligations, investment law represents one example which has been identified as a form of Global Administrative Law.[34] In this view, investment law restrains states in their sovereignty. On the substantive level, investor rights discipline states through balancing investors' interests with the public interest.[35] Considering enforcement, tribunals allow for individual remedies by the investor against the state similar to domestic administrative courts.[36]

---

32 Kingsbury and others (n 28) 3; Kingsbury (n 30) 31–33; Cassese and D'Alterio (n 30) 3–9; Richard B Stewart, 'The Normative Dimensions and Performance of Global Administrative Law' (2015) 13(2) International Journal of Constitutional Law 499, 500–506; for a critical reflection on general principles and values that Global Administrative Law may entail see Carol Harlow, 'Global Administrative Law: The Quest for Principles and Values' (2006) 17(1) European Journal of International Law 187, 195–214.

33 Lorenzo Casini, 'Beyond Drip-Painting? Ten Years of GAL and the Emergence of a Global Administration' (2015) 13(2) International Journal of Constitutional Law 473, 473.

34 Gus van Harten and Martin Loughlin, 'Investment Treaty Arbitration as a Species of Global Administrative Law' (2006) 17(1) European Journal of International Law 121, 148–149; Gus van Harten, *Investment Treaty Arbitration and Public Law* (Oxford University Press 2007) 45, 71 who consider investment law to be a part of the states' administrative law systems and to follow public law principles. See also Daniel Kalderimis, 'Investment Treaty Arbitration as Global Administrative Law: What This Might Mean in Practice' in Chester Brown (ed), *Evolution in Investment Treaty Law and Arbitration* (Cambridge University Press 2011) 155 who observes that investment treaty law follows a public law paradigm, calling for more transparency; Stephan W Schill, 'Enhancing International Investment Law's Legitimacy: Conceptual and Methodological Foundations of a New Public Law Approach' (2011) 52(1) Virginia Journal of International Law 57, 71–85 who elaborates on the hybrid nature of investment law which combines traditions of commercial arbitration with principles and functions of public law; Andreas Kulick, *Global Public Interest in International Investment Law* (Cambridge University Press 2012) 81–85 on the administrative review that investment tribunals provide.

35 van Harten and Loughlin (n 34) 146–147.

36 ibid, 127–139.

2. Investor obligations as part of global administrative space

Investor obligations qualify as phenomena of Global Administrative Law too. The fact that private actors become direct addressees of global regulation constitutes a key feature of Global Administrative Law.[37] In this regard, *Kingsbury*, *Krisch* and *Stewart* have observed: '[T]he real addressees of […] global regulatory regimes are now increasingly the same as in domestic law: namely, individuals […] and collective entities like corporations […].'[38] Investor obligations do precisely that. They set standards of conduct that directly address foreign investors instead of focussing on the relations between states.

The notion of a 'global administrative space' describes rather well the many different sources on which investor obligations have drawn to define their content. To recall, they do not only create novel standards but also build on states' international obligations, soft law and domestic law. Two constellations are particularly indicative of Global Administrative Law: Investor obligations overcome the distinction between domestic and international law while IIAs internationalise domestic standards.[39] In doing so they further expand investment law's 'hybrid foundations'.[40] What is more, some obligations provide standards with legal effects that have not been created by states. Recurrently, the analysis has encountered obligations which build on CSR and other soft law[41] – hence, on norms also created by corporations and other private institutions.

Furthermore, as Chapter 10 has shown, investor obligations can exert an international regulatory effect independent of domestic activities by the host state. It is such processes beyond traditional regulation by the sovereign state that Global Administrative Law describes. Functionally, to regulate the behaviour of foreign investors by balancing their economic freedoms with the public interest is the ambit of administrative law.

Notwithstanding, the values and rights that investor obligations aim to protect remain hard to define with precision. Due to a lack of awareness that investor obligations have already been established to a considerable degree, it is still open for discussion how investors' economic freedoms

---

37 Kingsbury, Krisch and Stewart (n 31) 23–25.

38 ibid, 23–24.

39 See for example Chapter 3.V, Chapter 3.VI, Chapter 7.I.2 and Chapter 7.II.5.

40 Zachary Douglas, 'The Hybrid Foundations of Investment Treaty Arbitration' (2004) 74(1) British Yearbook of International Law 151.

41 See for example Chapter 3.III and Chapter 7.II.3.

should be balanced with any duties towards the public interest. This is a question for the states to decide by concretising investor obligation clauses in IIAs and interpreting the identified existing mechanisms of investor obligations.

And investor obligations remain disparate and contested in their doctrinal mechanisms so far. There is not one regulatory agency, one administrative court or even a collective and coordinated effort of states to create and flesh out investor obligations. Rather, many different actors engage in creating and applying investor obligations, sometimes even only implicitly: Primarily states in drafting and concluding new IIAs, arbitral tribunals (without a coordinating appellate instance or a doctrine of precedent) and in addition scholars and institutions like UNCTAD who reflect on investment law reform. Such decentral law-making decoupled from classic state legislation and treaty-making is, however, precisely characteristic for rule-making in the global administrative space. It is thus fair to say that investor obligations are Global Administrative Law in the – chaotic and decentral – making.

However, in contrast to Global Administrative Law approaches, this book has methodologically focussed on the traditional sources of international and domestic law. It laid out that investor obligations *do* conform with international law's canonical sources as reflected in Art 38 (1) ICJ-Statute. They constitute binding rules of public international law. Thus, international investor obligations as depicted here are *not* private rules. In addition, investors do not create the obligations, instead states do so by concluding respective IIAs.[42]

In addition, investor obligations are not *global*. The reason is that they arise only between the parties of IIAs and foreign investors of the corresponding nationalities. Hence, they do not comprehensively cover all foreign investment in a host state. Their reach is more limited than, for example, the mentioned ISO standards.

42 cf Schmidt-Aßmann, 'The Internationalization of Administrative Relations as a Challenge for Administrative Law Scholarship' (2008) 9(11) German Law Journal 2061, 2067–2068 who highlights that states still remain the most important regulators in matters of administration. On the interest in private actors and international organisations as regulators, see for example Kingsbury, Krisch and Stewart (n 31) 18–19.

3. Following administrative law functions and principles

Investor obligations also reinforce administrative or public law as the field's dominant paradigm in line with Global Administrative Law.

As to which 'paradigms' investment law follows has been intensively discussed. To think in paradigms means to understand which values structurally affect investment law, and which principles it should follow. The field originally developed out of ideas of commercial arbitration which favoured a private law paradigm – the delineating of private risks and interests. Especially the right to regulate-debate has shown that investment law has increasingly adopted a paradigm of (international) public law: Investor rights entail the balancing of private interests of investors with the public interest.[43]

In line with Global Administrative Law, investor obligations strongly support a public law paradigm. Chapter 9.II.3 has shed light on a new, 'public' role of investors from which is expected to contribute actively to the public interest. Chapter 9.III has shown that investor obligations turn the field into a 'sustainable investment law'. These developments follow structures of domestic administrative law. They embody the setting of public obligations and defining how the host state should develop – towards an economy in harmony with society and the environment.

In an institutional perspective, investment tribunals take over functions additional to the challenging of host state regulation.[44] As they apply investor obligations, they become more general fora which comprehensively address disputes arising out of a foreign investment.[45] Then, investment tribunals can be seen as institutions beyond the state, exerting judicial powers over general matters of public administration.[46]

---

43 See Anthea Roberts, 'Clash of Paradigms: Actors and Analogies Shaping the Investment Treaty System' (2013) 107(1) American Journal of International Law 45, 45–75; for a support of the public law paradigm see only Harten (n 34).

44 Roberts (n 43) 45–46.

45 cf the juxtaposition by Mark W Friedman and Ina C Popova, 'Can State Counterclaims Salvage Investment Arbitration?' (2014) 8(2) World Arbitration & Mediation Review 139, 169.

46 That the perspective of Global Administrative Law is overly limited to administration instead of appreciating the legislative and judiciary functions as well, is rightly observed by Armin v Bogdandy, Philipp Dann and Matthias Goldmann, 'Developing the Publicness of Public International Law: Towards a Legal Framework for Global Governance Activities' in Armin v Bogdandy and others (eds), *The Exercise of Public Authority by International Institutions: Advancing International Institutional Law* (Springer 2010) 16; Kulick (n 34) 84.

The study has also shown that investor obligations apply principles of domestic public law.[47] In particular, all obligations entailed a weighing and balancing between public and private interests which resemble the proportionality principle.[48] Another good example is the requirement to comply with domestic and international law which follows an underlying understanding that investments should be legal – implying the principle of legality that Global Administrative Law has studied in other contexts.

III. Individual responsibility as a fundamental value?

Global Administrative Law offers a perspective that is external to international law and observes how investor obligations contribute to global governance. But investor obligations also prompt asking how they relate to general developments within international law.

This Section will analyse how they stand to international law's shift from the state to the individual. In the last hundred years, international law has developed from an inter-state character to a legal order which centres on the individual as a subject (1.). In part, investor obligations reflect this development because they bring about individual responsibility (2.). However, they do so in a less value-based manner than other areas of international law, for example compared to human rights and criminal law. Instead, they realise such individual positions in a more pragmatic way (3.).

1. The idea of individual international law

The role of the individual in international law has changed over time. By and large, until the early 20th century, only the state was considered the subject of international rights and obligations. Individuals were mediatised by the state of their nationality. Indirectly, states could, at their discretion, defend their nationals' interests through diplomatic protection.[49]

---

47 Supported and demanded for example by Stephan W Schill, 'International Investment Law and Comparative Public Law – an Introduction' in Stephan W Schill (ed), *International Investment Law and Comparative Public Law* (Oxford University Press 2010) 10–37; Schill, 'Enhancing' (n 34) 85–102.

48 See only Chapter 9.II.

49 For a viewpoint from general international law see Antônio AC Trindade, 'The Historical Recovery of the Human Person as Subject of the Law of Nations'

In the last hundred years, international law has changed substantially in this matter as individuals have moved into its centre. In particular, as states created international human rights, they acknowledged that individuals are subjects of international law, too. Increasingly, international law has awarded individual rights to them. They are not mediatised by the state anymore but rather are the respective right's bearers. Thus, they can themselves invoke a violation without depending on the state, and international law has increasingly provided procedures for them to do so. This shift towards the (direct) recognition of the individual is still ongoing.[50]

The awarding of individual rights has emerged from a growing consensus on fundamental human values: to guarantee human dignity, freedom and equality.[51] To that end, individual rights embody an emancipatory potential because they understand individuals as persons empowered to actively defend themselves.[52] But even beyond human rights, many other areas have accepted individual rights, such as international humanitarian, environmental protection and labour law.[53] Investment law is another often-mentioned example because of its awarding of individual investor *rights*.[54] Constitutional theories of international law have given these indi-

---

(2012) 1(3) Cambridge Journal of International and Comparative Law 8, 20–21; for the investment law context see also Chapter 2.IV and Chapter 6.VIII.

50 See for example Rosalyn Higgins, *Problems and Process: International Law and How We Use It* (Clarendon Press 1995) 53–55 who considers the increasing role of investment arbitration as evidence for an increasing recognition of the individual as the bearer of international rights accompanied with sanctions, building on an understanding of law based on *Austin* and *Kelsen*; Ratner (n 7) 475–488 on the recognition of international human rights and international criminal law which reflects that corporations may have directly applicable international rights and obligations; Gerhard Hafner, 'The Emancipation of the Individual from the State Under International Law' (2011) 358 Recueil des Cours 263, 315–436 with the more nuanced observation that the emancipation of the individual as a subject of international law depends on the particular applicable legal regime and that international law is subject to a state- and an individual-oriented trend at the same time; Peters (n 1) 194–471, 526 mapping the many different individual legal positions in international law 'beyond human rights' and identifying the individual as the primary international legal person.

51 For a particularly strong representation of a value-based approach see Trindade (n 49) 48–49.

52 Peters (n 1) 536–541.

53 See the comprehensive analysis by ibid.

54 José E Alvarez, 'Are Corporations "Subjects" of International Law?' (2011) 9(1) Santa Clara Journal of International Law 1, 1–35; Stephan W Schill, 'Cross-Regime Harmonization Through Proportionality Analysis: The Case of International Investment Law, the Law of State Immunity and Human Rights'

vidual rights a prominent role. In their view, the status of the individual as a subject that enjoys rights constitutes an important constitutional principle itself.[55]

In contrast to rights, individuals do not have many directly applicable obligations under international law as seen.[56] Nevertheless, many proponents of individual rights have also demanded the creation of comprehensive individual obligations. Often, they bring forward similar fundamental reasons: Some perceive that individuals who enjoy protection should also be accountable under international law.[57] Others argue that individuals are the real, original subjects of international law, and hence should also be subject to obligations.[58] Some follow the same from a constitutional

---

(2012) 27(1) ICSID Review 87, 91; Tillmann R Braun, *Ausprägungen der Globalisierung: Der Investor als partielles Subjekt im Internationalen Investitionsrecht: Qualität und Grenzen dieser Wirkungseinheit* (Nomos 2012) 266–268; Laurence B de Chazournes and Brian McGarry, 'What Roles Can Constitutional Law Play in Investment Arbitration?' (2014) 15(5–6) Journal of World Investment & Trade 862, 883; Peters (n 1) 282–338; on the controversy if investor rights are individual in character see already Chapter 3.VII.2.b).

55 See for example Bruno Simma, 'From Bilateralism to Community Interest in International Law' (1994) 250(VI) Recueil des Cours 217, 242–243, 285–301 who reflects on how individual human rights have entered as a community interest into the traditionally bilateral international law, elaborating *inter alia* on how they express themselves as *ius cogens* and obligations *erga omnes*; Andreas L Paulus, *Die internationale Gemeinschaft im Völkerrecht: Eine Untersuchung zur Entwicklung des Völkerrechts im Zeitalter der Globalisierung* (C.H. Beck 2001) 254–260 who acknowledges a minimum consensus on (practical) human rights as a common value of the international community notwithstanding the debate on universalism versus regionalism.

56 See Chapter 2.IV.

57 See for example Trindade (n 49) 14–16, 29–31, 50–57.

58 See for example Hersch Lauterpacht, 'The Subjects of the Law of Nations' in Elihu Lauterpacht (ed), *International Law Being the Collected Papers of Hersch Lauterpacht,* vol 3 The Law of Peace Parts II-VI (Cambridge University Press 1977) 487–533; Hersch Lauterpacht, 'State Sovereignty and Human Rights' in Elihu Lauterpacht (ed), *International Law Being the Collected Papers of Hersch Lauterpacht,* vol 3 The Law of Peace Parts II-VI (Cambridge University Press 1977) 426–430 who understands international law as a system that bases on the individual, not on states, but which needs practical realisation in a world dominated by states, for example by the recognition of individual obligations; Peters (n 1) 538, 541, 551–555 argues that already today the individual is the 'natural subject of international law'.

understanding of international law as a system, for example building on human rights.[59]

2. Investor obligations as individual international law

Investor obligations contribute to further the development of international law with the individual as its central subject. Investment law may serve as a case study of a field which not only accords individual rights but also obligations.

Of course, direct obligations are most relevant in this regard. Construed similarly to obligations in international criminal law, they turn investment law into a new field of international law with directly applicable obligations. Importantly, these obligations have a much broader substantive scope than international criminal law. They are not limited to the gravest atrocities but cover how every day business activity affects public goods and individual rights.

At first glance, indirect obligations appear to conform less with the described calls for individual obligations because they form part of investor rights. However, such a perspective would be too formalistic. Rather, this Chapter's insight that both direct and indirect obligations bring about a specific new form of international investor responsibility is decisive. As it is a form of *individual* responsibility, also indirect obligations represent means to sanction investors' misconduct. They serve as a potential model for sanctioning private actors in other fields of international law with legal force.

Investor obligations' new emphasis on the individual becomes even clearer if one reflects on investment law's history. As seen, neither direct nor indirect obligations existed as part of its predecessor: the law of aliens and diplomatic protection.[60] It appears that the newly-created ambit of individual rights in IIAs was a fertile ground for the delayed establishment of obligations. The analysis has also pointed out that investor obligations

59 See for example Ernst-Ulrich Petersmann, *Multilevel Constitutionalism for Multilevel Governance of Public Goods: Methodology Problems in International Law* (Bloomsbury Publishing 2017) 3–75, 147–219, 233–372 who envisages a system of multi-level-governance including individual rights and accountability based on human rights.

60 See Chapter 2.V.1 and Chapter 6.VIII.

build more broadly on increased expectations from corporations in society.[61]

Moreover, in some cases, investor obligations even directly individualise existing international obligations of states. A number of investor obligations studied define their content by referring to these external obligations that originally addressed the state.[62] Herein, the IIA serves as a vehicle for making a certain norm directly applicable to individuals by taking away their mediatisation by the state. For example, an IIA which contains an obligation that requires investors to abide by the ICCPR makes the ICCPR directly applicable to this extent – and thus brings about a feature that international human rights law has not developed so far on its own.

3. More pragmatic, less value-oriented

At the same time, there are some reservations against reading investor obligations as contributing to international law's development to place the individual at its centre.

Firstly, investment law conserves states' pivotal importance because foreign investors' nationality remains decisive. Investors only enjoy rights and, increasingly, obligations if they have the nationality of a state that is party to an IIA and, conversely, operate in the territory of another state party. Hence, investor obligations still give substantial weight to territory and nationality as core elements of state sovereignty.[63]

Similarly, investor obligations exclude civil society from participating in the legal relationship they bring about. As seen, investors owe direct obligations to the host state.[64] And it is only the host state which can enforce them through counterclaims.[65] As indirect obligations are intertwined with investor rights, they only relate to the host state as well. When breached, they deprive the investor of protection from the host state. Hence, the actual victims of violations have no say. They do not appear

61 See Chapter 9.II.3.

62 See for example Chapter 3.II and Chapter 7.I.3.

63 In the same vein Barnali Choudhury, 'Investor Obligations for Human Rights' (2020) 35(1–2) ICSID Review 82, 101 who highlights that investor human rights obligations would still 'leave governance gaps since international investment law does not offer a multilateral approach to governing foreign investment.'

64 See Chapter 3.VII.3.

65 See Chapter 4.

as the corresponding right bearers and cannot enforce a violation of an investor obligation. In short, they remain mediatised by the host state.[66]

Furthermore, there is an even more fundamental reservation: investor obligations' relative character. They do not share the multilateral and communal nature of many other individual norms of international law. Branches such as international human rights, criminal, environmental law and labour law embody objective standards of community interests beyond the *quid pro quo* constellation of IIAs.[67] For this reason, these norms often constitute *erga omnes* obligations, meaning that states may invoke them against other states without having suffered any harm themselves.[68]

In contrast, investor obligations form part of IIAs that are often bilateral in nature.[69] Even where they start to develop in plurilateral settings, they follow a reciprocal logic: IIAs' primary purpose is not to create companies' international responsibility. They exist to attract investors by granting

66 In the same vein Silvia Steininger, 'The Role of Human Rights in Investment Law and Arbitration, State Obligations, Corporate Responsibility and Community Empowerment' in Ilias Bantekas and Michael A Stein (eds), *The Cambridge Companion to Business & Human Rights Law* (Cambridge University Press 2021) 422–423; UNGA 'Human Rights-Compatible International Investment Agreements. Report of the Working Group on the Issue of Human Rights and Transnational Corporations and Other Business Enterprises' (27 July 2021) UN Doc A/76/238, paras 67–71; for a discussion of the potentials of host citizen-investor disputes see Martin Jarrett, 'A New Frontier in International Investment Law: Adjudication of Host Citizen-Investor Disputes?' (2021) 81(4) Zeitschrift für ausländisches öffentliches Recht und Völkerrecht 969, 972–999; for a consideration that the host state can act as *parens patriae* on behalf of human rights victims, see Tomoko Ishikawa, 'Counterclaims in Investment Arbitration: Is the Host State the Right Claimant?' in Jean Ho and Mavluda Sattorova (eds), *Investors' International Law* (Hart 2021) 205–211.

67 On the communal and multilateral character see Simma (n 55) 256–287; Paulus (n 55) 250–284.

68 They are owed 'towards the international community as a whole', see *Case Concerning the Barcelona Traction, Light and Power Company, Limited (Belgium v Spain) (Second Phase)* (Judgment) [1970] ICJ Rep 3, para 33; see further Christian Tomuschat, 'International Law: Ensuring the Survival of Mankind on the Eve of a New Century: General Course on Public International Law' (1999) 281 Recueil des Cours 9, 82–84; generally on doctrinal manifestations see Simma (n 55) 285–321.

69 The bilateral character of most international investment law in the context of global public goods is also highlighted by Giorgio Sacerdoti, 'Investment Protection and Sustainable Development: Key Issues' in Steffen Hindelang and Markus Krajewski (eds), *Shifting Paradigms in International Investment Law: More Balanced, Less Isolated, Increasingly Diversified* (Oxford University Press 2016) 38; it forms part of the criticism of investor obligations by Braun (n 54) 201.

them international protection. Even if, as seen, the choice of who should be attracted is becoming more selective, as the field adopts the concept of sustainable development,[70] international investor rights and obligations remain the result of an inter-state bargain to foster state parties' development. Consequently, they are less value-oriented in the way they centre on the individual than the other described branches of international law such as human rights norms which aim to realise freedom, equality and dignity as common overarching values.

The findings on investor obligations' regulatory potential in Chapter 10 point in the same direction. In contrast to criminal law, they do not serve as an instrument to answer and punish investor misconduct unconditionally. Rather, they may operate as a sophisticated tool that incentivises proper behaviour – a rather pragmatic approach to the protection of public interest.

Nevertheless, investor obligations may still play an important role in international law's shift towards the individual. It should be appreciated that investment law has already gone a long way from its original focus on protecting investors. Investor obligations contribute to the 'generalisation of international investment law'[71] which may transform investment law into a more value-based field in the long term. The bilateral or plurilateral settings of IIAs and investment arbitration allow for quick and decentral developments. Therefore, investment law may even provide a useful testing field for creating a new form of individual obligations and responsibility – and in that regard inspire other areas of international law.

---

70 See Chapter 9.III.

71 Peter-Tobias Stoll and Till P Holterhus, 'The "Generalization" of International Investment Law in Constitutional Perspective' in Steffen Hindelang and Markus Krajewski (eds), *Shifting Paradigms in International Investment Law: More Balanced, Less Isolated, Increasingly Diversified* (Oxford University Press 2016).

Chapter 12.
Conclusion: Towards an International Responsibility of Investors

> IIAs can do more to enhance responsible investment. Although (foreign) investment can create positive conditions for improving peoples' lives, it can also carry the risk of negatively impacting on the environment, peoples' health and the enjoyment of their human rights. These effects can be aggravated due to domestic regulatory lacunae. It is important, therefore, that while IIAs continue to provide a firm basis for investment protection, they should also begin to address more directly investor responsibilities.[1]

With these words, UNCTAD called for reforming international investment governance in 2015. The present study has shown that investment law is one step ahead: it *already gives rise* to investor responsibilities to a significant extent. The field has already begun the process of complementing investor rights with obligations.

Already today, IIAs do more than solely protect the investor, they also contain investor obligations. They impose binding standards of conduct towards the public interest: how the investor should behave towards, for example, the environment and human rights of others. It seems as though reform discussions so far have not paid enough attention to this development. Focussing on strengthening the host state's right to regulate remains important – but the right to regulate only accords a passive role to the public interest, as an argumentative means to justify that the host state infringes on investor rights. In contrast, the investor obligations analysed in this book actively expect public interest-friendly conduct from the investor.

---

1 UNCTAD, *World Investment Report: Reforming International Investment Governance* (United Nations Publications 2015) 126; in the same vein UNGA 'Human Rights-Compatible International Investment Agreements. Report of the Working Group on the Issue of Human Rights and Transnational Corporations and Other Business Enterprises' (27 July 2021) UN Doc A/76/238 paras 24–25, 63–66.

The findings of this book join UNCTAD in observing that 'the IIA regime is going through a period of reflection, review and revision'.[2] There are dynamics to provide IIAs with a new function: to hold investors responsible instead of only disciplining states. On the UN level, the Open-Ended Intergovernmental Working Group on Transnational Corporations and other Business Enterprises with Respect to Human Rights has been discussing the creation of legally binding international obligations of corporations. However, given that states have, so far, not agreed on such a treaty, these discussions are yet to come to fruition and have recently concentrated more on new obligations of states towards companies. Investment law has been more successful in this regard. Hence, paradoxically, a field that many have criticised for its pro-investor bias has started to offer solutions for holding transnationally operating corporations accountable. This, of course, is contrary to its original exclusive purpose – to protect the investors.

More precisely, this study has identified two different types of obligations in investment law practice: direct (Part I) and indirect (Part II), allowing for common conclusions (Part III). The former have emerged in first IIAs and arbitral awards. The latter are already substantially established in arbitral jurisprudence – and constitute a new doctrinal category that this book introduced.

I. The dawn of direct obligations (Part I)

Direct obligations are similarly construed as obligations in international criminal law. They are international obligations directly applicable to investors as private actors – without the state having to act as an intermediary (Chapter 2). In international law, such obligations exist only exceptionally. Yet, they have recently emerged in investment practice. Most likely, it is IIAs' bilateral setting that made possible what states have failed to achieve multilaterally so far. In other words, IIAs serve as a tool in which like-minded states can create direct investor obligations in their mutual relations. As a corollary, they only apply to investors of the state parties' nationality.

The ICSID Tribunals' rulings in *Burlington v Ecuador* and *Perenco v Ecuador* in 2017 and 2019 present good examples of direct obligations. They concerned Ecuador's counterclaims against the companies Burlington and

2 ibid, 120.

Perenco. Here, the Tribunals applied a direct obligation to prevent environmental pollution. They held that the investor must pay a compensation of USD 54.539.517 and USD 39.199.373 to Ecuador for polluting soil and groundwater, respectively.[3]

Findings like these indicate that such direct obligations already have stronger ground in investment practice than usually perceived (Chapter 3). On the one hand, many developing countries have invented new treaty clauses with direct obligations. They feature in new model BITs and IIAs, *inter alia* by Brazil, India and many African countries as well as the African Union. This development is remarkable on its own. However, even investors from developed countries may be subject to direct obligations pursuant to 'conventional' IIAs. In such constellations, five arbitral tribunals have recently accepted direct obligations in different forms. These are the UNCITRAL awards in *Al-Warraq v Indonesia* in 2014 and in *Aven v Costa Rica* in 2018 as well as the ICSID awards in *Urbaser v Argentina* in 2016, *Perenco v Ecuador* in 2015 and 2019 and *Burlington v Ecuador* in 2017.

Existing practice has even developed to the point that it allowed this study to systematise different techniques of creating direct obligations in investment law. Most of these techniques have in common that they refer to existing standards of conduct outside of investment law. These include international obligations of states under international treaties and customary law, domestic investor obligations and CSR norms. As of today, the interplay with domestic obligations has the greatest potential for bringing about direct obligations. These norms are already tailored to private actors. And they comprehensively cover different facets of the public interest in branches such as administrative law, human rights and environmental law. In particular, domestic obligations can form part of the applicable law in an investment arbitration. The arbitration internationalises these domestic obligations in a manner tantamount to the actual creation of an international norm.

Counterclaims provide states with an international means of enforcing these direct obligations (Chapter 4). They are not new instruments. However, only in the course of the last couple of years, states have discovered their potential to take on a new function: enforcing direct obligations against investors who have impaired the public interest. Arbitral awards

3 *Burlington Resources Inc. v Republic of Ecuador*, ICSID Case No. ARB/08/5, Decision on Counterclaims (7 February 2017) para 889; *Perenco Ecuador Ltd. v The Republic of Ecuador*, ICSID Case No. ARB/08/6, Award (27 September 2019) para 1023; see above Chapter 3.VI.2.

allow host states to do so even against investors' assets outside of their territory. To that end, these awards qualify as part of the ICSID or New York Convention's global enforcement systems. The analysis revealed that the requirements for filing a counterclaim are lenient – already today, many IIAs allow for counterclaims. The five arbitral awards mentioned above form the forefront of this new development. For the first time, the awards in *Burlington v Ecuador* and *Perenco v Ecuador* in 2017 and 2019 successfully applied a direct obligation to the detriment of an investor[4] – a milestone in investment law history. Of course, the encountered new practice is still small, considering the many investment arbitrations and IIAs worldwide. Notwithstanding, the findings reflect dynamics indicative of a new qualitative approach – possibly even signaling the dawn of direct obligations in the field (Chapter 5).

II. The presence of indirect obligations (Part II)

Beyond these direct obligations, Part II has identified even better-established indirect obligations. They are standards of conduct which the state cannot force the investors to observe. However, if the investors do not comply, they suffer negative legal consequences. They forfeit investment protection in full or in part (Chapter 6). Although one could also understand them as conditions for investor rights, this book chooses to describe them as a sub-type of an obligation. The term 'indirect obligations' reflects that investors face actual expectations regarding their behaviour. It also shows that they have a partly compulsory character. Even though states cannot enforce them through counterclaims, they automatically accord a sanction in case of a breach. Hence, they change investors' legal position under an IIA against their will.

For example, one could imagine an indirect obligation as an IIA clause with the following content:

> If the investor does not comply with the duty to protect human rights as enshrined in the ICCPR, the right to protection against expropriation granted in this treaty does not apply.

Arbitral jurisprudence has already established many such indirect obligations (Chapter 7). Yet, tribunals have thus far not employed this term. Instead, they have interpreted different requirements of investment law

4 ibid.

in a manner which is functionally equivalent to an indirect obligation: as being conditional on proper investor behaviour. Sometimes, tribunals have built on explicit IIA clauses. More often, they have interpreted 'conventional' IIAs in a manner which brings about indirect obligations. Such jurisprudence can be found for a broad range of different investment law requirements. And they impose standards of conduct relating to very different aspects of the public interest. They include environmental protection, human rights, the national economy, and the rule of law, to name but a few. This is another reason why this book chooses to identify them as structurally common indirect obligations.

More specifically, one can find them implied in jurisdiction and admissibility requirements of investment arbitration. Here, they condition the procedural right to file an investment claim against the host state. Furthermore, indirect obligations have been accepted as part of investor rights' requirements. Non-compliance disqualifies investors from substantive investment protection – such as in the above-mentioned example of protection against expropriation. Finally, rules on compensation contain indirect obligations too. If investors violate them, tribunals reduce the amount of damages which investors otherwise could have claimed from the host state for violating their investor rights. Apart from arbitral awards, new IIAs have invented new explicit clauses on indirect obligations, too.

However, so far, these obligations have developed rather chaotically. Largely, arbitral jurisprudence has discussed the respective requirements of investor rights only in a case by case manner – without being conscious of their common character as obligations. Nevertheless, indirect obligations appear to follow a certain basic order. Those which form part of jurisdiction and admissibility requirements operate as a filter which sanction *prima facie* or particularly grave violations of the public interest. Within the substantive requirements of investor rights, tribunals were generally reluctant to automatically deprive investors of protection for their misbehaviour. Here, indirect obligations build especially on defined domestic and international norms outside of investment law. In contrast, rules on compensation allow for more flexible sanctions for the breach of an indirect obligation: Tribunals may reduce compensation only in part. This allows for more nuanced results which weigh the appropriate sanction against the gravity of the investor's and the host state's misconduct.

And arbitral jurisprudence is still developing. The study has also shown that not all awards which examined investors' misconduct bring about indirect obligations. Sometimes, tribunals merely considered misconduct as one balancing factor amongst others within the analysis of an investor right. In these instances, there is, thus, no automatic sanction for breaching a standard of conduct. It is a different way of giving weight to investors' behaviour. Here, infringing with the public interest 'tips the scales' against the investor in the legal analysis. This book was careful in distinguishing these instances from other treaty clauses and cases which gave rise to indirect obligations as defined here.

Nevertheless, even to consider misconduct as a balancing factor is a novelty. It contributes to broader dynamics that investment protection should be dependent on proper investor behaviour. Together, arbitral jurisprudence and new IIAs outline a new interpretation of investment law. Therein, indirect obligations constitute the most stringent way of imposing standards of conduct on investors without creating direct obligations (Chapter 8).

III. Common implications (Part III)

1. Rebalancing investment law

Together, direct and indirect investor obligations contribute to rebalancing investment law from within (Chapter 9). They alter a traditional characteristic of the field: its asymmetry. Originally, it only accorded rights without obligations. To rest within this type of wording, investor obligations make investment law more symmetrical. As a corollary, IIAs in which investor rights and obligations go hand in hand have a stronger emphasis on the public interest. They depart from an exclusive focus on defending investors' economic interests.

This change alters the overall purpose that IIAs serve. Originally, they aimed to attract any foreign investment to foster the host state's development. By providing international protection, investors should experience less risk and hence be more ready to invest abroad in the first place. Investment law with investor obligations operates differently. Only public interest-friendly investments receive unconditional protection. Investors who violate the public interest either face direct obligations – and respective compensation counterclaims by the host state – or forfeit investment protection. Both neutralise IIAs' risk reducing effect. This means that such IIAs only attract selected, public interest-friendly investments: quality comes before quantity. In other words, such IIAs do not rely on the assumption that any increase of the investment volume will preponderantly serve the public interest. In doing so, IIAs build on the concept of sustainable development that there must be an equilibrium between the economy, the environment, and society.

To achieve sustainability within investment law, investor obligations offer a reform approach that is complementary to reinforcing the right to regulate. Both serve to strengthen the public interest in the analysis of investor rights. The right to regulate focusses on the state as the guardian of the public interest. Investor obligations express that investors take an active part in that task, too.

However, investor obligations also interact with the right to regulate. On the one hand, they contribute to strengthening it. On the other hand, investor obligations may also limit the host state's right to regulate. With regard to the former, generally, to the extent they prohibit investor misconduct, the IIA also allows the host state to interfere with the investor domestically. Nevertheless, investor obligations do not provide host states with a *carte blanche*. Investor rights and obligations must be interpreted in harmony; hence, especially the manner in which the host state interferes with the investor will still remain under scrutiny. As for the limits that investor obligations may impose on the right to regulate, it is useful to consider that they constitute international standards of conduct. This entails that states to some extent lose control of their interpretation and application – for example, arbitral tribunals can interpret them autonomously in unexpected ways. In this respect they are no different from other international standards.

2. Regulating investment based on incentives

Furthermore, in contrast to right to regulate clauses, investor obligations have the potential to serve as a new international regulatory instrument (Chapter 10). IIAs could, for example, alleviate the problem of regulating corporations which operate beyond national borders. The study has examined two different ways in which investor obligations could serve to regulate investors' behaviour.

First, as a command-and-control tool which responds to unwanted behaviour, possibly by force, and punishes it. Yet, in contrast to domestic legal systems with courts and executive agencies, investor obligations lack the international institutions and procedures to serve this regulatory approach effectively. Investment law only provides for counterclaims to enforce direct obligations in an international procedure. And by their nature, counterclaims remain a *reactive* enforcement means. States may file them after investors themselves have raised an arbitral claim.

However, IIAs may fulfil an incentive-based regulatory approach. Such regulatory strategies operate by offering advantages or the menace of sanctions. Then, their addressees comply voluntarily and pre-emptively to receive the former or avoid the latter.

The prospect of receiving investment protection constitutes such an incentive. Investor rights have an economic value for investors. They reduce their investment risk in an unknown, potentially unstable regulatory environment. In addition, investors may receive better financing conditions. In this view, the threat of losing investment protection deters investors from breaching an investor obligation. Serving their own interest, they will comply in order to qualify for protection in case they need it. Direct and indirect obligations both produce this incentivising effect. In the case of direct obligations, investors face a counterclaim which would offset any potential gain that investor rights offer. The indirect ones automatically neutralise investor rights by depriving them of protection. In short, investor obligations use investor rights as leverage to induce public interest-friendly behaviour.

In contrast to the right to regulate, this regulatory effect operates in a way detached from the host state's domestic legal system. It only builds on the presence of international investment protection. Even if the host state shows no domestic regulatory activity, there is an incentive for investors to comply with investor obligations pre-emptively. Otherwise, they run the risk that, at a later point in time, they will not have investment protection available. And indeed, investment protection was precisely invented to provide a more stable investment environment even though host states' policies and governments may change unpredictably. With this pre-emptive steering effect, investor obligations may, to a certain extent, compensate for the lack of regulatory action by an unwilling or unable host state.

The study also describes the limits of this regulatory effect. For example, much depends on the actual economic value of the concrete IIA to the specific investor. Hence, IIAs' steering potential is best understood as complementing other regulatory approaches, especially on the domestic level.

3. A case study for the individual's role in international law

Looking at the broader picture, the recent development of investor obligations allowed to outline what they imply for the individual's role in international law (Chapter 11). Herein, the investor as a natural or private legal person serves as a case study for general international law.

This book has shown that investor obligations bring about a new form of international 'civil' responsibility of individuals. The concept of responsibility has been established in particular for states. So far, individuals are subject to such responsibility only in international criminal law. Conceptually, foreign investors now face a new form of individual responsibility. In analogy to the ILC's terminology on the responsibility of states, investor obligations contain primary rules – the substantive standards of conduct not to harm, for example, the environment or human rights of others. Furthermore, investor obligations also imply secondary rules on the legal consequences for breaching these primary rules. They are reflected in the division between direct and indirect obligations: to pay compensation or to lose an investor right, respectively. This understanding allows for further insights. In particular, the fact that investors are responsible does not mean that states are relieved of their obligations. On the contrary, it is established in international law that two subjects can be separately responsible for the same harmful outcome – the so-called shared responsibility which can also apply to investors and states.

Furthermore, in bringing about international responsibility, investor obligations can be understood as phenomena of Global Administrative Law. In this sense, investor obligations 'administer' how investors, as private actors, relate to public goods and individual rights of others – similar to how domestic administrative law defines what private actors must do to safeguard the environment, the health of others, and so on. In doing so, investor obligations follow public law principles. For example, the public law principle of proportionality requires a weighing and balancing of all interests affected in a certain case. Most investor obligations reflect such a weighing and balancing and thus build on this principle. Furthermore, investor obligations govern investor behaviour beyond traditional state regulation in the state's domestic legal system. They combine many different sources such as international obligations of states, CSR norms and domestic law. Moreover, investment tribunals acquire new functions as comprehensive fora to adjudicate if investors' behaviour towards the public interest was appropriate – similar to the role of domestic administrative courts.

Turning to a more fundamental perspective, the study has put investor obligations into the context of international law's general development. In this view, they serve as a reference field for how international law increasingly addresses individuals directly – without mediatising them through states. So far, many consider investment law as an example of a field of international law that has awarded individual rights. This study shows that it fuels this development even further by also according individual obligations.

However, in contrast to international law's general trend, investor obligations rest less on a fundamental concern for values. Especially international human rights build on the idea that they empower all persons because of their human dignity, liberty and equality. Here, individual rights embody a universal value that is protected *erga omnes*. In comparison, investor obligations serve a more pragmatic telos. IIAs are a result of a bilateral bargain. Any contained investor obligations merely have effect *inter partes* for investors of the right nationality. And IIAs give no corresponding individual rights to the actual victims of violations that investors committed. This shows that even IIAs which contain obligations still follow the main economic goal of fostering sustainable development by attracting quality investment. Investor obligations remain but a means to that end.

IV. Outlook

Investor obligations reflect a changing understanding of the investor's role in society. In UNCTAD's words:

> As the global community's views on development have evolved, societies' expectations about the role of foreign investment have become more demanding. Today, it is no longer enough that investment creates jobs, contributes to economic growth or generates foreign exchange. Countries increasingly look for investment that is not harmful for the environment, which brings social benefits, promotes gender equality, and which helps them to move up the global value chain.[5]

These societal expectations have found their way into investment law. It is a welcome development as it reacts to foreign investments' high and rising impact on society. At the same time, what is necessary is a reasonable rebalancing of the field. Investor obligations can only unfold their poten-

5 UNCTAD (n 1) 127.

tial if they operate hand in hand with effective investment protection.[6] Investor rights provide the fertile soil in which obligations may grow.

This book's main contribution is to shed light on investor obligations' recent, sometimes chaotic 'growth'. It invites further research on questions that it could not cover. For example, one should further discuss which of the two, direct or indirect obligations, or perhaps even both in certain situations, are the most preferable for investment law. It is open to discussion whether different aspects of the public interest should be treated differently – for example, if investor obligations should vary in the way they function and are structured if they protect the environment as opposed to third parties' human rights and *vice versa*. Further thinking is required if the identified investor obligations produce those risks against which scholars have warned who are generally sceptical of international obligations directly applicable to non-state-actors.[7] Suggestions should be made on how civil society and victims of investor misconduct could invoke their rights against investors on the international level. Currently, they have no say in this matter that is exclusively between the state and the investor. Furthermore, empirical studies are needed to measure the extent to which investor obligations can actually steer foreign investors' behaviour in practice. Beyond investment law, this book may inspire exploration of indirect international obligations of non-state actors in other areas of international law.

For the time being, the present study may serve to raise awareness of the fact that investor obligations are a complex but promising concept. Their further development remains precarious. Only a small portion of IIAs have so far brought about direct obligations. It remains to be seen if other IIAs follow suit. In addition, tribunals may still change their jurisprudence on indirect obligations. There is also the danger that tribunals may interpret MFN and national treatment rights in a way that undermines investor obligations.[8] Much depends on states' willingness to support investor obligations in the future. While investment law is currently in a transitional stage, it remains in the hands of the states to decide in which direction to steer its development. In this sense, investor obligations may prove a

6 Andrea K Bjorklund, 'The Role of Counterclaims in Rebalancing Investment Law' (2013) 17(2) Lewis & Clark Law Review 461, 479; Patrick Abel, 'Counterclaims Based on International Human Rights Obligations of Investors in International Investment Arbitration: Fallacies and Potentials of the 2016 ICSID Urbaser v. Argentina Award' [2018] Brill Open Law 1, 25.

7 See above Chapter 11.I.3.

8 See Chapter 3.VII.4.b).

valuable new element of investment law and serve to further the field's legitimacy that has been under attack for quite some time.

Table of International Treaties

Accord entre le Gouvernement de la République française et le Gouvernement de la République de l'Équateur sur l'encouragement et la protection réciproques des investissements (adopted 7 September 1994, entered into force 10 June 1996, date of termination 23 May 2018) ‹https://investmentpolicy.unctad.org/international-investment-agreements/treaty-files/1052/download› accessed 7 December 2021

Additional Protocol to the Criminal Law Convention on Corruption (adopted 15 May 2003, entered into force 1 February 2005) 2466 UNTS 168

Additional Protocol to the Framework Agreement of the Pacific Alliance (adopted 10 February 2014, entered into force 1 May 2016) ‹https://investmentpolicy.unctad.org/international-investment-agreements/treaty-files/2940/download› accessed 7 December 2021

African Charter on Human and Peoples' Rights (adopted 27 June 1981, entered into force 21 October 1986) 1520 UNTS 217

African Union Convention on Preventing and Combating Corruption (adopted 11 July 2003, entered into force 5 August 2006) 2860 UNTS 113

Agreement between the United States of America, the United Mexican States, and Canada (adopted 30 November 2018, revised 10 December 2019 by the Protocol of Amendment, entered into force 1 July 2020) ‹https://investmentpolicy.unctad.org/international-investment-agreements/treaty-files/6008/download› accessed 7 December 2021

Agreement on Promotion, Protection and Guarantee of Investments among Member States of the Organisation of the Islamic Conference (adopted 5 June 1981, entered into force 23 September 1986) ‹https://investmentpolicy.unctad.org/international-investment-agreements/treaty-files/2399/download› accessed 7 December 2021

American Convention on Human Rights (adopted 22 November 1969, entered into force 18 July 1978) 1144 UNTS 123

Argentina-Spain BIT (adopted 3 October 1991, entered into force 28 September 1992) ‹https://investmentpolicy.unctad.org/international-investment-agreements/treaty-files/119/download› accessed 7 December 2021

Basel Protocol on Liability and Compensation for Damage Resulting from Transboundary Movements of Hazardous Waste and their Disposal (adopted 10 December 1999) UN Doc UNEP/CHW.1/WG.1/9/2

Belgium-Luxembourg Economic Union Model BIT (28 March 2019) ‹https://investmentpolicy.unctad.org/international-investment-agreements/treaty-files/5854/download› accessed 7 December 2021

Bolivia-Chile BIT (adopted 22 September 1994, entered into force 21 July 1999, date of termination 11 April 2020) ‹https://investmentpolicy.unctad.org/international-investment-agreements/treaty-files/448/download› accessed 7 December 2021

Brazil Model BIT (2015) ‹https://investmentpolicy.unctad.org/international-investment-agreements/treaty-files/4786/download› accessed 7 December 2021

Brazil-Angola Investment Cooperation and Facilitation Agreement (adopted 1 April 2015, entered into force 28 July 2017) ‹https://investmentpolicy.unctad.org/international-investment-agreements/treaty-files/4720/download› accessed 7 December 2021

Brazil-Chile Investment Cooperation and Facilitation Agreement (adopted 24 November 2015) ‹https://investmentpolicy.unctad.org/international-investment-agreements/treaty-files/4712/download› accessed 7 December 2021

Brazil-Colombia Investment Cooperation and Facilitation Agreement (adopted 9 October 2015) ‹https://investmentpolicy.unctad.org/international-investment-agreements/treaty-files/5765/download› accessed 7 December 2021

Brazil-Malawi Investment Cooperation and Facilitation Agreement (adopted 25 June 2015) ‹https://investmentpolicy.unctad.org/international-investment-agreements/treaty-files/4715/download› accessed 7 December 2021

Brazil-Mexico Investment Cooperation and Facilitation Agreement (adopted 26 May 2015, entered into force 7 October 2018) ‹https://investmentpolicy.unctad.org/international-investment-agreements/treaty-files/4718/download› accessed 7 December 2021

Brazil-Mozambique Investment Cooperation and Facilitation Agreement (adopted 30 March 2015) ‹https://investmentpolicy.unctad.org/international-investment-agreements/treaty-files/4717/download› accessed 7 December 2021

Brazil-Peru Economic and Trade Expansion Agreement (adopted 29 April 2016) ‹https://investmentpolicy.unctad.org/international-investment-agreements/treaty-files/5402/download› accessed 7 December 2021

Canada-Ecuador BIT (adopted 9 April 1996, entered into force 6 June 1997, date of termination 19 May 2018) ‹https://investmentpolicy.unctad.org/international-investment-agreements/treaty-files/609/download› accessed 7 December 2021

Canada-Peru FTA (adopted 29 May 2008, entered into force 1 August 2009) ‹https://investmentpolicy.unctad.org/international-investment-agreements/treaty-files/2568/download› accessed 7 December 2021

Charter of the United Nations (adopted 26 June 1945, entered into force 24 October 1945) 1 UNTS XVI

China Model BIT (1998) printed in Wenhua Shan and Norah Gallagher, 'China' in Chester Brown (ed), Commentaries on Selected Model Investment Treaties (Oxford University Press 2013)

Civil Law Convention on Corruption (adopted 4 November 1999, entered into force 1 November 2003) 2246 UNTS 3

Comprehensive and Progressive Agreement for Trans-Pacific Partnership (adopted 8 March 2018, entered into force 30 December 2018) ‹https://investmentpolicy.unctad.org/international-investment-agreements/treaty-files/5672/download› accessed 7 December 2021

Comprehensive Economic and Trade Agreement (adopted 30 October 2016) ‹https://investmentpolicy.unctad.org/international-investment-agreements/treaty-files/3593/download› accessed 7 December 2021

Convention Concerning the Protection of the World Cultural and Natural Heritage (adopted 16 November 1972, entered into force 17 December 1975) 1037 UNTS 151

Convention entre l'Union Économique Belgo-Luxembourgeoise et la République du Burundi Concernant l'Encouragement et la Protection Réciproques des Investissements (adopted 13 April 1989, entered into force 12 September 1993) ‹https://www.investorstatelawguide.com/documents/documents/BIT-0137%20-%20Belgium-Luxembourg-Burundi%20BIT%20(1989)%20[french].pdf› accessed 7 December 2021

Convention for the Protection of Human Rights and Fundamental Freedoms (adopted 4 November 1950, entered into force 3 September 1953) CETS No 5

Convention on the Elimination of All Forms of Discrimination against Women (adopted 18 December 1979, entered into force 3 September 1981) 1249 UNTS 1

Convention on the Prevention and Punishment of the Crime of Genocide (adopted 9 December 1948, entered into force 12 January 1951) 78 UNTS 278

Convention on the Recognition and Enforcement of Foreign Arbitral Awards (adopted 10 June 1958, entered into force 7 June 1959) 330 UNTS 3

Convention on the Settlement of Investment Disputes between States and Nationals of other States (adopted 18 March 1965, entered into force 14 October 1966) 575 UNTS 159

Convention on Third Party Liability in the Field of Nuclear Energy (adopted 29 July 1960, entered into force 1 April 1968) 956 UNTS 251

Criminal Law Convention on Corruption (adopted 27 January 1999, entered into force 1 July 2002) 2216 UNTS 225

Declaration of the Government of the Democratic and Popular Republic of Algeria concerning the Settlement of Claims by the Government of the United States of America and the Government of the Islamic Republic of Iran, Algiers Accords (19 January 1981) ‹https://iusct.com/wp-content/uploads/2021/02/1-General-Declaration_.pdf› accessed 7 December 2021

Dominican Republic-Central America FTA (adopted 5 August 2004, entered into force 1 March 2006) ‹https://investmentpolicy.unctad.org/international-investment-agreements/treaty-files/2482/download› accessed 7 December 2021

Draft Pan-African Investment Code E/ECA/COE/35/18, AU/STC/FMEPI/EXP/18(II) (26 March 2016)

ECOWAS Supplementary Act A/SA.3/12/08 Adopting Community Rules on Investment and the Modalities for their Implementation with ECOWAS (adopted 19 December 2008, entered into force 19 January 2009)

EU-Singapore Investment Protection Agreement (adopted 15 October 2018) ‹https://investmentpolicy.unctad.org/international-investment-agreements/treaty-files/5714/download› accessed 7 December 2021

EU-South Korea Free Trade Agreement (adopted 6 October 2010, entered into force 13 December 2015) ‹https://investmentpolicy.unctad.org/international-investment-agreements/treaty-files/2602/download› accessed 7 December 2021

EU-Vietnam FTA (adopted 30 June 2019, entered into force 1 August 2020) ‹https://policy.trade.ec.europa.eu/eu-trade-relationships-country-and-region/countries-and-regions/vietnam/eu-vietnam-agreement/texts-agreements_en› accessed 7 December 2021

EU-Vietnam Investment Protection Agreement (adopted 30 June 2019) ‹https://investmentpolicy.unctad.org/international-investment-agreements/treaty-files/5868/download› accessed 7 December 2021

Geneva Convention for the Amelioration of the Condition of the Wounded and Sick in Armed Forces in the Field (adopted 12 August 1949, entered into force 21 October 1950) 75 UNTS 31

Germany-Poland BIT (adopted 10 November 1989, entered into force 24 February 1991, date of termination 18 October 2019) ‹https://investmentpolicy.unctad.org/international-investment-agreements/treaty-files/1393/download› accessed 7 December 2021

Ghana Model BIT (2008) ‹https://investmentpolicy.unctad.org/international-investment-agreements/treaty-files/2866/download› accessed 7 December 2021

Ghana-Germany BIT (adopted 24 February 1995, entered into force 23 November 1998) ‹https://investmentpolicy.unctad.org/international-investment-agreements/treaty-files/1328/download› accessed 7 December 2021

Greece-Romania BIT (adopted 23 May 1997, entered into force 11 June 1998) ‹https://edit.wti.org/document/show/f236f60e-3166-4763-a8bc-00bee9e4fc18› accessed 7 December 2021

ILO Convention (No 98) Concerning the Application of the Principles of the Right to Organise and To Bargain Collectively (adopted 1 July 1949, entered into force 19 July 1951) 96 UNTS 257

ILO Convention (No 105) Concerning the Abolition of Forced Labour (adopted 25 June 1957, entered into force 17 January 1959) 320 UNTS 291

ILO Convention (No 169) Concerning Indigenous and Tribal Peoples in Independent Countries (adopted 27 June 1989, entered into force 5 September 1991) 1650 UNTS 383

India Model BIT (28 December 2015) ‹https://investmentpolicy.unctad.org/international-investment-agreements/treaty-files/3560/download› accessed 7 December 2021

Inter-American Convention against Corruption (adopted 29 March 1996, entered into force 6 March 1997) 35 ILM 724

International Convention on Civil Liability for Oil Pollution Damage (adopted 29 November 1969, entered into force 19 June 1975) 973 UNTS 3

International Convention on the Suppression and Punishment of the Crime of Apartheid (adopted 30 November 1973, entered into force 18 July 1976) 1015 UNTS 243

International Covenant on Civil and Political Rights (adopted 16 December 1966, entered into force 23 March 1976) 999 UNTS 171

International Covenant on Economic, Social and Cultural Rights (adopted 16 December 1966, entered into force 3 January 1976) 993 UNTS 3

Investment Agreement for the COMESA Common Investment Area (adopted 23 May 2007) ‹https://investmentpolicy.unctad.org/international-investment-agreements/treaty-files/3092/download› accessed 7 December 2021

Netherlands Model BIT (22 March 2019) ‹https://investmentpolicy.unctad.org/international-investment-agreements/treaty-files/5832/download› accessed 7 December 2021

North American Free Trade Agreement (adopted 18 December 1992, entered into force 1 January 1994, date of termination 1 July 2020) ‹https://investmentpolicy.unctad.org/international-investment-agreements/treaty-files/2412/download› accessed 7 December 2021

OECD Convention on Combating Bribery of Foreign Public Officials in International Business Transactions (adopted 17 December 1997, entered into force 15 February 1999) 2802 UNTS 225

Reciprocal Investment Promotion and Protection Agreement Between the Government of the Kingdom of Morocco and the Government of the Federal Republic of Nigeria (adopted 3 December 2016) ‹https://investmentpolicy.unctad.org/international-investment-agreements/treaty-files/5409/download› accessed 7 December 2021

Rome Statute of the International Criminal Court (adopted 17 July 1998, entered into force 1 July 2002) 2187 UNTS 3

Southern African Development Community, Model Bilateral Investment Treaty Template with Commentary (July 2012) ‹https://www.iisd.org/itn/wp-content/uploads/2012/10/sadc-model-bit-template-final.pdf› accessed 7 December 2021

The Energy Charter Treaty (adopted 17 December 1994, entered into force 16 April 1998) 2080 UNTS 95

Transpacific Partnership (adopted 4 February 2016) ‹https://investmentpolicy.unctad.org/international-investment-agreements/treaty-files/3573/download› accessed 7 December 2021

Treaty between the United States of America and the Republic of Ecuador concerning the Encouragement and Reciprocal Protection of Investment (adopted 27 August 1993, entered into force 11 May 1997, date of termination 18 May 2018) ‹https://investmentpolicy.unctad.org/international-investment-agreements/treaty-files/1065/download› accessed 7 December 2021

Ukraine-Germany BIT (adopted 15 February 1993, entered into force 29 June 1996) ‹https://investmentpolicy.unctad.org/international-investment-agreements/treaty-files/1442/download› accessed 7 December 2021

United Nations Convention against Corruption (adopted 31 October 2003, entered into force 14 December 2005) 2349 UNTS 41

United Nations Convention on the Law of the Sea (adopted 10 December 1982, entered into force 16 November 1994) 1833 UNTS 396

US-Colombia Trade Promotion Agreement (adopted 22 November 2006, entered into force 15 May 2012) ‹https://investmentpolicy.unctad.org/international-investment-agreements/treaty-files/2737/download› accessed 7 December 2021

US-Korea FTA (adopted 30 June 2007, entered into force 15 March 2012) ‹https://www.iisd.org/toolkits/sustainability-toolkit-for-trade-negotiators/wp-content/uploads/2016/09/US-Korea.pdf› accessed 7 December 2021

US-Peru Trade Promotion Agreement (adopted 12 April 2006, entered into force 1 February 2009) ‹https://investmentpolicy.unctad.org/international-investment-agreements/treaty-files/2721/download› accessed 7 December 2021

US-Rwanda BIT (adopted 19 February 2008, entered into force 1 January 2012) ‹https://investmentpolicy.unctad.org/international-investment-agreements/treaty-files/2241/download› accessed 7 December 2021

US-Uruguay BIT (adopted 4 November 2005, entered into force 31 October 2006) ‹https://investmentpolicy.unctad.org/international-investment-agreements/treaty-files/2380/download› accessed 7 December 2021

Vienna Convention on Civil Liability for Nuclear Damage (adopted 21 May 1963, entered into force 12 November 1977) 1063 UNTS 265

Vienna Convention on Consular Relations (adopted 24 April 1963, entered into force 19 March 1967) 596 UNTS 261

Vienna Convention on the Law of Treaties (adopted 22 May 1969, entered into force 27 January 1980) 1155 UNTS 331

WHO Framework Convention on Tobacco Control (adopted 21 May 2003, entered into force 27 February 2005) 2302 UNTS 166

Table of Declarations and Documents of International Organisations

Committee on Economic, Social and Cultural Rights 'General Comment No 3: The Nature of States Parties' Obligations (Art 2, Para 1, of the Covenant)' (14 December 1990) UN Doc E/1991/23

Council of the European Union 'Negotiating Directives for a Convention Establishing a Multilateral Court for the Settlement of Investment Disputes' (1 March 2018) 12981/17 ADD 1

IBRD 'Report of the Executive Directors on the Convention of the Settlement of Investment Disputes Between States and Nationals of Other States' (18 March 1965) ICSID/15/Rev.1, 35–49

ILC 'Articles on Responsibility of States for Internationally Wrongful Acts, with Commentaries' (53rd session of the International Law Commission, 23 April-1 June and 2 July 2001) (2001) II(2) Yearbook of the International Law Commission, 31

ILC 'Draft Articles on the Responsibility of International Organizations' (2011) ‹http://legal.un.org/ilc/texts/instruments/english/draft_articles/9_11_2011.pdf› accessed 7 December 2021

ILC 'Draft Articles on the Responsibility of International Organizations, with Commentaries' ‹http://legal.un.org/ilc/texts/instruments/english/commentaries/9_11_2011.pdf› accessed 7 December 2021

ILC 'Fragmentation of International Law: Difficulties Arising from the Diversification and Expansion of International Law, Report of the Study Group of the International Law Commission, Finalized by Martti Koskenniemi' (13 April 2006) UN Doc. A/CN.4/L.682

ILC 'Principles of International Law Recognized in the Charter of the Nürnberg Tribunal and in the Judgment of the Tribunal' [1950] Yearbook of the International Law Commission, vol II 374

ILC 'Report of the International Law Commission on the Work of Its Twenty-Second Session, 4 May-10 July 1970' UN Doc A/8010/Rev.1

ILC 'Second Report on State Responsibility, by Mr. James Crawford, Special Rapporteur' (17 March, 1 and 30 April, 19 July 1999) UN Doc A/CN.4/498 and Add.1 – 4

ILC 'Sixth Report on Diplomatic Protection, by Mr. John Dugard, Special Rapporteur' (11 August 2004) UN Doc A/CN.4/546

ILO 'Declaration on Fundamental Principles and Rights at Work' (18 June 1998) adopted by the International Labour Conference at its Eighty-sixth Session, Geneva, 37 ILM 1233

ILO 'Tripartite Declaration of Principles Concerning Multinational Enterprises and Social Policy' (16 November 1977) adopted by the Governing Body of the International Labour Office at its 204th Session (Geneva, November 1977) and amended at its 279th (November 2000), 295th (March 2006) and 329th (March 2017) Sessions, (1978) 17 ILM 422 ‹www.ilo.org/wcmsp5/groups/public/---ed_emp/---emp_ent/---multi/documents/publication/wcms_094386.pdf› accessed 7 December 2021

OECD 'Guidelines for Multinational Enterprises' (2011) ‹http://dx.doi.org/10.1787/9789264115415-en› accessed 7 December 2021

Office of the UN High Commissioner for Human Rights 'Frequently Asked Questions About the Guiding Principles on Business and Human Rights' (2014) HR/PUB/14/3

UN 'Global Compact' ‹www.unglobalcompact.org/what-is-gc/mission/principles› accessed 7 December 2021

UN Commission on Human Rights 'Human Rights, Trade and Investment, Report of the High Commissioner for Human Rights' (2 July 2003) UN Doc E/CN.4/Sub.2/2003/9 ‹http://daccess-ods.un.org/access.nsf/Get?Open&DS=E/CN.4/Sub.2/2003/9&Lang=E› accessed 7 December 2021

UN Commission on Human Rights 'Norms on the Responsibilities of Transnational Corporations and Other Business Enterprises with Regard to Human Rights' (13 August 2003) UN Doc E/CN.4/Sub.2/2003/12/Rev.2 (2003)

UN Human Rights Council 'Elaboration of an Internationally Legally Binding Instrument on Transnational Corporations and Other Business Enterprises with Respect to Human Rights' (14 July 2014) UN Doc A/HRC/RES/26/9

UN Human Rights Council 'Elements for the Draft Legally Binding Instrument on Transnational Corporations and Other Business Enterprises with Respect to Human Rights' (29 September 2017) ‹www.ohchr.org/Documents/HRBodies/HRCouncil/WGTransCorp/Session3/LegallyBindingInstrumentTNCs_OBEs.pdf› accessed 7 December 2021

UN Human Rights Council 'Guiding Principles on Business and Human Rights Implementing the United Nations "Protect, Respect and Remedy" Framework' (2011) UN Doc HRC/RES/17/4

UN Human Rights Council 'Protect, Respect and Remedy: A Framework for Business and Human Rights. Report of the Special Representative of the Secretary-General on the Issue of Human Rights and Transnational Corporations and Other Business Enterprises, John Ruggie' (7 April 2008) UN Doc A/HRC/8/5

UN Human Rights Council 'Report of the Independent International Commission of Inquiry on the Syrian Arab Republic' (22 February 2012) UN Doc A/HRC/19/69

UN Human Rights Council 'Report of the Working Group on the Issue of Human Rights and Transnational Corporations and Other Business Enterprises' (2 May 2018) UN Doc A/HRC/38/48

UNCITRAL 'Arbitration Rules (With New Article 1, Paragraph 4, as Adopted in 2013)' (16 December 2013) UN Doc A/RES/68/109

UNCITRAL 'Arbitration Rules' (15 December 1976) UN Doc A/40/17

UNCITRAL 'Model Law on International Commercial Arbitration 1985 (With Amendments as Adopted in 2006)' UN Doc A/40/17, Annex I and UN Doc A/61/17, Annex I

UNCITRAL 'Possible Reform of Investor-State Dispute Settlement (ISDS), Multiple Proceedings and Counterclaims' (22 January 2020) UN Doc A/CN.9/WG.III/WP.193

UNCTAD 'Development Indications of International Investment Agreements, IIA Monitor No. 2' (2007) UNCTAD/WEB/ITE/IIA/2007/2

UNCTAD 'IIA Mapping Project' ‹https://investmentpolicy.unctad.org/international-investment-agreements/iia-mapping› accessed 7 December 2021

UNCTAD 'Investment Policy Framework for Sustainable Development' (2015) UNCTAD/DIAE/PCB/2015/5

UNGA 'Formulation of the Nuremberg Principles' (12 December 1950) UN Doc A/RES/488 (V)

UNGA 'Human Rights-Compatible International Investment Agreements. Report of the Working Group on the Issue of Human Rights and Transnational Corporations and Other Business Enterprises' (27 July 2021) UN Doc A/76/238

UNGA 'Responsibility of States for Internationally Wrongful Acts' (12 December 2001) UN Doc A/RES/56/83

UNGA 'Rio Declaration on Environment and Development' (12 August 1992) UN Doc A/CONF.151/26 (Vol. I)

UNGA 'Towards Global Partnerships: A Principle-Based Approach to Enhanced Cooperation Between the United Nations and All Relevant Partners' (20 December 2013) UN Doc A/RES/68/234

UNGA 'Transforming Our World: The 2030 Agenda for Sustainable Development' (21 October 2015) UN A/RES/70/1

UNGA 'United Nations Declaration Against Corruption and Bribery in International Commercial Transactions' (21 February 1997) UN Doc A/RES/51/191

UNGA 'United Nations Declaration on the Rights of Indigenous Peoples' (13 September 2007) UN Doc A/RES/61/295

UNGA 'Universal Declaration of Human Rights' (10 December 1948) UN Doc A/RES/217 (III) A

UNSC 'The Situation in Somalia' (8 April 2003) UN Doc S/RES/1474 (2003)

Table of Cases

International Arbitrations

ADC Affiliate Limited and ADC & ADMC Management Limited v The Republic of Hungary, ICSID Case No. ARB/03/16, Award (2 October 2006)

Alasdair Ross Anderson et al v Republic of Costa Rica, ICSID Case No. ARB(AF)/07/3, Award (19 May 2010)

Alpha Projektholding GmbH v Ukraine, ICSID Case No. ARB/07/16, Award (8 November 2010)

Álvarez y Marín Corporación S.A. and Others v República de Panamá, ICSID Case No. ARB/15/14, Laudo (12 October 2018)

American Manufacturing & Trading, Inc. v Republic of Zaire, ICSID Case No. ARB/93/1, Award (21 February 1997)

Antoine Goetz & Consorts and S.A. Affinange des Métaux v Republic of Burundi (Goetz II), ICSID Case No. ARB/01/2, Sentence (21 June 2012)

Antoine Goetz et consorts v République du Burundi (Goetz I), ICSID Case No. ARB/95/3, Award (10 February 1999)

Asian Agricultural Products Ltd. v Republic of Sri Lanka, ICSID Case No. ARB/87/3, Final Award (27 June 1990)

Austrian Airlines v The Slovak Republic, Final Award (UNCITRAL, 9 October 2009)

Award in the Arbitration Regarding the Delimitation of the Maritime Boundary Between Guyana and Suriname (Guyana v Suriname) (Award) (2007) 30 RIAA 1

Azurix Corp. v The Argentine Republic, ICSID Case No. ARB/01/12, Award (14 July 2006)

Bear Creek Mining Corporation v Republic of Perú, ICSID Case No. ARB/14/21, Partial Dissenting Opinion by Professor Philippe Sands QC (12 September 2017)

Bear Creek Mining Corporation v Republic of Perú, ICSID Case No. ARB/14/21, Award (30 November 2017)

BG Group Plc. v Republic of Argentina, Final Award (UNCITRAL, 24 December 2007)

Biloune and Marine Drive Complex Ltd v Ghana Investments Centre and the Government of Ghana, Award on Jurisdiction and Liability (UNCITRAL, 27 October 1989)

Biwater Gauff (Tanzania) Ltd v United Republic of Tanzania, ICSID Case No. ARB/05/22, Award (24 July 2008)

Blusun S.A, Jean-Pierre Lecorcier and Michael Stein v Italian Republic, ICSID Case No. ARB/14/3, Award (27 December 2016)

Bureau Veritas, Inspection, Valuation, Assessment and Control, BIVAC B.V. v The Republic of Paraguay, ICSID Case No. ARB/07/9, Decision of the Tribunal on Objections to Jurisdiction (29 May 2009)

Burlington Resources Inc. v Republic of Ecuador, ICSID Case No. ARB/08/5, Decision on Liability (14 December 2012)

Burlington Resources Inc. v Republic of Ecuador, ICSID Case No. ARB/08/5, Decision on Counterclaims (7 February 2017)

Ceskoslovenska Obchodni Banka, A.S. v The Slovak Republic, ICSID Case No. ARB/97/4, Decision of the Tribunal on Objections to Jurisdiction (24 May 1999)

Charanne and Construction Investments v The Kingdom of Spain, SCC Case No. V 062/2012, Award (21 January 2016)

Chemtura Corporation v Government of Canada, Award (UNCITRAL, 2 August 2010)

Chevron Corporation (USA) and Texaco Petroleum Corporation (USA) v The Republic of Ecuador, Interim Award (UNCITRAL, 1 December 2008)

CMS Gas Transmission Company v The Argentine Republic, ICSID Case No. ARB/01/8, Decision of the Ad Hoc Committee on the Application for Annulment of the Argentine Republic (25 September 2007)

Compañía del Desarrollo de Santa Elena, S.A. v The Republic of Costa Rica, ICSID Case No. ARB/96/1, Final Award (17 February 2000)

Computer Sciences Corporation v The Government of the Islamic Republic of Iran and Others (Award) (1986) 10 Iran-USCTR 269

Consortium R.F.C.C. v Kingdom of Morocco, ICSID Case No. ARB/00/6, Decision on Jurisdiction (16 July 2001)

Consorzio Groupement L.E.S.I.-DIPENTA v People's Democratic Republic of Algeria, ICSID Case No. ARB/03/08, Award (10 January 2005)

Copper Mesa Mining Corporation v The Republic of Ecuador, PCA Case No. 2012–2, Award (15 March 2016)

Corn Products International, Inc. v United Mexican States, ICSID Case No. ARB(AF)/04/01, Decision on Responsibility (15 January 2008)

Cortec Mining Kenya Limited, Cortec (PTY) Limited and Stirling Capital Limited v Republic of Kenya, ICSID Case No. ARB/15/29, Award (22 October 2018)

David Aven et al. v The Republic of Costa Rica, Case No. UNCT/15/3, Final Award (UNCITRAL, 18 September 2018)

Desert Line Projects LLC v The Republic of Yemen, ICSID Case No. ARB/05/17, Award (6 February 2008)

Duke Energy Electroquil Partners & Electroquil S.A. v Republic of Ecuador, ICSID Case No. ARB/04/19, Award (18 August 2008)

EDF International S.A. SAUR International S.A. and León Participaciones Argentinas S.A. v Argentine Republic, ICSID Case No. ARB/03/23, Award (11 June 2012)

Electrabel S.A. v Republic of Hungary, ICSID Case No. ARB/07/19, Decision on Jurisdiction, Applicable Law and Liability (30 November 2012)

Emilio Agustín Maffezini v The Kingdom of Spain, ICSID Case No. ARB/97/7, Decisión del Tribunal sobre Excepciones a la Jurisdicción (25 January 2000)

Emilio Agustín Maffezini v The Kingdom of Spain, ICSID Case No. ARB/97/7, Award (13 November 2000)

Emmis International Holding, B.V. Emmis Radio Operating, B.V. MEM Magyar Electronic Media Kereskedelmi és Szolgáltató Kft. v The Republic of Hungary, ICSID Case No. ARB/12/2, Award (16 April 2014)

EuroGas Inc. and Belmont Resources Inc. v Slovak Republic, ICSID Case No. ARB/14/14, Procedural Order No. 3: Decision on the Parties' Request for Provisional Measures (23 June 2015)

Fraport AG Frankfurt Airport Services Worldwide v Republic of Philippines, ICSID Case No. ARB/03/25, Decision on the Application for Annulment of Fraport AG Frankfurt Airport Services Worldwide (23 December 2010)

Fraport AG Frankfurt Airport Services Worldwide v The Republic of Philippines (Fraport I), ICSID Case No. ARB/03/25, Award (16 August 2007)

Fraport AG Frankfurt Airport Services Worldwide v The Republic of Philippines (Fraport I), ICSID Case No. ARB/03/25, Dissenting Opinion of Mr Bernardo Cremades (16 August 2007)

Fraport AG Frankfurt Airport Services Worldwide v The Republic of the Philippines (Fraport II), ICSID Case No. ARB/11/12, Award (10 December 2014)

Gabon v Société Serete S.A. ICSID Case No. ARB/76/1, Order Taking Note of the Discontinuance Issued by the Tribunal (27 February 1978)

Gas Natural SDG, S.A. v The Argentine Republic, ICSID Case No. ARB/03/10, Decision of the Tribunal on Preliminary Questions of Jurisdiction (17 June 2005)

GEA Group Aktiengesellschaft v Ukraine, ICSID Case No. ARB/08/16, Award (31 March 2011)

Glamis Gold, Ltd. v The United States of America, Award (UNCITRAL, 8 June 2009)

Global Trading Resource Corp. and Globex International, Inc. v Ukraine, ICSID Case No. ARB/09/11, Award (1 December 2010)

Government of the Province of East Kalimantan v PT Kaltim Prima Coal and Others, ICSID Case No. ARB/07/3, Award on Jurisdiction (28 December 2009)

Grand River Enterprises Six Nations, Ltd. and Others v United States of America, Award (UNCITRAL, 12 January 2011)

Gustav FW Hamester GmbH & Co KG v Republic of Ghana, ICSID Case No. ARB/07/24, Award (18 June 2010)

Helnan International Hotels A/S v Arab Republic of Egypt, ICSID Case No. ARB/05/19, Decision of the Tribunal on Objection to Jurisdiction (17 October 2006)

Hesham Talaat M. Al-Warraq v The Republic of Indonesia, Award on Respondent's Preliminary Objections to Jurisdiction and Admissibility of the Claims (UNCITRAL, 21 June 2012)

Hesham Talaat M. Al-Warraq v The Republic of Indonesia, Final Award (UNCITRAL, 15 December 2014)

Hochtief AG v The Argentine Republic, ICSID Case No. ARB/07/31, Decision on Jurisdiction (24 October 2011)

Hussein Nuaman Soufraki v The United Arab Emirates, ICSID Case No. ARB/02/7, Decision of the ad hoc Committee on the Application for Annulment of Mr Soufraki (5 June 2007)

Impregilo S.p.A. v Argentine Republic, ICSID Case No. ARB/07/17, Award (21 June 2011)

Inceysa Vallisoletana, S.L. v Republic of El Salvador, ICSID Case No. ARB/03/26, Award (2 August 2006)

Inmaris Perestroika Sailing Maritime Services GmbH and Others v Ukraine, ICSID Case No. ARB/08/8, Decision on Jurisdiction (8 March 2010)

Inmaris Perestroika Sailing Maritime Services GmbH and Others v Ukraine, ICSID Case No. ARB/08/8, Award (1 March 2012)

Ioannis Kardassopoulos v The Republic of Georgia, ICSID Case No. ARB/05/18, Decision on Jurisdiction (6 July 2007)

Jan de Nul N.V. and Dreging International N.V. v Arab Republic of Egypt, ICSID Case No. ARB/04/13, Decision on Jurisdiction (16 June 2006)

Joseph Charles Lemire v Ukraine, ICSID Case No. ARB/06/18, Award (28 March 2011)

Joy Mining Machinery Limited v Arab Republic of Egypt, ICSID Case No. ARB/03/11, Award on Jurisdiction (6 August 2004)

Klöckner Industrie-Anlagen GmbH, Klöckner Belge S.A. et Klöckner Handelsmaatschappij v République unie du Cameroun et Sté camerounaise des engrais (SOCAME), ICSID Case No. ARB/81/2, Sentence (21 October 1983)

KT Asia Investment Group B.V. v Republic of Kazakhstan, ICSID Case No. ARB/09/8, Award (17 October 2013)

L.E.S.I. S.p.A. and ASTALDI S.p.A. v People's Democratic Republic of Algeria, ICSID Case No. ARB/05/3, Decision (12 July 2006)

L.F.H. Neer and Pauline Neer (U.S.A.) v United Mexican States (Decision) (1926) 4 Reports of International Arbitral Awards 60

LG&E Energy Corp. LG&E Capital Corp. and LG&E International, Inc. v Argentine Republic, ICSID Case No. ARB/02/1, Decision on Liability (3 October 2006)

LG&E Energy Corp. LG&E Capital Corp. and LG&E International, Inc. v Argentine Republic, ICSID Case No. ARB/02/1, Award (25 July 2007)

Limited Liability Company AMTO v Ukraine, SCC Case No 080/2005, Final Award (26 March 2008)

Malaysian Historical Salvors SDN BHD v The Government of Malaysia, ICSID Case No. ARB/05/10, Dissenting Opinion of Judge Mohamed Shahabuddeen (19 February 2009)

Malaysian Historical Salvors SDN BHD v The Government of Malaysia, ICSID Case No. ARB/05/10, Decision on the Application for Annulment (16 April 2009)

Malaysian Historical Salvors SDN, BHD v The Government of Malaysia, ICSID Case No. ARB/05/10, Award on Jurisdiction (17 May 2007)

Mamidoil Jetoil Greek Petroleum Products Societe S.A. v Republic of Albania, ICSID Case No. ARB/11/24, Award (30 March 2015)

Marion Unglaube and Reinhard Unglaube v Republic of Costa Rica, ICSID Case No. ARB/08/1, ARB/09/20, Award (16 May 2012)

Metalclad Corporation v The United Mexican States, ICSID Case No. ARB(AF)/97/1, Award (30 August 2000)

Methanex Corporation v United States of America, Final Award of the Tribunal on Jurisdiction and Merits (UNCITRAL, 3 August 2005)

Millicom International Operations B.V. and Sentel GSM S.A. v The Republic of Senegal, ICSID Case No. ARB/08/20, Decision on Jurisdiction of the Arbitral Tribunal (16 July 2010)

Mr. Franck Charles Arif v Republic of Moldova, ICSID Case No. ARB/11/23, Award (8 April 2013)

Mr. Patrick Mitchell v Democratic Republic of the Congo, ICSID Case No. ARB/99/7, Decision on the Stay of Enforcement of the Award (9 February 2004)

MTD Equity Sdn. Bhd. and MTD Chile S.A. v Republic of Chile, ICSID Case No. ARB/01/7, Award (25 May 2004)

MTD Equity Sdn. Bhd. and MTD Chile S.A. v Republic of Chile, ICSID Case No. ARB/01/7, Decision on Annulment (21 March 2007)

National Grid PLC v The Argentine Republic, Award (UNCITRAL, 3 November 2008)

National Grid PLC v The Argentine Republic, Decision on Jurisdiction (UNCITRAL, 20 June 2006)

Occidental Petroleum Corporation and Occidental Exploration and Production Company v Republic of Ecuador, ICSID Case No. ARB/06/11, Award (5 October 2012)

Oxus Gold v Republic of Uzbekistan, Award (UNCITRAL, 17 December 2015)

Pantechniki S.A. Contractors & Engineers (Greece) v Republic of Albania, ICSID Case No. ARB/07/21, Award (30 July 2009)

Perenco Ecuador Ltd. v The Republic of Ecuador, ICSID Case No. ARB/08/6, Interim Decision on the Environmental Counterclaim (11 August 2015)

Perenco Ecuador Ltd. v The Republic of Ecuador, ICSID Case No. ARB/08/6, Decision on Jurisdiction (30 June 2011)

Perenco Ecuador Ltd. v The Republic of Ecuador, ICSID Case No. ARB/08/6, Decision on Remaining Issues of Jurisdiction and on Liability (12 September 2014)

Perenco Ecuador Ltd. v The Republic of Ecuador, ICSID Case No. ARB/08/6, Award (27 September 2019)

Philip Morris Brands Sàrl, Philip Morris Products S.A. and Abal Hermanos S.A. v Oriental Republic of Uruguay, ICSID Case No. ARB/10/7, Award (8 July 2016)

Phoenix Action, Ltd. v The Czech Republic, ICSID Case No. ARB/06/5, Award (15 April 2009)

Piero Foresti and Others v The Republic of South Africa, ICSID Case No. ARB(AF)/07/1, Award (4 August 2010)

Plama Consortium Limited v Republic of Bulgaria, ICSID Case No. ARB/03/24, Decision on Jurisdiction (8 February 2005)

Plama Consortium Limited v Republic of Bulgaria, ICSID Case No. ARB/03/24, Award (27 August 2008)

PSEG Global Inc. The North American Coal Corporation, and Konya Ilgin Elektrik Üretim ve Ticaret Limited Sirketi v Republic of Turkey, ICSID Case No. ARB/02/5, Decision on Jurisdiction (4 June 2004)

Quiborax S.A. and Non Metallic Minerals S.A. v Plurinational State of Bolivia, ICSID Case No. ARB/06/2, Award (16 September 2015)

Quiborax S.A., Non Metallic Minerals S.A. and Allan Fosk Kaplún v Plurinational State of Bolivia, ICSID Case No. ARB/06/2, Decision on Jurisdiction (27 September 2012)

Railroad Development Corporation (RDC) v Republic of Guatemala, ICSID Case No. ARB/07/23, Second Decision on Objections to Jurisdiction (18 May 2010)

RSM Production Corporation v Grenada, ICSID Case No. ARB/05/14, Award (13 March 2009)

Rumeli Telekom A.S. and Telsim Mobil Telekomikasyon Hizmetleri A.S. v Republic of Kazakhstan, ICSID Case No. ARB/05/16, Award (29 July 2008)

Rusoro Mining Limited v The Bolivarian Republic of Venezuela, ICSID Case No. ARB(AF)/12/5, Award (22 August 2016)

S.D. Myers, Inc. v Government of Canada, Partial Award (UNCITRAL, 13 November 2000)

Saba Fakes v Republic of Turkey, ICSID Case No. ARB/07/20, Award (14 July 2010)

Saipem S.p.A. v The People's Republic of Bangladesh, ICSID Case No. ARB/05/07, Decision on Jurisdiction and Recommendation on Provisional Measures (21 March 2007)

Saipem S.p.A. v The People's Republic of Bangladesh, ICSID Case No. ARB/05/7, Award (30 June 2009)

Salini Costruttori S.P.A. and Italstrade S.P.A. v Kingdom of Morocco, ICSID Case No. ARB/00/4, Decision on Jurisdiction (23 July 2001)

Salini Costruttori S.p.A. and Italstrade S.p.A. v The Hashemite Kingdom of Jordan, ICSID Case No. ARB/02/13, Decision on Jurisdiction (15 November 2004)

Saluka Investments BV v The Czech Republic, Decision on Jurisdiction over the Czech Republic's Counterclaim (UNCITRAL, 7 May 2004)

Saluka Investments BV v The Czech Republic, Partial Award (UNCITRAL, 17 March 2006)

SAUR International S.A. v Republic of Argentina, ICSID Case No. ARB/04/4, Decision on Jurisdiction and Liability (6 June 2012)

Señor Tza Yap Shum v La República del Perú, ICSID Case No. ARB/07/6, Decisión sobre Jurisdicción y Competencia (19 June 2009)

Sergei Paushok, CJSC Golden East Company, CJSC Vostokneftegaz Company v The Government of Mongolia, Award on Jurisdiction and Liability (UNCITRAL, 28 April 2011)

SGS Société Générale de Surveillance S.A. v Islamic Republic of Pakistan, ICSID Case No. ARB/01/13, Procedural Order No. 2 (16 October 2002)

Siemens A.G. v The Argentine Republic, ICSID Case No. ARB/02/8, Award (6 February 2007)

Siemens A.G. v The Argentine Republic, ICSID Case No. ARB/02/8, Decision on Jurisdiction (3 August 2004)

South American Silver Limited (Bermuda) v The Plurinational State of Bolivia, PCA Case No. 2013–15, Award (22 November 2018)

Southern Pacific Properties (Middle East) Limited v Arab Republic of Egypt, ICSID Case No. ARB/84/3, Award on the Merits (20 May 1992)

Suez, Sociedad General de Aguas de Barcelona S.A. and Vivendi Universal S.A. v The Argentine Republic, ICSID Case No. ARB/03/19, Decision on Jurisdiction (3 August 2006)

Suez, Sociedad General de Aguas de Barcelona S.A. and Vivendi Universal S.A. v The Argentine Republic, ICSID Case No. ARB/03/19, Decision on Liability (30 July 2010)

Swembalt AB, Sweden v The Republic of Latvia, Decision (UNCITRAL, 23 October 2000)

Syridion Roussalis v Romania, ICSID Case No. ARB/06/1, Award (7 December 2011)

Syridion Roussalis v Romania, ICSID Case No. ARB/06/1, Declaration of Arbitrator Reisman (28 November 2011)

Tanzania Electric Supply Company Limited v Independent Power Tanzania Limited, ICSID Case No. ARB/98/8, Final Award (12 July 2001)

Tecnicas Medioambientales Tecmed S.A. v The United Mexican States, ICSID Case No. ARB (AF)/00/2, Award (29 May 2003)

Telenor Mobile Communications A.S. v The Republic of Hungary, ICSID Case No. ARB/04/15, Award (13 September 2006)

The Loewen Group, Inc. and Raymond L. Loewen v United States of America, ICSID Case No. ARB(AF)/98/3, Award (26 June 2003)

Tokios Tokelės v Ukraine, ICSID Case No. ARB/02/18, Decision on Jurisdiction (29 April 2004)

Toto Costruzioni Generali S.P.A. v Republic of Lebanon, ICSID Case No. ARB/07/12, Decision on Jurisdiction (11 September 2009)

Trail Smelter Case (United States/Canada) (Award) (1938 and 1941) 3 RIAA 1905

Urbaser S.A. and Consorcio de Aguas Bilbao Bizkaia, Bilbao Biskaia Ur Partzuergoa v The Argentine Republic, ICSID Case No. ARB/07/26, Decision on Jurisdiction (9 December 2012)

Urbaser S.A. and Consorcio de Aguas Bilbao Bizkaia, Bilbao Biskaia Ur Partzuergoa v The Argentine Republic, ICSID Case No. ARB/07/26, Award (8 December 2016)

Víctor Pey Casado and President Allende Foundation v Republic of Chile, ICSID Case No. ARB/98/2, Award (8 May 2008)

Vladimir Berschader and Moïse Berschader v The Russian Federation, SCC Case No 080/2004, Award (21 April 2006)

Vladislav Kim and Others v Republic of Uzbekistan, ICSID Case No. ARB/13/6, Decision on Jurisdiction (8 March 2017)

Waste Management, Inc. v United Mexican States, ICSID Case No. ARB(AF)/00/3, Award (30 April 2004)

Wena Hotels Limited v Arab Republic of Egypt, ICSID Case No. ARB/98/4, Decision (5 February 2002)

World Duty Free Company Limited v Republic of Kenya, ICSID Case No. ARB/00/7, Award (4 October 2006)

Yukos Universal Limited (Isle of Man) v The Russian Federation, PCA Case No. AA 227, Final Award (18 July 2014)

Yukos Universal Limited (Isle of Man) v The Russian Federation, PCA Case No. AA 227, Interim Award on Jurisdiction and Admissibility (UNCITRAL, 30 November 2009)

International Courts and Tribunals

Permanent Court of International Justice and International Court of Justice

Anglo-Iranian Oil Co. Case (United Kingdom v Iran) (Preliminary Objection) [1952] ICJ Rep 93

Application of the Interim Accord of 13 December 1995 (the former Yugoslav Republic of Macedonia v Greece) (Separate Opinion of Judge Simma) [2011] ICJ Rep 695

Case Concerning Avena and Other Mexican Nationals (Mexico v United States of America) (Judgment) [2004] ICJ Rep 12

Case Concerning Certain Questions of Mutual Assistance in Criminal Matters (Djibouti v France) (Judgment) [2008] ICJ Rep 177

Case Concerning Elettronica Sicula S.p.A. (ELSI) (USA v Italy) (Judgment) [1989] ICJ Rep 15

Case Concerning Military and Paramilitary Activities in and against Nicaragua (Nicaragua v United States of America) (Jurisdiction of the Court and Admissibility of the Application) [1984] ICJ Rep 392

Case Concerning Military and Paramilitary Activities in and against Nicaragua (Nicaragua v United States of America) (Dissenting Opinion of Judge Schwebel) [1986] ICJ Rep 259

Case Concerning Oil Platforms (Islamic Republic of Iran v United States of America) (Preliminary Objection) [1996] ICJ Rep 803

Case Concerning the Arrest Warrant of 11 April 2000 (Democratic Republic of the Congo v Belgium) (Dissenting Opinion of Judge van den Wyngaert) [2002] ICJ Rep 137

Case Concerning the Barcelona Traction, Light and Power Company, Limited (Belgium v Spain) (Second Phase) (Judgment) [1970] ICJ Rep 3

Case Concerning the Gabčikovo-Nagymaros Project (Hungary v Slovakia) (Judgment) [1997] ICJ Rep 7

Case Concerning the Payment in Gold of Brazilian Federal Loans Contracted in France (France v Brazil) (Judgment) [1929] PCIJ Rep Series A No 15

Case Concerning the Payment of Various Serbian Loans Issued in France (France v Yugoslavia) (Judgment) [1929] PCIJ Rep Series A No 20

Case of the Free Zones of Upper Savoy and the District of Gex (Switzerland v France) (Judgment) [1932] PCIJ Rep Series A/B No 46

Certain German Interests in Polish Upper Silesia (Germany v Poland) (Merits) [1926] PCIJ Rep Series A No 7

Certain Iranian Assets (Islamic Republic of Iran v United States of America) (Preliminary Objections) [2019] ICJ Rep 7

Dispute Regarding Navigational and Related Rights (Costa Rica v Nicaragua) (Judgment) [2009] ICJ Rep 213

Interhandel Case (Switzerland v USA) (Preliminary Objections) [1959] ICJ Rep 6

Interpretation of Peace Treaties with Bulgaria, Hungary and Romania (Second Phase) (Advisory Opinion) [1950] ICJ Rep 221

LaGrand Case (Germany v USA) (Judgment) [2001] ICJ Rep 466

Legality of the Use by a State of Nuclear Weapons in Armed Conflict (Advisory Opinion) [1996] ICJ Rep 66

Reparation for Injuries Suffered in the Service of the United Nations (Advisory Opinion) [1949] ICJ Rep 174

Rights of Minorities in Upper Silesia (Minority Schools) (Germany v Poland) (Judgment) [1928] PCIJ Rep Series A No 15

Status of Eastern Carelia (Advisory Opinion) [1923] PCIJ Rep Series B No 5

The Case of the S.S. 'Lotus' (France v Turkey) (Judgment) [1927] PCIJ Rep Series A No 10

The Corfu Channel Case (UK v Albania) (Preliminary Objection) [1948] ICJ Rep 15

The Diversion of Water From the Meuse (Netherlands v Belgium) (Dissenting Opinion of M. Anzilotti) [1937] PCIJ Rep Series A/B No 70

The Diversion of Water From the Meuse (Netherlands v Belgium) (Individual Opinion By Mr. Hudson) [1937] PCIJ Rep Series A/B No 70

The Mavrommatis Palestine Concessions (Greece v Britain) (Objection to the Jurisdiction of the Court) [1924] PCIJ Rep Series A No 2

International Criminal Tribunals

Prosecutor v Anto Furundžija (Judgement) IT-95–17/1-T (ICTY, 10 December 1998)

Prosecutor v Duško Tadić (Decision on the Defence Motion for Interlocutory Appeal on Jurisdiction) IT-94–1-AR72 (ICTY, 2 October 1995)

Prosecutor v Duško Tadić (Judgment) IT-94–1-T (ICTY, 7 May 1997)

The United States of America, the French Republic, the United Kingdom of Great Britain and Northern Ireland, and the Union of Soviet Socialist Republics v Hermann Wilhelm Göring and Others (Proceedings) (International Military Tribunal, 1948) XXII Trial of the Major War Criminals Before the International Military Tribunal

The United States of America, the Republic of China, the United Kingdom of Great Britain and Northern Ireland, the Union of Soviet Socialist Republics, the Commonwealth of Australia, Canada, the Republic of France, the Kingdom of the Netherlands, New Zealand, India, and the Commonwealth of the Philippines Against Araki, Sadao and Others (Judgment) (International Military Tribunal for the Far East, 4 November 1948) printed in Röling BV and Rüter CF (eds), *The Tokyo Judgment: The International Military Tribunal for the Far East (I.M.T.F.E.), 29 April 1946–12 November 1948* (University Press Amsterdam 1977)

International Tribunal for the Law of the Sea

Responsibilities and Obligations of States Sponsoring Persons and Entities with Respect to Activities in the Area (Advisory Opinion, 1 February 2011) ITLOS Rep 2011

WTO Dispute Settlement Body

United States—Standards for Reformulated and Conventional Gasoline (29 April 1996) WT/DS2/AB/R

UN Human Rights Committee

Lilian Celiberti de Casariego v Uruguay Comm No. R.13/56 (Individual Opinion of Mr. Christian Tomuschat) UN Doc Supp No 40 (A/36/40) 185 (1981) (UN Human Rights Committee, 29 July 1981)

M.A. v Italy Comm No. 117/1981 (Decision on Inadmissibility) UN Doc Supp No 40 (A/39/40) 190 (1981) (UN Human Rights Committee, 21 September 1981)

Sergio Euben Lopez Burgos v Uruguay Comm No R.12/52 (Individual Opinion of Mr. Christian Tomuschat) UN Doc Supp No 40 (A/36/40) 176 (1981) (UN Human Rights Committee, 29 July 1981)

European Court of Human Rights

Case of Brumărescu v Romania App no 28342/95, ECHR 1999-VII 201 (European Court of Human Rights, 28 October 1999)

Case of James and Others v The United Kingdom App no 8793/79, ECHR Series A no 98 (European Court of Human Rights, 21 February 1986)

Case of Kasymakhunov and Saybatalov v Russia App no 26261/05, 26377/06, ECLI:CE:ECHR:2013:0314JUD002626105 (European Court of Human Rights, 14 March 2013)

Case of Lawless v Ireland (No. 3) App no 332/57, ECHR Series A no 3 (European Court of Human Rights, 1 July 1961)

Case of Leroy v France App no 36109/03, ECLI:CE:ECHR:2008:1002JUD003610903 (European Court of Human Rights, 2 October 2008)

Case of Matos e Silva, Lda. and Others v Portugal App no 15777/89, ECHR 1996-IV (European Court of Human Rights, 16 September 1996)

Case of Mellacher and Others v Austria App no 10522/83, 11011/84, 11070/84, ECHR Series A no 169 (European Court of Human Rights, 19 December 1989)

Case of Paksas v Lithuania App no 34932/04, ECLI:CE:ECHR:2011:0106JUD003493204 (European Court of Human Rights, 6 January 2011)

Case of Pressos Compania Naviera S.A. and Others v Belgium App no 17849/91, ECHR Series A no 332 (European Court of Human Rights, 20 November 1995)

Case of Refah Partisi (the Welfare Party) and Others v Turkey App no 41340/98, 41342/98, 41343/98, 41344/98, 13.2.2003, ECHR 2003-II 267 (European Court of Human Rights, 13 February 2003)

Case of Stran Greek Refineries and Stratis Andreadis v Greece App no 13427/87, ECHR Series A no 301-B (European Court of Human Rights, 9 December 1994)

Case of United Communist Party of Turkey and Others v Turkey App no 19392/92, ECHR 1998-I (European Court of Human Rights, 30 January 1998)

Court of Justice of the European Union

Free Trade Agreement between the European Union and the Republic of Singapore (Opinion C-2/15) [2017] ECLI:EU:C:2017:376

Slovak Republic v Achmea BV (Case C-284/16) [2018] ECLI:EU:C:2018:158

Inter-American Court of Human Rights

Compulsory Membership in an Association Prescribed by Law for the Practice of Journalism (Arts 13 and 29 American Convention on Human Rights) OC-5/85 (Advisory Opinion) Inter-American Court of Human Rights Series A No 5 (13 November 1985)

Domestic Courts

Kiobel and Others v Royal Dutch Petroleum Co. and Others (2010) 621 F.3d 111 (US Court of Appeals for the Second Circuit)

Precision Instrument Mfg. Co. v Automotive Co. (1945) 324 U.S. 806 (US Supreme Court)

The Russian Federation v Veteran Petroleum Limited (2016) C/09/477160/HA ZA 15–1 (The Hague District Court)

United States v Alfried Felix Alwyn Krupp von Bohlen und Halbach and Others ('The Krupp Case') (1948) IX Trials of War Criminals Before the Nuernberg Military Tribunals Under Control Council Law No 10 (US Military Tribunal III)

United States v Karl Krauch and Others ('The Farben Case') (1948) VIII Trials of War Criminals Before the Nuernberg Military Tribunals Under Control Council Law No 10 (US Military Tribunal VI)

Bibliography

van Aaken A and Simsek B, 'Rewarding in International Law' (2021) 115(2) American Journal of International Law 195

Abbott KW and Snidal D, 'Hard and Soft Law in International Governance' (2000) 54(3) International Organization 421

Abel P, 'Menschenrechtsschutz durch Individualbeschwerdeverfahren: Ein regionaler Vergleich aus historischer, normativer und faktischer Perspektive' (2013) 51(3) Archiv des Völkerrechts 369

—— 'Comparative Conclusions on Arbitral Dispute Settlement in Trade-Labour Matters Under US FTAs' in Henner Gött (ed), *Labour Standards in International Economic Law* (Springer International Publishing 2018)

—— 'Counterclaims Based on International Human Rights Obligations of Investors in International Investment Arbitration: Fallacies and Potentials of the 2016 ICSID Urbaser v. Argentina Award' [2018] Brill Open Law 1

—— 'Negative Zuständigkeitskonflikte internationaler Gerichte durch Subsidiaritätsklauseln: Zur Bedeutung des Maritime Delimitation in the Indian Ocean-Urteils des IGH für die internationale Streitbeilegung' (2018) 78(2) Zeitschrift für ausländisches öffentliches Recht und Völkerrecht 339

Alston P, '"Core Labour Standards" and the Transformation of the International Labour Rights Regime' (2004) 15(3) European Journal of International Law 457

Alston P and Quinn G, 'The Nature and Scope of States Parties' Obligations Under the International Covenant on Economic, Social and Cultural Rights' (1987) 9 Human Rights Quarterly 156

Alston P and Robinson M (eds), *Human Rights and Development: Towards Mutual Reinforcement* (Oxford University Press 2005)

Alvarez JE, 'Are Corporations "Subjects" of International Law?' (2011) 9(1) Santa Clara Journal of International Law 1

—— 'ISDS Reform: The Long View' (2021) 36(2) ICSID Review 253

Alvarez JE and others (eds), *The Evolving International Investment Regime: Expectations, Realities, Options* (Oxford University Press 2011)

Amado JD, Kern JS and Rodriguez MD, *Arbitrating the Conduct of International Investors* (Cambridge University Press 2018)

Anderson AM and Beaumont B (eds), *The Investor-State Dispute Settlement System: Reform, Replace or Status Quo?* (Wolters Kluwer 2020)

de Andrade PP and Monebhurrun N, 'Mapping Investors' Environmental Commitments and Obligations' in Jean Ho and Mavluda Sattorova (eds), *Investors' International Law* (Hart 2021)

Anning M, 'Counterclaims Admissibility in Investment Arbitration' in Julien Chaisse, Leïla Choukroune and Sufian Jusoh (eds), *Handbook of International Investment Law and Policy* (Springer 2021)

Antonopoulos C, *Counterclaims Before the International Court of Justice* (T.M.C. Asser Press 2011)

Anzilotti D, *Cours de droit international: 1 Introduction, théories générales* (Sirey 1929)

Atanasova D, Martínez Benoit A and Ostransky J, 'The Legal Framework for Counterclaims in Investment Treaty Arbitration' (2014) 31(3) Journal of International Arbitration 357

Audit M and Schill SW (eds), *Transnational Law of Public Contracts* (Bruylant 2016)

Aust HP, 'Investment Protection and Sustainable Development: What Role for the Law of State Responsibility?' in Steffen Hindelang and Markus Krajewski (eds), *Shifting Paradigms in International Investment Law: More Balanced, Less Isolated, Increasingly Diversified* (Oxford University Press 2016)

Baetens F (ed), *Investment Law Within International Law: Integrationist Perspectives* (Cambridge University Press 2013)

Balcerzak F, *Investor – State Arbitration and Human Rights* (Brill Nijhoff 2017)

Baltag C (ed), *ICSID Convention After 50 Years: Unsettled Issues* (Wolters Kluwer 2017)

Bantekas I and Stein MA (eds), *The Cambridge Companion to Business & Human Rights Law* (Cambridge University Press 2021)

Baxi U, *The Future of Human Rights* (Oxford University Press 2002)

Beaulieu E and O'Neill K, 'The Economics of Foreign Direct Investment and International Investment Agreements' in John Anthony VanDuzer and Patrick Leblond (eds), *Promoting and Managing International Investment: Towards an Integrated Policy Approach* (Routledge 2020)

Bedjaoui M (ed), *International Law: Achievements and Prospects* (UNESCO, Nijhoff 1991)

Ben Hamida W, 'L'arbitrage Etat-investisseur cherche son équilibre perdu: Dans quelle mesure l'État peut introduire des demandes reconventionnelles contre l'investisseur privé?' (2005) 7(4) International Law FORUM du droit international 261

Benveništi E and Nolte G (eds), *Community Interests Across International Law* (Oxford University Press 2018)

Bernasconi-Osterwalder N, 'Inclusion of Investor Obligations and Corporate Accountability Provisions in Investment Agreements' in Julien Chaisse, Leïla Choukroune and Sufian Jusoh (eds), *Handbook of International Investment Law and Policy* (Springer 2021)

Bernasconi-Osterwalder N and others, *Harnessing Investment for Sustainable Development: Inclusion of Investor Obligations and Corporate Accountability Provisions in Trade and Investment Agreements* (IISD, 2018)

Beyerlin U, 'Sustainable Development' in Anne Peters (ed), *Max Planck Encyclopedia of Public International Law* (October 2013)

Bianchi A, 'The Fight for Inclusion: Non-State Actors and International Law' in Ulrich Fastenrath and others (eds), *From Bilateralism to Community Interest: Essays in Honour of Judge Bruno Simma* (Oxford University Press 2011)

Biersteker TJ, Eckert SE and Tourinho M (eds), *Targeted Sanctions: The Impacts and Effectiveness of United Nations Action* (Cambridge University Press 2016)

Binder C and others (eds), *International Investment Law for the 21st Century: Essays in Honour of Christoph Schreuer* (Oxford University Press 2009)

Bischoff JA and Happ R, 'The Scope of Application of International Investment Agreements' in Marc Bungenberg and others (eds), *International Investment Law* (Nomos 2015)

Bismuth R, 'Customary Principles Regarding Public Contracts Concluded with Foreigners' in Mathias Audit and Stephan W Schill (eds), *Transnational Law of Public Contracts* (Bruylant 2016)

Bjorklund AK, 'The Role of Counterclaims in Rebalancing Investment Law' (2013) 17(2) Lewis & Clark Law Review 461

Bjorklund AK and Reinisch A (eds), *International Investment Law and Soft Law* (Edward Elgar Publishing 2012)

Bjorklund AK and Vanhonnaeker L, 'Yukos: The Clean Hands Doctrine Revisisted' (2015) 9(2) Diritti Umani e Diritto Internazionale 365

Blackaby N and others, *Redfern and Hunter on International Arbitration* (6th edn, Oxford University Press, Wolters Kluwer Law & Business 2015)

von Bogdandy A and others (eds), *The Exercise of Public Authority by International Institutions: Advancing International Institutional Law* (Springer 2010)

von Bogdandy A, Dann P and Goldmann M, 'Developing the Publicness of Public International Law: Towards a Legal Framework for Global Governance Activities' in Armin von Bogdandy and others (eds), *The Exercise of Public Authority by International Institutions: Advancing International Institutional Law* (Springer 2010)

Bogojević S, 'Ending the Honeymoon: Deconstructing Emissions Trading Discourses' (2009) 21(3) Journal of Environmental Law 443

Boisson de Chazournes L, Kohen MG and Viñuales JE (eds), *Diplomatic and Judicial Means of Dispute Settlement* (Martinus Nijhoff Publishers 2013)

Bollecker-Stern B, *Le préjudice dans la théorie de la responsabilité internationale* (Editions A. Pedone 1973)

Bonnitcha J, *Substantive Protection Under Investment Treaties: A Legal and Economic Analysis* (Cambridge University Press 2014)

Bonzon A-J, 'Balance Between Investment Protection and Sustainable Development in BITs' (2014) 15(5–6) Journal of World Investment & Trade 809

Bormann C, *Transnationale Informationsgewinnung durch Nachrichtendienste und Polizei: Eine Untersuchung von Zulässigkeit und Verwertbarkeit* (Peter Lang GmbH Internationaler Verlag der Wissenschaften 2016)

Bose D, 'David R Aven v Costa Rica: The Confluence of Corporations, Public International Law and International Investment Law' (2020) 35(1–2) ICSID Review 20

Bothe A, *Die 'Corruption Defence' des Gaststaats in internationalen Investitionsschiedsverfahren* (Nomos 2021)

de Brabandere E, *Investment Treaty Arbitration as Public International Law: Procedural Aspects and Implications* (Cambridge University Press 2015)

—— 'Human Rights and International Investment Law' in Markus Krajewski and Rhea Hoffmann (eds), *Research Handbook on Foreign Direct Investment* (Edward Elgar Publishing 2019)

—— 'The (Ir)Relevance of Transnational Public Policy in Investment Treaty Arbitration – a Reply to Jean-Michel Marcoux' (2020) 21(6) Journal of World Investment & Trade 847

de Brabandere de and Hazelzet M, *Corporate Responsibility and Human Rights – Navigating Between International, Domestic and Self-Regulation* (Grotius Centre Working Paper 2017/056-HRL)

Braun TR, *Ausprägungen der Globalisierung: Der Investor als partielles Subjekt im Internationalen Investitionsrecht: Qualität und Grenzen dieser Wirkungseinheit* (Nomos 2012)

Bray HL, 'SOI – Save Our Investments! International Investment Law and International Humanitarian Law' (2013) 14(3) Journal of World Investment & Trade 578

Brown C (ed), *Evolution in Investment Treaty Law and Arbitration* (Cambridge University Press 2011)

—— (ed), *Commentaries on Selected Model Investment Treaties* (Oxford University Press 2013)

Brownlie I, *Principles of Public International Law* (6th edn, Oxford University Press 2003)

Bücheler G, *Proportionality in Investor-State Arbitration* (Oxford University Press 2015)

Buergenthal T, 'To Respect and to Ensure: State Obligations and Permissible Derogations' in Louis Henkin (ed), *The International Bill of Rights* (Columbia University Press 1981)

Bungenberg M and others (eds), *International Investment Law* (Nomos 2015)

Bungenberg M and Reinisch A, *Draft Statute of the Multilateral Investment Court* (Nomos 2021)

Bungenberg M and Reinisch A, *From Bilateral Arbitral Tribunals and Investment Courts to a Multilateral Investment Court* (2nd edn, Springer 2020)

Cafaggi F, 'Transnational Private Regulation: Regulating Global Private Regulators' in Sabino Cassese (ed), *Research Handbook on Global Administrative Law* (Edward Elgar Publishing 2016)

Carducci G, 'Dealing with Set-Off and Counterclaims in International Commercial and Investment Arbitration' (2013) 3 Yearbook on International Arbitration 173

Carlsnaes W, Risse T and Simmons BA (eds), *Handbook of International Relations* (2nd edn, Sage 2013)

Casini L, 'Beyond Drip-Painting? Ten Years of GAL and the Emergence of a Global Administration' (2015) 13(2) International Journal of Constitutional Law 473

—— 'Global Administrative Law Scholarship' in Sabino Cassese (ed), *Research Handbook on Global Administrative Law* (Edward Elgar Publishing 2016)

Cassese S (ed), *Research Handbook on Global Administrative Law* (Edward Elgar Publishing 2016)

Cassese S and D'Alterio E, 'Introduction: The Development of Global Administrative Law' in Sabino Cassese (ed), *Research Handbook on Global Administrative Law* (Edward Elgar Publishing 2016)

Chaisse J, Choukroune L and Jusoh S (eds), *Handbook of International Investment Law and Policy* (Springer 2021)

Chaisse J and Donde R, 'The State of Investor-State Arbitration' (2018) 51(1) The International Lawyer 47

de Chazournes LB and McGarry B, 'What Roles Can Constitutional Law Play in Investment Arbitration?' (2014) 15(5–6) Journal of World Investment & Trade 862

Cheng B, *General Principles of Law as Applied by International Courts and Tribunals* (Stevens & Sons Limited 1953)

—— 'Introduction to Subjects of International Law' in Mohammed Bedjaoui (ed), *International Law: Achievements and Prospects* (UNESCO, Nijhoff 1991)

Chinkin C, *Third Parties in International Law* (Clarendon Press 1993)

Choudhury B, 'Recapturing Public Power: Is Investment Arbitration's Engagement of the Public Interest Contributing to the Democratic Deficit?' (2008) 41(3) Vanderbilt Journal of Transnational Law 775

—— 'Investor Obligations for Human Rights' (2020) 35(1–2) ICSID Review 82

—— 'The Role of Soft Law Corporate Responsibilities in Defining Investor Obligations in International Investment Agreements' in Jean Ho and Mavluda Sattorova (eds), *Investors' International Law* (Hart 2021)

Choudhury B and Petrin M, *Corporate Duties to the Public* (Cambridge University Press 2019)

Choukroune L (ed), *Judging the State in International Trade and Investment Law* (Springer Singapore 2016)

Clapham A, *Human Rights Obligations of Non-State Actors* (Oxford University Press 2006)

—— 'The Role of the Individual in International Law' (2010) 21(1) European Journal of International Law 25

Clara R and Christoph S, 'Human Rights and International Investment Arbitration' in Pierre-Marie Dupuy, Ernst-Ulrich Petersmann and Francesco Francioni (eds), *Human Rights in International Investment Law and Arbitration* (Oxford University Press 2009)

Clodfelter MA and Tsutieva D, 'Counterclaims in Investment Treaty Arbitration' in Catherine Yannaca-Small (ed), *Arbitration Under International Investment Agreements: A Guide to the Key Issues* (2nd edn, Oxford University Press 2018)

Cogan JK, 'The Regulatory Turn in International Law' (2011) 52(2) Harvard International Law Journal 321

Cordonier Segger M-C and Gehring MW (eds), *Sustainable Development in World Trade Law* (Kluwer Law International 2005)

Cordonier Segger M-C, Gehring MW and Newcombe AP (eds), *Sustainable Development in World Investment Law* (Kluwer Law International 2011)

—— (eds), *Sustainable Development in World Investment Law* (Kluwer Law International 2011)

Cottier T and others, 'The Principle of Proportionality in International Law: Foundations and Variations' (2017) 18(4) Journal of World Investment & Trade 628

Coyle JF, 'The Treaty of Friendship, Commerce, and Navigation in the Modern Era' (2013) 51(2) Columbia Journal of Transnational Law 302

Crawford E, 'Proportionality' in Anne Peters (ed), *Max Planck Encyclopedia of Public International Law* (May 2011)

Crawford J, 'Treaty and Contract in Investment Arbitration' (2008) 24(3) Arbitration International 351

—— *Brownlie's Principles of Public International Law* (8th edn, Oxford University Press 2012)

—— *State Responsibility: The General Part* (Cambridge University Press 2013)

Crawford J, Pellet A and Olleson S (eds), *The Law of International Responsibility* (Oxford University Press 2010)

Crescenzi MJC, *Of Friends and Foes: Reputation and Learning in World Politics* (Oxford University Press 2018)

d'Aspremont J and others, 'Sharing Responsibility Between Non-State Actors and States in International Law: Introduction' (2015) 62(1) Netherlands International Law Review 49

Dari-Mattiacci G and de Geest G, 'Carrots vs. Sticks' in Francesco Parisi (ed), *The Oxford Handbook of Law and Economics*, vol I Methodology and Concepts (Oxford University Press 2017)

Desierto DA, 'Development as an International Right: Investment in the New Trade-Based IIAs' (2011) 3(2) Trade, Law and Development 296

—— 'ICESCR Minimum Core Obligations and Investment: Recasting the Non-Expropriation Compensation Model During Financial Crises' (2012) 44(3) George Washington International Law Review 473

—— 'Conflict of Treaties, Interpretation, and Decision-Making on Human Rights and Investment During Economic Crises' (2013) 10(1) Transnational Dispute Management 1

—— 'Deciding International Investment Agreement Applicability: The Development Argument in Investment' in Freya Baetens (ed), *Investment Law Within International Law: Integrationist Perspectives* (Cambridge University Press 2013)

—— *Public Policy in International Economic Law: The ICESCR in Trade, Finance, and Investment* (Oxford University Press 2015)

Deva S, 'Conclusion: Investors' International Law: Beyond the Present' in Jean Ho and Mavluda Sattorova (eds), *Investors' International Law* (Hart 2021)

Deva S and Bilchitz D (eds), *Building a Treaty on Business and Human Rights: Context and Contours* (Cambridge University Press 2017)

Diel-Gligor K and Hennecke R, 'Investment in Accordance with the Law' in Marc Bungenberg and others (eds), *International Investment Law* (Nomos 2015)

Dinstein Y, 'Par in Parem Non Habet Imperium' (1966) 1(3) Israel Law Review 407

Dixon J and Haslam PA, 'Does the Quality of Investment Protection Affect FDI Flows to Developing Countries? Evidence from Latin America' (2016) 39(8) The World Economy 1080

Dolzer R and Schreuer C, *Principles of International Investment Law* (2nd edn, Oxford University Press 2012)

Donno D and Neureiter M, 'Can Human Rights Conditionality Reduce Repression? Examining the European Union's Economic Agreements' (2018) 13(3) The Review of International Organizations 335

Douglas Z, 'The Hybrid Foundations of Investment Treaty Arbitration' (2004) 74(1) British Yearbook of International Law 151

—— *The International Law of Investment Claims* (Cambridge University Press 2009)

—— 'The Enforcement of Environmental Norms in Investment Treaty Arbitration' in Pierre-Marie Dupuy and Jorge E Viñuales (eds), *Harnessing Foreign Investment to Promote Environmental Protection: Incentives and Safeguards* (Cambridge University Press 2013)

Douglas Z, Pauwelyn J and Viñuales JE (eds), *The Foundations of International Investment Law: Bringing Theory into Practice* (Oxford University Press 2014)

Drahos P (ed), *Regulatory Theory: Foundations and Applications* (Australian National University Press 2017)

Dudas S, 'Treaty Counterclaims Under the ICSID Convention' in Crina Baltag (ed), *ICSID Convention After 50 Years: Unsettled Issues* (Wolters Kluwer 2017)

Dufey A and Grieg-Gran M, 'The Linkages Between Project Finance and Sustainable Development' in Sheldon Leader (ed), *Global Project Finance, Human Rights and Sustainable Development* (Cambridge University Press 2011)

Dumberry P, 'State of Confusion: The Doctrine of "Clean Hands" in Investment Arbitration After the Yukos Award' (2016) 17(2) Journal of World Investment & Trade 229

—— 'The Clean Hands Doctrine as a General Principle of International Law' (2020) 21(4) Journal of World Investment & Trade 489

Dumberry P and Dumas-Aubin G, 'How to Impose Human Rights Obligations on Corporations Under Investment Treaties?' (2011–2012) 4 Yearbook on International Investment Law and Policy

—— 'When and How Allegations of Human Rights Violations Can Be Raised in Investor-State Arbitration' (2012) 13 Journal of World Investment & Trade 349

—— 'A Few Pragmatic Observations on How BITs Should Be Modified to Incorporate Human Rights Obligations' (2014) 11(1) Transnational Dispute Management 1

Dupont C, Schultz T and Angin M, 'Political Risk and Investment Arbitration: An Empirical Study' (2016) 7(1) Journal of International Dispute Settlement 136

Dupuy P-M, 'International Law and Domestic (Municipal) Law' in Anne Peters (ed), *Max Planck Encyclopedia of Public International Law* (April 2011)

Dupuy P-M, Petersmann E-U and Francioni F (eds), *Human Rights in International Investment Law and Arbitration* (Oxford University Press 2009)

Dupuy P-M and Viñuales JE (eds), *Harnessing Foreign Investment to Promote Environmental Protection: Incentives and Safeguards* (Cambridge University Press 2013)

—— 'Human Rights and Investment Disciplines: Integration in Progress' in Marc Bungenberg and others (eds), *International Investment Law* (Nomos 2015)

Ehle B, 'Article I' in Reinmar Wolff (ed), *New York Convention* (C.H. Beck 2012)

Ejims O, 'The 2016 Morocco–Nigeria Bilateral Investment Treaty: More Practical Reality in Providing a Balanced Investment Treaty?' (2019) 34(1) ICSID Review 62

El-Hosseny F and Devine P, 'Contributory Fault Under International Law: A Gateway for Human Rights in ISDS?' (2020) 35(1–2) ICSID Review 105

Endicott M, 'The Definition of Investment in ICSID Arbitration: Development Lessons for the WTO?' in Marie-Claire Cordonier Segger and Markus W Gehring (eds), *Sustainable Development in World Trade Law* (Kluwer Law International 2005)

Fastenrath U, 'Das UNESCO-Übereinkommen zum Schutz des Kultur- und Naturerbes der Welt und seine Wirkungen im deutschen Recht' (2016) 54(4) Archiv des Völkerrechts 382

Fastenrath U and others (eds), *From Bilateralism to Community Interest: Essays in Honour of Judge Bruno Simma* (Oxford University Press 2011)

Fauchald OK, 'The Legal Reasoning of ICSID Tribunals – an Empirical Analysis' (2008) 19(2) European Journal of International Law 301

Fitzmaurice G, 'The General Principles of International Law, Considered from the Standpoint of the Rule of Law' (1957) 92 Recueil des Cours 1

Footer M, *An Institutional and Normative Analysis of the World Trade Organization* (Nijhoff 2006)

Footer ME, 'Bits and Pieces: Social and Environmental Protection in the Regulation of Foreign Investment' (2009) 18(1) Michigan State Journal of International Law 33

Foster GK, 'Investors, States, and Stakeholders: Power Asymmetries in International Investment and the Stabilizing Potential of Investment Treaties' (2013) 17(2) Lewis & Clark Law Review 361

Friedman MW and Popova IC, 'Can State Counterclaims Salvage Investment Arbitration?' (2014) 8(2) World Arbitration & Mediation Review 139

Friedrich J, 'Legal Challenges of Non-Binding Instruments: The Case of the FAO Code of Conduct for Responsible Fisheries' in Armin von Bogdandy and others (eds), *The Exercise of Public Authority by International Institutions: Advancing International Institutional Law* (Springer 2010)

Frowein JA, 'Artikel 17' in Jochen A Frowein and Wolfgang Peukert (eds), *Europäische Menschenrechtskonvention: EMRK-Kommentar* (2nd edn, N.P. Engel 1996)

Frowein JA and Peukert W (eds), *Europäische Menschenrechtskonvention: EMRK-Kommentar* (2nd edn, N.P. Engel 1996)

Gaillard E and Banifatemi Y, 'The Meaning of "And" in Article 42(1), Second Sentence, of the Washington Convention: The Role of International Law in the ICSID Choice of Law Process' (2003) 18(2) ICSID Review 375

—— 'The Long March Towards a Jurisprudence Constante on the Notion of Investment: Salini v. Morocco, ICSID Case No. ARB/00/4' in Mairée Uran Bidegain and others (eds), *Building International Investment Law: The First 50 Years of ICSID* (ICSID, Wolters Kluwer 2016)

Gazzini T, 'Bilateral Investment Treaties and Sustainable Development' (2014) 15(5–6) Journal of World Investment & Trade 929

—— *Interpretation of International Investment Treaties* (Hart Publishing 2016)

Gazzini T and Radi Y, 'Foreign Investment with a Human Face – with Special Reference to Rights of Indigenous Peoples' in Rainer Hofmann and Christian J Tams (eds), *International Investment Law and Its Others* (Nomos 2012)

Gebauer M, 'Ordre Public (Public Policy)' in Anne Peters (ed), *Max Planck Encyclopedia of Public International Law* (May 2007)

Gehne K, 'Soft Standards and Hard Consequences: Why Transnational Companies Commit to Respect International Labour and Social Standards, and How This Relates to Business and Regulation' in Henner Gött (ed), *Labour Standards in International Economic Law* (Springer International Publishing 2018)

Gleason T, 'Examining Host-State Counterclaims for Environmental Damage in Investor-State Dispute Settlement from Human Rights and Transnational Public Policy Perspectives' (2021) 21(3) International Environmental Agreements 427

Gött H (ed), *Labour Standards in International Economic Law* (Springer International Publishing 2018)

Gött H and Holterhus TP, 'Mainstreaming Investment-Labour Linkage Through "Mega-Regional" Trade Agreements' in Henner Gött (ed), *Labour Standards in International Economic Law* (Springer International Publishing 2018)

Gritsenko M, 'Relevance of the Host State's Development Status in Investment Treaty Arbitration' in Freya Baetens (ed), *Investment Law Within International Law: Integrationist Perspectives* (Cambridge University Press 2013)

Gunningham N and Sinclair D, 'Smart Regulation' in Peter Drahos (ed), *Regulatory Theory: Foundations and Applications* (Australian National University Press 2017)

Guntrip E, 'Urbaser v. Argentina: The Origins of a Host State Human Rights Counterclaim in ICSID Arbitration?' [2017] EJIL:Talk! ‹www.ejiltalk.org/urbaser-v-argentina-the-origins-of-a-host-state-human-rights-counterclaim-in-icsid-arbitration/#more-14978› accessed 7 December 2021

Hafner G, 'The Emancipation of the Individual from the State Under International Law' (2011) 358 Recueil des Cours 263

Hallward-Driemeier, 'Do Bilateral Investment Treaties Attract Foreign Direct Investment? Only a Bit ... And They Could Bite' [2003] World Bank Policy Research Working Paper 3121

Hansen JS, '"Missing Links" in Investment Arbitration: Quantification of Damages to Foreign Shareholders' (2013) 14(3) Journal of World Investment & Trade 434

Harlow C, 'Global Administrative Law: The Quest for Principles and Values' (2006) 17(1) European Journal of International Law 187

Harrison J, 'Environmental Counterclaims in Investor-State Arbitration: Perenco Ecuador Ltd v Republic of Ecuador, ICSID Case No ARB/08/6, Interim Decision on the Environmental Counterclaim, 11 August 2015 (Peter Tomka, Neil Kaplan, J Christopher Thomas)' (2016) 17(3) Journal of World Investment & Trade 479

Hart HL, *The Concept of Law* (2nd edn, Clarendon Press 1994)

van Harten G, *Investment Treaty Arbitration and Public Law* (Oxford University Press 2007)

van Harten G and Loughlin M, 'Investment Treaty Arbitration as a Species of Global Administrative Law' (2006) 17(1) European Journal of International Law 121

Hauriou A, 'Les Dommages Indirects Dans Les Arbitrages Internationaux' (1924) 31 Revue Générale de Droit International Public 203

Heinemann A, 'Business Enterprises in Public International Law: The Case for an International Code on Corporate Responsibility' in Ulrich Fastenrath and others (eds), *From Bilateralism to Community Interest: Essays in Honour of Judge Bruno Simma* (Oxford University Press 2011)

Henckels C, 'Protecting Regulatory Autonomy Through Greater Precision in Investment Treaties: The TPP, CETA, and TTIP' (2016) 19(1) Journal of International Economic Law 27

Henkin L (ed), *The International Bill of Rights* (Columbia University Press 1981)

Hepburn J, *Domestic Law in International Investment Arbitration* (Oxford University Press 2017)

Hepburn J and Kuuya V, 'Corporate Social Responsibility and Investment Treaties' in Marie-Claire Cordonier Segger, Markus W Gehring and Andrew P Newcombe (eds), *Sustainable Development in World Investment Law* (Kluwer Law International 2011)

—— 'Corporate Social Responsibility and Investment Treaties' in Marie-Claire Cordonier Segger, Markus W Gehring and Andrew P Newcombe (eds), *Sustainable Development in World Investment Law* (Kluwer Law International 2011)

Herstein OJ, 'A Normative Theory of the Clean Hands Defense' (2011) 17(3) Legal Theory 171

Higgins R, *Problems and Process: International Law and How We Use It* (Clarendon Press 1995)

Hindelang S and Krajewski M, 'Conclusion and Outlook: Whither International Investment Law?' in Steffen Hindelang and Markus Krajewski (eds), *Shifting Paradigms in International Investment Law: More Balanced, Less Isolated, Increasingly Diversified* (Oxford University Press 2016)

—— (eds), *Shifting Paradigms in International Investment Law: More Balanced, Less Isolated, Increasingly Diversified* (Oxford University Press 2016)

Hirsch M, 'Interactions Between Investment and Non-Investment Obligations' in Peter Muchlinski, Frederico Ortino and Christoph Schreuer (eds), *The Oxford Handbook of International Investment Law* (Oxford University Press 2008)

—— 'Investment Tribunals and Human Rights Treaties: A Sociological Perspective' in Freya Baetens (ed), *Investment Law Within International Law: Integrationist Perspectives* (Cambridge University Press 2013)

—— 'The Sociology of International Investment Law' in Zachary Douglas, Joost Pauwelyn and Jorge E Viñuales (eds), *The Foundations of International Investment Law: Bringing Theory into Practice* (Oxford University Press 2014)

Ho J, 'The Creation of Elusive Investor Responsibility' (2019) 113 AJIL Unbound 10

Ho J and Sattorova M (eds), *Investors' International Law* (Hart 2021)

Hobér K and Fellenbaum J, 'Political Risk Insurance and Financing of Foreign Direct Investment' in Marc Bungenberg and others (eds), *International Investment Law* (Nomos 2015)

Hoffmeister F, 'The Contribution of EU Trade Agreements to the Development of International Investment Law' in Steffen Hindelang and Markus Krajewski (eds), *Shifting Paradigms in International Investment Law: More Balanced, Less Isolated, Increasingly Diversified* (Oxford University Press 2016)

Hofmann R and Tams CJ (eds), *International Investment Law and Its Others* (Nomos 2012)

Hohmann J and Weller M (eds), *The UN Declaration on the Rights of Indigenous Peoples: A Commentary* (Oxford University Press 2018)

Howse R, 'Designing a Multilateral Investment Court: Issues and Options' (2017) 36(1) Yearbook of European Law 209

IISD, *Model International Agreement on Investment for Sustainable Development* (2005)

—— *A Sustainability Toolkit for Trade Negotiators: Trade and Investment as Vehicles for Achieving the 2030 Sustainable Development Agenda* (2017)

—— *Investment-Related Dispute Settlement: Towards an Inclusive Multilateral Approach* (2017)

—— *Integrating Investor Obligations and Corporate Accountability Provisions in Trade and Investment Agreements: Report of the Expert Meeting Held in Versoix, Switzerland, January 11–12, 2018* (2018)

International Commission of Jurists, *Needs and Options for a New International Instrument in the Field of Business and Human Rights* (International Commission of Jurists 2014)

International Committee of the Red Cross, *Commentary on the First Geneva Convention* (1952)

Ishikawa T, 'Counterclaims and the Rule of Law in Investment Arbitration' (2019) 113 AJIL Unbound 33

—— 'Counterclaims in Investment Arbitration: Is the Host State the Right Claimant?' in Jean Ho and Mavluda Sattorova (eds), *Investors' International Law* (Hart 2021)

Jacob M, 'Faith Betrayed: International Investment Law and Human Rights' in Rainer Hofmann and Christian J Tams (eds), *International Investment Law and Its Others* (Nomos 2012)

Jarrett M, *Contributory Fault and Investor Misconduct in Investment Arbitration* (Cambridge University Press 2019)

—— 'A New Frontier in International Investment Law: Adjudication of Host Citizen-Investor Disputes?' (2021) 81(4) Zeitschrift für ausländisches öffentliches Recht und Völkerrecht 969, 972

Jarrett M, Puig S and Ratner SR, 'Towards Greater Investor Accountability: Indirect Actions, Direct Actions by States and Direct Actions by Individuals' (2021) Journal of International Dispute Settlement 1, 6, advance article version ‹https://doi.org/10.1093/jnlids/idab035› accessed 7 December 2021

Jessup PC, *Transnational Law* (Yale University Press 1956)

Jeżweski M, 'Development Considerations in Defining Investment' in Marie-Claire Cordonier Segger, Markus W Gehring and Andrew P Newcombe (eds), *Sustainable Development in World Investment Law* (Kluwer Law International 2011)

Johannsen SLE, *Der Investitionsbegriff nach Art. 25 Abs. 1 der ICSID-Konvention* (Martin-Luther-Universität Halle-Wittenberg Institut für Wirtschaftsrecht 2009)

Kalderimis D, 'Investment Treaty Arbitration as Global Administrative Law: What This Might Mean in Practice' in Chester Brown (ed), *Evolution in Investment Treaty Law and Arbitration* (Cambridge University Press 2011)

Kalicki JE and Joubin-Bret A (eds), *Reshaping the Investor-State Dispute Settlement System: Journeys for the 21st Century* (Brill 2015)

Kammerhofer J, 'The Theory of Norm Conflict Solutions in International Investment Law' in Marie-Claire Cordonier Segger, Markus W Gehring and Andrew P Newcombe (eds), *Sustainable Development in World Investment Law* (Kluwer Law International 2011)

Karavias M, *Corporate Obligations Under International Law* (Oxford University Press 2014)

—— 'Corporations and Responsibility Under International Law' in Photini Pazartzis and Panos Merkouris (eds), *Permutations of Responsibility in International Law* (Brill Nijhoff 2019)

Kelsen H, *Reine Rechtslehre* (Franz Deuticke 1934)

Kendra T, 'State Counterclaims in Investment Arbitration – a New Lease of Life?' (2013) 29(4) Arbitration International 575

Kessedjian C, 'Rebalancing Investors' Rights and Obligations' (2021) 22(5–6) Journal of World Investment & Trade 645

Keohane RO, 'Rational Choice Theory and International Law: Insights and Limitations' (2002) 31(1) Journal of Legal Studies 307

Kern JS, 'Investor Responsibility as Familiar Frontier' (2019) 113 AJIL Unbound 28

Kim Y-I, 'Investment Law and the Individual' in Marc Bungenberg and others (eds), *International Investment Law* (Nomos 2015)

Kingsbury B, 'The Concept of "Law" in Global Administrative Law' (2009) 20(1) European Journal of International Law 23

Kingsbury B, Krisch N and Stewart RB, 'The Emergence of Global Administrative Law' (2005) 68(3) Law and Contemporary Problems 15

Kingsbury B and others, 'Foreword: Global Governance as Administration – National and Transnational Approaches to Global and Administrative Law' (2005) 68(3 & 4) Law and Contemporary Problems 1

Kingsbury B and Schill SW, 'Public Law Concepts to Balance Investors' Rights with State Regulatory Actions in the Public Interest – the Concept of Proportionality' in Stephan W Schill (ed), *International Investment Law and Comparative Public Law* (Oxford University Press 2010)

Kinnear M and Le Cannu PJ, 'Concluding Remarks: ICSID and African States Leading International Investment Law Reform' (2019) 34(2) ICSID Review 542

Kjos HE, *Applicable Law in Investor-State Arbitration* (Oxford University Press 2013)

Kläger R, '"Fair and Equitable Treatment" and Sustainable Development' in Marie-Claire Cordonier Segger, Markus W Gehring and Andrew P Newcombe (eds), *Sustainable Development in World Investment Law* (Kluwer Law International 2011)

—— 'Revising Treatment Standards – Fair and Equitable Treatment in Light of Sustainable Development' in Steffen Hindelang and Markus Krajewski (eds), *Shifting Paradigms in International Investment Law: More Balanced, Less Isolated, Increasingly Diversified* (Oxford University Press 2016)

Klausegger C and others (eds), *Austrian Yearbook on International Arbitration* (Stämpfli Verlag 2010)

Knahr C, 'Investments "In Accordance with Host State Law"' (2007) 4(5) Transnational Dispute Management 1

Kneer D, *Investitionsschutz und Menschenrechte: Eine Untersuchung zum Einfluss menschenrechtlicher Standards auf die Investitionssicherung* (Nomos 2013)

Knoll-Tudor I, 'The Fair and Equitable Treatment Standard and Human Rights Norms' in Pierre-Marie Dupuy, Ernst-Ulrich Petersmann and Francesco Francioni (eds), *Human Rights in International Investment Law and Arbitration* (Oxford University Press 2009)

Knox JH, 'Horizontal Human Rights Law' (2008) 102(1) American Journal of International Law 1

Krajewski M, 'A Nightmare or a Noble Dream? Establishing Investor Obligations Through Treaty-Making and Treaty-Application' (2020) 5(1) Business and Human Rights Journal 105

Krajewski M and Hoffmann R (eds), *Research Handbook on Foreign Direct Investment* (Edward Elgar Publishing 2019)

Kriebaum U, 'Human Rights of the Population of the Host State in International Investment Arbitration' (2009) 10(5) Journal of World Investment & Trade 653

—— 'Investment Arbitration – Illegal Investments' in Christian Klausegger and others (eds), *Austrian Yearbook on International Arbitration* (Stämpfli Verlag 2010)

—— 'Foreign Investments & Human Rights: The Actors and Their Different Roles' (2013) 10(1–17) Transnational Dispute Management

—— 'Expropriation' in Marc Bungenberg and others (eds), *International Investment Law* (Nomos 2015)

Krisch N, 'The Decay of Consent: International Law in an Age of Global Public Goods' (2014) 108(1) American Journal of International Law 1

Krommendijk J and Morijn J, '"Proportional" by What Measure(s)? Balancing Investor Interests and Human Rights by Way of Applying the Proportionality Principle in Investor-State Arbitration' in Pierre-Marie Dupuy, Ernst-Ulrich Petersmann and Francesco Francioni (eds), *Human Rights in International Investment Law and Arbitration* (Oxford University Press 2009)

Kryvoi Y, 'Economic Crimes in International Investment Law' (2018) 67(3) International & Comparative Law Quarterly 577

Kube V and Petersmann E-U, 'Human Rights Law in International Investment Arbitration' (2016) 11(1) Asian Journal of WTO & International Health Law and Policy 65

Kulesza J, *Due Diligence in International Law* (Brill Nijhoff 2016)

Kulick A, *Global Public Interest in International Investment Law* (Cambridge University Press 2012)

—— 'About the Order of Cart and Horse, Among Other Things: Estoppel in the Jurisprudence of International Investment Arbitration Tribunals' (2016) 27(1) European Journal of International Law 107

—— (ed), *Reassertion of Control over the Investment Treaty Regime* (Cambridge University Press 2017)

Laborde G, 'The Case for Host State Claims in Investment Arbitration' (2010) 1(1) Journal of International Dispute Settlement 97

Larschan B and Mirfendereski G, 'The Status of Counterclaims in International Law, with Particular Reference to International Arbitration Involving a Private Party and a Foreign State' (1986–1987) 15(1) Denver Journal of International Law and Policy 11

Lauterpacht E (ed), *International Law Being the Collected Papers of Hersch Lauterpacht*, vol 3 The Law of Peace Parts II-VI (Cambridge University Press 1977)

Lauterpacht H, *International Law and Human Rights* (Garland Publishing, Inc. 1973)

—— 'State Sovereignty and Human Rights' in Elihu Lauterpacht (ed), *International Law Being the Collected Papers of Hersch Lauterpacht*, vol 3 The Law of Peace Parts II-VI (Cambridge University Press 1977)

—— 'The Subjects of the Law of Nations' in Elihu Lauterpacht (ed), *International Law Being the Collected Papers of Hersch Lauterpacht*, vol 3 The Law of Peace Parts II-VI (Cambridge University Press 1977)

Le Moullec C, 'The Clean Hands Doctrine: A Tool for Accountability of Investor Conduct and Inadmissibility of Investment Claims' (2018) 84(1) Arbitration: The International Journal of Arbitration, Mediation and Dispute Management 13

Leader S (ed), *Global Project Finance, Human Rights and Sustainable Development* (Cambridge University Press 2011)

Leinhardt SB, 'Some Thoughts on Foreign Investors' Responsibilities to Respect Human Rights' (2013) 10(1) Transnational Dispute Management 1

Lejour A and Salfi M, 'The Regional Impact of Bilateral Investment Treaties on Foreign Direct Investment' [2014] CPB Netherlands Bureau for Economic Policy Analysis Discussion Paper 298

Levine MAJ, 'Emerging Practice on Investor Diligence: Jurisdiction, Admissibility, Merits' in Julien Chaisse, Leïla Choukroune and Sufian Jusoh (eds), *Handbook of International Investment Law and Policy* (Springer 2021)

Liberti L, 'The Relevance of Non-Investment Treaty Obligations in Assessing Compensation' in Pierre-Marie Dupuy, Ernst-Ulrich Petersmann and Francesco Francioni (eds), *Human Rights in International Investment Law and Arbitration* (Oxford University Press 2009)

Llamzon A, 'Yukos Universal Limited (Isle of Man) v the Russian Federation: The State of the "Unclean Hands" Doctrine in International Investment Law: Yukos as Both Omega and Alpha' (2015) 30(2) ICSID Review 315

López Escarcena S, *Indirect Expropriation in International Law* (Edward Elgar Publishing 2014)

Lorz RA and Busch M, 'Investment in Accordance with the Law – Specifically Corruption' in Marc Bungenberg and others (eds), *International Investment Law* (Nomos 2015)

Macqueen HL and Bogle S, 'Private Autonomy and the Protection of the Weaker Party: Historical' in Stefan Vogenauer (ed), *General Principles of Law: European and Comparative Perspectives* (Bloomsbury Publishing 2017)

Maljean-Dubois S and Richard V, 'The Applicability of International Environmental Law to Private Enterprises' in Pierre-Marie Dupuy and Jorge E Viñuales (eds), *Harnessing Foreign Investment to Promote Environmental Protection: Incentives and Safeguards* (Cambridge University Press 2013)

Mann H, 'Civil Society Perspectives: What Do Key Stakeholders Expect from the International Investment Regime?' in José E Alvarez and others (eds), *The Evolving International Investment Regime: Expectations, Realities, Options* (Oxford University Press 2011)

—— 'Reconceptualizing International Investment Law: Its Role in Sustainable Development' (2013) 17(2) Lewis & Clark Law Review 521

Marboe I, *Calculation of Compensation and Damages in International Investment Law* (2nd edn, Oxford University Press 2017)

Marcoux J-M, 'Transnational Public Policy as a Vehicle to Impose Human Rights Obligations in International Investment Arbitration' (2020) 21(6) Journal of World Investment & Trade 809

Marcoux J-M and Newcombe A, 'Bear Creek Mining Corporation v Republic of Peru: Two Sides of a "Social License" to Operate' (2018) 33(3) ICSID Review 653

Mares R, 'Legalizing Human Rights Due Diligence and the Separation of Entities Principle' in Surya Deva and David Bilchitz (eds), *Building a Treaty on Business and Human Rights: Context and Contours* (Cambridge University Press 2017)

Marzal T, 'Quantum (In)Justice: Rethinking the Calculation of Compensation and Damages in ISDS' (2021) 22(2) Journal of World Investment & Trade 249

Mayeda G, 'Sustainable International Investment Agreements: Challenges and Solutions for Developing Countries' in Marie-Claire Cordonier Segger, Markus W Gehring and Andrew P Newcombe (eds), *Sustainable Development in World Investment Law* (Kluwer Law International 2011)

Mbengue MM, 'Africa's Voice in the Formation, Shaping and Redesign of International Investment Law' (2019) 34(2) ICSID Review 455

Mbengue MM and Schacherer S, 'The Africanization of International Investment Law: The Pan-African Investment Code and the Reform of the International Investment Regime' (2017) 18(3) Journal of World Investment & Trade 414

Menaker AJ, 'The Determinative Impact of Fraud and Corruption on Investment Arbitrations' (2010) 25(1) ICSID Review 67

Merrills JG, *International Dispute Settlement* (6th edn, Cambridge University Press 2017)

Meshel T, 'Use and Misuse of the Corruption Defence in International Investment Arbitration' (2013) 30(3) Journal of International Arbitration 267

Miles CA, 'Corruption, Jurisdiction and Admissibility in International Investment Claims' (2012) 3(2) Journal of International Dispute Settlement 329

Miles K, *The Origins of International Investment Law: Empire, Environment and the Safeguarding of Capital* (Cambridge University Press 2013)

—— (ed), *Research Handbook on Environment and Investment Law* (Edward Elgar Publishing 2019)

Miles W and Lawry-White M, 'Arbitral Institutions and the Enforcement of Climate Change Obligations for the Benefit of All Stakeholders: The Role of ICSID' (2019) 34(1) ICSID Review 1

Mitra T and Donde R, 'Claims and Counterclaims Under Asian Multilateral Investment Treaties' in Leïla Choukroune (ed), *Judging the State in International Trade and Investment Law* (Springer Singapore 2016)

Moinuddin H, *The Charter of the Islamic Conference and Legal Framework of Economic Co-Operation Among Its Member States: A Study of the Charter, the General Agreement for Economic, Technical and Commercial Co-Operation and the Agreement for Promotion, Protection and Guarantee of Investments Among Member States of the OIC* (Clarendon Press 1987)

Moloo R, 'A Comment on the Clean Hands Doctrine in International Law' (2011) 8(1) Transnational Dispute Management 1

Monebhurrun N, 'Mapping the Duties of Private Companies in International Investment Law' (2017) 14(2) Brazilian Journal of International Law 50

Monebhurrun N, 'Novelty in International Investment Law: The Brazilian Agreement on Cooperation and Facilitation of Investments as a Different International Investment Agreement Model' (2017) 8(1) Journal of International Dispute Settlement 79

Monnheimer M, *Due Diligence Obligations in International Human Rights Law* (Cambridge University Press 2021)

Morosini F and Sanchez MR (eds), *Reconceptualizing International Investment Law from the Global South* (Cambridge University Press 2018)

Muchlinski P, '"Caveat Investor"? The Relevance of the Conduct of the Investor Under the Fair and Equitable Treatment Standard' (2006) 55(3) International & Comparative Law Quarterly 527

—— *Multinational Enterprises and the Law* (2nd edn, Oxford University Press 2007)

—— 'Regulating Multinationals: Foreign Investment, Development, and the Balance of Corporate and Home Country Rights and Responsibilities in a Globalizing World' in José E Alvarez and others (eds), *The Evolving International Investment Regime: Expectations, Realities, Options* (Oxford University Press 2011)

—— 'Negotiating New Generation International Investment Agreements: New Sustainable Development Oriented Initiatives' in Steffen Hindelang and Markus Krajewski (eds), *Shifting Paradigms in International Investment Law: More Balanced, Less Isolated, Increasingly Diversified* (Oxford University Press 2016)

—— 'The Impact of a Business and Human Rights Treaty on Investment Law and Arbitration' in Surya Deva and David Bilchitz (eds), *Building a Treaty on Business and Human Rights: Context and Contours* (Cambridge University Press 2017)

Muchlinski P, Ortino F and Schreuer C (eds), *The Oxford Handbook of International Investment Law* (Oxford University Press 2008)

Nedumpara JJ and Laddha A, 'Human Rights and Environmental Counterclaims in Investment Treaty Arbitration' in Julien Chaisse, Leïla Choukroune and Sufian Jusoh (eds), *Handbook of International Investment Law and Policy* (Springer 2021)

Nolte G, *Eingreifen auf Einladung: Zur völkerrechtlichen Zulässigkeit des Einsatzes fremder Truppen im internen Konflikt auf Einladung der Regierung* (Springer 1999)

Nowak M, *U.N. Covenant on Civil and Political Rights: CCPR Commentary* (2nd edn, N.P. Engel 2005)

Nowrot K, 'How to Include Environmental Protection, Human Rights and Sustainability in International Investment Law?' (2014) 15(3/4) Journal of World Investment & Trade 612

—— 'Obligations of Investors' in Marc Bungenberg and others (eds), *International Investment Law* (Nomos 2015)

—— 'Termination and Renegotiation of International Investment Agreements' in Steffen Hindelang and Markus Krajewski (eds), *Shifting Paradigms in International Investment Law: More Balanced, Less Isolated, Increasingly Diversified* (Oxford University Press 2016)

Oppenheim LF, *International Law: A Treatise* (2nd edn, Longmans, Green and Co. 1912)

Palombino FM, *Fair and Equitable Treatment and the Fabric of General Principles* (T.M.C. Asser Press 2018)

Paparinskis M, 'MFN Clauses and International Dispute Settlement: Moving Beyond Maffezini and Plama?' (2011) 26(2) ICSID Review 14

—— 'Investment Treaty Arbitration and the (New) Law of State Responsibility' (2013) 24(2) European Journal of International Law 617

Paparinskis M, *The International Minimum Standard and Fair and Equitable Treatment* (Oxford University Press 2013)

Parisi F (ed), *The Oxford Handbook of Law and Economics*, vol I Methodology and Concepts (Oxford University Press 2017)

—— (ed), *The Oxford Handbook of Law and Economics*, vol III Public Law and Legal Institutions (Oxford University Press 2017)

Parlett K, *The Individual in the International Legal System: Continuity and Change in International Law* (Cambridge University Press 2011)

—— 'The Individual and Structural Change in the International Legal System' (2012) 1(3) Cambridge Journal of International and Comparative Law 60

Parra A, 'The Convention and Centre for Settlement of Investment Disputes' (2014) 374 Recueil des Cours 313

Paulsson J, 'Arbitration Without Privity' (1995) 10(2) ICSID Review 232

Paulus AL, *Die internationale Gemeinschaft im Völkerrecht: Eine Untersuchung zur Entwicklung des Völkerrechts im Zeitalter der Globalisierung* (C.H. Beck 2001)

—— 'Treaties of Friendship, Commerce and Navigation' in Anne Peters (ed), *Max Planck Encyclopedia of Public International Law* (March 2011)

Paust JJ, 'Human Rights Responsibilities of Private Corporations' (2002) 35(3) Vanderbilt Journal of Transnational Law 801

Pauwelyn J, *Conflict of Norms in Public International Law: How WTO Law Relates to Other Rules of International Law* (Cambridge University Press 2003)

Pazartzis P and Merkouris P (eds), *Permutations of Responsibility in International Law* (Brill Nijhoff 2019)

Peinhardt C and Allee T, 'Political Risk Insurance as Dispute Resolution' (2016) 7(1) Journal of International Dispute Settlement 205

Pellet A, 'Judicial Settlement of International Disputes' in Anne Peters (ed), *Max Planck Encyclopedia of Public International Law* (July 2013)

Perrone NM, 'The "Invisible" Local Communities: Foreign Investor Obligations, Inclusiveness, and the International Investment Regime' (2019) 113 AJIL Unbound 16

Peters A, *Beyond Human Rights: The Legal Status of the Individual in International Law* (Cambridge University Press 2016)

—— (ed), *Max Planck Encyclopedia of Public International Law* ‹https://opil.ouplaw.com/home/mpil› accessed 7 December 2021

Petersmann E-U, 'Constitutional Theories of International Economic Adjudication and Investor-State Arbitration' in Pierre-Marie Dupuy, Ernst-Ulrich Petersmann and Francesco Francioni (eds), *Human Rights in International Investment Law and Arbitration* (Oxford University Press 2009)

—— *Multilevel Constitutionalism for Multilevel Governance of Public Goods: Methodology Problems in International Law* (Bloomsbury Publishing 2017)

Pinelli C, 'Conditionality' in Anne Peters (ed), *Max Planck Encyclopedia of Public International Law* (November 2013)

Pomson O, 'The Clean Hands Doctrine in the Yukos Awards: A Response to Patrick Dumberry' (2017) 18(4) Journal of World Investment & Trade 712

Popova IC and Poon F, 'From Perpetual Respondent to Aspiring Counterclaimant? State Counterclaims in the New Wave of Investment Treaties' (2015) 2(2) BCDR International Arbitration Review 223

Portmann R, *Legal Personality in International Law* (Cambridge University Press 2010)

Posner EA and Sykes AO, *Economic Foundations of International Law* (Belknap Press of Harvard University Press 2013)

Prislan V, 'Non-Investment Obligations in Investment Treaty Arbitration: Towards a Greater Role for States?' in Freya Baetens (ed), *Investment Law Within International Law: Integrationist Perspectives* (Cambridge University Press 2013)

Protopsaltis PM, 'Compliance with the Laws of the Host Country in Bilateral Investment Treaties' (2015) 12(6) Transnational Dispute Management 1

Quashigah K, 'Scope of Individual Duties in the African Charter' in Manisuli Ssenyonjo (ed), *The African Regional Human Rights System: 30 Years After the African Charter on Human and Peoples' Rights* (Martinus Nijhoff Publishers 2012)

Rama-Montaldo M, 'International Legal Personality and Implied Powers of International Organizations' (1970) 44 British Yearbook of International Law 111

Ranjan P, 'Investor Obligations in Investment Treaties: Missing Text or a Matter of Application?' in Jean Ho and Mavluda Sattorova (eds), *Investors' International Law* (Hart 2021)

Ratner SR, 'Corporations and Human Rights: A Theory of Legal Responsibility' (2001) 111(3) Yale Law Journal 443

—— 'International Investment Law Through the Lens of Global Justice' (2017) 20(4) Journal of International Economic Law 747

Raz J, *The Morality of Freedom* (Clarendon Press 1988)

Reinisch A, 'The Interpretation of International Investment Agreements' in Marc Bungenberg and others (eds), *International Investment Law* (Nomos 2015)

—— 'Enforcement of Investment Treaty Awards' in Catherine Yannaca-Small (ed), *Arbitration Under International Investment Agreements: A Guide to the Key Issues* (2nd edn, Oxford University Press 2018)

Reinsch PS, 'International Administrative Law and National Sovereignty' (1909) 3(1) American Journal of International Law 1

Reisman WM, 'The Regime for Lacunae in the ICSID Choice of Law Provision and the Question of Its Threshold' (2000) 15(2) ICSID Review 362

Ripinsky S and Williams K, *Damages in International Investment Law* (British Institute of International and Comparative Law 2008)

Rivas JA, 'ICSID Treaty Counterclaims: Case Law and Treaty Evolution' in Jean E Kalicki and Anna Joubin-Bret (eds), *Reshaping the Investor-State Dispute Settlement System: Journeys for the 21st Century* (Brill 2015)

Roberts A, 'Clash of Paradigms: Actors and Analogies Shaping the Investment Treaty System' (2013) 107(1) American Journal of International Law 45

Rousseau C, *Droit international public*, vol V Les rapports conflictuels (Sirey 1983)

Ruffert M and Walter C, *Institutionalised International Law* (Nomos 2015)

Ruggie JG, *Just Business: Multinational Corporations and Human Rights* (Norton 2013)

Sabahi B, *Compensation and Restitution in Investor-State Arbitration: Principles and Practice* (Oxford University Press 2011)

Sabahi B and Ziyaeva D, 'Yukos v. Russian Federation: Observations on the Tribunal's Ruling on Damages' (2015) 13(5) Oil, Gas & Energy Law 1

Sacerdoti G, 'Investment Protection and Sustainable Development: Key Issues' in Steffen Hindelang and Markus Krajewski (eds), *Shifting Paradigms in International Investment Law: More Balanced, Less Isolated, Increasingly Diversified* (Oxford University Press 2016)

Salacuse JW, *The Law of Investment Treaties* (3rd edn, Oxford University Press 2021)

Salmon JJ, 'Des «Mains Propres» comme condition de recevabilité des réclamations internationales' (1964) 10 Annuaire Français de Droit International 225

Sanchez Badin MR and Morosini F, 'Navigating Between Resistance and Conformity with the International Investment Regime: The Brazilian Agreements on Cooperation and Facilitation of Investments (ACFIs)' in Fabio Morosini and Michelle R Sanchez (eds), *Reconceptualizing International Investment Law from the Global South* (Cambridge University Press 2018)

Sant'ana M, 'Risk Managers or Risk Promoters? The Impact of Export Credit and Investment Insurance Agencies on Human Development and Human Rights' in Johan F M Swinnen, Jan Wouters and Olivier de Schutter (eds), *Foreign Direct Investment and Human Development: The Law and Economics of International Investment Agreements* (Routledge 2013)

Sattorova M, 'Investor Responsibilities from a Host State Perspective: Qualitative Data and Proposals for Treaty Reform' (2019) 113 AJIL Unbound 22

Saul B, Kinley D and Mowbray J, *The International Covenant on Economic, Social and Cultural Rights: Commentary, Cases, and Materials* (Oxford University Press 2014)

Schabas W, *The European Convention on Human Rights: A Commentary* (Oxford University Press 2015)

Schacherer S, *Sustainable Development in EU Foreign Investment Law* (Brill 2021)

Scheinin M and Åhrén M, 'Relationship to Human Rights, and Related International Instruments' in Jessie Hohmann and Marc Weller (eds), *The UN Declaration on the Rights of Indigenous Peoples: A Commentary* (Oxford University Press 2018)

Scherer M, Bruce S and Reschke J, 'Environmental Counterclaims in Investment Treaty Arbitration' (2021) ICSID Review 36(2) 413

Scheu J, *Systematische Berücksichtigung von Menschenrechten in Investitionsschiedsverfahren* (Nomos 2017)

—— 'Trust Building, Balancing, and Sanctioning: Three Pillars of a Systematic Approach to Human Rights in International Investment Law and Arbitration' (2017) 48(2) Georgetown Journal of International Law 449

Schill SW, *The Multilateralization of International Investment Law* (Cambridge University Press 2009)

—— (ed), *International Investment Law and Comparative Public Law* (Oxford University Press 2010)

—— 'International Investment Law and Comparative Public Law – an Introduction' in Stephan W Schill (ed), *International Investment Law and Comparative Public Law* (Oxford University Press 2010)

—— 'Enhancing International Investment Law's Legitimacy: Conceptual and Methodological Foundations of a New Public Law Approach' (2011) 52(1) Virginia Journal of International Law 57

—— 'W(h)ither Fragmentation? On the Literature and Sociology of International Investment Law' (2011) 22(3) European Journal of International Law 875

—— 'Cross-Regime Harmonization Through Proportionality Analysis: The Case of International Investment Law, the Law of State Immunity and Human Rights' (2012) 27(1) ICSID Review 87

—— 'Illegal Investments in Investment Treaty Arbitration' (2012) 11(2) The Law & Practice of International Courts and Tribunals 281

—— 'Investitionsschutzrecht als Entwicklungsvölkerrecht' (2012) 72(2) Zeitschrift für ausländisches öffentliches Recht und Völkerrecht 261

—— 'The Sixth Path: Reforming Investment Law from Within' in Jean E Kalicki and Anna Joubin-Bret (eds), *Reshaping the Investor-State Dispute Settlement System: Journeys for the 21st Century* (Brill 2015)

—— 'Reforming Investor–State Dispute Settlement: A (Comparative and International) Constitutional Law Framework' (2017) 20(3) Journal of International Economic Law 649

Schill S and Djanic V, 'International Investment Law and Community Interests' in Eyāl Benveniśtî and Georg Nolte (eds), *Community Interests Across International Law* (Oxford University Press 2018)

Schill SW, Tams CJ and Hofmann R, 'International Investment Law and Development: Friends or Foes?' in Christian J Tams, Rainer Hofmann and Stephan W Schill (eds), *International Investment Law and Development: Bridging the Gap* (Edward Elgar Publishing 2015)

Schmidt R, *Die Obliegenheiten: Studien auf dem Gebiet des Rechtszwanges im Zivilrecht unter besonderer Berücksichtigung des Privatversicherungsrechts* (Karlsruhe 1953)

Schmidt-Aßmann, 'The Internationalization of Administrative Relations as a Challenge for Administrative Law Scholarship' (2008) 9(11) German Law Journal 2061

Schorkopf F, 'European Arrest Warrant' in Anne Peters (ed), *Max Planck Encyclopedia of Public International Law* (January 2009)

Schreuer C, 'Fair and Equitable Treatment in Arbitral Practice' (2005) 6(3) Journal of World Investment & Trade 357

—— *The ICSID Convention: A Commentary* (2nd edn, Cambridge University Press 2009)

—— 'The Protection of Investments in Armed Conflicts' in Freya Baetens (ed), *Investment Law Within International Law: Integrationist Perspectives* (Cambridge University Press 2013)

Schreuer C and Kriebaum U, 'From Individual to Community Interest in International Investment Law' in Ulrich Fastenrath and others (eds), *From Bilateralism to Community Interest: Essays in Honour of Judge Bruno Simma* (Oxford University Press 2011)

de Schutter O, *International Human Rights Law: Cases, Materials, Commentary* (2nd edn, Cambridge University Press 2014)

Schwebel SM, 'A BIT About ICSID' (2008) 23(1) ICSID Review 1

—— 'Clean Hands, Principle' in Anne Peters (ed), *Max Planck Encyclopedia of Public International Law* (March 2013)

Seibert-Fohr A, 'Transnational Labour Litigation: The Ups and Downs Under the Alien Tort Statute' in Henner Gött (ed), *Labour Standards in International Economic Law* (Springer International Publishing 2018)

Sepúlveda-Amor B, 'Opening Remarks' in Laurence Boisson de Chazournes, Marcelo G Kohen and Jorge E Viñuales (eds), *Diplomatic and Judicial Means of Dispute Settlement* (Martinus Nijhoff Publishers 2013)

Shan W and Gallagher N, 'China' in Chester Brown (ed), *Commentaries on Selected Model Investment Treaties* (Oxford University Press 2013)

Shao X, 'Environmental and Human Rights Counterclaims in International Investment Arbitration: at the Crossroads of Domestic and International Law' (2021) 24(1) Journal of International Economic Law 157

Shapovalov A, 'Should a Requirement of "Clean Hands" Be a Prerequisite to the Exercise of Diplomatic Protection? Human Rights Implications of the International Law Commission's Debate' (2005) 20(4) American University International Law Review 829

Sheppard A, 'Interim ILA Report on Public Policy as a Bar to Enforcement of International Arbitral Awards' (2003) 19(2) Arbitration International 217

Shihata IF, 'Towards a Greater Depoliticization of Investment Disputes: The Roles of ICSID and MIGA' (1986) 1(1) ICSID Review 1

Simma B, 'From Bilateralism to Community Interest in International Law' (1994) 250(VI) Recueil des Cours 217

—— 'Foreign Investment Arbitration: A Place for Human Rights?' (2011) 60(3) International & Comparative Law Quarterly 573

Simma B and Kill T, 'Harmonizing Investment Protection and International Human Rights: First Steps Towards a Methodology' in Christina Binder and others (eds), *International Investment Law for the 21st Century: Essays in Honour of Christoph Schreuer* (Oxford University Press 2009)

Simma B and Paulus AL, 'The Responsibility of Individuals for Human Rights Abuses in Internal Conflicts: A Positivist View' (1999) 93(2) American Journal of International Law 302

Simmons BA, 'International Law' in Walter Carlsnaes, Thomas Risse and Beth A Simmons (eds), *Handbook of International Relations* (2nd edn, Sage 2013)

Sornarajah M, *The International Law on Foreign Investment* (5th edn, Cambridge University Press 2021)

Ssenyonjo M, *Economic, Social and Cultural Rights in International Law* (Hart Publishing 2009)

—— (ed), *The African Regional Human Rights System: 30 Years After the African Charter on Human and Peoples' Rights* (Martinus Nijhoff Publishers 2012)

von Stein L, 'Einige Bemerkungen über das internationale Verwaltungsrecht' (1882) 6(2) Jahrbuch für Gesetzgebung, Verwaltung und Volkswirtschaft im Deutschen Reich 395

Steininger S, 'The Role of Human Rights in Investment Law and Arbitration, State Obligations, Corporate Responsibility and Community Empowerment' in Ilias Bantekas and Michael A Stein (eds), *The Cambridge Companion to Business & Human Rights Law* (Cambridge University Press 2021)

Stern B, 'The Future of International Investment Law: A Balance Between the Protection of Investors and the States' Capacity to Regulate' in José E Alvarez and others (eds), *The Evolving International Investment Regime: Expectations, Realities, Options* (Oxford University Press 2011)

Stewart RB, 'The Normative Dimensions and Performance of Global Administrative Law' (2015) 13(2) International Journal of Constitutional Law 499

Stifter L and Reinisch A, 'Expropriation in the Light of the UNCTAD Investment Policy Framework for Sustainable Development' in Steffen Hindelang and Markus Krajewski (eds), *Shifting Paradigms in International Investment Law: More Balanced, Less Isolated, Increasingly Diversified* (Oxford University Press 2016)

Stiglitz JE, 'Regulating Multinational Corporations: Towards Principles of Cross-Border Legal Frameworks in a Globalized World Balancing Rights with Responsibilities' (2007–2008) 23(3) American University International Law Review 451

Stoll P-T and Holterhus TP, 'The "Generalization" of International Investment Law in Constitutional Perspective' in Steffen Hindelang and Markus Krajewski (eds), *Shifting Paradigms in International Investment Law: More Balanced, Less Isolated, Increasingly Diversified* (Oxford University Press 2016)

Stone RW, 'The Scope of IMF Conditionality' (2008) 62(4) International Organization 589

Sullivan J and Kirsey V, 'Environmental Policies: A Shield or a Sword in Investment Arbitration?' (2017) 18(1) Journal of World Investment & Trade 100

Surminski S, 'The Role of Insurance Risk Transfer in Encouraging Climate Investment in Developing Countries' in Pierre-Marie Dupuy and Jorge E Viñuales (eds), *Harnessing Foreign Investment to Promote Environmental Protection: Incentives and Safeguards* (Cambridge University Press 2013)

Swinnen JFM, Wouters J and de Schutter O (eds), *Foreign Direct Investment and Human Development: The Law and Economics of International Investment Agreements* (Routledge 2013)

Sykes AO, 'Public Versus Private Enforcement of International Economic Law: Standing and Remedy' (2005) 34(2) Journal of Legal Studies 631

Sykes AO and Guzman A, 'Economics of International Law' in Francesco Parisi (ed), *The Oxford Handbook of Law and Economics*, vol III Public Law and Legal Institutions (Oxford University Press 2017)

Tams CJ, Hofmann R and Schill SW (eds), *International Investment Law and Development: Bridging the Gap* (Edward Elgar Publishing 2015)

Tan Y, *Resettlement in the Three Gorges Project* (Hong Kong University Press 2008)

Thomé H, 'Holding Transnational Corporations Accountable for Environmental Harm Through Counterclaims in Investor-State Dispute Settlement: Myth or Reality?' (2021) 22(5–6) Journal of World Investment & Trade 651

Thompson A, 'Applying Rational Choice Theory to International Law: The Promise and Pitfalls' (2002) 31(1) Journal of Legal Studies 285

Tienhaara K, 'Regulatory Chill and the Threat of Arbitration: A View from Political Science' in Chester Brown (ed), *Evolution in Investment Treaty Law and Arbitration* (Cambridge University Press 2011)

Tietje C, *Individualrechte im Menschenrechts- und Investitionsschutzbereich – Kohärenz von Staaten- und Unternehmensverantwortung?* (Martin-Luther-Universität Halle-Wittenberg 2012)

Titi A, *The Right to Regulate in International Investment Law* (Nomos 2014)

Tomuschat C, 'Grundpflichten des Individuums nach Völkerrecht' (1983) 21(3) Archiv des Völkerrechts 289

—— 'Obligations Arising for States Without or Against Their Will' (1993) 241 Recueil des Cours 195

—— 'International Law: Ensuring the Survival of Mankind on the Eve of a New Century: General Course on Public International Law' (1999) 281 Recueil des Cours 9

—— 'The Responsibility of Other Entities: Private Individuals' in James Crawford, Alain Pellet and Simon Olleson (eds), *The Law of International Responsibility* (Oxford University Press 2010)

—— *Human Rights: Between Idealism and Realism* (3rd edn, Oxford University Press 2014)

Toral M and Schultz T, 'The State, a Perpetual Respondent in Investment Arbitration? Some Unorthodox Considerations' in Michael A Waibel (ed), *The Backlash Against Investment Arbitration: Perceptions and Reality* (Wolters Kluwer Law & Business 2010)

Trindade AAC, 'The Historical Recovery of the Human Person as Subject of the Law of Nations' (2012) 1(3) Cambridge Journal of International and Comparative Law 8

Tyler TR, 'Value-Driven Behavior and the Law' in Francesco Parisi (ed), *The Oxford Handbook of Law and Economics*, vol I Methodology and Concepts (Oxford University Press 2017)

UNCTAD, *World Investment Report: Reforming International Investment Governance* (United Nations Publications 2015)

—— *World Investment Report: Investment and the Digital Economy* (United Nations Publications 2017)

—— *World Investment Report: International Production Beyond the Pandemic* (United Nations Publications 2020)

—— *World Investment Report: Investing in Sustainable Recovery* (United Nations Publications 2021)

Uran Bidegain M and others (eds), *Building International Investment Law: The First 50 Years of ICSID* (ICSID, Wolters Kluwer 2016)

Vandenbogaerde A, *Towards Shared Accountability in International Human Rights Law* (Intersentia 2016)

VanDuzer JA, 'Sustainable Development Provisions in International Trade Treaties: What Lessons for International Investment Agreements?' in Steffen Hindelang and Markus Krajewski (eds), *Shifting Paradigms in International Investment Law: More Balanced, Less Isolated, Increasingly Diversified* (Oxford University Press 2016)

VanDuzer JA and Leblond P (eds), *Promoting and Managing International Investment: Towards an Integrated Policy Approach* (Routledge 2020)

Veenstra-Kjos HE, 'Counterclaims by Host States in Investment Treaty Arbitration' (2007) 4(4) Transnational Dispute Management 1

Vidigal G and Stevens B, 'Brazil's New Model of Dispute Settlement for Investment: Return to the Past or Alternative for the Future?' (2018) 19(3) Journal of World Investment & Trade 475

Viljoen F, 'Communications Under the African Charter: Procedure and Admissibility' in Manisuli Ssenyonjo (ed), *The African Regional Human Rights System: 30 Years After the African Charter on Human and Peoples' Rights* (Martinus Nijhoff Publishers 2012)

Villiger ME, *Commentary on the 1969 Vienna Convention on the Law of Treaties* (Martinus Nijhoff Publishers 2009)

Viñuales JE, *Foreign Investment and the Environment in International Law* (Cambridge University Press 2012)

—— 'The Environmental Regulation of Foreign Investment Schemes Under International Law' in Pierre-Marie Dupuy and Jorge E Viñuales (eds), *Harnessing Foreign Investment to Promote Environmental Protection: Incentives and Safeguards* (Cambridge University Press 2013)

—— 'Investment Law and Sustainable Development: The Environment Breaks into Investment Disputes' in Marc Bungenberg and others (eds), *International Investment Law* (Nomos 2015)

—— 'Investor Diligence in Investment Arbitration: Sources and Arguments' (2017) 32(2) ICSID Review 346

—— 'Foreign Investment and the Environment in International Law: Current Trends' in Kate Miles (ed), *Research Handbook on Environment and Investment Law* (Edward Elgar Publishing 2019)

Vogenauer S (ed), *General Principles of Law: European and Comparative Perspectives* (Bloomsbury Publishing 2017)

Vohryzek-Griest, 'State Counterclaims in Investor-State Disputes: A History of 30 Years of Failure' (2009) 15 Revista Colombiana de Derecho Internacional 83

Waibel MA (ed), *The Backlash Against Investment Arbitration: Perceptions and Reality* (Wolters Kluwer Law & Business 2010)

Walter C, 'Subjects of International Law' in Anne Peters (ed), *Max Planck Encyclopedia of Public International Law* (May 2007)

Weber J and Titi C, 'UNCTAD's Roadmap for IIA Reform of Investment Dispute Settlement' (2015) 21(4) New Zealand Business Law Quarterly 319

Weil P, 'The State, the Foreign Investor, and International Law: The No Longer Stormy Relationship of a Menage À Trois' (2000) 15(2) ICSID Review 401

Weiler T, 'Balancing Human Rights and Investor Protection: A New Approach for a Different Legal Order' (2004) 27(2) Boston College International and Comparative Law Review 429

Wilske S, 'Sanctions for Unethical and Illegal Behavior in International Arbitration: A Double-Edged Sword?' (2010) 3 Contemporary Asia Arbitration Journal 211

Woicke P, 'Putting Human Rights Principles into Development Practice Through Finance: The Experience of the International Finance Corporation' in Philip Alston and Mary Robinson (eds), *Human Rights and Development: Towards Mutual Reinforcement* (Oxford University Press 2005)

Wolff R (ed), *New York Convention* (C.H. Beck 2012)

Wongkaew T, *Protection of Legitimate Expectations in Investment Treaty Arbitration* (Cambridge University Press 2019)

World Commission on Environment and Development, *Our Common Future* (Oxford University Press 1987)

Yackee JW, 'Do BITs "Work"? Empirical Evidence from France' (2016) 7(1) Journal of International Dispute Settlement 55

Yala F, 'The Notion of "Investment" in ICSID Case Law: A Drifting Jurisdictional Requirement? Some "Un-Conventional" Thoughts on Salini, SGS and Mihaly' (2005) 22(2) Journal of International Arbitration 105

Yang SL, Zhang J and Xu XJ, 'Influence of the Three Gorges Dam on Downstream Delivery of Sediment and Its Environmental Implications, Yangtze River' (2007) 34(10) Geophysical Research Letters 37

Yannaca-Small C (ed), *Arbitration Under International Investment Agreements: A Guide to the Key Issues* (2nd edn, Oxford University Press 2018)

Zagel GM, 'Achieving Sustainable Development Objectives in International Investment Law' in Julien Chaisse, Leïla Choukroune and Sufian Jusoh (eds), *Handbook of International Investment Law and Policy* (Springer 2021)

Zee E van der, 'Incorporating the OECD Guidelines in International Investment Agreements: Turning a Soft Law Obligation into Hard Law' (2013) 33(1) Legal Issues of Economic Integration 33

Zimmer R, 'Implications of CETA and TTIP on Social Standards' in Henner Gött (ed), *Labour Standards in International Economic Law* (Springer International Publishing 2018)

Zin SM, 'Reappraising Access to Justice in ISDS: A Critical Review on State Recourse to Counterclaim' in Alan M Anderson and Ben Beaumont (eds), *The Investor-State Dispute Settlement System: Reform, Replace or Status Quo?* (Wolters Kluwer 2020)

Zugliani N, 'Human rights in International Investment Law: The 2016 Morocco-Nigeria Bilateral Investment Treaty' (2019) 68(3) International and Comparative Law Quarterly 761